The Creation of the World According to Gersonides

BROWN UNIVERSITY
BROWN JUDAIC STUDIES
Edited by
Jacob Neusner
Wendell S. Dietrich, Ernest S. Frerichs,
Alan Zuckerman

Board of Editors

Number 24

THE CREATION OF THE WORLD ACCORDING TO GERSONIDES

Jacob J. Staub

THE CREATION OF
THE WORLD
ACCORDING TO
GERSONIDES

by
Jacob J. Staub

Scholars Press

Published by
SCHOLARS PRESS
101 Salem Street
P.O. Box 2268
Chico, CA 95927

THE CREATION OF THE WORLD ACCORDING TO GERSONIDES

by

Jacob J. Staub

B
759
.L4
57
1982

Library of Congress Cataloging in Publication Data

Staub, Jacob J.
    The creation of the world according to Gersonides.

    (Brown Judaic studies ; no. 24) (ISSN 0147–927X)
    "The translation of and commentary to The wars of
the Lord 6:2:1–8": p.
    Originally presented as the author's thesis (Ph.D.)
    Bibliography: p.
    1. Levi ben Gershom, 1288–1344. 2. Creation—
History of doctrines. 3. Philosophy, Jewish. 4. Philosophy,
Medieval. I. Levi ben Gershom, 1288–1344. Milḥamot ha-
Shem. English. 1981. II. Title. III. Series.
B759.L4S7 1981   296.3'4   81-13523
ISBN 0-89130-526-2 (pbk.)   AACR2

Printed in the United States of America

Dedicated to the Memory
of my Father
Andrew H. Staub

"And he shall turn the heart of the fathers to the children,
And the heart of the children to their fathers."
(Malachi 3:24)

TABLE OF CONTENTS

THE TRANSLATION OF AND COMMENTARY TO THE WARS
OF THE LORD 6:2:1-8

ACKNOWLEDGMENTS

The present work is substantially identical with my doctoral
dissertation (Temple University, January, 1981). It was written
under the direction of Professor Norbert M. Samuelson. I thank
him for the generous way in which he shared innumerable hours with
me as he helped to prepare me to write this work, for his reading
of the various drafts with an exemplary degree of care and atten-
tiveness, and for the comments and suggestions which he offered at
all stages and which invariably spurred me to better my efforts.

Thanks are also due to other teachers of mine: to Professor
Ronald Hathaway, for sharing his knowledge of the Aristotelian
tradition with me; to Professor Zalman Schachter, for teaching me
about biblical exegesis of all kinds; and to Professor Robert
Wright, for insisting on a sensitivity to the process of translation. I would also like to acknowledge the support and advice of
Professor Jacob Neusner and the valuable suggestions and encourage-
ment of Professor David Blumenthal. Needless to say, I take full
responsibility for the contents of this book including any errors,
opinions or interpretations to be found therein.

My work on this project was assisted by a Dissertation
Research Fellowship granted by the National Foundation of Jewish
Culture. Preparation of the manuscript for publication was
assisted by a grant from the Committee on Advanced Study and
Research of Lafayette College. I am indebted to the librarians
of the Bodleian, Vatican, Paris National, Jewish Theological
Seminary, Hebrew Union College, Hebrew University, Bavarian State
and Parma libraries for the use of microfilm copies of manuscripts.

Thanks are due to Oxford University Press, for permission to
reprint passages from Plato's Timaeus, translated by Benjamin
Jowett, from The Works of Aristotle Translated into English, edited
by J. A. Smith and W. D. Ross, and from The Compact Edition of the
Oxford English Dictionary; to the University of Chicago Press, for
permission to reprint passages from Maimonides' The Guide of the
Perplexed, translated by Shlomo Pines; and to the Jewish Publication Society of America, for permission to reprint passages from
the 1962 translation of The Torah.

In addition, I offer my gratitude to my wife, Barbara, whose
confidence in me exceeded mine at all points and who graciously
became something of an expert in medieval philosophy so that she
could help me to work through particular problems; to my ḥaver,

Rabbi Michael Paley, with whom I studied large sections of the first part of the sixth treatise, learning both from his acute intellect and from his love of learning; to the secretarial staff of Lafayette College and Mrs. M. J. Lutz in particular, without whose cooperation this book could not have been completed; to Helen Lakatos, for the competent way in which she typed and often corrected this manuscript; and to Mr. Dick Everett and the entire staff of the reference department of Lafayette's Skillman Library, for their assistance in locating and obtaining research materials.

Finally, I am thankful, in Gersonides' terms, to the Lord, may He be blessed, and to the divine nomos which He graciously causes to overflow from Him, for endowing me with the nature to seek my end, which has included the writing of this book.

Jacob J. Staub
Easton, Pennsylvania

September 20, 1981
21 Elul 5741

INTRODUCTION

PART ONE

The Scope of the Project

Gersonides (1288-1344) stands as one of the leading Jewish thinkers of the medieval period.[1] He distinguished himself through his work in the fields of astronomy, mathematics and Biblical exegesis, but he is known primarily for his contributions to philosophy and is generally regarded by students of the period as the leading philosophical successor to Maimonides.

His major work of philosophy is The Wars of the Lord (Milḥamot Ha-Shem), a part of which is translated below. In this work, he does not aspire to deal with every issue of importance nor to construct a comprehensive philosophical system. The work is rather divided into six treatises, each of which focuses upon a single issue. The issues with which he chooses to deal are those the solutions of which, in Gersonides' view, are inadequately addressed by Maimonides in The Guide of the Perplexed. The first five treatises deal respectively with: 1) the immortality of the soul and the nature of the human intellect; 2) dreams, divination and prophecy; 3) divine knowledge of particular things; 4) providence; and 5) astronomy, the heavenly bodies and separate intellects. In each case, he reviews the opinions of his predecessors and arrives at his own independent and often controversial conclusions.

The sixth and final treatise of The Wars of the Lord deals with the question of the origin of the world. It is divided into two parts. The first part contains his philosophical arguments for his own view of the creation of the world. In the first eight chapters of the second part, he shows that the conclusions which he reaches through philosophical speculation in the first part are identical with the teachings of the Torah as they are revealed in the creation narrative of Genesis. The last section of the second part contains his discussion of the nature of marvels and a brief discussion of the ways in which a prophet's authenticity can be tested.

It is the first eight chapters of the second part of the sixth treatise which are translated below and to which the commentary below has been written. Thus, the subject of this book is Gersonides' view of the creation of the world. His philosophical demonstration and his exposition of his view of creation in 6:1

1

are summarized in the third part of this introduction. The primary
focus of this book, however, is his argument in 6:2:1-8 that the
demonstrated conclusions which he reaches by means of speculation
in 6:1 are identical to the view of creation which is revealed in
the Genesis narrative. That argument for the agreement of speculation and the Torah on the issue of creation is the subject of
the text of 6:2:1-8, which is translated and annotated below and
which is explicated in Part IV of this introduction and evaluated
in Part V of this introduction.

An understanding of Gersonides' account of creation and of
his reading of the creation narrative of Genesis in 6:2:1-8 is
important for several reasons. First, it stands as the most complete and systematic discussion with which Gersonides provides
us of his understanding of the way in which the world came to be.
It is true that sections of his discussion here are paralleled in
his Commentary to the Torah. The Commentary, however, is not
systematic and has the structural disadvantage of moving from
passage to passage of the Biblical text. Similarly, his discussion
of creation in 6:1, where he argues for his view of creation, contains a number of important passages in which he describes the process in which the world came to be and which are cited in the
commentary below when they illumine our text. Indeed, as mentioned
above, the account of creation in 6:2:1-8 is based upon his argument in 6:1. Nevertheless, a complete exposition of the implications of his argument is contained only in 6:2:1-8.

Second, the text of 6:2:1-8 stands as a model exercise in the
enterprise of medieval philosophy. As Wolfson describes that
enterprise, all philosophers, beginning with Philo Judaeus and
ending with Spinoza—Muslim, Jewish and Christian—can be characterized as working towards a synthesis between their respective
revealed traditions and the methods and teachings of Greek philosophy.[2] Insofar as Gersonides can be characterized as one of the
most independent medieval Jewish philosophers who was willing to
accept and pursue philosophical demonstrations even when his conclusions diverged significantly from the accepted teachings of his
tradition, his reading of the Biblical text is particularly note-
worthy as an illustration of the premises and methods employed by
medieval Jewish philosophers to achieve a synthesis of reason and
revelation.

Third, the account of creation presented by Gersonides in the
text translated below is remarkable for its originality. Gersonides' view that the world came to be out of a body which persisted

prior to creation is not only distinctive in the history of Jewish
exegesis of the creation narrative of Genesis. It also offers us
an original cosmology in the history of philosophy. Gersonides
was heir to a number of alternative views of the origin of the
world: the view that there had been a succession of created
worlds; the view that the world had been created out of absolutely
nothing; the view that the creation of the world had been an ordering of disorderly motions; and the view that the world had existed
eternally and had not been created in time. Each of these preceding views had attempted to resolve a number of difficult philosophical issues, including: the relationship of God's immutability
and His willful causation; the relationship of God's self-
sufficiency and His governance of the created world; the relationship of God's omnipotence and the imperfect state of affairs of
the created world; and the relationship of God's immateriality and
the material world.

In rejecting the preceding views and in constructing an
original account of creation, Gersonides offers a new and significant way of dealing with these issues. Most significantly, he
develops an original view of the characteristics of matter and the
manner in which it becomes disposed to receive the causation of the
divine will. As is discussed below in Parts III, IV and V of this
introduction and in the commentary to the translated test (especially notes #49 and #51), his view of a formless body with absolute
dimensionality which persisted prior to creation is significant
not only in the history of cosmology but also for its consequences
for his view of the nature of God and of the nature and the purpose
of the created world.

The present work is based upon and is indebted to preceding
scholarly discussions of Gersonides' account of creation. Charles
Touati's La pensée philosophique et théologique de Gersonide
(Paris: Minuit, 1973) is a monumental work which deals comprehen-
sively with the entirety of Gersonides' thought and which must
necessarily serve as a reference point for all subsequent Gersonidean scholarship. Specifically, Part Three, in which Touati presents Gersonides' arguments for creation, as well as his interpretation of the Genesis narrative of creation, has been recapitulated
in various sections of this introduction. Also, two articles by
Seymour Feldman—"Gersonides' Proofs for the Creation of the
Universe," Proceedings of the American Academy for Jewish Research
35 (1967): 113-137; and "Platonic Themes in Gersonides' Cosmology,"
Salo Wittmayer Baron Jubilee Volume, pp. 383-405—deal directly

with the first part of the sixth treatise of The Wars. They have
been consulted in the summary of 6:1 below in Part Three of this
introduction.

The distinctive contribution of this work to Gersonidean
scholarship, however, is the depth of its investigation of Gersonides' understanding of body which does not preserve its shape and
the implications of that understanding for his entire philosophic
system. As is apparent from the lengthy discussions below, it is
not sufficient to note that he posits a formless body which persisted prior to creation, out of which the world comes to be. This
assertion assumes a number of controversial and innovative propositions about the nature of matter, of formal causation and of God
which demand explication and evaluation. It reverberates throughout
The Wars, not only in his discussion of creation but in his discussions of immortality, prophecy, marvels, divine knowledge, providence and the purpose of the supralunar world as well. Touati's
discussion of the issue indicates Gersonides' position but, in the
context of the comprehensive nature of his survey of all of Gersonides' thought, does not devote a full analysis to all of its
implications. Feldman's analyses of Gersonides' arguments are
valuable but are limited in scope. Insofar as they do not fully
take into account Gersonides' view of body which does not preserve
its shape, they do not present his arguments in their proper context. This book intends neither to refute nor to correct previous
work on this subject but rather to supplement and clarify by offering a fuller exposition of the problems and solutions entailed by
Gersonides' view of creation.

The purpose of the commentary which accompanies the
translation of the text of 6:2:1-8 is primarily to clarify the
meaning of the text. Insofar as the text forms the conclusion of
the entire The Wars of the Lord, the commentary refers back to
earlier treatises, as well as to the first part of the sixth treatise, in order to establish some of the conceptions which Gersonides
has already discussed and demonstrated and which he therefore
assumes. He explicitly states that this last treatise depends upon
the issues discussed in the preceding treatises.[3] Also, cross
references to his Commentary to the Torah are included in the
commentary when they shed light upon the meaning of the text.
Though his discussions of the creation narrative of Genesis in his
Commentary most often parallel his comments in our text, his discussions there occasionally do diverge from or add to our text.

Thus, the commentary attempts to establish Gersonides' meaning
primarily through his own words and arguments—by examining and
comparing his own statements throughout The Wars of the Lord and
his Commentary. Working with the assumption that he was a competent and consistent thinker, the notes of the commentary attempt
to resolve apparent inconsistencies and errors by referring them
to other of his statements and by seeking to construct the common
assumptions which underlie all of those statements.

        The commentary also makes frequent reference to Gersonides'
predecessors, most notably Aristotle, Maimonides and Averroes.
The purpose of those references, however, is to clarify Gersonides'
own meaning. No attempt has been made to establish the accurate
meaning of those sources. Rather, the commentary attempts to read
them as Gersonides would have read them. This is particularly
true with reference to Aristotle, to whom Gersonides had access
primarily through Hebrew translations of Averroes' commentaries to
his works. To establish most accurately Gersonides' understanding
of Aristotle, an examination of Gersonides' supercommentaries to
Averroes' commentaries is required. Though portions of his supercommentaries have been examined with regard to several issues, a
thorough examination fell beyond the scope of this project. Therefore, translations of the original passages from Aristotle's works
have been cited when Gersonides explicitly refers to them or when
a citation of them was judged to clarify the text's meaning. Again,
the purpose of the commentary is a clarification of Gersonides'
meaning in his own terms and not a description of his philosophical
sources.

        A word of explanation about the length of the text translated
and annotated below is needed. Though Gersonides' discussion of
marvels and of the authenticity of prophets in the latter section
of the second part of treatise six (6:2:9-14) is based upon the
discussion of creation which precedes it, it forms a separate unit
which does not illuminate his discussion of creation and which
therefore has been judged to be beyond the scope of the present
project. On the few occasions when his comments in 6:2:9-14 were
judged to shed light on his meaning in 6:2:1-8, those comments have
been cited in the notes of the commentary.

        The remainder of this introduction falls into four parts.
First, Part II is a discussion of the text which underlies the
translation and the method used to translate the text. Second,
Part III is a critical summary of Gersonides' argument for his

view of creation as he presents it in 6:1. It is this argument
which directly precedes our text in The Wars of the Lord and it is
the conclusions reached by this argument which he seeks in 6:2:1-8
to find in the Torah. Third, a more systematic presentation of the
major ideas contained in our commentary to the translated text is
provided in Part IV, including: a discussion of the consequences
of Gersonides' view of creation for his other physical and metaphysical views; and analysis of the way in which he views the text
of the Torah; a review of his understanding of key terms in the
Genesis narrative; an exposition of his view of the unity of all
created things; and a word-by-word review of his reading of the
text of the creation narrative of Genesis. Fourth, Part V concludes
with a discussion of the validity and the importance of Gersonides'
account of creation. With regard to its validity, the discussion
focuses primarily upon his discussion of the body which does not
preserve its shape, examining his statements to determine whether
they are consistent with other of his views and with his epistemology in particular. With regard to its importance, there is a
discussion of the philosophical consequences of his view for problems of cosmology, and the religious consequences of his view for
traditional Jewish doctrines.

PART TWO

On the Translation

The translation below of 6:2:1-8 is not based upon a critical edition of the text established by consulting all available manuscripts. The text which underlies the translation is that of the two printed editions of The Wars of the Lord: Riva di Trento, 1569 and Leipzig, 1866. The pages and lines of the Leipzig edition have been noted in the margins of the translation. The pages and columns of the Riva di Trento edition have been noted also in the margins and are underlined. A nonexhaustive comparison of the printed editions of the text of 6:2:1-8 with several of the more reliable manuscript witnesses reveals that the printed editions are reliable. Three manuscript witnesses have been consulted and were chosen on the basis of Touati's evaluation that they are among the most reliable:[4] Pococke 376 (A. Neubauer, Catalogue of the Hebrew Manuscripts in the Bodleian Library; [Oxford, 1886], #1286), from the Bodleian Library; Urbinate 28, from the Vatican Library; and Hebrew Manuscript #723, from the Bibliothèque Nationale in Paris. Where the Riva di Trento and the Leipzig editions disagree, preference has been given to the Riva di Trento reading, except in the following cases: when the Leipzig reading was supported by the manuscripts and could thus be justified as a correction of the Riva di Trento text; and when the Riva di Trento reading was unintelligible. When the Riva di Trento and the Leipzig editions agreed about a text which seemed problematic or unintelligible, the manuscript witnesses were consulted and, when they differed from the text of the printed editions, the alternate manuscript reading was cited in the notes of the commentary. In these latter cases, our translation is based upon the version of the printed texts and every effort has been made to make sense of the printed version. It has not been assumed that manuscript readings which clarify the text's meaning necessarily represent Gersonides' original words.

The translation of 6:2:1-8 endeavors to present the reader of the English translation with a text that resembles, as closely as possible, the text with which the reader of the Hebrew original is confronted. The purpose of the translation, therefore, is not to attempt to recover Gersonides' true intentions—that attempt is made in the commentary and, in summary form, in the introduction—but to reproduce, as accurately as possible, what Gersonides said. To the extent that this translation has realized this purpose,

7

the reader of the English translation who does not have access to
the Hebrew original will be able to approach and interpret Gersonides' statements without the intervention of a translator who has
already consciously sought to clarify the text.

This approach has been chosen because of the nature of the
text being translated here. The Wars of the Lord is a work of
philosophy in which Gersonides pays a great deal of attention to
the precise use of technical terms and to the construction of carefully formulated arguments in which the order of his premises and
conclusions matters to the success of the argument. It is often
the case that one's understanding of an argument will depend upon
one's understanding of a single clause and its relationship to the
other parts of the argument. Though the contents of 6:2:1-8 do
not take the form of the rigorous philosophical argumentation that
can be found, for example, in 6:1, it can fairly be stated that
both the exegesis involved in his discussion of the Biblical text
and the implicit and explicit references which he makes back to
his preceding arguments demand the kind of detailed attention
required by earlier treatises. Given the nature of the text, the
translation seeks to maintain a verbal faithfulness to the original
in which both the syntax and the terminological consistency employed
by its author have been retained, as far as possible.

One direct consequence of this approach is that the translation
seeks to be only as clear and as graceful as the original. Where
Gersonides seems unclear, the translation seeks to replicate his
apparent lack of clarity so that the reader of the translation can
understand the text as well as—but no "better" than—the reader of
the original. Two examples will illustrate the point. The first
sentence of 6:2:4, p. 421, l. 3f., has been translated as follows:

> Tohu and bohu are used in our language to refer to
> "the matter most distant from (a given) existent thing
> and to its last form which is prior in order."

No claim is being made here for the grace or clarity of this
translation. The parenthetical addition is made not for the purpose of clarification but rather to reproduce in English, as
closely as possible, the original phrase, ha-nimṣaʾ ha-huʾ. If the
reader cannot, on the basis of this translation, understand Gersonides' definitions of the Biblical terms, tohu and bohu, it is
because the original is awkward and unclear. It is nevertheless
the original syntax and terminology of the sentence which serves
as one of the bases for the understanding of Gersonides' view of
prime matter and last form, as is discussed in note #49 of the

commentary. And it is precisely the awkwardness of this sentence in the original Hebrew that would lead the reader to embark upon a more thorough investigation of Gersonides' intentions. To the extent that the awkwardness of the translation also leads the reader to such an investigation or explains to the reader the reason that the matter is pursued at length in the commentary, it has realized the intended goal.

Another example can be found in 6:2:8, p. 436, ll. 5-8, which has been translated as follows:

> Furthermore, if it had discussed the creation of the stars (immediately) after the creation of the heavenly body, it would have been possible for the speculator to think erroneously that the stars were in the spheres for their own sake and that the benefit which is realized from them in these (lower) existent things came from them in a secondary way.

Neither from the original nor, it is hoped, from this translation can the reader infer definitively whether the erroneous view to which Gersonides is referring here is that the stars are in the spheres for the sake of the spheres of that they are in the spheres for the sake of the stars. Nor can one determine whether he is being critical here of the view that the benefits which overflow to the sublunar world come in a secondary way from the stars or from the spheres or from both the stars and the spheres. These are questions which are addressed in the commentary to this passage. If the intent of the translation has been effected, however, the conclusions reached in the commentary, which depend on his statements elsewhere and not here, have not been used to clarify the ambiguity in the text here.

Of course, the weakness of any translation is that it is inevitably an interpretation of the original. This translation, however, seeks to avoid some of the unfortunate consequences which accompany translations of all kinds. As noted above, the translation attempts to avoid textual emendations and reconstructions which have resolved apparent inconsistencies in and problematic passages of the text, so that Gersonides' true meaning would not be covered over by the imposition upon him of preconceived notions of what he meant to say. In addition, consistency in the translation of his terminology has been attempted, so that one English term is employed to translate a single one of his terms, as far as that is possible, and so that different English terms are employed to translate each of several of his terms, even when he seems to be using those terms synonymously. For example, the two phrases,

havayat ha-ᶜolam and ḥidush ha-ᶜolam apparently do not have two
distinct meanings. Two different translations have nevertheless
been employed for each of his two different phrases—"the coming to
be of the world" and "the generation of the world"—in order to
retain a verbal faithfulness to the original and in order to allow
the reader of the translation to determine for himself whether these
phrases are, in fact, used synonymously.

In some cases English terms which depart from common usage
have been employed deliberately in order to attempt to produce a
translation which replicates for the English reader the text of the
original. The term ᶜiyun has been translated as "speculation"
rather than "philosophy" because Gersonides uses the term to refer
to the study of a great deal more than what is indicated today by
the term "philosophy." Inasmuch as the occupations of the philosopher have changed over the last six centuries, the term "philosophy"
no longer serves as a literal translation of ᶜiyun, which involves
the study of logic, mathematics, the natural and physical sciences
and astronomy, as well as metaphysics. The term madregah has been
translated as "degree" in order to allude to the technical sense
in which Gersonides uses the term, i.e., as referring to different
levels of being or reality. In both cases, the choice of terms was
made to alert the reader of the translation to the fact that Gersonides' referents in these instances differ significantly from our
common assumptions. A third example is the translation of niflaᵓot
as "marvels" rather than as "miracles." As explained below in note
#4 of the commentary, his notion of the nature of the marvelous
differs significantly from our common assumptions about the miracu-
lous. Thus, a different, somewhat eccentric term was chosen to
avoid confusion.

In most cases it was found that the semantic range of any one
of Gersonides' terms could be reproduced by a single English term.
Sometimes, however, this was not possible. The term which has the
widest semantic range is ᶜinyan, which has been translated below
as "context," "definition," "notion," "case," "sense," "state" and
"state of affairs." In such a case, terminological consistency had
to be abandoned and the meaning of the term was determined from its
context. Similarly, the verb ᶜasah has been translated as "to
cause," "to make," "to perform" and "to produce," and the root yḥd
has been translated in its various forms to indicate simultaneity,
togetherness, individuation, specificity and uniqueness. Gersonides' apparent meaning was determined from context. Although such
contextual judgments were unavoidable in such cases, in principle

it would have been preferable to avoid them because of the
inevitable consequence that the translation becomes more interpretation and less replication. Therefore, the number of different
English terms used to translate each Hebrew term has been minimized,
to the greatest extent possible. Each additional English term was
chosen only when all previous terms used to translate the Hebrew
term proved to be inadequate.

There are many less radical examples of terms which function,
in Gersonides' usage, in more than one sense: <u>keliy</u> means "organ"
and "instrument;" <u>ʾot</u> means "letter" and "sign;" <u>mofet</u> means
"demonstration" and "wonder;" <u>dimyon</u> means "analogy" and "imagination;" <u>ḥiluf</u> means "diversity" and "contrariety." In these cases
the context again served as a guide to the text's meaning, but
there was less difficulty in making these judgments.

In some cases, it would have been possible to use only one
term in the translation, but more than one term was used in order
to evoke the different nuances of the Hebrew term. For example:
<u>takhlit</u> might have been translated in all cases as "end," but
"purpose" was employed when the context suggested a teleological
end; perhaps <u>hasagah</u> could have been translated consistently as
"apprehension" instead of alternating between "perception" (for
sensible objects) and "conception" (for intelligible objects);
<u>devekut</u> has been translated as both "cleaving" and "inhering,"
when either of the terms could have been used in all instances.
In these cases, terminological consistency was judged to be less
important in replicating the meaning of the original text than was
an explication of the nuances of a single Hebrew term.

Insofar as the text being translated is an exercise in Biblical
exegesis, the translator confronts additional challenges. This is
because Gersonides takes Biblical terms and invests them with his
own meaning. As a consequence, he often cites a Biblical passage
which he is reading in an entirely different way than any modern
Biblical translation would present it. In all such cases, the
Biblical passage has been translated in accordance with Gersonides'
interpretation, without reference to the literal meaning of the
Biblical text. When his citation and comparison of Biblical texts
depend upon similarities of Hebrew roots that cannot easily be
made apparent through translation, a transliteration of the Hebrew
terms has been included within the body of the translation.

In the case of the Biblical terms, <u>tohu</u> and <u>bohu</u> (Gen 1:2), the
Hebrew terms have been left untranslated because there is no
scholarly consensus about their exact literal meaning and because

Gersonides' translation—"last form" and "prime matter"—is not
easily inserted into the Biblical verse. It was thought that it
is less intelligible to have the translation say, for example, that
"formless" means "last form" and "void" means "prime matter" than
to leave the original terms transliterated. The Biblical term
raqi^ca has also been left transliterated, because the literal ren-
dering "firmament" bears virtually no relation to Gersonides'
understanding of the term and because his understanding of the term
gives it a semantic range which makes a translation impossible. No
single English term could be found which meant "that which is
stretched out," "the heavenly body as a whole," "the all-encompass-
ing sphere" and "the heavenly spheres." Inasmuch as a clear presentation of his exegesis required a single term, the original Hebrew
term was not translated. In other similar cases, when he explicitly
states that a Biblical term-e.g., ^ʔereṣ, ^cal, ruaḥ—is equivocal,
the meaning of his exegesis has been preserved by retaining the
original Hebrew term.

PART III

Gersonides' Discussion of His Argument
For the Creation of the World

A. Gersonides' Introduction

This Part of the introduction is the summary of Treatise Six,
Part One of The Wars of the Lord. It is in 6:1:1-29 that Gersonides makes his philosophical argument for his view of the creation
of the world. In 6:2:1-8, which is explicated in Part IV of this
introduction and is translated and annotated below, it is the
argument and exposition of 6:1 which he identifies as the truth of
speculation and which he claims is identical to the truth revealed
in the Genesis narrative of creation. What follows immediately
below is a brief review of 6:1:1-29, which in turn is summarized
more fully in the remainder of this Part of the introduction. The
review indicates where the various parts of 6:1 are summarized in
this introduction.

After discussing some of the difficulties involved in pursuing
an investigation of the origins of the universe (6:1:1—Part III,
A, 1 of this introduction), Gersonides proceeds to examine the
views of his predecessors. He lists them (6:1:2—Part III, A, 2),
examines the aspects of plausibility which each of them possesses
(6:1:3—Part III, A, 3), and after concluding that only Aristotle's
view of the world's eternity is viable, he offers a preliminary
refutation of Aristotle's arguments (6:1:4—Part III, A, 4).

Gersonides then embarks upon his own investigation of the
question. He asserts that the proper subjects for investigation
are those things whose existence is continuous and which may therefore be thought to be beginningless—i.e., the heavenly bodies and
their movers, time, motion and the elevated, visible part of the
earth. If it can be demonstrated that these continuous things were
generated, then the world as a whole must have come to be. If it
can be demonstrated that these things could not have been generated,
then the world as a whole could not have come to be. He discusses
three characteristics which are possessed by generated things and
are not possessed by things which do not come to be (6:1:5-6—
Part III, B, 1) and then proceeds to show that the heavens (6:1:7-
9—Part III, B, 2-4) and the visible part of the earth (6:1:12—
Part III, B, 5) possess these characteristics. He discusses the
nature of time and demonstrates that it cannot be infinite and
then proceeds similarly with regard to motion (6:1:10-12—Part III,

13

B, 6). He then considers John Philoponus' argument for creation
from finitudes (6:1:14—Part III, B, 7) and offers another, independent demonstration of the generation of the world from the
perfectibility of human culture (6:1:15—Part III, B, 8).

Having demonstrated that the world came to be, Gersonides
proceeds to argue that its generation does not entail its destructi-
bility (6:1:16—Part III, B, 9). He then reexamines the Platonic
view of creation out of eternal matter and the Maimonidean view of
creation ex nihilo. He rejects both views and offers his own view
that the world came to be out of formless body which does not preserve its shape (6:1:17—Part III, C, 1), a view which he claims
is not subject to the doubts and contradictions entailed by the
alternate views. He then resolves a number of doubts which he
poses to his own view (6:1:18—Part III, C, 2), argues for the
impossibility of the simultaneous existence of more than one world
(6:1:19—Part III, C, 3), and responds to each of the arguments
for the eternity of the world which he attributed to Aristotle
in 6:1:3 (6:1:20-28—Part III, D, 1). Gersonides' concluding
chapter serves more as a conclusion to the entire work, The Wars
of the Lord (6:1:29—Part III, D, 2).

1. The Difficulties of the Investigation (6:1:1)

Gersonides mentions five indications of the difficulty of the
issue. First, he notes the great diversity among his philosophical
predecessors. Second, a demonstration of the origins of the world
requires the most perfect possible knowledge of the true conceptions of existent things in their totality. He has already stated
elsewhere that even the most developed human intellect can aspire
at most to a limited knowledge of existent things.[5] Third, the
investigation requires a knowledge of the First Cause in order to
determine if we can attribute to Him a volitional creative act
which causes the world's existence after it did not exist. Our
knowledge of the First Cause, however, is very weak. Fourth, the
conclusion one reaches is determined by which conceptions are
chosen as the basis of the argument. The appropriate bases, however, are anything but self-evident. Fifth, he notes Aristotle's
own admission,[6] as it is related by Maimonides,[7] that the truth of
the question cannot be demonstrated.

2. The Views of Gersonides' Predecessors (6:1:2)

Gersonides categorizes the preceding views as follows:
1) The view that the world has been generated and has passed away
an infinite number of times.[8]   2) The view that the world was

generated only one time. This view is subdivided into two views:
2a) The view of Plato and his followers that the world was generated from something;[9] 2b) The view that the world was generated
from absolutely nothing, which is held by the early Kalam,[10] John
Philoponus,[11] Maimonides[12] and many of the sages of the Torah.[13]
3) The Aristotelian view that the world is eternal.[14]

The polemical value of this categorization becomes clear
when it is compared with Maimonides' presentation in the Guide
(2:13). Whereas Maimonides sharply distinguishes his own view from
that of Plato, Gersonides lists them as related subcategories of
the second view. The implications of this become clear later in
the argument when Gersonides takes Maimonides at his word when the
latter states that either the Platonic view or the view of creation
out of absolutely nothing accords with the Torah.[15] What is crucial is that the Torah is founded upon willful, purposeful creation
and not upon necessary generation. As Maimonides rejects the
Platonic view because it has not been demonstrated, Gersonides
similarly will reject both the Platonic and the Maimonidean views
because of the unresolvable doubts they entail. In their place,
he will propose a third version of the second view which will be,
in his view, both philosophically demonstrable and in accord with
the principles of the Torah.

Gersonides attributes the diversity of views concerning the
origins of the world to the following causes: 1) As he notes in
6:1:1, one's conclusion depends upon which principles and states
of affairs are used to construct one's argument. For his part,
he will choose (6:1:5) to investigate those things whose existence
is continuous, the eternity of which would entail the eternity of
the world and the generation of which would entail the generation
of the world. 2) They were compelled to reach conclusions which
would agree with what they thought was the view of the Torah. This
may refer only to Maimonides and the sages, or he may be using the
term Torah to refer more generally to Islamic and Christian Scripture. The most obvious referent here is Maimonides who explicitly
states that his choice of creation ex nihilo over eternity is made
because of the requirements of the Torah.[16] 3) A combination of
(1) and (2).

3. Aspects of Plausibility of the Views of Gersonides'
   Predecessors (6:1:3)

In support of the first view that the world has been generated
and has passed away an infinite number of times, Gersonides lists
six arguments.

a) An argument from analogy with existent things. As all things
come to be and pass away in succession, one might infer that this
is true of the world in its totality.[17] Here Gersonides adds an
additional consideration. One way to resolve the problem that
results from positing that God acts at one time and not at
another,[18] he says, is to posit that He continually creates and
destroys worlds in infinite succession.

b) An argument from the eternity of time. Gersonides cites two
arguments for the eternity of time which he attributes to Aristotle.
First, if time came to be, it would have come to be in time. Since
this is impossible, time could not have come to be.[19] Second, if
time came to be, there would be an actual existent "now" at which
it came to be. Since every part of time has only a potential existence, no such "now" could exist. Therefore, time could not have
come to be.[20] Given the eternity of time, and given that the world
as a whole is subject to generation and corruption as established
in the first argument, the world must have come to be and passed
away an infinite number of times in infinite time.

c) An argument from the nature of motion. Given Aristotle's
assertion that motion cannot be absolutely generated,[21] if the
world is generable and destructible as the first argument claims,
then there must have been an infinite succession of worlds in such
a way that motion was never generated.

d) An argument from the nature of prime matter. Given that matter
cannot exist without form,[22] and given that matter underlies and
remains through all changes of form,[23] if the world came to be, as
the first argument maintains, then there must have been a world
which existed before the generation of this one in a way that this
matter did not exist without form. Implicitly, the argument applies
to each preceding world, ad infinitum.

e) An argument from the nature of generated things. Aristotle
states that everything which comes to be passes away.[24] Given the
first argument that the world came to be, it necessarily follows
that the world passes away. Implicitly, the argument applies to an
infinite succession of worlds.

f) An argument from the nature of an infinite power. Aristotle
states that it is impossible for an infinite power to exist in a
finite body[25] and that the heavens are finite in magnitude.[26] If

the heavens were indestructible, a power would exist in them which
would sustain and move them endlessly. But such a power would be
infinite and thus could not exist in a finite world. Therefore,
the heavens are destructible and (based upon the implicit premise
that all possibilities must be realized in an infinite time)[27] they
must necessarily pass away. But everything that passes away must
come to be.[28] Therefore, the heavens must have come to be.
Assumed is the final conclusion that, given the infinite time
established in the second argument, there must be an infinite succession of worlds which come to be and pass away. He cites John
Philoponus as the source of this argument, as his argument is
related by Averroes in his Commentary to the Metaphysica.[29]

The first version of the second view that the world came to
be once is the Platonic one which characterizes that coming to be
as a move from disorder to order. As Gersonides presents the argument, it is the intellect which is the principle of all things and
is the source of the good and of order. As he has argued in the
first treatise of The Wars of the Lord, it is the Active Intellect
which conceives of all of the forms of lower existent things in
their oneness and order and which actualizes in the human, hylic
intellect the conception of the material instantiations of the
forms. All individuals of a species are one in conception and all
species are one in the divine order which governs the sublunar
world. Arguing from analogy, as all things come to be through this
formal and final causation of the intellect so the world as a
whole must come to be in a similar way.[30] Given that the world
came to be and given that all things come to be from something,[31]
the world must have come to be from something. But since motion
cannot have had an absolute beginning,[32] there must have been
motion in that which preceded the generation of the world—disorderly motion, since order is caused by the intellect.

The Platonic view also affirms the indestructibility of the
world after its generation, because there is nothing in the nature
of the heavens which could cause it to pass way.[33] Things pass
away because of the nature of sublunar matter which the supralunar
world does not have.[34] Therefore, the heavens cannot pass away and
it necessarily follows from this that the world cannot pass away.[35]

Here Gersonides mentions the following objection. Given that
Aristotle has explained that that which does not pass away does
not come to be,[36] if the heavens are indestructible then they are
ungenerated. Gersonides responds by citing the acquired intellect,

which he has shown in the first treatise to be generated and indestructible,[37] as a way of disproving the universal applicability of Aristotle's principle. He also refers the reader to his own refutation of Aristotle on this point below.[38]

The second version of the second view that the world came to be once argues that it came to be out of nothing. Gersonides offers two arguments in support of it, both of which assume a prior demonstration that the world was generated and which argue for creation out of nothing. As a third point, he mentions the Atomistic physics of the Kalam as supporting this view.

a) An argument from analogy with the nature of the generation of all things. All things which come to be come to be from nothing. Therefore the world came to be from nothing.[39] By way of explaining the argument's first premise, he states that it is the form which comes to be in any process of generation and not the matter, which serves as the substratum of both the anterior and the posterior form.[40] But the form of a generated thing does not come to be from another form or from anything else. Since a thing comes to be insofar as it is form and not insofar as it is matter, it can be said to come to be from nothing. Gersonides adds here that this analogy is true only if it is possible for matter to be generated from nothing.

b) An argument from the indefensibility of the Platonic view. Assuming that the world came to be, the Platonic view that it came to be from disorderly motion entails several impossible consequences, as Aristotle demonstrated in his refutation of Plato. This is what caused Maimonides to reject the Platonic position which otherwise he found to be reconcilable with the Torah.[41] The Platonic view entails the following: 1) That the unactualized possibility of the world's generation existed for an infinite time prior to its generation. Since no possibility can exist unactualized for an infinite time,[42] the Platonic view is untenable. But if it is posited that the world came to be from nothing, then there was no matter in which such a possibility could reside. 2) That the world existed, in its disorderly motion, prior to its coming to be.[43] This absurdity would not be entailed if the world came to be from nothing.

c) Gersonides notes that the Atomism of the Kalam, as it is described by Maimonides, was used to strengthen the view of creation out of nothing,[44] in that it posits that the world is perpetually caused by God at every instant. Based upon the report of

Maimonides, however, Gersonides concludes that the doctrine of
continuous causation cannot be used, as it is used by the Kalam,
to prove that the world had an absolute generation, since God
causes the world continually and not at a particular moment.[45]

In support of the third, Aristotelian view that the world is
eternal, Gersonides offers nine arguments.

a) An argument from the nature of time. If time came to be, it
must have come to be in time. Therefore, time could not have come
to be in an absolute sense.[46] But time, the definition of which
is the measure of continuous motion, is inseparable from motion.[47]
Therefore, motion could not have come to be in an absolute sense.
But there is no motion apart from a moved object.[48] Aristotle
explains that this is possible only if the object moves in a
single, continuous, circular motion.[49] This argument can also be
used to establish that time cannot pass away, for if it passed
away, it would pass away in time. Thus, time is endless as it is
beginningless, and there always has been and always will be a thing
moved in a circle.

b) An argument from the definition of the "now." As Aristotle
defines the "now," it is a middle point which divides the "before"
from the "after."[50] If time came to be absolutely, there would be
an actual "now" at which time began. But such a "now" would not
divide the "before" from the "after," because there would be no
time before that "now." Therefore, there is no such "now" and
time did not come to be absolutely.[51] Gersonides leaves unstated
here the remainder of the argument, elaborated in the first argument from time, that beginningless time entails beginningless
motion and an object moved perpetually in a circular motion.

b') An argument from temporal language. If we were to posit that
time absolutely came to be or passed away, there would be no way
to avoid temporal references to before time came to be or to after
it passed away. But such references imply that time exists prior
to its coming to be and after its passing away. Therefore, time
can have neither a beginning nor an end.[52] Here he refers the
reader back to the first argument for the completion of the proof
for an eternal world.

c) An argument from the nature of motion. Aristotle explains that
locomotion is the first of all motions[53] and that it is ultimately
caused by a single moved object.[54] If we were to posit that the
heavenly bodies came to be, it would follow necessarily that there
was moved object which caused their coming to be. But if that
first moved object itself came to be, it would again follow

necessarily that it would have been caused by another object in
motion. But an infinite series of causes in this manner is an
impossibility, because there cannot be an infinite number of
(simultaneously existing) bodies.[55] Therefore, there must be a
first moved object which did not come to be which moves, as discussed above in the first argument, in a single, perpetual, circular motion.[56] But if such an object exists, the world is eternal.
d) An argument from the nature of generated things. This argument
has two parts. The first concludes that time has no absolute
coming to be. The second employs a different approach than the
one used in the first argument to demonstrate that the eternity of
time entails an object which moves perpetually. The first part of
the argument begins with Aristotle's assertion that everything
which comes to be has a potential existence which is temporally
prior to its actualization.[57] If we were to posit that the world
came to be, it would have existed potentially before its actual
existence. But our use of temporal references implies that time
must have existed prior to the generation of the world. Therefore,
time has no beginning. The second part of the argument proceeds
as follows: If time is beginningless, then motion is also. Beginningless motion entails an object perpetually in motion. But all
things in motion are moved either by nature or by compulsion.[58]
If it was moved by compulsion, then natural motion existed because,
by definition, compulsory motion is contrary to natural motion.[59]
But there can be no natural motion apart from the existence of
things with natures to move. Therefore, if we were to posit that
the world came to be, prior in time to its generation there would
exist existent things with natural motions, i.e., the world would
exist prior to its generation. Therefore, the world could not
have come to be.
e) An argument from the impossibility of a first motion. If we
were to posit a first generated motion, the moved object would
either have come to be or not have come to be. If it came to be,
then the motion of its generation would precede its first motion
and hence the latter would not be "first."[60] But we cannot posit
that the motion of the generation of the first moved object is the
first motion for two reasons. First, there must have been an agent
which caused its generation. When an agent causes at one moment
after not having caused, its causal activity is itself a change
which must have a causal agent, and this would be necessary of an
infinite succession of agents.[61] Second, with regard to everything
which comes to be, the motion of its generation is preceded by the

motion of the generation of the possibility of its generation.
Therefore, the first moved object could not have come to be if its
motion is a first motion. Nor is the motion of the first moved
object first if we posit that it did not come to be. To account
for its initial motion, we can posit either of two different sets
of circumstances. Either we can assume that the nature of its
mover had always been to move and the nature of the moved object
had always been to be moved. If this was the case, then we must
assume that there was some obstructing condition which had pre-
vented the first mover from moving the first moved object. But the
removal of such a condition would require a motion prior to the
initial motion of the first moved object, so that the motion
posited to be "first" would not be first. Or we can assume that
a change was necessary either in the first mover or in the first
moved object before the one could move the other, and that initial
motion would be prior to the posited "first" motion. In either
case, the argument could be applied to the prior change, leading
to an infinite succession of motions prior to any posited "first"
motion. Therefore, there cannot be a first generated motion
whether or not the first moved object came to be.[62] This argument
can be applied similarly to the hypothesis that there is a last
motion. Thus, motion must be eternal and there must be a thing
moved perpetually in a continuous circular motion, as explained
above.

f) An argument from the nature of prime matter.[63] Aristotle
states that matter cannot come to be or pass away insofar as it
is matter[64] and that matter is the substratum of all change,
including generation.[65] If we were to posit that the world in its
totality came to be, there must have been a substratum from which
it came to be and in which its potentiality resided prior to its
actualization. But that substratum of potentiality cannot be
distinguished from matter, since substrata are distinguishable
only with reference to the substances which they underlie. In
itself, all potentiality is one and resides in matter.[66] Therefore,
if we posit that the world in its totality came to be, matter would
have existed prior to its own generation, which is clearly a false,
self-contradictory consequence which invalidates the premise. In
addition, if matter existed, existent things existed, because
matter cannot exist apart from the forms which it underlies.[67]
Therefore, the world in its totality could not have come to be
without the prior existence of matter and form. But this would
mean that the world existed before its generation. Therefore, the
world in its totality could not have come to be.

g) An argument from the nature of the fifth body.[68] Everything
which comes to be comes to be from its contrary and everything
which passes away passes away to its contrary. It is the action
of the contrary qualities of the sublunar elements upon each other
which cause all changes in the sublunar world. But the fifth body,
i.e., the matter of the heavenly body, has no contrary. Therefore,
there is no cause of the coming to be or of the passing away of
the heavens.[69] He leaves unstated here the conclusion that if the
heavens have no beginning, neither does the world as a whole, as
explained above.

h) An argument from the incorruptibility of the heavens. Given
the fact, established in the preceding argument, that the heavens
as they are currently constituted have no cause of passing away
and thus exist perpetually in infinite future time, it can be
demonstrated that they could not have come to be. Aristotle
claims that the incorruptible is ungenerated for the following
reason:[70] If we were to posit that the heavens came to be, the
potential for their existence would have existed for an infinite
time prior to their generation. But if this were the case, the
potential for the existence of the heavens would exist for an
infinite time and the potential for the nonexistence of the heavens
would exist for an infinite time. But this is impossible, because
contraries cannot exist simultaneously in a single substratum
unless they are defined, and there is only one undifferentiated
infinite time. Therefore, the heavens could not have come to be.
For this reason, Aristotle rejects the possibility that infinite
time can be limited at its beginning or at its end. He maintains
that a thing is either subject to generation and corruption or it
is not, so that the incorruptible cannot be generated.[71] Gersonides
concludes the discussion of the eternity of the heavens with two
final remarks. First, he advances an argument from analogy. That
is, since everything in this world which comes to be is observed
to pass away, therefore if the heavens came to be they must necessarily pass away. But since they cannot pass away, they cannot
come to be. Second, he notes that Aristotle also appealed, in
support of this position, to the generally recognized view in his
time that the heavens were eternal.[72]

i) An argument from the impossibility of a void. Aristotle defines
a void as that in which the presence of a body, though not actual,
is possible,[73] and he does not admit the possibility of the existence of a void.[74] If we were to posit that the world came to be

from nothing, then body in its totality came to be from no body.
But if this were the case, a void would have existed prior to the
generation of the world, because there must have been the possibility of a body prior to its actualization and this is the definition
of a void. But a void is an impossibility. Therefore, the world
could not have come to be from nothing. Nor could the world have
come to be from potential body, i.e., formless matter, because
formless matter cannot exist in actuality. Insofar as it is
potential, it is a void.

Gersonides closes his discussion of the arguments in support
of the Aristotelian position with two remarks about Aristotle.
First, he offers the opinion that Aristotle was motivated to argue
for eternity primarily because he believed it inappropriate to
posit of God that He causes at one time and not at another.[75]
Also, Aristotle thought it inappropriate for God, who is the nomos
of all things and from whom the world derives its existence through
His conception of that nomos in His self-conception, to have existed
without the world, for if this were the case, He would conceive
without there being an object of conception. Second, he notes that,
as Alexander of Aphrodisias, Averroes and Maimonides all relate,
Aristotle was aware that his arguments for the eternity of the
world were not a demonstration of the truth of the question.[76]

4. Preliminary Response to Aristotle's View (6:1:4)

The title of 6:1:4 reads: "in which we shall explain in some
way that the arguments which we have mentioned in support of each
of the views do not necessitate that that view is correct." The
substance of the chapter, however, is a preliminary refutation of
the arguments in support of the Aristotelian view that the world
is eternal. Gersonides begins by stating that it is clear that
only the Aristotelian view is viable, because Aristotle himself
has already refuted the other views.[77] In fact, however, Gersonides
will refute the other views later. His demonstration that time is
not infinite (6:1:11) refutes the first view that there was an
infinite succession of worlds. In 6:1:17, he explains the difficulties entailed by the Platonic and Maimonidean views before he
offers his own alternative. A complete response to the Aristotelian arguments, which employs his own view of creation, can be found
in 6:1:20-28.

The first part of the preliminary response implicitly addresses
the two considerations which, at the end of 6:1:3, Gersonides
states are the reasons which motivated Aristotle to affirm the

eternity of the world though he could not demonstrate it. The two
considerations are: 1) It is inappropriate to posit of God, the
Unmoved Mover, that He creates at one time and not at another,
because this would entail a change in His unchanging will. 2) It
is inappropriate to posit of God, from whom the world overflows
from His conception of the nomos of existent things which is His
self-conception, that He eternally conceives that nomos before it
came to be.[78]

    Gersonides responds as follows: He begins by referring to
his explanation in the fifth treatise that God is not the cause of
the world in the sense that He is the mover of the sphere of the
fixed stars.[79] Therefore, one cannot argue for the eternity of
the world on the grounds that the single, perpetual circular motion
of the first moved object is eternally related to the eternal,
unchanging divine will. Nor can one argue that Gersonides' understanding of the way in which God is the cause of all existent things
entails that existent things exist eternally with Him. God is the
primary cause of all existence in that God, in His self-conception,
perpetually conceives of the nomos of existent things and, through
His self-conception, that nomos overflows from Him to the world.
This occurs when the separate intellects long to approximate His
conception and so move their spheres. From the motions of the
heavens, the nomos of existent things overflows to the sublunar
world. Gersonides argues that this manner of causation does not
entail the eternity of the world for the following reasons:
1) God does not acquire His perfection form the world. His causation occurs out of His goodness and grace, not out of His need.
Thus, there is nothing about God that would change if we posit
that at one time He conceives of Himself without the world's existence and at another time He conceives of Himself and the world
overflows from His self-conception. Both before and after creation
He performs the same, single, unchanging function. Here Gersonides
refers the reader to his discussion below (6:1:18) for a more complete discussion of the issue. He will explain there that it is
the nature of the material receptacle that requires a choice of
the moment in which the world comes to be.
2) It is appropriate to posit that God conceived of the nomos of
existent things prior to the coming to be of the world. This is
because He does not acquire His knowledge of the nomos from existent
things as we do. Rather, they acquire their existence from the
nomos which He conceives. Thus, while we cannot acquire a true
conception of that which does not exist, God is not constrained in

this way. Gersonides offers the example of an artisan who
conceives of an artifact before he produces it, and he refers to
his explanation of this in the first treatise.[80]

As a general refutation of the other arguments in support of
the Aristotelian view, Gersonides states that they are based on an
illegitimate use of an analogy between the coming to be of the
world as a whole and the coming to be of parts of the world which
are generated according to the laws of nature. Unlike Maimonides,
who asserts that there is no parallel between the two,[81] Gersonides
is willing to admit that certain aspects of each kind of generation
are related. He does not, however, accept the notion upon which
the Aristotelian arguments are based that the two are parallel in
all respects. To illustrate the false consequences entailed by
this assumption, he offers the example of the distinction that
needs to be drawn between the birth of a man and his subsequent
nutrition.[82] As the human organs cannot exist independent of the
organism of which they are a part, and as the man exists in his
totality prior to his nutrition,[83] similarly the parts of the world
cannot exist independent of the world, and the world actually
exists in its totality logically prior to the coming to be of its
parts. The coming to be of its parts are caused by the laws of
nature and prior motions in the world.[84] Thus, if one confuses
the distinction between the absolute generation of a human being
in his totality with the partial, nutritional generation that
occurs subsequently, as the Aristotelian arguments confuse this
distinction with regard to the world, one might also demonstrate
that an individual man could not have come to be. He would, for
example, have existed prior to his (partial) coming to be.

Gersonides cites an objection to his analogy between the
partial and total generation of a human being and the partial and
total generation of the world. The objection attempts to distinguish between a man's generation and the generation of the world,
because a man does not come to be absolutely but is rather preceded
by another member of his species who causes his generation. Similarly, Aristotle affirms that the world is preceded by some prior
moved object which causes its generation.

Gersonides maintains, however, that his analogy is legitimate
for the following reasons: First, it is only insofar as a man is
part of the world that he is preceded by members of his species.
Insofar as a man is a man, no part of him causes his coming to be.
Second, one's father can die before one's birth. Thus, as with
the generation of the world, the coming to be of a man requires

that we posit a separate mover as its cause.[85] For these reasons,
the generation of the human microcosm is parallel to the generation
of the universal macrocosm, and the Aristotelian arguments for
eternity can be refuted by the absurdities which arise when they
are applied to human generation.

B.   Gersonides' Argument

1.   The Proper Method of Investigation (6:1:5-6)

As Gersonides mentions in the first two chapters, the
conclusions which one reaches about the origins of the world
depend upon the method one uses to investigate the issue and the
things which one investigates. For example, he would fault Maimonides' method of investigation. Maimonides chooses to examine the
arguments for the eternity of the world, and, having shown that
the world's eternity cannot be demonstrated, he opts for the
undemonstrated view of creation out of nothing. Similarly, Gersonides faults the Aristotelian method for basing its investigation
on the generation of existent things which come to be and pass
away, because nothing conclusive about the generation of the world
in its totality can be inferred from these instances of natural
generation. It is based upon this methodological consideration
that Gersonides states that he does not begin by investigating
whether it is appropriate to posit of God that He caused the generation of the world. Our knowledge of God is very weak and an
investigation which was founded on that weak knowledge could not
yield a demonstration of the truth. Rather, he bases his argument
on certain existent things in the world.

Gersonides proposes that the proper subjects for investigation
are those things in the world which have continuous existence. It
is these things which might reasonably be thought to be ungenerated.
They are: the heavenly bodies and their movers, time, motion and
the visible part of the earth which is elevated above the waters.
If it can be demonstrated that it is necessarily the case that
these things came to be, then the world as a whole must have come
to be. If it can be demonstrated that it is impossible for these
things to have come to be, then the world as a whole could not
have come to be. If neither alternative is demonstrable, then the
investigation will show that both the hypothesis of a generated
world and the hypothesis of an ungenerated world are possible.
That is, the heavens cause the existence of the sublunar world.
If the heavens are generated, then their effects could not have

existed prior to them. If the heavens are ungenerated, they could
not have existed without the effects for the sake of which they
move, because in that case their motions would be in vain, which
is contrary to nature,[86] and because the possibility of sublunar
existence would have existed unrealized for an infinite time prior
to its generation. This is an impossibility.[87] The generation or
the eternity of the visible part of the earth entails similar
consequences with regard to the sublunar species, because its
existence entails the possibility of their existence—a possibility
which cannot be unactualized over an infinite period of time—and
its nonexistence precludes the possibility of their existence. If
time and motion are generated, then the world must be generated,
and if they are ungenerated, then the world must be eternal, because
there is no time apart from motion and there is no motion apart from
objects in motion, as the Aristotelian arguments from time and
motion demonstrate.[88]

In order to determine whether these things came to be,
Gersonides lists three properties which generated things possess
and which distinguish them from ungenerated things.
1) Things which come to be have a final cause.[89] The end of a
thing is the function it performs to fulfill its nature. All
things generated in nature and in artisanship exhibit a purpose
which reflects the fact that they are the effects of an agent who
conceives of this purpose and causes them to fulfill the purpose.
The exception to this are accidents, but chance occurrences are
infrequent and of short duration.[90] Because of accidental generation, the absence of a final cause does not entail eternity.
Rather, the presence of a final cause entails generation. By contrast, mathematical entities, for example, do not come to be as
the effect of an agent and do not have a teleological purpose.
Here Gersonides admits the possibility that a teleologically
structured thing might not have a temporal beginning if it perpetually comes to be as the effect of the continuous action of a
cause. Though such perpetual generation is possible by definition
and accords with the definition he is offering here of the properties of generated things, he will demonstrate the impossibility of
the continuous causation of the heavens later by limiting the
category to accidental things (6:1:7).
2) Things which come to be possess nonessential properties which
neither define them nor follow from their definitions. For example,
a piece of wood is accidentally a chair or box. Neither is

necessary from the nature of the wood and their accidental
existence reflects the causal action of the artisan. On the other
hand, things which are not generated cannot have unessential properties insofar as they are ungenerated. Their nature does not
require those accidents, so that one would have to posit a cause
of the perpetual existence of those accidents within them.[91]
3) Things which come to be may have something in their essence
which functions for the sake of some other thing.[92] An example of
this with regard to naturally generated things is the way plants
serve as nutrition for animals. An example of this with regard to
things generated by will is the way that clothes serve human welfare. By contrast, something which does not come to be cannot
function for the sake of some other things, because such a function
entails a teleological cause, which an ungenerated thing cannot
have. Also, a thing which functions essentially for the sake of
some other thing has a connection with that other thing which an
ungenerated thing would possess perpetually. But such a perpetual
connection could only exist as an effect of a providential cause,
so that that "ungenerated" thing would be essentially the effect
of an agent.

Though the first and the third properties are related and
though something which possesses the third property must also
possess the first, the two are not identical. The heavens, for
example, move for the sake of the sublunar world. Their final
cause, however, is the divine nomos which the separate movers long
to approximate. Or, the final cause of a seed is the tree which
is its nature to become. It exists, however, for the sake of animal nutrition. Thus, we may assume that Gersonides distinguishes
between these two properties because with regard to any given
generated thing the investigator might note one and not the other
property. The existence of either property entails generation.
Nevertheless, his demonstrations below that the heavens possess
both of these properties will necessarily overlap because they are
interrelated.

2. <u>That the Heavens Have a Final Cause</u> (6:1:7)

Gersonides' argument that the heavens are teleologically
caused is based upon his discussion in the fifth treatise where
he shows that all aspects of the motions of the heavenly bodies
exist in the most perfect possible way for the purpose of perfecting sublunar existence so that the slightest alteration of the
heavenly bodies' shapes, distances, velocities, radiations,

arrangements, etc. would result in the passing away of the sublunar world.[93] All of the motions of the spheres combine to form a single nomos which overflows from them. From this marvelous unity, Gersonides infers that there must be a single causal principle which created them in this unified perfection for the purpose of generating the overflow of the divine nomos. By definition, then, the heavens must have come to be as the effect of an agent because of their teleological structure. For this reason, Aristotle stated that it is more of an error to attribute chance as the cause of the heavens than to do so with regard to the sublunar species, because nothing in the heavens is accidental.[94]

Gersonides then argues that the heavens must have been generated absolutely by their cause and cannot have been caused by perpetual overflow from their cause as sunlight, for example, overflows from the sun. This argument attempts to show that if we accept Aristotle's view that the universe has a teleological structure, then it follows necessarily that the world cannot have been caused perpetually without beginning. As Touati points out, the object of his attack here significantly resembles the Atomistic view of the Kalam that the world is continuously caused by God at every moment.[95] Aristotle would not have argued for continuous re-creation. He does argue, however, that if the existence of a cause necessarily entails the existence of an effect, then if the cause is eternal, the effect is eternal.[96] Gersonides wants to claim that, though we can posit the continuous causation of an accident such as motion,[97] it is more difficult to posit this of a thing which exists essentially. In what sense can we posit that the heavens are created if they are not created at a given moment and are not given at that moment a nature according to which they can function subsequently? His answer to this implicit question is that the heavens must be created at every moment, according to this hypothesis, in the sense that they are moved at every moment.[98] But the hypothesis that the motions of the heavens overflow perpetually from God entails the following false consequences:
1) They must pass away to nothing immediately after overflowing from Him so that they can again, at the next moment, overflow into existence from nothing. We can't say that the subsequent existence of the heavens is caused by God in the sense that He causes their existence from their prior existence. If this were the case, the generation of the heavens would have occurred just once. By definition, the coming to be of a thing is from something other than itself.

2) The heavens must come to be and pass away in a single "now."
If we were to posit that the heavens come to be at moment A and
pass away at moment B and come to be at moment C, their existence
would not be continuous,[99] and their existence would not overflow
perpetually from God. Therefore, they must come to be and pass
away in a single "now." But the latter is impossible because two
contraries would be gathered together undefined in a single substratum perpetually, i.e., the heavens simultaneously would exist
and would not exist for an infinite time.

3) The heavens must come to be at each and every "now." Thus, the
"nows" would be continuous and time would be composed of "nows."
There could be not time between "nows" because the heavens would
not exist at those times and they are posited to overflow perpetually. But, by definition, time cannot be composed of "nows"
because the "now," which measures time, is not a part of time. The
"now" is indivisible, unlike time, and there is no motion in a
"now."[100]

4) The heavenly bodies would exist only potentially, because their
existence would endure only for a "now." But things which exist
only for a "now" exist potentially.[101]

5) The heavenly bodies would not have continuous motion, because
continuous motion requires a single moved object.[102] But if the
heavens are re-created at every moment, their existence cannot be
continuous.

6) There would be no motion in the heavens because they would
exist only in the "now" and there is no motion in the "now."[103]

     On the basis of all of these false consequences, Gersonides
rejects the hypothesis that the heavens perpetually overflow from
God. Since they have a final cause, however, they must be generated.
Therefore, they must be generated by God at the moment of generation. They cannot be said to endure perpetually with God as their
form, as the matter of lower existent things endures because of its
form, for the following reasons: First, this hypothesis would
account for the cause of their duration, but it does not address
the question of their efficient cause which, since it cannot cause
them perpetually, must cause them at the moment of their generation.
Second, the analogy is faulty because matter endures through its
form because its form predominates over contraries which are potential causes of passing away. The heavens, however, are not composite and do not have contraries.

Thus, it has been demonstrated that the heavens are generated and that they are generated at a particular moment in time and are not caused perpetually without beginning. It is impossible that their variety of functions occur accidently because they function to form a single, perfect nomos which requires a purposeful cause.[104]

He concludes the discussion with two arguments that the generation of the heavens entails the generation of the world. 1) Without the heavens, there would be no above and below. If there were no above and below, there would be no elements, because the nature of the elements is to be at rest above and below one another and to move up and down to their natural positions.[105] If there were no elements, the world, which is composed of the elements, would not exist.

2) Since the heavens are the principle which causes natural things, the effects of that causal principle cannot exist without the cause.

3. That the Heavens Have Nonessential Properties (6:1:8)

The fifth body of which the heavens are composed is simple, of homogeneous parts and without contraries.[106] Thus, the nature of the heavens does not require the great diversity of its species. All characteristics of all heavenly bodies are therefore nonessential characteristics which serve as evidence that the heavens are generated. For example, the separate movers of the spheres should not have specific differences in the way they each move their respective spheres; the spheres should not be of diverse quantities; the heavenly body whould be one in number; all parts of a sphere should be homogeneous without variations in thickness and without the stars; and all stars should be identical in quantity, color, radiation, and influence upon the sublunar world.

None of these diverse characteristics are accounted for either by the view that the heavens are eternal or by the view that the heavens come to be naturally. If the heavens are eternal, then we cannot account for their nonessential characteristics, because those characteristics do not follow from their definition. Nor can we account for their nonessential characteristics if we posit that they came to be naturally, because the nature of the heavens does not require this diversity of characteristics. That is, the separate movers of the supralunar spheres do not acquire their perfection from the variegated structures and motions of their spheres and the nature of the substance of the heavens, which is homogeneous, also does not account for this diversity.

To resolve this problem, Gersonides returns to his distinction
between the generation of the world in its totality and the generation of its parts after it has come to be in its totality. The
latter generation occurs naturally, according to the natural laws
of the divine nomos which governs the sublunar world. Each thing
acts according to its nature and the diversity which exists among
individual members of species is caused by the accidental action
of contraries in natural generation, for the purpose of the preservation of each of the species. The generation of the world in its
totality, however, must be posited, on account of the diversity in
the heavens, to be generated by will. God created the world in its
totality by a single act of will. As the artisan can vary the
shape and size of his artifact according to his will, so God created
the world according to His will and He willed the diversity in the
heavens, which is not required by their nature, in order to fulfill
His purposes.[107]

4.   That the Heavens Act for the Sake of Some Other Thing (6:1:9)

The heavens also have the third property of generated things,
i.e., all of their motions are for the sake of the perfection of
the sublunar world. It cannot be posited that they move, as sublunar animals move, for their own sake, in order, for example, to
approach what they need or to flee from that which is harmful to
them,[108] because the heavens need nothing to perfect their existence
and have no contraries from which to flee. Gersonides undertakes
here to refute Aristotle's attempts to show that everything in the
supralunar world follows necessarily from the nature of the heavens.
He deals with the following claims:
1) The heavens move because they are animate and motion is the
life of living things.[109] Therefore, the heavens would move for
their own sake. Gersonides rejects this argument on two counts.
First, if the premise is granted, what follows is that the heavens
move in some way and not that they move to perfect the sublunar
world in the marvelous way that it is perfected. Thus, their
motion cannot be said to perfect themselves alone. Second, the
premise is faulty. Living things move to achieve their ends.
There is no gratuitous motion in nature that endures for very long.
The heavens, which are perfect in themselves, have no need to move
for the sake of fulfilling their end and it cannot be posited that
they perpetually act gratuitously.
2) The heavens move so that the intellects which move them can have
the pleasure of conception, as the human intellect derives pleasure

from the conception of motion.[110] Therefore, the heavens move for
the sake of the intelligible world. Gersonides rejects this argument for the following reasons: First, the motion involved in human
conception is a function of the hylic nature of that conception.
The human intellect acquires conceptions by abstracting them from
their material instantiations. It is a cumulative process which
requires the intellect to actualize its potential conceptions, and
it is in this sense that it involves motion. By contrast, the conception of the spheres' intellects is separate so that it is
totally actual and perpetual. For this reason Aristotle refers to
their conception as "rest."[111] Thus, the spheres' motion cannot
be for the sake of their own conception. Second, if we were to
grant that the spheres need motion for the sake of their own conception, it would not necessarily follow that they would move in
the marvelous way that perfects the sublunar world. Third, the
premise is faulty because, as Aristotle states, motion inhibits
conception.[112] Therefore, the only way to posit that the motions
of the spheres are for the sake of their own conception is to say
that the separate intellects conceive of the divine nomos and that
they long to move their spheres in a way that this nomos overflows
from them to the sublunar world. But if this is the case, then
they are, in fact, moving for the sake of the sublunar world.
3) In several places, Aristotle attempts to account for the motions
and diversity of the heavenly bodies by attributing necessary and
natural causes to them. Gersonides cites the following three
examples: a) Aristotle states that the motion of the daily sphere
is from east to west because east is right and motion from right to
left is more venerable than from left to right.[113] b) Aristotle
states that the upper stars move more slowly than the lower stars
because of their proximity to the outermost sphere which moves in
the opposite direction.[114] c) Aristotle states that the sphere
of the fixed stars contains many stars while the lower spheres each
contain only one star because, if the lower spheres each had more
than one star, the separate intellect of the outermost sphere would
not have the strength to move them.[115] Gersonides raises objections
to each of these claims and concludes that Aristotle is incorrect
in assuming that the heavens' properties follow from their nature.
    Thus, the supralunar bodies move for the sake of perfecting
the sublunar world, as Aristotle himself admits,[116] and they must
therefore be caused. Here Gersonides reviews some of the positions
of the followers of Aristotle who did not recognize that his arguments do not demonstrate the world's eternity and who posit that

the world perpetually emanates from God as a single thing—a
separate intellect, we assume—and that compositeness arises out
of the duality of that thing's conception of both itself and its
cause. He states that Averroes' discussion of the matter in his
Commentary to the Metaphysica does not explain adequately how the
materiality of the spheres could overflow from God as well as the
separate intellects, if it is posited that this all occurs by
nature and not by will. He also states that Averroes' predecessors
posited the perpetual overflow of the world from God and that consequently their view was vulnerable to the objections which Gersonides
raises in his discussion of continuous causation. Thus, Averroes
modified the view and posited that God perpetually unites and
orders the spheres. This view, however, entails absolute generation at a moment in time, as Gersonides has already explained
above.[117]

In summary, Gersonides has demonstrated that the heavens
possess all three of the properties which distinguish generated
things from ungenerated things. They have a marvelous purpose;
they have nonessential properties; and they act for the sake of
some other thing.

5. On the Visible Part of the Earth (6:1:13)

Gersonides applies the same method of investigation to the
visible part of the earth as he does to the heavens and reaches
the conclusion that it possesses all three of the properties
possessed by generated things. That the visible part of the earth
must be posited to have continuous existence is apparent because if
it were to pass away for a moment, all the species which live upon
it would pass away and would not have the capacity to be regener-
ated.[118] Thus, as a thing which has continuous existence, it is one
of the proper subjects for investigation. If it necessarily is
generated, then the world is generated, for the heavens and the
elements could not have existed for an infinite period of time
prior to the generation of the visible part of the earth. If this
were the case, the heavens would have moved for an unrealized purpose for an infinite time and the possibility of the earth's elevation would have been unrealized for an infinite time.[119]

First, the elevated part of the earth clearly has a final
cause. Its existence makes possible the existence of all sublunar
species which live upon it. This purpose cannot be posited to
occur by chance, because accidents are infrequent and of short
duration. This benefit, however, is not only long-lasting—it is

continuous. Therefore, a purposeful cause must be posited to
account for the generation of the elevated part of the earth.

Second, the elevation of the earth does not follow from the
definitions of the elements earth and water. The natures of earth
and water require that the earth be encompassed by the water, so
that the elevation of the earth is a nonessential property. Nor can
the earth's elevation be posited to follow necessarily from the
overflow of the motions of the heavenly bodies to the sublunar
world. All other influences from the celestial world vary according
to the proximity of the influential star to the earth and cause
their effects upon whole sections of the earth. But there is no
star to which we can attribute the constant and perpetual elevation
of the earth, and no star to which we can attribute the fact that
only some parts of the earth are elevated perpetually.[120] Since
the elevation of the earth follows neither from the natures of the
elements nor from the necessary influence of the heavens, it must
be a nonessential property which is caused by the willful action
of an agent at the moment of its creation. Its subsequent perpetual
duration, however, is a result of supralunar influence.

Gersonides rejects Aristotle's claim that the cause of the
earth's visibility is the heat of the sun in the northern hemisphere which dries the water.[121] If this were the case, the
entire earth ought to be visible except for the two poles, because
the influence of the sun predominates in both the north and the
south. Thus, Averroes assigns the heat of the illuminations of
the stars as an additional cause of the elevation of the earth in
the north, because there are more stars in the north than in the
south.[122] Gersonides rejects this suggestion because the drying
action of the stars' illuminations cannot account for the elevation
of the earth above the water. The generation of the element earth
is related to the cold and not to heat.[123]

Third, the elevation of the visible part of the earth is for
the sake of something other than itself, i.e., for the sake of the
species which live upon it. Thus, it has the third property of
generated things.

In addition to the fact that the generation of the elevated
part of the earth must be posited, as explained above, to have
been by divine will and not by nature, the generation of land
species upon it must also have been by will and not be nature. By
nature, individual members of species come to be from members of
their own species. The first member of the succession of

individuals, therefore, must have been generated by will. The
Creator willed that the species should come to be and that they
should endure by nature.

6. <u>On the Finite Nature of Time and Motion</u> (6:1:10-12)

Though he has already demonstrated that the heavens are
generated and though time and motion are accidents which inhere in
moved objects so that they could not have existed prior to the
generation of a first moved object, Gersonides investigates the
question of the eternity of time and motion independently of his
investigation of the eternity of the heavens. He offers two reasons for this independent investigation. First, if he can demonstrate that time is generated, he will refute the view that there
has been an infinite succession of created worlds, because that
view is based on the eternal, infinite nature of time. Second,
Aristotle's arguments for the eternity of the heavens are based
upon the infinite nature of time. Unless Gersonides can demonstrate
that time must necessarily have a beginning, his own demonstration
of the generation of the heavens will lack credibility.

He begins with a discussion of the nature of time upon which
he can found his argument. In this discussion, he makes five
observations about the nature of time.

1) Time is a quantity. This can be shown clearly because we speak
of parts of time as equal or unequal, and these are characteristics
of quantity.[124]

2) Time is a continuous quantity, because it has the following
characteristics: its parts are referred to as long and short;[125]
it is measured hypothetically, not by nature;[126] and its end is
the "now" which is the single extremity of both past and future
time[127] and which is not itself continuous.[128]

3) Time resides in a substratum in one respect and is separate in
another respect. Time is separable from its substratum, because
if it were in its substratum, it would be multiple and multiplied
by the number of subjects in which it resides. But there is only
one time.[129] Therefore, time is separate in one respect. In
another respect, however, time is not separate. First, it has
distinguishable parts, because present time is distinct from past
and from future time and because if it did not have different parts,
the impossible consequence would be entailed that contraries would
simultaneously reside in a single substratum in a single respect.[130]
Second, given that time is composed of homogeneous parts,[131] it

must not be separate. If it were separate, it would not have
different parts, because homogeneous parts can be distinguished
only in respect to their different substrata. Also, if it were
separate, any part of time would be identical to the whole of time,
because homogeneous parts are identical to their whole in definition and are different from the whole only with respect to their
substrata. Therefore, time is separate in one respect and is not
separate in another respect. Its subject is motion of which it is
an accident and which it numbers, but it is separate from motion
in that it is not multiplied by the multiple motions which it
numbers.[132]

4) Past time is actual in some way and future time is absolutely
potential. Time is an accident which inheres in and numbers motion.
As the existence of motion is partly potential and partly actual,[133]
so is the existence of time. Future time is potential.[134] Time is
actualized in the present so that past time is in some sense actual,
though, unlike motion for which an actual trace of the perfection
acquired by the moved object remains,[135] there is no actual trace
of past time which remains except in terms of the motion it has
measured. We cannot posit that time is totally potential, for if
this were the case, contrary possibilities would exist with regard
to the past as well as the future. All possibilities would remain
unactualized.[136]

5) Time is one and it is multiple neither in respect to simultaneous
nor to successive parts. Many times cannot exist simultaneously,
because time is present equally everywhere and with all things.[137]
Nor can times be multiple successively. If this were the case,
this multiplicity would exist as it does, for example, in the human
species. Individual human beings are essentially distinguishable
by nature and not by hypothesis as is the case with time. But
since time is divisible only hypothetically and has no defined
extremities that cannot be posited as middles of other periods of
time, time is one in actuality though potentially multiple in its
measurement. Therefore, times cannot be multiple in succession.

Having established these characteristics about time, Gersonides
proceeds to argue that time must have been generated. The first
two and the fifth arguments are based upon the logic of quantitative
discourse. The other seven arguments list the difficulties entailed
by the hypothesis that time is infinite.

1) Quantity insofar as it is quantity is finite, because quantity
is measurable and knowable and the infinite is neither measurable

nor knowable.[138] Aristotle explains that all classes of quantity
are finite, i.e., there can neither be an actual infinite body[139]
nor an infinite surface[140] nor an infinite magnitude[141] nor an
infinite number.[142] Therefore, since time is a quantity, time
cannot be infinite. Though Aristotle admits the infinite augmenta-
bility of number and the infinite divisibility of magnitude,[143]
the infinite in these cases exists potentially in the functions of
augmentation and division. Every member in the succession of
addition is finite and every magnitude which is divided has a finite
number of parts. Number and magnitude can only be number and magnitude and these always remain finite in actuality. It is not
possible to suggest that time need not have been generated absolutely even though it is finite in quantity because one can posit
an infinite succession of finite times, as might be posited by
those who believe in an infinite succession of worlds. This is
not possible because time is one, continuous and not multiple.
Nor can one object that, as Aristotle asserts, time may be infinite
insofar as it is potential as the augmentation of number or the
division of magnitude is infinite in potentiality. Gersonides
agrees that time can be said to be infinite in the sense that it,
like all magnitude, is infinitely divisible and it, like all number,
is infinitely augmentable. But neither of these properties entails
that time itself is infinite in quantity. In addition, he rejects
the objection on the following grounds: a) If augmentation and
division are infinite in potentiality, then time is infinitely
augmentable only with respect to the future, in which time is
potential. In respect to actualized past time, time will always
remain finite. b) He rejects the assertion that body, number and
magnitude are finite in quantity because they are actual. As
Aristotle himself shows with regard to the numerability of number,
quantity is finite because it is measurable.[144] c) He rejects the
assumption that all things which are potential are necessarily
infinite and offers the contrary example of rectilinear motion
which is not actual but is necessarily finite in quantity.[145]
2) All classes and concepts of body are finite in quantity. Time
is a concept of body, since it inheres, in some sense, in motion
and there is no motion without a moved body. Therefore, time must
be finite in quantity. He offers here an exhaustive list of the
categories and concepts of body and shows how each is necessarily
finite because it is defined.

3) If time were infinite in quantity, past time would be infinite
in quantity and the world would be eternal, because there cannot
be eternal, continuous time without eternal, continuous motion.
If this were the case, there could be no variation in the velocities of the motion of the spheres. If there were variations in
these velocities, a sphere which moves at a greater velocity would
accumulate a greater number of rotations than a sphere which moves
at a lesser velocity. But if past time were infinite, the number
of rotations of all spheres would be infinite. But since large and
small are terms which apply to finite quantities, no infinite magnitude can be greater than any other.[146] Therefore, all spheres
would have an equal number of rotations in past infinite time and
would thus have an equal velocity. But since the conclusion conflicts with empirical observation of the variation in the velocities
of the spheres, the premise is false. Therefore, past time is
finite in quantity.[147]

4) Arguing again from the premise that no infinite can be greater
than another, Gersonides proceeds to show that if past time were
infinite in quantity, the following absurdities would be entailed:
since the time of past lunar eclipses would be infinite, the moon
would have been eclipsed perpetually and since the time in which
the moon was not eclipsed would be infinite, the moon would have
never been eclipsed; the luminous part of the moon would perpetually have faced east of the sun and west of the sun; the light of
the moon would have perpetually been increasing and decreasing
simultaneously; the planets would have been perpetually east and
west of the sun, would have been perpetually moving forward and
backward and would have been perpetually inclined towards the north
and towards the south. He refers here to Aristotle's own argument
that the heavens' motion must be regular as based on similar
premises.[148]

5) This argument is based on his assertion that time is subject to
the logic of quantitative discourse. No "when" is infinite, since
every part of time is finite and the "when" measures the finite.
Since time is composed of homogeneous parts, all parts of time
share a single meaning. Since no "when" is infinite, no part of
past time is an infinite distance to the present "now." But if
time were posited to be infinite, given any "when" in the past,
the relation of the time before it to the time between it and the
present would be the relation of an infinite to a finite. But
since every "when" in time has a single meaning, this is impossible.
Therefore, time must be finite.

6) Given that the nature of time is to come to be continuously as
the measure of perpetually augmented motion, past time cannot be
infinite. If past time were infinite, the motion which it has
measured would be actually infinite and, since one infinite cannot
be greater than another infinite, the motion which occurs in the
present would not augment infinite past motion and would not be
measurable. Therefore, time would have to be posited to exist
without motion, which is contrary to its definition. Therefore,
past time must be finite.[149] If we were to posit that time can be
generated as the measure of an infinite succession of motions and
that there is no trace of temporal measurement in the infinite
motion, it is necessarily the case that time must have first been
finite before it became infinite. If it had always been infinite,
it would not be connected to motion at all. But if time was first
finite, then it had a beginning and it can never become an actual
infinite quantity through its perpetual augmentation.

7) By definition, time measures actual motion as it is generated.
Since time is one and continuous, it is necessarily the case that
time measures successive motion in its totality. Since the infinite
cannot be measured or defined,[150] time must be finite insofar as
it is the measure of motion.

8) By definition, time comes to be in a forward direction as the
measure of the succession of generated motion.[151] If we were to
posit that past time is infinite, we would have to posit that for
any past time which is measured there exists past time before that
measurement. But if this were the case, time would come to be in
a backwards direction. Therefore, past time cannot be infinite.
Two additional considerations apply here. First, there would be
no way for finite time to become infinite because the intermediate
between the finite and the infinite would be neither finite nor
infinite. Since no such intermediate can exist, there is no way
for finite time to become infinite.[152] Second, the infinite cannot
be generated from an endless succession of finite quantities. No
matter how large the augmented finite magnitude becomes, it remains
finite.

9) If time were infinite in quantity, it would be more likely that
this would occur in respect to the future, which is absolutely
potential, rather than in respect to the actual past. But future
time can never become infinite in quantity, because no matter which
point in past time we choose to begin our measurement, that measurement will remain finite in quantity. But if future time cannot be

infinite in quantity, certainly past time cannot be infinite in quantity.

10) If past time were infinite, it would measure the motion of a moved object which moves continuously in a circle, as Aristotle explains. This moved object would be the heavens, since it is they who move in this way. Since it has been demonstrated above that the heavens were generated, there is no such motion for an infinite time to measure in the past. Therefore, past time is finite.

As a demonstration that motion is generated (6:1:12), Gersonides shows that the ten arguments for the finite nature of time can also be employed to demonstrate that motion is finite.

Both with regard to time and to motion, Gersonides concludes his demonstration by arguing against the claims that past time and past motion do not exist in themselves. He is apparently responding to the argument, made by Maimonides and Averroes, that an infinite succession is not an impossibility with respect to time and motion because they are accidents and because an infinite series of successive motions would not actually exist simultaneously.[153] Gersonides does not admit a distinction between an accidental and essential infinite series. Both time and motion, he iterates, are existent things which are actualized as the motion of the moved object is generated. There is no intelligent way to speak of the perfection which is realized in a moved object without positing the existence of motion, and there is no motion without time. Though they are both accidents and though they pass away as they move forward, they are numerable quantities and must therefore be finite.

7. Philoponus' Argument from Finitudes (6:1:14)

After having demonstrated that things with continuous existence—i.e., the heavens, the visible part of the earth which is elevated, time and motion—are generated, and that the world must thus have come to be, Gersonides proceeds to investigate the validity of the argument for creation from finitudes which he attributes to John Philoponus. He cites Averroes' refutation of the argument and shows that the refutation is not valid. Nevertheless, he does not accept the argument as valid, because the argument is based on the corruptibility of the world and he does not believe that the world is corruptible once it has been generated.

He presents the argument in the following way: Aristotle states that it is impossible for an infinite force to exist in a finite body.[154] Given that the heavens are a finite body,[155] no

infinite force can exist within them. Since a finite force cannot
cause motion for an infinite time,[156] the heavens must pass away.
Since everything which passes away must come to be, the heavens,
and consequently the world, must have come to be.[157]

According to Gersonides, Averroes sought to refute the
argument by noting that the heavenly bodies only have potential
with regard to place. In all other respects they are actual and
possess no contingency. Thus, what follows from the argument is
not that the heavens must eventually pass away but that their
motion must eventually cease. But the latter does not occur because
the heavens are moved by separate causes which are not in the finite
body of the heavens and can thus have an infinite power.[158]

In his consideration of Averroes' claim, Gersonides makes the
following arguments:

1) When a moved object has a finite possibility to be moved, it
becomes weak as it approaches its limit to be in motion. The
cessation of its motion is always caused by a weakness in the
moved object and not in the mover. For example, a musician moves
his limbs because of the conception of the music in his soul.
When he grows tired and ceases to play his instrument, the conception of the song remains unchanged. Thus, Averroes would seem to
be confusing the efficient and final causes of the motion of the
heavens. The infinite existence of the separate intellects may
persist everlastingly and, in fact, is not subject to temporal
measurement since it is not material and in motion. But if the
body of the heavens is posited to have a finite possibility for
motion, we must infer that, if it is moved perpetually, it must be
compelled to move against its nature through contact with another
body. But this is clearly false, because there is no body outside
the heavens and because a separate mover does not move in this way.
Therefore, the heavens' motion must be finite.

2) If Averroes is correct, then the motion of the heavens must be
posited to be perpetually possible with respect to themselves and
perpetually necessary with respect to their cause. If this were
the case, the heavens, in their motion, would be coerced against
their nature perpetually for infinite past time. But Aristotle
explicitly states that compulsory motion cannot be long-lasting,
let alone continuous and eternal.[159] Therefore, the motion of the
heavens cannot be compulsory and must be finite.

3) The movers of the heavens do not move them by compulsion. The
heavens have motion in respect to conception and apprehension which

their movers have and which make them long to move the spheres.
Thus, the motion of the heavens is not perpetually caused by the
power of the separate intellects but rather by their longing to move
in accordance with the conception of the divine nomos. Therefore,
since their motion cannot be posited to be compulsory, it must be
finite.

4) Averroes' argument is undercut by Aristotle's statement that if
the lower spheres each contained more than one star, the separate
mover of the outermost sphere would be weak in moving them.[160]
This would suggest that the separate movers are in fact limited in
their power to move by the substance of the spheres.

Thus, Gersonídes concludes that Philoponus is correct in
inferring from Aristotle's premises that the heavens are corruptible. He maintains, however, that this inference is not valid
because, as he will explain below (6:1:16), the heavens are not
composite, have no contrary and therefore have no cause of passing
away.

8. An Argument from the Imperfection of Human Culture (6:1:15)

Gersonides concludes his argument for the generation of the
world with a proof that he presents as independent of everything
that precedes it. It appears to be related, however, to his sixth
argument for the generation of time and motion: if past time were
infinite, past motion would be infinite and would thus not be
augmentable. Thus, one of the premises upon which this argument
is based is that one infinite cannot be larger than another. A
second premise which he assumes here is that all possibilities are
realized in an infinite time.

Given that human knowledge of the sciences—e.g., mathematics,
physics, astronomy—is gradually augmented over long periods of
time because of the nature of human beings to long and to strive
for a perfect conception of these sciences, the human species cannot have existed for an infinite past time. If this were the case,
no developments in the knowledge of these sciences could have been
made within recent human history. Given our potential to know these
things, the perfection of our knowledge would have been realized
previously in infinite time. Implicit in this argument is Gersonides' understanding of knowledge as that which encompasses and
defines and which is therefore finite.[161] Also implicit is his
understanding that the generation of the human species entails the
generation of all subordinate sublunar species which exists to

serve the end of human perfection.[162] It also entails the
generation of the heavens, the motions of which are for the sake of
the perfection of all sublunar existence, so that these motions
cannot be posited to have moved in vain for an infinite period of
time in the past. Therefore, given that the generation of the
heavens entails the generation of the world, this argument is
intended as a demonstration of the generation of the world.

Gersonides applies the argument to several other examples to
make the identical point. Given that the Torah is a perfect nomos
which is very superior to all other nomoi and which was revealed
to Moses because of the perfection of Moses' conception which
enabled him to apprehend it in its totality,[163] we can infer that
the human species must have had a finite past existence. If its
existence had been infinite, the potential for the level of conception attained by Moses would have been realized in the infinite
time before him.

Similarly, given that languages are conventional,[164]
Gersonides suggests a theory of the development of language in
which a people must precede its language so that it can establish
linguistic conventions. Since the human species requires language
for its preservation, it cannot be posited that the human species
existed for an infinite time before linguistic conventions were
established. Nor can an infinite series of languages be posited
to have been developed successively in the past. Therefore, he
concludes that the existence of the human species must have
preceded language only for a finite time.

9. That the World is Incorruptible (6:1:16)

Having demonstrated that the world is generated, Gersonides
offers a preliminary argument that the world cannot pass away after
having been generated. His discussion here is an elaboration of
his reasons for disagreeing with Philoponus' assumption (6:1:14)
that the heavens must pass away. Later (6:1:27), he will offer a
thorough examination of the Aristotelian argument that generability
and corruptibility entail each other. His argument here has two
parts. First, the heavens, and therefore the world, have no natural
cause of passing away. Second, the world can have no cause of passing away with respect to the divine will.

Natural passing away occurs in respect to the matter of the
thing which passes away and not in respect to its form. That is,
the form of a thing strives to preserve a given existent thing

and passing away occurs when a contrary power predominates over
the prior form, i.e., when the matter's affection predominates
over the form's activity.[165] Thus, passing away in nature occurs
insofar as a thing is composite and has contraries. Since the
heavenly body neither has a contrary nor is composed of contraries,[166] it is impossible for it to pass away naturally. Since the
heavens cannot pass away, the world as a whole cannot pass away,
because the nomos which sustains the sublunar world overflows from
the heavens.

Gersonides does not agree with Maimonides that the world can
pass away through the action of the divine will as it has come to
be through the action of the divine will.[167] As a preliminary
consideration he observes that the state of affairs of the heavens
requires that they be posited to have come to be by willful creation. Their state of affairs does not require, however, that they
be posited to pass away by willful action. Furthermore, things
which pass away as a result of willful action are caused either by
good intentions or by destructive intentions. As examples of
destruction for good intentions, he mentions the artisan who
destroys an imperfect artifact in order to create a more perfect
artifact, or who destroys an artifact to make some other thing
which he needs. As examples of destruction for evil intentions,
he mentions the angry actions of wicked men who destroy things
gratuitously or out of vengeance.

Neither of these possibilities are appropriate to posit of
the divine will. God does not destroy things gratuitously or in
anger. Nor can we posit that God would destroy this world to create
a better one. Given the nature of God, whose knowledge is actual
and perpetual, whose wisdom cannot be improved and whose will cannot have been previously obstructed, the world which has overflowed
from His self-conception is the most perfect possible world. Nor
can God be posited to destroy out of need, because He needs nothing.
Thus, though it is natural for the divine will to create,[168] it is
not natural for the divine will to destroy.

C. Gersonides' View

1. The Way in Which the World Came to Be (6:1:17)

Since the world has been demonstrated to be generated,
Gersonides proceeds to investigate the manner in which that generation occurred. He examines the Platonic and the Maimonidean
alternatives—the two versions of the second view that the world

came to be only once—and finds each of them deficient. He then
offers his own view in which he attempts to avoid the difficulties
entailed by the two other views.

The list of impossible consequences which he lists as being
entailed by the Platonic view stems from his application of
Aristotelian physics to it. That is, Plato posits that the world
came to be as an ordering of pre-existent disorderly motion.[169]
Since this pre-existent matter had disorderly motion, it cannot
have been formless, because matter cannot move itself without
form.[170] As Gersonides understands Plato's view, the disorderly
motion would have occurred in what is now the sublunar world. The
heavens would have existed in some form, though not necessarily
with motions or with stars identical to those which now exist
perpetually. The heavens must have existed because circular motion
is prior to rectilinear motion in that up and down are determined
by the location of a center and a circumference.[171] Given that
prior matter had form and was moved in disorderly motions, i.e.,
motions which are not the motions of this world, the following
impossible consequences are entailed:

1) Given that the motions of the prior world cannot, by definition,
be posited to be identical to the motions of this world, because
this hypothesis entails that the world itself existed prior to its
own coming to be, the prior world would have passed away over the
course of infinite past time and would not have had a subsequent
cause to come to be. That is, if the prior motions did not have
the order of the motions of this world, then the heavens would not
have had the stars and/or the motions which perfect sublunar existence. But if this were the case, the balance between the contrary
powers of the elements would not have been maintained and one of
the contraries would have predominated over the others. For example, fire might have burned the other elements. If this had
occurred, the four elements, from which the sublunar world is
ordered by the actions of the heavens, would not have existed at
the subsequent point in time at which Plato posits they were
ordered.[172]

2) Given that the hypothesis of eternal pre-existent disorderly
motion requires that the elements would have existed without interacting to form the hierarchy of composite species for the sake of
which the elements exist, the elements would have existed gratuitously for an infinite time. But gratuitous existence occurs
infrequently and for short durations.[173]

3) Given the inevitable predominance of one contrary over the other, as explained above, the pre-existent world out of which this world was ordered would not have been in motion as Plato claimed. This is because the motion of sublunar things occurs because of the interactions of contraries and because each of the elements strives to move upwards or downwards to its natural position. But if one of the elements had predominated over the others, there could have been no such motions.

4) The motion of the heavens would have been gratuitous for an infinite time, since no order would overflow from them to the sublunar world for the sake of which they move. As noted above, it is impossible to posit that perpetual motion is gratuitous.

5) Given that the hypothesis of prior disorderly motion requires that there was circular motion and that the heavens therefore did exist in some form with at least some stars, that prior state of affairs must be posited to have itself been created by an act of will. That is, circular motion requires as its cause a separate intellect because the motion is single and must therefore have a noncomposite cause which perpetually longs with a single conception to fulfill the divine nomos by causing the perfect motion. But if this were the case, the motions of the heavens would have been for the sake of the perfection, in some way, of the sublunar world. But the existence of even one star in the spheres has been shown above (6:1:8) to require that we posit a creator who acts by will, since the nature of the heavens requires no diversity. Therefore, the prior state of affairs which Plato posits also entails a coming to be by will and therefore, according to Plato, we must posit that God willed more than one world. But it has already been explained that this is impossible (6:1:16).

6) Given Plato's hypothesis, time and motion must be infinite in quantity. Given the above demonstrations that they are finite (6:1:10-12), Plato's view is false.

The alternative version of the second view that the world was generated once is that it came to be from nothing. Gersonides proceeds to show that this version also entails a series of impossible consequences. He makes the following points:

1) He begins with a discussion of the first argument which he lists in its support above (6:1:3). That argument attempts to draw an analogy between individual instances of coming to be in nature and the coming to be of the world as a whole. It argues that all things which come to be come to be from nothing. That is,

a generated thing comes to insofar as its form comes to be, and
its form comes to be from nothing. Gersonides observes here that
this argument actually provides evidence against the view of creation from nothing. That is, in any process of generation, the
material substratum is not generated. Bodies are not generated.
All generation occurs when forms come to be from the composition
of their material substrata.[174] Therefore, if we are going to argue
from analogy, we must observe that no body comes to be from non-
body.

2) He then turns to the impossible consequences which are entailed
by the hypothesis that body came to be from non-body. All of these
consequences depend on Aristotle's discussion of the void or vacuum. First, Gersonides restates the ninth argument in support of
the Aristotelian view above (6:1:3). That is, if the world came
to be from nothing, it came to be from a void. Since it is impossible that a void exist, this is clearly false.[175]

3) Second, if we were to posit that the world came to be from a
void—i.e., from a place in which the presence of a body, though
not actual, is possible[176]—then the part of the void in which it
is posited the world now exists would not have had a greater disposition than the other parts of the void to contain the body of
the world, since a void, insofar as it is a void, admits no
diversity in possibility.[177] Therefore, even after the generation
of the world in one part of the void, the void outside of the
world would remain infinite. But this is clearly false, since the
void would be limited by the body of the world.[178]

4) Third, the causal action of a separate intellect such as God is
not realized in a specific place, because a separate intellect is
immaterial and the category of place does not apply to it. Rather,
its causal action is realized in whatever place is disposed to
receive it. Now, if the world had come to be from a void, there
would have been no diversity among the parts of the void so that
all of its parts would have been disposed equally to receive God's
causal action. Assuming that body can come to be from non-body,
the body of the world would have overflowed from God to all parts
of the void and the world should have been infinite. But since
the world is finite, it is necessary to posit that the finite
place in which the world came to be was disposed to receive God's
causal action in a way that the rest of place was not disposed.[179]

5) Prior to the coming to be of the world, the existence of the
world must have been possible. If it had been necessary, it would

have always existed. If it had been impossible, it could not have
come to be. But possibility requires a substratum in which it
resides and which has the possibility to receive the action of the
creative will. Thus, it cannot have been the case that there was
no material substratum from which the world came to be.
6) Prior to the coming to be of the world, the cause of its
generation, as yet unactualized, must have been potential. But
when the cause of a generated thing is potential, its effect must
also be potential, because correlatives come to be simultaneously.[180] Since potential effect is body, there must have been
body prior to the world's generation. Thus, the world cannot have
come to be from nothing because body does not come to be from
non-body.

Having explained the difficulties entailed by the preceding
views concerning the way in which the world came to be, Gersonides
proceeds to offer a way of resolving these difficulties. He dis-
misses as a solution the use of the distinction that he has previously made between the generation of the parts of the world and
the generation of the world in its totality. This is the method
of Maimonides, who allows no inferences from the nature of the
world after creation to the manner of its generation before it was
completed.[181] Gersonides accepts Maimonides' distinction only
partially. That is, he thinks that it is not valid to draw an
analogy between the characteristics which the world now has because
its generation is complete and the laws which existed prior to the
completion of its generation. A valid inference about the generation of the world can be made, however, from the characteristics
which the world now has which are not the specific consequences of
its being in a completed state. Thus, as he argues in 6:1:4, the
Aristotelian arguments for eternity make invalid inferences when
they assume an identity between partial and total generation. It
is incorrect, for example, to assume that no first motion is possible because all motions within the completed world are preceded by
prior motions. This is the case only because these motions are a
part of the completed world. Nevertheless, there are some characteristics of natural law which are not a function of the fact that
the world is in a completed state. One such characteristic is that
potentiality resides in a material substratum. Another such characteristic is that the causal action of a separate intellect can
be realized only if there is a material substratum which is disposed
to receive its causal action. Thus, the doubts which occur when

the world is posited to have come to be from nothing cannot be
resolved by making a distinction between partial and total generation.

Gersonides then notes that Maimonides did not believe that the
view that the world came to be from nothing was necessarily the
view of the Torah. If he had believed this, he would not have
stated that the Platonic view does not contradict the Torah's view
and that, if it were demonstrable, there would be no difficulty in
interpreting the words of the Torah in accordance with it.[182]
Rather, all things which the Torah describes as created come to
be from something[183] except for the world of the separate intellects which the Torah refers to as "light."[184] Maimonides stated
that the view of creation out of nothing is a principle of the
Torah because he believed the Platonic view was vulnerable to
Aristotle's criticisms and because he believed that the view of
creation out of nothing was philosophically defensible, though not
demonstrable. His true aim was to establish a willful and not a
necessary creation.[185] As is demonstrated above, however, the
view of creation out of nothing is not philosophically defensible.

Furthermore, Maimonides is incorrect when he states that
belief in the creation of the world out of nothing is required if
one is to believe in wonders.[186] According to his own argument,
no inference can be drawn from the state of affairs of the world
after creation to the state of affairs of the world prior to the
completion of its generation. Since wonders occur after creation,
their nature is not related to the nature of creation, according
to Maimonides. In fact, his argument that everything that occurs
in the world after its generation is subject to natural law would
seem to weaken one's belief in the possibility of wonders.[187]
Therefore, there is no religious need to believe in creation out
of nothing given the philosophical indefensibility of that view.

Thus, Gersonides continues, it should not be thought that the
view of creation which he is about to suggest conflicts with the
view of the Torah. As Maimonides stated, there can be no conflict
between the teachings of the Torah and the truth; whatever opinion
is demonstrable should be believed. He went as far as to state
that, if it were philosophically demonstrable, even the Aristotelian
view that the world is eternal could be reconciled with the Torah
by the interpretation of the Torah's words.[188]

Since it has been shown that the world could have come to be
neither from something, as Plato defines the term, nor from nothing,

as Maimonides defines the term, Gersonides concludes that the world
must have come to be from something in one respect and from nothing
in another respect. That is, the world came to be from something
in that it came to be from body. Thus, all the doubts entailed by
the Maimonidean view are resolved. The world came to be from
nothing in that it came to be from a formless body. Thus, all the
doubts entailed by the Platonic view are resolved, because they
are all consequences of Plato's assertion that there was prior
disorderly motion. Formless body, however, can have no motion,
because matter cannot move itself.

From his description here and elsewhere, it can be inferred
that Gersonides conceives of this formless body, which he calls
"body which does not preserve its shape," as indefinite dimensionality—a mass with no particular dispositions, with potentially
definite dimensions, which serves as the substratum which receives
the forms which overflow from the divine will.[189] As he describes
the coming to be of the world here, God willed that some of the
formless body should assume the definite dimensions of the spheres
and the stars and that some of it should persist between the
spheres to separate their respective motions, so that the heavens
would move in a way that there would overflow from them what is
needed for the perfection of the sublunar world. God willed that
some of this body have the nature to receive all of the hylic
forms by receiving the elemental forms which then combine to form
the composites of all existent sublunar species.[190]

Gersonides concludes the discussion here with several
clarifying remarks. First, he explains why he thinks that this
formless body lacked "preservation of shape," i.e., had indefinite
dimensionality. He notes that defined dimensions can be observed
to correlate with the degree of the form of a given thing. That
is, the shapes of animals are more definite than those of inanimate
objects and the shapes of the stars are perpetually unchanging.
The inference to be drawn is that the degree of a thing's definition increases with the venerability of its form. Since this body
is absolutely formless, it must have been utterly without dimensional definition.

He then explains that this single, undifferentiated matter,
which has no specific disposition whatever, was able to receive a
diversity of forms because the creation of the world occurred
through a particularizing act of divine will which gave this body
different forms and different dispositions. It is in this way that

the fifth body of the heavens became diversified in its nature, as
explained above (6:1:8), and can move in a variety of ways which
combine to form the divine nomos which overflows to the sublunar
world.

That there should be a single body without diversity which
underlies all matter is proper, since all forms overflow from a
single nomos conceived by God in His self-conception. The unity of
sublunar and supralunar matter undercuts the view of those who base
their belief in two divinities on the incorrect assumption that
there are two principles for sublunar and supralunar matter.

Finally, he concludes the discussion emphasizing that "body
which does not preserve its shape" does not have disorderly motion.
It is body which lacks all form and is thus deprived of motion and
of any nature from which definite dimensionality follows.

2. Resolution of Doubts Concerning Gersonides' View (6:1:18)

Immediately following his discussion of the way in which the
world came to be, Gersonides lists nine doubts which may occur to
the reader and which may therefore lead the reader to question the
validity of Gersonides' view. After listing the nine doubts,
Gersonides makes note of the limitations of our knowledge about
"body which does not preserve its shape." He then responds to
each of the doubts.

He lists the doubts as follows:
1) If the world were to have come to be from a formless body, after
the generation of the world either a remainder of this body persists
or it does not. We cannot posit that a remainder persists, because
it would persist gratuitously for perpetuity and gratuitous things
are infrequent and of short duration. Therefore, there cannot be
a remainder of this body, and the body in its entirety must have
received the forms of the divine nomos to constitute the world.
But if this were the case, two difficulties are entailed. First,
there would be no way to account for the spherical shape of the
world. The body could not have been spherical by nature because
it has no nature. It would also be highly unlikely that it accidently was in the perfect spherical shape of the world. But if
this body was not spherical in shape prior to creation and its
shape was altered to form the sphere of the world, then we must
posit the falsehood that a void now exists in the place in which
this body once persisted but no longer persists. Second, it is
highly unlikely that this body was exactly the proper size for the

world to be generated from it so that no remainder of it persists
after the world's creation. We cannot posit that the size of the
world was determined accidentally by the size that this body happened to be. The size of the world could not be other than what
it is. The size of sublunar and supralunar species are defined
by their natures which are part of the nomos which overflows from
God and which is one and unchangeable. Thus, one might have reason
to be skeptical about the suggestion that this formless body was
accidentally exactly the proper size to receive the action of the
perfect divine nomos.[191]

2) This formless body from which the world came to be is uncaused
and has no nature, so that its magnitude is accidental. Given that
the world could be no other size than its present size, if the body
had not happened to have the proper magnitude for the world to come
to be from it, then the divine nomos would never have been able to
overflow from God's conception to create the world, and God's creative will would have been in vain. Furthermore, if the world was
able to come to be because the body accidentally happened to be
the proper size, then the world can be said to have come to be
accidentally.[192]

3) This prior formless body would have pre-existed eternally before
creation. Since eternal things are divine, this body would be a
divinity like God.[193]

4) This body would either be in motion or at rest. If it was in
motion, all the doubts entailed by the Platonic position (6:1:17)
are entailed. But if it was at rest, it would have been at rest
by nature or by compulsion, and in either case it must have had a
nature and a form,[194] which contradicts its posited definition.
Similarly, if the body was at rest, the world must have existed
prior to its generation, because the notion of rest entails the
existence of elements which are light and heavy and which naturally
move above and below. Thus, if it was at rest, the existence of
the circular motion of the heavens is entailed by this body and
again the doubts entailed by the Platonic view are entailed
(6:1:17).

5) Matter does not exist naked of form.[195] But this body would
exist naked of form for an infinite past time.

6) This formless body is posited to have existed without a nature
for all of infinite past time prior to its reception of a nature
for the finite time since creation. But things which lack a
nature occur infrequently and they exist with their natural characteristics for much longer than they exist without them.[196]

7) The generation of all things—whether by nature or by will—
does not occur from accidental substrata. The substratum of a
thing is predisposed to receive the action of its cause. For
example, the artisan makes a ring from metal and not from any
substance whatsoever. Similarly, individual members of species
come to be from members of their own species. Thus, it is difficult to believe that there was one undifferentiated body with no
dispositions which received all of the natures of existent things.
If this body did not have the predisposition to receive the forms
which overflowed from the divine nomos, and its initial efficient
cause was the will of a separate intellect which causes only when
a given thing is receptive to its causal action, it is difficult
to understand how this natureless body was compelled to receive
the hierarchy of forms in the divine nomos. [197]

8) If the world came to be from this body, then the dimensions of
the created world would seem to have existed before creation. But
if there were dimensions, it would seem to be the case that the
world existed prior to its generation, because dimensions entail
an above and a below, which in turn entails the existence of
elements, which move up and down, and that which encompasses
them. [198]

9) In what sense can it be posited that God willed the generation
of the world after not having willed it? We can posit neither
that new knowledge was generated in Him nor that He needed it at
the particular moment of creation nor that a prior obstacle to His
willing of the generation of the world was removed, as explained
above (6:1:16). [199]

    Prior to responding to each of these nine doubts, Gersonides
undertakes a discussion of the limitations of human knowledge with
regard to the origins of the world. Some questions in any science
are not subject to resolution. In order to attain the most perfect possible knowledge of any field, one needs to establish which
questions are relevant and which have answers.

    With regard to the body from which the world came to be, we
must begin by acknowledging that we cannot know it. [200] It is not
the effect of an agent and therefore it has no final cause and no
nature. Thus, we cannot investigate the state of affairs of its
shape or its quantity, for example, to determine the purpose of its
shape or quantity or to determine the shape or quantity required
for it to fulfill its natural function.

    It may be noted that the agnostic position which Gersonides
assumes with reference to formless body renders him vulnerable to

the charge that he directs at Maimonides' approach to the knowledge
of God. He objects in the third treatise to Maimonides' assertion
that language is applied to God with absolute equivocation, so that
we can have no knowledge of Him. Gersonides argues there that
though language is used equivocally when we speak about God, the
manner of equivocation is pros hen equivocation. That is, attributes can be applied to God and to human beings in the sense that
He is the prior cause of these perfections and we possess these
perfections as effects. Though the knowledge of a cause which can
be inferred from its effects is very weak, it is knowledge in an
intelligible sense of the term.[201]

In his discussion of creation Gersonides attempts to avoid
the error which he attributes to Maimonides with regard to divine
predication by rejecting the absolute distinction which Maimonides
makes between the laws which govern the generation of things within
the world after creation and the laws which govern the state of
affairs which persisted prior to the completion of creation (6:1:4,
17). Unlike Maimonides, Gersonides argues that valid inferences
from the generation of things within the world can be made about
the state of affairs which existed prior to the world's coming to
be. To be valid, however, these inferences must be drawn upon
aspects of the generation of things within the world which are not
consequences of the partial nature of their generation. It is on
the basis of these inferences that he suggests that the world came
to be out of formless body.

Nevertheless, his method of procedure remains open to
criticism. He offers no demonstrated method to determine which
aspects of natural law are consequent upon the world having come
to be already and which would apply prior to its generation. Since
all natural law is a consequence of the overflow of the divine
nomos which occurs at the moment of creation, nothing intelligible
can be said with certainty about what ought to have been the state
of affairs of this body before creation. In fact, we may note that
his argument for formless body in 6:1:17 relies more upon his need
to posit a receptacle for the actions of a separate intellect. But
he has stated at the very beginning of this treatise (6:1:1) that
our knowledge of the First Cause is too weak to be used as a basis
for a theory of creation. He is left therefore with a very weak
knowledge of the First Cause and a material receptacle which,
because of its formlessness, is not the proper object of true
knowledge. In his own defense, he would argue that, unlike

Maimonides, he makes use of the limited inferences that can be
drawn from our knowledge of God and from the nature of generation.
At least in the case of his hypothesis of formless body, however,
his admission that it is unknowable makes any alternate hypothesis
equally (in)defensible. It may be difficult to see, therefore,
how he can call his argument a philosophical demonstration. A
more complete discussion of the viability of Gersonides' theory is
offered below, in Part V of this introduction.

     After his discussion of the limitations of our knowledge,
Gersonides proceeds to respond to each of the nine doubts. In
response to the first doubt, he iterates that we can know neither
what the size of the formless body was nor if a remainder of it
persists after the creation of the world. From our observations
of the existence of the world, however, we can make the following
inferences: First, we can know that the quantity of this body was
sufficient for the world to have been created from it. Second, we
can know that it is possible that a remainder of this body persists
after creation which is not a part of the world. The persistence
of such a remainder is not an impossibility because it would not
be the effect of an agent. Without a final cause, there can be no
objection to its gratuitous persistence. It may, however, have
been exactly the proper size for the world accidentally, though
this is unlikely.[202] Third, we may infer with certainty that the
shape of the body was such that the sphere of the world could be
generated within it, so that no void persists after creation in a
place which once contained this body but which is not a part of the
sphere of the world. Fourth, with regard to his entire view, he
suggests that it is reasonable, though very uncertain, to posit
that there be an intermediate between existent body, which is
informed and living, and absolute privation—i.e., formless body.

     In response to the second doubt, he distinguishes between
necessary causation and necessary affection. That is, with respect
to God's constant and unchanging will, it is necessary that He
perpetually perform His single function of self-conception from
which the cause of the generation of the world overflows. With
respect to the effects caused by His will, the generation of the
world was not necessary. Rather, it was contingent on the existence of a substratum of the proper size to receive His causal
action. If no such receptacle had existed, there would have been
no deficiency in God's causation. As explained above (6:1:4;
cf. Treatise 3), God's knowledge of the world occurs through His

self-conception and thus does not entail the existence of the
world. Also, it has been explained that God does not will out of
His own need or for His own perfection but rather out of His goodness and grace (6:1:4). Therefore, it is reasonable to posit that
the world would never have come to be if the proper receptacle for
the divine will had not persisted prior to creation.

In response to the third doubt, Gersonides attacks the
assumption that the eternal existence of a thing entails its
divinity. God's divinity is not a function of His eternity. Even
if the world were eternal, we would still attribute divinity to
God alone, because He exercises providence over all things in the
world through the overflow from Him of the divine nomos. It is the
wisdom, power and perfection of the degree of His conception which
cause us to attribute divinity to Him. By contrast, the formless
body from which the world comes to be is utter privation of good
and, deprived of any form of the divine nomos, it is the most distant thing from divinity. As God, the source of form and order in
the world, is the cause of good, so this material receptacle, and
the contrary qualities of the elemental forms which it receives
so that it is disposed to receive the forms of the divine nomos,
are the source of all evil, change and passing away in the sublunar
world.[203]

In response to the fourth doubt, Gersonides explains that it
is incorrect to state that the body must be posited to have been
either in motion or at rest. A body which has no nature, and
therefore has no natural motion and no natural place, cannot be
described as being "at rest." Rest is the contrary of motion and
can therefore be posited only of something which has motion.[204]
To apply the term to formless, motionless body is a category mistake similar to describing a wall as "blind."[205] He also notes
here that it is incorrect to assume the existence of time prior to
creation, since there was neither motion nor rest, and time is the
measure of motion.[206] This observation is applicable also to the
third doubt, which assumes the existence of time in calling the
body "eternal," and to the first doubt, which assumes the existence
of time in claiming that a remainder of the body would persist
gratuitously for a long time.

In response to the fifth doubt, Gersonides argues that a
valid inference from the fact that matter never exists naked of
form in the sublunar world cannot be made concerning the state of
affairs which persisted prior to creation. That matter is never

naked of form in the sublunar world is a result of the nature
which God willed for sublunar matter at the moment of creation.
That is, He willed that formless body receive the forms of the
elements which contain contrary qualities which interact and combine in the series of changes that occur in the generation of all
sublunar species. In this process, matter persists through all of
these contrary qualities so that it can be disposed to receive the
forms of all existent things. That this state of affairs is not
applicable beyond the sublunar world can be seen in the persistence
of formless body in the supralunar world between the spheres, as
Gersonides has explained in the fifth treatise. Also relevant here
is the fact that the fifth body of the heavens, which does not
change, is not composed of matter and form.[207] Thus, we need not
infer that matter cannot exist naked of form. Rather, it is
reasonable to assume that just as forms exist hylically in the
sublunar world and separately in the supralunar world, matter
similarly exists informed in the sublunar world and formless elsewhere.[208] Furthermore, the body cannot be said to have existed in
a formless state for an infinite time, because there is no time
prior to creation.

In response to the sixth doubt, Gersonides observes that it
cannot be claimed that this body persists without its nature for
a longer time than it exists with its nature, because prior to
creation the body has no nature[209] and because there is no time
prior to creation. In addition, he notes that the premise of the
sixth doubt is false even with reference to the sublunar world.
That is, the component parts of the human body, for example, exist
abstracted from the human body for a longer time than they exist
as parts of the human body.[210]

In response to the seventh doubt, Gersonides suggests that
it is only in the sublunar world that the assumption applies.
That is, the natural law of the divine nomos which governs sublunar matter is such that things only receive causation when they
are properly predisposed. This is a function of generation which
occurs in the world's parts, from things which already have natures,
and thus does not apply to the coming to be of the world in its
totality from something which has no nature. In addition, he notes
that the generation of the world is by will and not by nature.
Thus, as he has argued above with regard to the diversity of the
fifth body of the heavens (6:1:7-9), a single, undifferentiated
matter can receive diverse forms when the cause wills that to

occur. An artisan, who is separate from the matter of his artifact,
can choose to make diverse shapes from a single matter. Thus, it
is reasonable to posit that the willful action of a separate
intellect could have chosen to endow a single, natureless matter
with diverse natures.

In response to the eighth doubt, Gersonides rejects the
assumption that the persistence of this potentially dimensional
body entails the existence of an above and a below and thus the
existence of an encompassing circular motion. The body has no
nature, and thus has no elements and nothing encompassing it.
Therefore, prior to creation there was no above and no below.[211]

In response to the ninth doubt which suggests that creation
at a particular moment entails a change in God's will or knowledge
or ability to act, Gersonides observes that God derives no benefit
from the existence of the world. He wills its creation out of
goodness and grace.[212] We may begin by observing, therefore, that
God is no more perfect after creation than He is before it, so
that He lacks nothing prior to creation and so that He would have
lacked nothing if the requisite receptacle had never been able to
receive the overflow of His conception. His conception is constant apart from any causation that does or does not overflow from
it.[213]

There is no need to posit that a change of any sort in God is
entailed by the fact that the world came to be at a particular
moment. This occurred because the nature of the material receptacle necessitated it. The order of existence must have a temporal
beginning because it requires some cause to have ordered it. The
privation which persists prior to creation is thus attributable
to the nature of matter and not to God, from whom goodness and order
overflow perpetually. To posit that the order of existence inhered
eternally in the matter is to assume that this order is not the
effect of an agent, because, as explained above (6:1:7), it is
impossible to posit eternal causation. Therefore, there had to be
a moment at which the world came to be. It makes no sense to
question why the particular moment was chosen, because the identical question would apply equally to any prior moment.[214]

To say that God cannot perform the impossible is not to
limit His power.[215] God cannot cause two contraries to exist
simultaneously in a single thing because of the nature of that
thing. Similarly, He does not have the power to cause goodness
perpetually because of the deficiency of the material receptacle
which necessitates that order be created.[216]

3. That There is Only One World (6:1:19)

The impossibility of successive multiple worlds has been
established above (6:1:16) by the demonstration that the world is
not corruptible and by the observation that any other world which
overflowed from the divine nomos would be identical to this one.
Gersonides here seeks to demonstrate that no other world exists
simultaneously with this one.[217]

He begins by defining the limitations of the investigation.
Insofar as formless body has no cause or nature, we can draw no
inferences from it with regard to whether more than one world could
have come to be in respect to it. Thus, he makes his argument on
the basis of empirical evidence.

His first argument, however, is hazardously based upon an
assumption about formless body. That is, he states that though
the body may have persisted in one place or in many places, it
seems proper that it was only in one place. This is because we
observe that accidents are few and infrequent.[218] He does not
deal here with the possibility that the infrequent occurrence of
accidents in the created world is a function of the governing
nomos which occurs only at creation, so that this state of affairs
ought not be applied to what persisted prior to creation. As a
second consideration, he observes that if this body was in many
places, that state of affairs would have entailed a number of
impossible consequences, including the existence of a void and the
existence of magnitude, differentiation and relation within the
absolute privation "between" the parts of this body.[219] Thus,
it is likely that this body persisted in only one place.

If we assume that this body was in only one place, then it is
reasonable to assert that there is only one world. That is, if
there were more than one world, the body between worlds would
either preserve its shape or would not preserve its shape. If it
preserves its shape—i.e., if it has form—then it would move and
be moved by the worlds with which it is in contact. Thus, confused
motions would occur in each of these worlds and their motions
would affect one another. In addition, in order for this state of
affairs to exist, we would have to posit falsely the existence of
a vacuum, so that there would be room for the body and the worlds
to move. If it does not preserve its shape, we should be able to
see the stars of other worlds, because the definition of formless
body requires that it be transparent. Given this transparency,

the light of the stars of the other worlds ought to affect the
stars of this world and a number of other changes in the state of
affairs of the heavens would occur. We cannot posit that the body
between worlds lacks preservation of shape and is not transparent.
If this were the case, it would receive the stars' illuminations
and be luminous. Thus, if the formless body was in a single place,
empirical observation indicates that there is only one world.

Second, given that if there were more than one world they
would all be identical, as he has argued above (6:1:16),[220] it
necessarily follows that the separate movers of the spheres of
each world would be identical. Thus, it is impossible to posit
that a single separate intellect with a single, perpetual conception could move multiple bodies in different places.

Third, oneness is more venerable than multiplicity. Therefore,
there is unity in things with respect to the form and multiplicity
in respect to the matter. Given that divine action is the most
venerable of all, it is proper to assume that there is only one
world.[221]

Fourth, we observe that multiplicity occurs in nature for the
purpose of the preservation of species. Sublunar species, whose
individuals come to be and pass away, are multiple. The heavenly
bodies which are not subject to generation and corruption have only
one member of each species. Since the world cannot pass away, it
is not proper to posit that it have a multiplicity of individuals.

On the basis of these observations, Gersonides concludes
that multiple worlds do not exist simultaneously just as they do
not exist successively.

D.   Gersonides' Conclusion

1.   Refutations of the Aristotelian Arguments for Eternity
     (6:1:20-28)

Gersonides concludes by devoting a chapter to each of the
arguments which he listed at the outset (6:1:3) in support of the
Aristotelian view that the world could not have come to be. In
substance, his responses to each of the nine Aristotelian arguments, which seek to demonstrate the impossibility of the generation of the world, are specific applications of the general principle which he set forth above (6:1:4) in his preliminary response
to Aristotle. That is, in each case he attempts to demonstrate why
the inferences which Aristotle draws from the state of affairs of
the generation of the parts of the world after creation to the

state of affairs of the generation of the world in its totality
are not valid. As discussed above, the weakness of this entire
final section of his argument is his failure to clearly define the
method he uses to determine which aspects of partial generation are
analogous to total generation and which aspects are not. An examination of his arguments here would seem to indicate that he regards
as analogous only the perpetual and unchanging causation of the
separate intellect and the need for a material substratum to underlie all generation. All other characteristics of this world after
creation cannot be used to infer anything about the state of
affairs which persisted prior to creation.

The first Aristotelian argument is from the nature of time
(6:1:20). As Gersonides summarizes it here, it is based on an
analogy between the parts of time and time as a whole. As everything which comes to be comes to be in time and as everything
which passes away passes away in time, similarly if time came to
be it must have come to be in time and if time were to pass away
it would pass away in time. In addition, the cause of time's
generation would have existed prior to its generation, so that
there must have been time before time's coming to be. Our use of
temporal distinctions such as "before" time's coming to be and
"after" time's passing away are indications that it cannot come to
be and pass away. Given eternal time, there is eternal motion and
a single moved object which moves in a single, continuous motion
perpetually.

Gersonides begins by noting that Aristotle appeals to the
consensus of his predecessors when he asserts that time is ungenerated.[222] Gersonides infers from this appeal that Aristotle was
aware of the weakness of his argument.

Gersonides argues that the whole of time is not identical to
each of its parts with regard to generation. He concedes that
each part of time cannot come to be except at the end of a previous
part of time. This is a function of time's continuous existence
so that the hypothetical end of one part of time is a hypothetical
beginning of the next part of time. Nevertheless, a given part of
time does not come to be in the previous part of time, so that its
coming to be does not require the existence of the previous part.
Rather, its time begins at the end of the prior change.

Not all generated things are generated in time. Here he
refers to Aristotle's distinction between change which occurs from
contrary to contrary and change in which "not-being" comes to be.[223]

In the former change, the prior contrary state is already in motion
and therefore in time, so that the change from contrary to contrary
is in time. In the latter change, a state of "not-being" is not
in motion nor in time until it comes to be. Thus, it is at the end
of the change that motion and time come to be; absolute generation
is instantaneous and atemporal.[224] Thus, there could have been no
time prior to the instantaneous generation of existent things at
the moment of creation. Since everything which comes to be in
time, which is preceded by a change, comes to be at the end of the
prior change, the coming to be of that which is not preceded by a
prior change does not come to be in time. Thus, if time came to
be, it did not come to be in time and the same argument can be
made with regard to its passing away.

Gersonides also rejects Aristotle's argument from our use of
temporal terms to refer to before time's coming to be and after
time's passing away. Such use of terms is absolutely equivocal.
Aristotle himself is vulnerable to this criticism in his use of
the term "outside" to refer to that which is beyond this world.[225]
This shows that language is conventional and must sometimes be
used with absolute equivocation.

Aristotle's second argument is from the nature of the "now"
(6:1:21). Given his definition of the "now" as that which divides
past time from future time,[226] Aristotle concludes that there cannot be a first "now" before which there is no past time.

Gersonides presents a second version of the argument from the
nature of the "now" which he did not attribute to Aristotle above
(6:1:3) but rather discussed as an argument in support of the first
view that there is infinite succession of worlds which come to be
and pass away. That is, the "now" can only have potential existence and can never be actual. It resembles the point on a circle
in this respect. That is, a point can be the actual beginning
or end of a straight line but it can only be a potential beginning
or end of a line which it divides. This is because a point, which
is indivisible, is not a part of the infinitely divisible quantity
of the line it measures. Similarly, time is analogous to the
circular line in that its continuous existence has no beginning or
end except hypothetically. The indivisible "now" divides time
only hypothetically, so that the future time which a given "now"
divides from past time can be posited to be past time in relation
to some other time which it precedes. Thus, the "now" only has
potential existence. But if time came to be absolutely, there

would be a first "now" which would be its actual indivisible
beginning, as the actual point which begins or end a straight line.
Since the "now" cannot be actual, time cannot come to be absolutely.

In response to the first argument from the nature of the
"now," Gersonides observes that everything which is imaginable is
not true and not all truths are necessarily imaginable. Thus,
that we cannot imagine a "now" before or after which there is no
time is not conclusive evidence of any sort. That we cannot
imagine that there is a void at the end of the world's body does
not prevent us from positing that void.

That the "now" invariably measures time in respect to the
before and the after is not a function of the nature of the "now."
It is rather a function of the nature of time which is the number
of motion in respect to the before and the after.[227] Thus, the
"now" which is in time must divide before and after because it is
in time, and not because it is a "now."

The "now" has existence in two respects. In addition to its
division of the before and the after, it also sets limits which
indicate the length of a part of time or motion, such as an hour
or a day. If the "now" only functioned to divide before and after,
there would be no difference between three hours or three days,
because the numbering of each would be identical—each period of
time would be divided by two "nows." The difference between the
two periods of time occurs because the "now" functions to indicate
diverse quantities of continuous time by limiting the distance
between "nows" and thus defining the intervening quantities. Thus,
we say that times are long or short in respect to the distance
between the two "nows" which limit those times. As the point both
limits the line by serving as its end and numbers the line by
dividing before and after, similarly the "now" serves to limit
and to number time and motion.[228] Thus, the "now" which limits
time need not be posited to have time existing before it.

In response to the second version of the argument from the
potential nature of the "now," Gersonides draws a distinction
between the potentiality of a point on a line and the potentiality
of the "now." The end which divides before and after is potential
in that, because of the continuous existence of that which it
divides, it is a beginning and an end simultaneously.[229] The
"now," on the other hand, is potential because it does not actually
exist when it is alluded to—i.e., when one refers to a "now,"
the "now" to which he refers is no longer a "now." Thus, given

that the "now" is not potential insofar as it is simultaneously a
beginning and an end, we can posit that it is the potential beginning of absolutely generated time. The first "now" need not be
posited to have been actual on the grounds that it is not simultaneously a beginning and an end.

As a postscript, Gersonides rejects the analogy between a
circular line and time. This analogy is made because continuous
time is associated with perpetual, circular motion and because no
rectilinear motion can be infinite. Gersonides notes that time is
not circular, as can be seen from the fact that time never returns
to the past. Thus, the "now" need not necessarily be beginning
and end as is the case with a point on a circle.

Aristotle's third argument is from the nature of motion
(6:1:22). Based on his assumption that locomotion is the first of
all motions, he argues that every motion of generation is preceded
by locomotion and the generation of that locomotion must be preceded by a prior locomotion, ad infinitum. Therefore, given the
impossiblity of an infinite succession of motions, there must be
a first moved object which is ungenerated.

Gersonides rejects the argument on three grounds. First, as
he has argued above (6:1:4), a valid inference from the generation
of parts of the world after creation cannot be made in this respect
with regard to the generation of the world as a whole. That is,
the fact that each thing comes to be in the world as the consequence of a prior motion of some other part of the world is a
function of the partial nature of this generation which cannot be
applied to the absolute generation of the world as a whole. Second,
as he has argued above (6:1:21), the first motion is not locomotion
but is rather the motion of coming to be, because before anything
came to be there was no motion. Third, the generation of the
world, as explained above (6:1:7, 17, 18), is caused by willful
action so that the laws which apply to natural generation do not
apply to it.

Aristotle's fourth argument is from the nature of generated
things (6:1:23). For all things which are generated, their actual
generation is temporally preceded by the potential for their generation. Thus, the generation of the world must have been preceded
in time by the potential for its generation. If it was preceded
by time, there were motions which preceded it. And if there were
motions, then the world existed before its own generation.

Gersonides rejects the argument as circular. The claim that every generated thing is preceded in time by its potential assumes that time has no beginning, which is the point at issue. In fact, no valid inference about the generation of the world as a whole can be made from the observation that the potentiality for the generation of all parts of the world precedes in time their actual generation. This occurs because their actual generation is preceded by other motions and therefore by time.

In principle, however, the potential for the generation of a thing need not exist in a time prior to its actual generation. As explained above with regard to Aristotle's first argument (6:1:20), there are two kinds of potentiality: the absolute potentiality, which exists when the potential actualized comes to be with the causal motion; and non-absolute potentiality, which exists when the potential is partially actualized in the process which precedes its complete actualization. Though motion, and hence time, must be posited to exist prior to the complete actualization of non-absolute potentiality, there is no motion prior to the moment that the world comes to be from formless body. The priority of its potential for generation is not temporal because there is no time prior to the completion of its generation.

Aristotle's fifth argument is from the impossibility of a first motion (6:1:24). A posited first motion must be preceded by the motion of the generation of the first moved object. The latter cannot be posited to be first because it requires that we posit a change in the cause which causes the generation and that we posit a motion which precedes the motion of generation. There is no escape from this impossible infinite regress even if the first moved object is posited to be ungenerated. Even in that case, we must still posit an actualization of a potential causation on the part of the first mover and a relation which is generated between the first mover and the first moved object prior to the posited first motion.

Gersonides responds to the argument in two parts, first with regard to the problems raised about the first mover and second with regard to the problems raised about the first moved object. He argues that, as he has explained the coming to be of the world (6:1:17), there is no necessity to posit a change either in the cause or in the effect prior to creation.

With regard to God, he has already explained (6:1:18) that the creation of the world at an arbitrary moment in time does not

entail a change in Him. It is a consequence of the nature of the
material receptacle that it can receive the causation of the
unchanging divine conception only at a moment of time and that this
causation is preceded by privation. In addition, Aristotle errs
in asserting that the actualization of a potential in a cause
requires a change in that cause. Though every motion is an
actualization of a potential, not every actualization of a potential
is a change.[230] This is because the change may occur in the
actualization of the potential which resides in the effect and not
in the cause. The definition of motion is the perfection of the
effect and change is in the moved object and not in the mover.
Not every mover changes when it moves, for if this were the case,
there would be two simultaneous motions in every change—one in
the mover and one in the moved object. But Aristotle himself
explains that motion occurs only in the moved object.[231] This is
most clearly the case with respect to a separate mover, which
causes by being desired and thus does not change in its causation.
The causation occurs when the moved object changes in a way that
it can receive the perpetual and unchanging causative action of
the separate mover.[232] Thus, a first motion does not entail a
prior change in the First Cause.

     Nor does a first motion entail a prior change in the first
moved object, in that the possibility of that motion had to first
be generated in that object. Natural change requires a preceding
change in the generation of the possibility of that change, so
that we can account for the receptivity which the effect now has
but previously lacked to the causal action of its cause. But the
world was generated by will, and change which is generated by will
is not necessarily preceded by a change in which the possibility
of the change is generated. An artisan who creates by will makes
an artifact at a time which he chooses to act and which is not
necessarily related to a prior change in the material with which
he works.

     Thus, Gersonides argues, the coming to be of the world need
not have been preceded by a change in God and it need not have
been preceded by a change in formless body. If his argument to
this point is examined, however, he has not yet shown that the
generation of the world need not have been preceded by either of
these two possibilities. What he has shown is that the causation
of a separate mover can be attributed to a change in the nature of
its effect without a change in that mover, and that a change in

an effect can be attributed to a change in the will of its cause
without a prior change in the effect. The object of his argument
is to show, however, that there was a change neither in God nor in
the formless body prior to creation.

He therefore continues with an additional observation. He
notes that the change in possibility of generation need not be
temporally prior to the generation of the change. For example,
fire is generated from the earth simultaneously with its potential
to move upwards. The potential for upwards motion did not exist in
the earth prior to the generation of the fire. Thus, the priority
of the possibility of a change to the change, which Aristotle
affirms, is a natural and not necessarily a temporal priority. We
may conclude, therefore, that, at the moment of creation, the
natureless body which lacked preservation of shape simultaneously
received the nature to receive the forms of the divine nomos and
received those forms. No prior change in the divine will from
which those forms overflow perpetually need be posited to account
for creation, since the change occurred in the nature of the
receptacle. And no temporally prior change in the receptacle need
be posited, since it received the forms when it received the nature
to receive them.

With regard to Aristotle's claim that a first motion entails
a prior change in the relation between the first mover and the
first moved object, Gersonides observes that a relation between
two things can be generated with a change in only one of the
related objects. For example, a change in A may cause it to
resemble B, so that B resembles A even though B did not change.
Similarly, a change in the relation between God and the world
occurs without a change in God. It occurs with the disposition
of body to receive the divine overflow and this occurs at the
moment of creation.

Aristotle's sixth argument is from the nature of prime
matter (6:1:25). In short, it maintains that the world must have
come to be from a material substratum and that, since matter does
not exist naked of form, matter and form, and hence the world,
must have existed prior to the generation of the world.

In response, Gersonides repeats that the nature of matter in
the sublunar world not to be formless is a consequence, as
explained above (6:1:18), of the action of the divine nomos at
the moment of creation. It cannot, therefore, be applied to the
state of affairs of formless body prior to creation.

Aristotle's seventh argument is from the nature of the fifth body (6:1:26). Since everything which comes to be and passes away comes to be from its contrary and passes away to its contrary, and since the fifth body of the heavens has no contrary, it necessarily follows that the heavens, and thus the world, cannot come to be or pass away.

Gersonides responds by noting that the coming to be from contraries and the passing away to contraries which occurs in the sublunar world is a function of the existence of the sublunar world and its governance by the divine nomos. It cannot be assumed to apply to the coming to be of the world in its totality. This is because even in nature most things which come to be do not come to be in themselves from their contraries but rather come to be as as forms which have no contraries. It is the material substratum which changes from contrary to contrary in order to be disposed to receive the form, and this is a function of its being partial generation. Additionally, the creation of the world is caused by will and not by nature. Willful causation does not necessarily occur from a contrary. For example, the shape of an artifact does not necessarily follow from the prior shape of its material. It rather follows from the will of the artisan. Thus, there can be no objection to our positing that the heavens came to be from formless body by willful causation.

Aristotle's eighth argument is from the incorruptibility of the heavens (6:1:27). That which comes to be must pass away. That which is incorruptible cannot have been generated. Since the heavens cannot pass away, they, and hence the world, cannot have come to be. Gersonides presents Aristotle's position as a series of arguments to which he responds.[233] The primary arguments which he attributes to Aristotle are as follows:

First, the contrary potentials which a thing possesses must be posited to be defined. They cannot exist simultaneously in a single thing and they certainly cannot exist simultaneously in a thing for an infinite time. Thus, a single thing cannot have the potential to exist for an infinite time and to not exist for an infinite time. Thus, if the world is posited to exist perpetually without passing away, it cannot be said to have a potential for nonexistence, because that potential will never be realized and is thus not a possibility. But if it does not have the potential for nonexistence, it cannot be posited to have come to be, because it must have existed prior to its generation. If it is posited to

have come to be, then it does have a potential for nonexistence
and thus the world must be posited to have the potential to pass
away.[234]

Second, the intermediate between the contraries always-
existing and never-existing must, as all intermediates do, negate
both extremes. Thus, the intermediate must both exist and not
exist. It therefore must come to be and pass away.[235]

Third, that which has the potential to act or to be acted upon
will act or be acted upon, as far as that is possible, and will be
defined by that potential. That which has the potential to come
to be and pass away has finite defined potentials. Infinite powers
have no limits because one infinite cannot be greater than another
infinite. Therefore, if the world came to be, its existence must
be finite.[236]

Fourth, if the world came to be and if it exists everlastingly
after its generation, the potential for its existence would have
preceded it in all past infinite time.[237]

Fifth, if the world came to be and remains everlastingly,
two contrary potentials would exist in it simultaneously and
undefined, because one cannot distinguish one infinite time from
another infinite time.[238]

Sixth, anything which does not pass away exists necessarily
because of its nature for perpetual existence. Such a thing cannot have come to be.[239]

Gersonides' responses to these arguments group some of the
arguments together and generally do not deal with each argument
individually. What follows is a general summary of his remarks,
many of which apply to more than one of Aristotle's arguments.

He begins with the assertion that there was no time prior to
creation. Thus, Aristotle's arguments which refer to the infinite
past time in which the potential for the world's existence existed
unactualized are not valid.

After the generation of the world, there is no potential for
it to not exist, as explained above (6:1:16). Its capacity for
nonexistence—which it does have since it is not necessary in
itself—was realized prior to creation and no longer exists given
the willful nature of its creation.

Nor can Aristotle refer legitimately to its infinite potential
to exist and to not exist. Prior to creation there was no time
and subsequent to creation time remains finite no matter how much
it is augmented through the everlasting existence of the world.

In general, Gersonides rejects Aristotle's linguistic analysis.
Though it is true that the intermediate between always-existing
and never-existing must negate both extremes, the intermediate need
not be that which comes to be and passes away. That which comes
to be and does not pass away, or that which passes away and does not
come to be, is intermediate between the extremes and both exists
and does not exist. Aristotle errs when he asserts that generated
and corruptible are convertible predicates. Gersonides argues that
contingent existence does not necessarily entail corruptibility;
rather, it entails either generability or corruptibility. The
world, by nature, cannot pass away; prior to its generation it had
no nature.

Aristotle's ninth argument is from the impossibility of a
void (6:1:28). That is, if the world as a whole came to be, then
body must have come to be out of non-body. But if this were the
case, a void would have existed prior to creation, because the
definition of a void is that which has the potential for body
without actually having body. Since the existence of a void is
impossible, the world could not have come to be. Additionally,
body cannot come to be from non-body, nor can it come to be from
potential body, because matter cannot be stripped of form.

Gersonides responds by referring back to his description of
the way in which the world came to be, i.e., out of formless body
(6:1:17, 18). He repeats his claim that the inability of sublunar
matter to be formless is a function of the nature and the elemental
forms which it received at the moment of creation but which it
necessarily did not have prior to creation.

2. Conclusion (6:1:29)

Gersonides concludes the first part of the sixth treatise with
a review of the entire book, The Wars of the Lord. He notes that
his predecessors were confused about the issues of the immortality
of the soul and the acquired intellect, dreams, divination and
prophecy, God's knowledge of particular things, providence, the
heavenly bodies and their movers, and the generation of the world.
Thus, he gives thanks to the Lord for giving him the ability to
clarify these previously obfuscated issues.

In his postscript, he notes that he initially conceived of the
book exclusively as a discussion of the generation of the world.
He found, however, that he needed to discuss the issues in the
first five treatises before he could resolve the complex question

of generation.   Thus, though the book is divided into six treatises,
all of the treatises are interrelated and shed light on one another.

PART FOUR

Gersonides' Interpretation
of the Creation Narrative of Genesis

Gersonides approaches the text of the creation narrative of
Genesis with the belief that his argument in 6:1 has refuted the
Platonic, the Maimonidean and the Aristotelian views of the origin
of the world and has irrefutably demonstrated the truth of his own
position, i.e., that the world came to be out of a body which was
deprived of preservation of shape. As will be discussed below in
Part IV, B of this introduction, he is convinced that there is only
one truth so that any view which is demonstrated by means of speculation must necessarily be the truth which the Torah reveals. In
the case of creation, he makes his claim even stronger. That is,
he asserts that the Genesis narrative guided him to the truth for
which he argues in 6:1. Thus, his reading of the Genesis narrative
of creation in 6:2:1-8 provides him with the opportunity both to
describe in detail his view of the process of creation and to indicate the ways in which the Torah guides the philosopher to the
truth of this investigation.

This Part of this introduction is a presentation of the major
ideas of 6:2:1-8 which have been explored below in the commentary
to the translation of 6:2:1-8. In a number of instances, the
statements made in this Part are conclusions about matters of controversy which have been reached on the basis of inquiries which
are documented and traced in the notes of the commentary below.
In all cases, specific references supporting the assertions made
here are given in the commentary's notes. Therefore, the notes to
this section of this introduction will primarily serve the purpose
of referring the reader to the notes of the commentary in which
these issues are often discussed in greater depth and in which
more complete documentation is provided.

This Part of the introduction will take the following form:
First, some of the underlying assumptions and some of the immediate
consequences of Gersonides' view that the world came to be out of
body which does not preserve its shape are explored (IV,A). Second,
his view of the relationship between speculative truth and revealed
truth is discussed (IV,B). Third, his understanding of key terms
in the Genesis narrative is reviewed (IV,C). Fourth, his view of
the unity and interrelatedness of all created things is discussed
(IV,D). Fifth, his understanding of body which does not preserve

73

its shape is discussed (IV,E). Finally, with all of this as
background, Gersonides' account of the creation of the world in
6:2:8 is reviewed (IV,F).

A. The Implications of the Argument in 6:1

      Though the bulk of 6:1 is structured as an argument against
the Aristotelian position based upon Aristotelian premises, the
assumptions which underlie Gersonides' conclusions as well as the
consequences of his position are perhaps best highlighted when his
view is contrasted with that of Maimonides. Gersonides presents
the latter's approach to the issue of creation as follows:
Maimonides professes to be open to any view of the world's origins
which can be demonstrated beyond doubt, and he asserts that any
view—even the Aristotelian view of eternity—could be reconciled
with the words of the Torah if it were demonstrably true. Having
dismissed the Platonic view as untenable and having shown that the
Aristotelian arguments for the eternity of the world are not conclusive, he chooses to accept the undemonstrated view of creation
ex nihilo. He does so because he believes that the Aristotelian
view, which is based upon the premise that things occur by necessity and not as a consequence of divine will, undermines the belief
in the Torah's promises of reward and punishment and the belief in
miracles. Since the Platonic view is indefensible, he asserts
that the view of creation ex nihilo is a foundation of Jewish
belief.[240]

      As is immediately apparent, Maimonides' position provides
Gersonides with a great deal of leeway. First, at no point does
Maimonides assert that creation ex nihilo is demonstrable. In
fact, he devotes a considerable amount of space to a refutation
of the Kalam arguments for this view. Second, he supports Gersonides' view that the Torah is the revelation of the truth and must
therefore be interpreted to agree with the demonstrated truth.
Third, his assertion that creation ex nihilo is a view upon which
Jewish belief is founded is made by default, i.e., because the
Platonic view is indefensible and because the Aristotelian view is
undemonstrable and is less easily reconciled with the Torah. On
the basis of all of these considerations, Gersonides can assert
with confidence that if Maimonides had had access to his own
demonstrated view, he would have accepted it as the truth.

      Gersonides would make this assertion not only because
Maimonides is committed to any view that can be demonstrated but
also because he believes that his own view is one upon which the

belief in the rewards and punishments promised by the Torah and
the belief in marvels can be founded. That is, Gersonides agrees
that the world was created by an act of divine will. Indeed, the
central core of his argument for creation is based upon his observation that both the supralunar world and the elevated part of the
earth have properties which can only be accounted for as the result
of the action of a First Cause who acts with will and purpose.[241]
They cannot be posited to have come to be by necessity. Thus,
given his view that everything in the intelligible, supralunar and
sublunar worlds has a final cause and acts for the sake of promoting the order and goodness of the governing divine nomos, his view
of creation provides no obstacles for belief either in the beneficial effects of following the Torah's commandments or the providential ends realized by marvels.

Gersonides disagrees, however, with Maimonides' assertion
that it is possible for God to have willed the creation of the
world out of absolutely nothing. Having listed his reasons for
rejecting this view as a possibility above (6:1:17), he offers the
alternate view that the world came to be out of body which does
not preserve its shape. His understanding of this body is discussed below in Part IV, section E, of this introduction. At this
point, it will suffice to observe that he offers this alternate
view because he agrees with the philosophers, to whom Maimonides
refers in the Guide,[242] who assert that to predicate that God can
create body out of non-body is to assert the impossible. The
causal action of a separate intellect has no reference to the
material and requires a material receptacle predisposed to receive
its formal causation. As no deficiency in God results from the
fact that He cannot cause it to rain and to not rain in the same
place at the same time, because that is impossible and contrary to
natural law, similarly the assertion that God requires a material
receptacle to receive the causal action of the divine nomos which
overflows from Him entails no deficiency in God.

Underlying this view is the assumption that God has only one
act of self-conception which is perpetual and unchanging. He can
be said to have willed the creation of the world in that He willed
that part of the divine nomos which He perpetually conceives should
overflow from Him so that other things could share in His goodness.
He knows the world only insofar as He knows Himself and the world
approximates the divine nomos. To affirm that He is perfect is not
to affirm that He is free to do anything He wills. The nomos which

overflows from His perfect conception is necessarily the way it
is, i.e., the most perfect possible nomos which could govern
existent things. He had no choice to will the nomos to be any
other way. His act of will was to choose to allow that nomos to
overflow from Him at the moment of creation. That is His single
action. Subsequent to the moment of creation, the world exists
according to the natural custom caused by the divine nomos. If
there had been no material receptacle, there would have been no
world and, in that case, God would not have been less perfect or
different in any way. He would continue as He had prior to creation and as He does now: engaged in His single, perpetual activity
of self-conception.[243]

    Thus, though he agrees in principle with Maimonides' view
that the world came to be as a consequence of the causation of the
divine will, Gersonides' understanding of the nature of divine
will differs from that of his predecessor. Though he agrees that
God's essence is beyond human conception, he believes that what
Maimonides calls divine actions—i.e., the overflow from God of
the divine nomos which governs this world—is, to some extent,
knowable not only as it governs the sublunar world but as it governs the supralunar and the intelligible worlds as well. The
divine nomos governs by natural law and, though God can be said to
will its overflow and to perpetuate its rule through His perpetual
self-conception, He cannot change it to perform a miracle and He
cannot have been the Cause of a supralunar world which is absolutely beyond human conception, as Maimonides would suggest.

    Thus, Gersonides' view of creation is based on an assumption
about the world which has consequences beyond his view of creation.
What follows is a brief discussion of several of the issues about
which he disagrees with Maimonides and which follow from his
assumptions about the nature of divine will and the nature of the
divine nomos which governs the world.

    First, as noted above in the previous section of this
introduction which summarizes Gersonides' argument in 6:1, he
rejects the absolute distinction which Maimonides draws between
the natural laws which govern the world after its creation and the
laws to which it was subject prior to the completion of its
creation.[244] As discussed above, Gersonides may be standing on
questionable ground in his attempts to distinguish between those
aspects of natural law which can be applied prior to creation and
those which cannot, but these attempts reflect his basic presupposition that the laws governing the causation of a separate intellect

and the affection of matter are constant and cannot be altered by
divine fiat. Maimonides, who in affirming creation ex nihilo
argues for our inability to know anything about what transpired
prior to the completion of creation, reflects, by contrast, his
own assumption that the actions of the divine will have a purpose
and a rationality which is absolutely beyond human reason and conception.

Second, Maimonides emphasizes the differences between sublunar
matter and the body of the supralunar world, going so far as to
assert that they are two different matters.[245] This assertion
follows from his view that the world was created out of absolutely
nothing so that the supralunar and sublunar worlds do not have a
common material origin. A further consequence of this view,
however, is his assertion that the diverse states of affairs of
the heavens are beyond human conception. By contrast, Gersonides,
who affirms that there is a body from which both the supralunar
and sublunar worlds came to be, stresses their common material
origins. As a consequence, he is able to assert that the diverse
states of affairs of the supralunar world are manifestly comprehensible to the human intellect, to the extent that their obvious
perfection can be utilized as evidence for a philosophical demonstration that they have come to be. Though Gersonides does
repeatedly note that our knowledge of the supralunar world is weak,
he nevertheless believes that the heavenly bodies are knowable to
some extent. This is another example of his belief that the
divine will works through a nomos which is subject to consistent
and perpetual laws and which is therefore the proper subject of
speculative inquiry.[246]

Third, Gersonides disagrees with Maimonides' view that the
supralunar world acts for its own sake and not, as Aristotle
asserts, for the sake of the sublunar world. As discussed below
in this introduction, Gersonides believes that, though the supralunar world is prior in venerability and in cause and nature to
the sublunar world, the actions of the heavenly bodies are for the
sake of the divine nomos which overflows from them to the sublunar
world and the end of which is the preservation of the human species
and its function of conception. This anthropocentric view is
intimately related to his view that the generation of the world is
subject to laws which are conceivable, to some extent, by the human
intellect. To the extent that all sublunar species exist and the
heavenly bodies move for the sake of the human species, the end of

which is the most perfect possible conception of the divine nomos,
it is reasonable to assume that that nomos governs in ways that
the human intellect can conceive.[247]

Finally, Gersonides' disagreement with Maimonides about the
nature of marvels can also be seen as a consequence of their dif-
fering views of creation. As mentioned above, the two issues are
interrelated by Maimonides in his assertion that the belief in
miracles is founded upon the view that the world was created ex
nihilo. Both depend on the belief that God can choose to will
that which does not conform to natural law as we know it. With
regard to creation, the divine will caused the generation of body
out of absolutely nothing, even though this is contrary to the
laws which govern the world after creation. With regard to marvels, God willed the suspension of natural law at specific moments
in time when He willed the creation of the world. To assert that
it is impossible for the divine will to cause the generation of
the world out of absolutely nothing because this is contrary to
natural law, Maimonides would argue, is to deny the possibility
that He could have suspended natural law to cause wonders. Both
views of Maimonides are founded on the premise that natural law, as
we know it through the natural custom which governs the created
world, is not universally applicable: prior to the completion of
creation, the laws which governed the states of affairs of things
differed from the natural laws which govern after creation, so that
a separate intellect could cause the generation of body out of
absolutely nothing; and during the generation of the world, natural
law is suspended. In both cases, Maimonides asserts that the
causation of the divine will is prior to natural law and thus cannot be limited by the natural custom of the created world.

As discussed above in Part III, section C, 1, of this introduction in our summary of 6:1:17, Gersonides questions this connection which Maimonides makes between creation and marvels. That is,
if it is true, as Maimonides asserts, that no inference can be
drawn from the state of affairs of the world after creation to the
state of affairs which existed before creation was completed, then
there is no relationship between the way in which the world came to
be and the marvels which are generated after creation. In fact,
however, Gersonides, who does believe that some inferences can be
drawn from the laws which govern this world to the state of affairs
which persisted prior to creation, offers a view of marvels which
is consistent with his overall position that nothing occurs in

this world which departs from natural custom (except for accidents
which are infrequent, of short duration and have no providential
effect). In his discussion of marvels (6:2:9-12), which immediately follows the text translated below, he asserts that marvels
do not depart from the divine nomos which governs this world. They
are marvelous insofar as they do not come to be from something
defined, i.e., from something which is customarily disposed to
receive them. They are caused by the Active Intellect as temporary
corrections to the occasionally imperfect nomos which overflows
from the supralunar world. They acquire their marvelous character
only if a prophet, whose conception sufficiently approximates that
of the Active Intellect to allow him to anticipate their occurrence,
utilizes them for providential ends. Thus, there is no need to
posit creation ex nihilo to support the belief in marvels, because
they are not generated by a divine will which temporarily suspends
the natural law. Rather, they are part of the divine nomos with
which the Active Intellect providentially governs the sublunar
world. Belief in them is founded, therefore, on the view that the
world has a teleological structure which culminates with the human
species. Maimonides is correct in arguing that they could not
occur if the world existed by necessity, as Aristotle asserts.
They can occur, however, in a world which has come to be as a consequence of the divine will that the most perfect possible nomos
should perpetually overflow from Him and should govern the world.[248]

    From these examples, it can be seen that Gersonides' view of
creation is both the cause and the consequence of other of his
views and that it has a central and integral place in his physical
and metaphysical system.

B. The Relationship of Speculation and the Torah

    An understanding of the way in which Gersonides reads the
Torah in general is necessary before one can evaluate his interpretation of the creation narrative in Genesis. Thus, what follows
is a discussion of Gersonides' view of the truth as it is revealed
in the Torah and as it is derived by means of speculation.[249]

    Gersonides introduces 6:2 as a whole by stating that his
purpose in it is to explain how the conclusion which he reached
by means of speculation in 6:1 is the view of the Torah. This
introduction is a repetition of a statement which he makes in the
Introduction to the entire work, The Wars of the Lord. The very
title of this work, as he explains in the Introduction, reveals

his intentions throughout the entire book: he is fighting the
wars of the Lord insofar as he is reaching true conclusions about
the issues with which he deals. As the purpose of the Torah is to
guide us to our ultimate end of realizing the most perfect possible
conception of the truth, any philosophical investigation which
leads to a conception of the truth contributes to the realization
of God's will.

In this view, Gersonides is typical of medieval philosophers
who, as Wolfson has characterized them, were engaged in a search
for the truth both through the guidance of revelation and through
the use of the Greek philosophical tradition to which they were
heir. The medieval philosophical enterprise has often been misunderstood in the modern age. Unsympathetic observers have questioned
whether the medievals can be said to have been engaged in philosophy
at all, since their use of philosophy was as a "handmaiden" of
Scripture. That is, they are charged with having used the methods
of philosophy not to determine the truth but rather to defend the
inherited doctrines of their respective religious traditions.
Gersonides, who so often departs so widely from the accepted teachings of the Jewish tradition, is not a likely target for this
accusation. Historically, he has rather been charged with manipulating the texts of the Torah without sensitivity to their obvious,
literal meaning in order to force them to agree with the conclusions he reaches by means of speculation. Indeed, the methodology
which he outlines in the Introduction to The Wars and which he
follows consistently—i.e., to investigate each issue by means of
speculation first and then to read the Torah in light of the demonstrated truth—may seem to justify this charge.

There is no denying that it is possible that the charge of
religious dishonesty may be justified: that Gersonides' first
allegiance was to philosophy and that he engaged in the practice
of reconciling his conclusions with the Torah only as a defense
against the charge of heresy. It is our view, however, that the
charge is not justified and is rather a reflection of a misunderstanding of Gersonides' purposes and of the medieval philosophic
enterprise in general. The charge is understandable when it is
made by Gersonides' contemporaries or by modern Orthodox Jews who
are devoted to traditional teachings and who are threatened by his
conclusions. It is not justified when it appears in the pages of
modern scholarly works.

Medieval philosophy is often characterized as an enterprise
of the harmonization or the reconciliation of the conflicting
truth claims of Greek philosophy and the philosopher's religious
tradition. In our view, this is an unfortunate choice of terms,
because it implies that the medieval philosopher was faced with
conflicting truths and conflicting loyalties and that he consciously
and explicitly sought to reconcile the two. Such a characterization cannot but cast doubt upon the intellectual integrity of the
enterprise. In the case of Gersonides' reading of the creation
narrative of Genesis, it leads the student to question whether
Gersonides really believed that the Torah meant to say all the
things which he reads into it with his philosophical mode of
interpretation.

A careful and sympathetic reading of Gersonides' writings
suggests that he did in fact believe that the truths of the Torah
can be understood best as consistent with the language of medieval
philosophy. Most modern readers of Scripture read Scripture with
the assumption that it was written or received by human beings
who lived in a specific socio-historical context and that the
literal meaning of the text is the meaning which those human beings
understood and intended in their time. By contrast, Gersonides
believed that the Torah was the repository of the infinite wisdom
of the divine nomos and that its meaning was not limited by its
historical context. He did not believe, therefore, that the
obvious meaning of the text—the meaning that is apparent to anyone
who opens Scripture—was its true meaning. An understanding of
divine wisdom, in his view, required a lifetime of preparation and
study and, even then, one's grasp of the truths revealed in the
Torah was very limited.

Gersonides believes that there is one truth: a truth that can
be conceived, to some extent, through the proper use of one's
intellect and the proper exercise of speculation, and that can be
learned from the Torah when it is read properly. His conviction
in this regard rests on his understanding of the purpose of the
Torah and of the ultimate end of human existence. He believes that
the Torah is a document which serves the providential end of guiding human beings to their ultimate felicity, viz., the most perfect
possible conception of the truth. Thus, the Torah is not intended
to coerce us into beliefs which conflict with the truth, because
such coercion would run counter to its purposes of leading us to
the truth. Its mode of persuasion is rather its self-evident

perfection. That is, when we recognize that it guides one who
studies it to true conception and one who follows its commandments
to moral perfection, we are drawn to follow and study this manifestly perfect nomos.

The Torah is a document which contains the true conceptions
which Moses acquired through the profound and unique development
of his intellect. There are other factors which contribute to
Mosaic and other, less profound and less complete prophecy which
allow the prophet to speak not only to the speculator but to the non-
philosophical masses as well. For our purposes, however, it is
sufficient to note that Gersonides believes that Moses was the
philosopher par excellence and that no other prophet or philosopher
has ever acquired a degree of true conception which remotely
approximates that of Moses. As a result of the high degree of the
development of his intellect, Moses came as close as is humanly
possible to approximating the conception of the Active Intellect.
Thus, the Torah, which documents Moses' conception, may be presumed
to be written with a profound wisdom about all issues of concern
to us. It is also written with the purpose of guiding the speculator to true conception, so that it often uses pedagogical techniques to lead us to correct conclusions and to stimulate us to
think about things in ways that otherwise would not occur to us.[250]

Thus, when Gersonides takes the conclusions which he reaches
by means of speculation to the text of the Torah and assumes that
any demonstrated truth must be the view of the Torah, he is not
consciously engaged in an insensitive manipulation of the obvious
meaning of the text. Nor does he believe that there is a need to
harmonize or to reconcile conflicting truth claims. What he
believes is that the Mosaic revelation must necessarily have been
aware of any true conception which he himself has acquired and that
the apparent meaning of the text and its preceding interpretations
by rabbis and philosophers alike have missed its true intentions.
He does not find this state of affairs surprising because the depths
of divine wisdom should be expected to be virtually inaccessible
except to the most well-trained speculators. The Torah has many
layers of meaning and its guidance is but vaguely comprehensible.
That its teachings accord with the conclusions of speculation is to
be expected since it is the repository of the wisdom of Moses, the
most accomplished of all philosophers.

Though Gersonides may be vulnerable to the charge that he lacks
humility in his assumption that his own conclusions more closely

approximate the truth than do any of the views of the sages who
preceded him, it should not be assumed that he has an inflated
view of the accomplishments of the human intellect. Rather, he
regularly and emphatically remarks about the limitations of human
knowledge. The first treatise of The Wars contains his argument
against those who suggest that the conjunction of the human intellect with the Active Intellect is possible, i.e., that it is possible for a human being to actualize the conception in his intellect to the extent that his conception is identical and therefore
united with the conception of the separate intellect which conceives of the sublunar world in its oneness. This is impossible,
he argues, primarily because our knowledge is multiple while the
knowledge of a separate intellect is single. That is, as he
explains in detail in the first treatise, the human intellect
begins without any actual conceptions. Potential conceptions exist
as a disposition in the hylic intellect and they are actualized
when we perceive existent things with our senses and use our
imagination and memory to abstract their definitions or essences
from the material embodiments of those essences. At the point at
which we conceive of the definition which inheres in a material
thing which is its essence and in which that material thing is one
with all other members of its species which share that definition,
we have acquired an actual conception which is abstracted from its
material embodiment and which does not come to be or pass away with
the coming to be or passing away of its material embodiment. To
the extent that a human intellect acquires true and everlasting
conceptions in this way, its intellect approximates the conception
of the Active Intellect. As a consequence, it achieves some degree
of immortality with its acquisition of everlasting conceptions,
and it is more subject to the providence which overflows from the
Active Intellect through the divine nomos which governs the sublunar world. If a human intellect acquires a sufficient number of
true conceptions, it may begin to understand their interrelationships and may begin to fathom the way in which all of the forms
of the divine nomos are one in the conception of the Active Intellect. The human intellect, however, can never achieve the perfect
conception of the Active Intellect in which all forms are known in
their unity, because the human intellect depends upon multiple
hylic forms—which are embodied in material things—to acquire its
knowledge.[251]

     Thus, Gersonides is emphatic about the limitations of human
knowledge. We can never know all of the definitions of all of
the sublunar species, let alone the way in which all of their

forms are interrelated as one. We can have only a very weak
knowledge of the Active Intellect and of the other separate intellects which are the movers of the spheres because we know them as
an effect knows its cause, i.e., by inferring from its own nature
the characteristics of its cause. Nor can we acquire anything
but a weak knowledge of the supralunar world, because of our physical distance from it and because of our distance in degree of
existence from its perpetual and unchanging nature.[252]

Given this view of the limitations of human knowledge, we may
take seriously Gersonides' humble statement in the Introduction to
The Wars that the issues which he is about to investigate are
extraordinarily difficult and will be discussed according to his
own limitations, and that the investigation of these issues could
not be accomplished without the guidance of the Torah. He is
especially insistent on the latter point with regard to the issue
of creation. That is, he states on a number of occasions that it
is the text of the creation narrative in Genesis which guided him
to the conclusions which he eventually reached by means of speculation. He does more than assert this point, however. His reading
of the text of Genesis in the section of The Wars translated below
is replete with instances in which he reads the Torah as a pedagogical tool which is designed to guide the speculator to true
conclusions about the issue of creation. One example may help to
clarify his meaning.

Gersonides reads the sequence of "days" of the creation
narrative as an indication of the priority of things created on
earlier "days" to things created on subsequent "days." His understanding of the different senses of priority and of the nontemporal
nature of creation is explained in detail below in this introduction. For our purposes here, we may note that this view is not a
method which he uses to circumvent the apparent suggestion of the
text that the days of creation are temporal designations. There
is no doubt in his mind that the Torah, which cannot, in principle,
contradict the truth, cannot possibly be suggesting that God
created the world with a series of temporally distinct creative
actions. Rather, he takes the order in which the creation story
is narrated very seriously and learns many things which plausibly
may have led him to the conclusions which he reaches in the first
part of this treatise. Among them are the lessons he learns from
the fact that the creation of the stars is narrated on the fourth
"day," after the narration of the creation of the visible part of
the earth on the third "day." He regards this inconsistency, in

which the stars, which are prior in cause and in nature to the
earth, are mentioned after it, as a technique which the Torah uses
to get the speculator to pause and to stimulate him to reach such
conclusions as that the earth is not elevated through the natural
causation which overflows from the stars' activities, and that the
spheres, the creation of which is narrated on the second "day," are
complete in themselves and derive no perfection from the stars
which they move or from the other actions of the stars. These are
data which he uses in his argument for creation in 6:1 and there is
no reason to doubt his assertion that he was led by the Torah to
note the nonessential characteristics of the supralunar world or of
the elevated part of the earth and to recognize these characteristics as demonstrations of the generation of the world.[253]

The notes of our commentary to the translation of the text of
6:2:1-8 below contain our discussions of many other examples of
the way the Torah guides him to speculative truth.[254] All of them
constitute evidence not that Gersonides gives priority to speculative truth over revealed truth but that he believes there is one
truth which can be partially discovered by means of speculation
but which can be more easily discovered when the speculator is
guided by the text of Torah. He thus considers the enterprise of
speculation to be the ultimate religious activity which is encour-
aged and aided by the Torah which exists for the providential end
of guiding the human intellect to its ultimate felicity of the most
perfect possible conception of the truth. For the most part, he
exhibits in The Wars none of the caution exercised by Maimonides in
revealing the secrets of ma^caseh bere^ʾshit—the esoteric study of
the account of creation—because, as he states in the Introduction
to The Wars, these matters are of such difficulty in themselves
that they demand clarification rather than obfuscation. Only in
the last chapter of the first treatise does he address the problem
that a person's faith might be shaken by the conclusions he reaches,
throughout The Wars, by means of speculation. There he advises
that the conclusions of speculation be disregarded by such a person, because the purpose of speculation is to support one's faith
which is in all cases of greater importance. Again, this chapter
may be read as an anomalous passage which contradicts his purposes
in The Wars and which is inserted as a way of defending his work
from the charge of undermining the faith of others. It is our
position, however, that it is consistent with his position throughout The Wars. His use of speculative inquiry is always with the

intention of seeking the truth of religions questions—the ultimate
religious activity—and never seeks to contradict the truth of
divine revelation.[255]

Gersonides' view of rabbinic statements and his use of Talmudic
and Midrashic texts which he cites in support of his own views is
less clear. In his Commentary to the Torah, he explicitly states
that rabbinic statements are not binding because they so often
contradict one another. In the text of 6:2:1-8 translated below,
he cites rabbinic texts with uncharacteristic frequency in order
to support his own interpretations of the text of Genesis. His
citations, however, are selective. He only cites texts which agree
with his views, even when those texts are surrounded by other
rabbinic statements which disagree with his views. On occasion,
he even quotes entire texts which support him in one respect but
which disagree with his views in other respects. His citations
invariably assume that the rabbis were acquainted with the principles of Aristotelian Physics, so that Rabbi Pinhas cannot mean,
for example, to assert the existence of a void with the term ḥalal,
since a void is an impossibility, or so that when Rabbi Aqiba uses
the term "water," he must mean to refer to the body which does not
preserve its shape which persists between the spheres.[256]

One motivation which he may have had in citing rabbinic
statements to which he attributed no authority may have been his
need to demonstrate that his own interpretations were not as out-
landish as they might appear. His apparent belief, however, that
the rabbis, when they understood the Torah correctly, understood
it as would a medieval philosopher, albeit imperfectly, strengthens
the argument that Gersonides sincerely believes that the truth
that the Torah intends to communicate can be expressed in the
language of Aristotle.

C.   Key Terms in the Genesis Narrative

After his introductory chapter (6:2:1), in which he asserts
that the existence of marvels does not presuppose creation ex
nihilo and in which he restates his claim that the text of the
Torah guided him to the truth of the issue of creation, Gersonides
devotes six chapters to a discussion of the meanings of terms in
the creation narrative in Genesis, the correct understanding of
which is crucial to a correct reading of the Torah. This section
of our introduction reviews his discussions in those chapters
(6:2:2-7).

This preliminary philological groundwork is a direct
consequence of his view, discussed above in the preceding section
of this introduction, that, insofar as the Torah is a document
which contains divine wisdom as it was revealed to Moses through
the profound development of his intellect, one can hope to be
guided by it only if one carefully prepares himself. His explication of the equivocal senses of terms as they occur in the Torah
presumes that its author, viz., Moses and other prophets, and its
source, viz., the Active Intellect and ultimately the conception
of God, necessarily have the most perfect possible knowledge of
speculative truth. In setting forth the senses of each term, he
resorts only to instances in which the term is used in Scripture.
He refers to at least two different kinds of equivocation, viz.,
analogy (dimyon), in which two things share a name and the second
possesses some attribute but not all attributes of the first, and
metaphor (hash'alah), in which the metaphorical usage of the term
is more remote than an analogous usage from the literal sense of
the term.[257]

In 6:2:2, he discusses the term re'shit (beginning) and lists
four different kinds of priority which the term designates when it
is said in the Torah: 1) temporal priority; 2) priority in order,
by which he means the priority of A to B when A is prior to B in
coming to be but A is posterior to B in nature, so that the existence of A is for the sake of the perfection of B, as the perfection
of the virtues is prior to intellectual perfection; 3) priority in
degree, in which A is said to be prior to B because A is more
venerable than B; and 4) priority in cause and in nature, in which
A is prior to B in the sense that the existence of A and B reciprocally imply each other but A is the cause of B and B is not the
cause of A. The relationship of this scheme to that of Aristotle
is discussed in the notes of the commentary below.[258] He refers
explicitly in this chapter only to the use of the term in Gen 1:1,
where he takes it in the fourth sense to refer to the priority in
cause and in nature of "light," i.e., the separate intellects, to
the rest of existent things. In general, however, his account of
the priority which is indicated by the "days" of creation depends
on his definitions here of the second and fourth senses of the
term.

In 6:2:3, he lists two senses of the term 'ereṣ (earth):
1) the element earth; and 2) all four of the sublunar elements.
The second, inclusive sense occurs when the term is said with the

term heaven, in which case it designates the sublunar world. It
is in the second sense that the term is said in Gen 1:1 and 1:2.

In 6:2:4, he discusses the meaning of tohu and bohu in Gen 1:2.
He takes them to refer to last form and prime matter, the first
principles of sublunar existence. Briefly, he understands prime
matter (bohu) to refer to the material receptacle which he refers
to elsewhere as body which does not preserve its shape, i.e.,
absolute dimensional body which has potentially definite dimensions.
By last form (tohu) he means the common characteristic of definite
dimensionality which is shared by all four of the elemental forms.
A fuller discussion of his understanding of the first principles
of sublunar existence is provided below in Part IV, section E, of
this introduction, in the discussion devoted to body which does
not preserve its shape.[259]

In 6:2:5, he discusses the following senses of the terms
ᵓor (light) and ḥoshekh (darkness): 1) perceptible light and the
privation of perceptible light; 2) clear sight and poor sight;
3) form and matter; and 4) the perfect conception of the separate
intellects and the privation of conception in a given human intellect. He takes the term "light," as it occurs in Gen 1:3, to refer
to the perfect conception of the separate intellects. He takes
the term "darkness," as it occurs in Gen 1:2, to refer to the
element earth, which is the most deprived of the form and goodness
of all of the elements. Though he does not discuss the term "darkness" in Gen 1:4 in this chapter, he devotes a considerable amount
of space in his discussion of the first "day" in 6:2:8 to possible
interpretations of its meaning. The interpretation which he prefers there refers the term to those of the separate intellects
which are less venerable in their conception than others. The
latter are referred to as "light" in Gen 1:4.[260]

In the course of his discussion in 6:2:5, he also mentions
that the term tehom (deep) in Gen 1:2 refers to the lowest part of
the element water, and that the term ᶜal in Gen 1:2 means "next to"
and not "on."[261]

In 6:2:6, he discusses the following senses of the term ruaḥ:
1) the wind; 2) the soul; and 3) elemental air. He takes the
term, as it occurs in Gen 1:2, to refer to elemental air and
explains that it is called ruaḥ ᵓelohim to indicate its magnitude,
which is great relative to the composite air with which we are
familiar. He also believes that the phrase also refers to elemental
fire and that the Torah chose not to use the term "fire" to name

elemental fire because the two are very dissimilar. He understands
the term merahefet in Gen 1:2 to mean "resting," so that the elemental air and elemental fire were resting next to the surface of
the water.[262]

In 6:2:7, he discusses the following senses of the term
raqiᶜa: 1) anything which is stretched out and has relatively
definite dimensions; and 2) the heavenly body, by which he means
the spheres, the dimensions of which are perpetually definite
and unchanging. As the term is said on the second "day" of the
creation narrative, it refers to the spheres.

The phrases "upper waters" and "lower waters" in the narrative
of the second "day" of creation refer respectively to the part of
the body which does not preserve its shape from which the supralunar world came to be and the part of that body from which the
sublunar world came to be. The term "water" is said analogously
of the body which does not preserve its shape, because the latter
has no actually definite dimensions and water is the substance
which most closely approximates absolute, indefinite dimensionality.
The distinction (mavdil) which is referred to on the second "day"
is the creation of the elemental forms which are received first by
the part of the body which does not preserve its shape from which
the sublunar world comes to be. The elemental forms distinguish
it from the perpetually unchanging nature of supralunar substance
because of their contrary qualities which interact under the
influence of supralunar motions, causing the processes of coming
to be and passing away in the sublunar world. The "water" above
and below each "raqiᶜa" refers to the body which does not preserve
its shape which persists between the spheres.[263]

D. On the Unity of All Created Things

Both in the introductory comments of 6:2:8, which precede his
direct discussion of the creation narrative, and throughout that
discussion in 6:2:8, Gersonides seeks to explain the text of Genesis as offering us guidance about the interrelationships which
exist among all created things. The creation narrative, he
believes, is designed to guide the speculator to the true conception of the way in which the divine nomos functions and of the ends
which the various parts of the world serve. Thus, he devotes a
considerable amount of his discussion of the account of the creation of the world to the ways in which some things are prior to
others and the way in which all degrees of existence are one in
the divine nomos.

Gersonides prefaces his account of creation in 6:2:8 by
correcting the common misunderstanding that the "days" of the
creation narrative are temporal designations. He refers back to
his argument in 6:1 in which he demonstrates that there is no time
prior to the creation of the world and that there is no time in the
process of its creation until it is completed.[264] Thus, the creation of all parts of the world described in the first six "days"
of the creation narrative was simultaneous. It occurred as the
instantaneous actualization of the single act of divine will at
the moment of creation that the hierarchy of forms of the divine
nomos should overflow from Him and should be received by the
material receptacle. He takes all instances of the recurring
phrase va-yehiy khen (and it was so) to be statements of this
instantaneous actualization, and only in the case of the generation
of the plant species does he suggest that the complete actualization of the species occurred at a later time.[265]

Rather, as mentioned above, the "days" indicate the priority
in cause and in nature and the priority in order of some things
to other things. On the first "day," the creation of the intelligible world of the separate intellects is described. The separate
intellects are prior in cause and in nature to all other created
things, in that they cause the motions of the spheres, on account
of which the divine nomos overflows to the sublunar world and
causes its existence.[266]

On the second "day," the creation of the spheres is described.
The spheres are also prior in cause and in nature to the sublunar
world which is caused by them. Also on the second "day," the
creation of the four concentric layers of the elements is described.
Though the details of this description are found in the first two
verses of the first chapter of Genesis after the word bere'shit,
that description is parenthetical and refers to the second "day."
The elements are prior in order to all other sublunar things which
are composed of them and for the sake of which they exist. He
often refers to this priority in order as hylic priority. That is,
A can be said to be hylically prior to B when the existence of A
is more material and less perfect than the existence of B. In
this way, the heavenly bodies are hylically prior to their separate
movers, and the hierarchy of sublunar species proceeds in degrees
from the relative privation of the elements to the relative perfection of the human species, for the sake of which all lower
sublunar species perform their natural, specific functions. Thus,

hylic priority is one form of priority in order, since the
hylically prior species exist for the sake of the species which
are hylically posterior to them. The hylically prior species are
prior in coming to be, in that higher species could not endure
without them, but they are posterior in venerability and in
nature.[267]

On the third "day," we would expect that the creation of the
stars would have been described, since the stars are prior in
cause and in nature to everything in the sublunar world. After his
discussion of the fourth "day," Gersonides explains why this is not
the case and his explanation is discussed below in Part IV, section
F, of this introduction. Rather, on the third "day," the creation
of the elevated, visible part of the earth is described as well as
the creation of the plant species. The visible part of the earth
is causally prior to the existence of all land species. The plant
species are hylically prior to fish, birds, walking animals and
humans.[268] On the fourth "day," the creation of the stars is
described as well as the three ways in which their activities are
for the sake of the causation of sublunar existence.[269]

On the fifth "day," the creation of the fish and bird species
is described. Both are hylically posterior to plants. Fish are
hylically prior to birds and birds are hylically prior to walking
animals. Their creation is described on the same "day" because
their mode of reproduction—i.e., by laying eggs outside the body—
is inferior and hence prior to the mode of reproduction of walking
animals, in which the gestation of the fetus occurs within the
womb.[270]

On the sixth "day," the creation of the walking animals is
first described. They are hylically posterior to lower species
and hylically prior to the human species. The description of the
six days culminates with the description of the creation of the
human species, to which all other sublunar existent things are
hylically prior and which is most perfect of all sublunar species
because of the relationship of the hylic intellect to the separate
intellects.[271]

Crucial to an understanding of Gersonides' view of priority
and of the hierarchy of existence is his repeated discussion of
how some things exist and/or act "for the sake of" (ba^cavur) other
things. As mentioned above, in our comparison of his orientation
with that of Maimonides in this section of our introduction,
Maimonides would say that if the natural functions of A are for

the sake of the perfection of B, then B is more venerable than A
insofar as the purpose or end of A is the existence of B. It is
for this reason that he rejects the notion that the supralunar
world acts for the sake of the sublunar world.

To a certain extent, Gersonides agrees with this position.
That is, in his view, the elemental forms, for example, exist for
the sake of the composite forms. They do not have an existence
apart from their existence in composite things—that is, there are
no pure, unmixed elements in the sublunar world—and so they derive
their perfection from the composite forms for the sake of which
they exist. This is a clear case in which that which exists for
the sake of something is less venerable. Similarly, the lower
sublunar species, who perform their specific functions for the
sake of the preservation of the human species and the perpetuation
of its ultimate end of conception, are also less venerable than
the human species, though it is less clear that they derive their
perfection from the human species.

Though Gersonides admits that there are instances in which A
acts for the sake of B and is less venerable than B, he argues
that, in such a case, A is less venerable than B not because it
functions for the sake of B but because it derives its perfection
from the existence of B. In general, however he believes that the
more venerable things always acts for the sake of the less venerable thing. God's self-conception can be said to be for the sake
of the divine nomos which overflows from Him. The conceptions of
the separate intellects can be said to be for the sake of the
motions of the spheres. Similarly, the conception of the Active
Intellect can be said to be for the sake of the governance of sublunar existence and the activities of the heavenly bodies can be
said to be for the sake of the divine nomos which is formed from
the combination of their activities and which overflows to the
sublunar world. All of these are cases in which the more venerable
things acts in a way that perfects the less venerable thing. In
none of these cases, however, does the more venerable thing derive
any perfection from the less venerable thing for the sake of which
it acts.[272]

This view depends on a fine distinction which Gersonides first
proposes in the first part of the sixth treatise in his discussion
of the properties of things which come to be (6:1:6-9, 13). Among
three such properties which he lists, he asserts: a) that things
which have a final cause must have come to be; and b) that things

which act for the sake of something else must have come to be.
On first glance, these two characteristics appear to be redundant
and, in fact, he asserts that anything which acts essentially for
the sake of something else must have a final cause. Furthermore,
when he attempts to demonstrate that the supralunar world and the
visible part of the earth have the characteristics of things which
come to be, in both cases he demonstrates both of the two characteristics mentioned here by showing that the activities of the heavens
and the visible part of the earth perfect the existence of the
sublunar world.

Thus, his distinction in the first part of the sixth treatise
may not become clear until his discussions of priority in 6:2:8.
His consistent assertion throughout his discussion of the creation
narrative is that, when the more venerable thing acts for the sake
of the less venerable thing, its final cause is not the less venerable thing but is rather the divine nomos. It is the divine nomos
which bestows the nature of a thing by which its natural functions
are determined, and which all things strive to fulfill, and it is
the divine nomos which, in its infinite wisdom, has created and
sustains the world in such a way that all things are interrelated
in the most perfect possible way for the sake of the preservation
of all species and for the sake of the most perfect possible per-
formance by those species of their natural function. Thus, the
separate intellects, for example, desire to approximate their final
cause—the divine nomos—and consequently they conceive the circular motion which moves their spheres. They derive no perfection
from the motion of their spheres; their conception includes neither
the actual position of their spheres as they move nor the nomos
which overflows from the motions of the supralunar world to the
sublunar world. They conceive only of themselves, their final
cause and the single, continuous conception of circular motion,
so that they have no need of their spheres or of the sublunar
world as the objects of their conception. He makes a similar
argument with regard to the other cases mentioned above. Though
the spheres move for the sake of the motions of the stars, they
derive no benefit from the diverse activities of the stars—their
final cause is their respective separate intellects. Though the
activities of the stars are for the sake of the sublunar world,
they derive no perfection from the overflow of the divine nomos—
their final cause is the divine nomos which caused them to come to
be in their diversity.

It is in this way that Gersonides can assert that the world
is anthropocentric. That is, all things in the intelligible,
supralunar and sublunar worlds act for the sake of the human
species and the human end of conception even though the human
species is not their end. The end of all things is the divine
nomos which governs a world which is a macrocosm, all of the components of which are interrelated.

Specifically with regard to the sublunar world, this view is
manifested in Gersonides' assertion that the hierarchy of hylic
forms in the divine nomos, which overflows from the activities of
the heavenly bodies, is one in the conception of the Active Intellect. The Active Intellect, which governs providentially the sublunar world, conceives of things insofar as they are one with all
other members of their species and it conceives of the forms of
all of the species insofar as they are one and interrelated in the
divine nomos. It is this perfect and single conception which
serves as the unattainable limit towards which human conception
approaches when the hylic intellect acquires actual conceptions
of hylic forms and begins to conceive of the overall scheme of the
universe, in which all things are one.

It is this conception of the interrelatedness of all things,
Gersonides believes, towards which the Torah seeks to guide us
with the recurring phrase, "and it was evening and it was morning"
(va-yehiy ᶜerev va-yehiy voqer). That is, the phrase occurs on
each "day" and denotes the unity of that particular degree of
creation and, in general, the unity of all creation. On the first
"day," the phrase teaches us that the separate intellects, with
their varying degrees of venerability, are one in the divine nomos;
on the second, that the spheres are the form and the perfection of
the elements; on the third, that the visible part of the earth is
elevated for the sake of the species which live upon it and that
all plant species, in their diversity, are interrelated; on the
fourth, that the diverse activities of the stars and the variations
in the intensity of the influence of each star upon the sublunar
world all combine to form the single divine nomos which overflows
to the sublunar world; on the fifth, that the diverse species of
fish and birds all are interrelated and serve a single function;
on the sixth, that the natural functions of walking animals are
for the sake of the human species; and finally, that all parts of
the world are united as a macrocosm, so that nothing in nature is
useless.[273]

Thus the purpose of the creation narrative in Genesis is to guide us towards a conception of the way in which the divine nomos governs the world which approximates, as closely as possible, the single, united conception of the Active Intellect. For this reason, the narrative does not describe the generation of accidents, which occur for short periods of time and infrequently, since they do not follow the natural custom by which the divine nomos governs. Neither does it attribute the creation of the elements, which are referred to indirectly in the parenthetical aside of Gen 1:1-2, to the will of God, because the existence of the elements is close to privation and their elemental forms only exist in composition, as discussed above. Nor does it mention the coming to be of homogeneous parts or of things which are spontaneously generated. Rather, the description of creation describes only those things which come to be from members of their own species and which thus are informed by the forms of the divine nomos. Even the plant species are not directly attributed to God's will because of their low degree of existence.[274] The creation narrative is not a pointlessly comprehensive scientific text. It is rather a vessel of providential revelation which seeks to guide us to the most perfect possible conception of those things which are the proper subjects of conception, i.e., which exist in such a way that form and goodness is dominant over matter and privation.

E.   On the Body Which Does Not Preserve Its Shape

Gersonides' argument in 6:1 for the persistence, prior to creation, of a body which does not preserve its shape (geshem biltiy shomer temunato) out of which the world came to be and his description of that body in 6:1 have been summarized above in Part III of this introduction. Having demonstrated that the world must have come to be, and having determined that it could have come to be neither as Plato suggests (because to posit disorderly motion prior to the creation of the world is to posit that the world existed prior to creation) nor as Maimonides suggests (because the nature of the causal action of a separate intellect cannot be posited to have brought body into existence out of absolutely nothing), he concludes that there must have been a material receptacle upon which the divine nomos, which overflowed from God at His will, acted. He calls this material receptacle "body which does not preserve its shape" and states that it persisted in a formless state prior to creation.

In positing the persistence of body which does not preserve
its shape prior to creation and apart from the causation of the
hierarchy of forms which overflows from the divine nomos, Gersonides
departs markedly and significantly from the assumptions of his
predecessors. According to the traditional medieval philosophical
model, formlessness entails absolute privation and potentiality.
Matter naked of form has no existence of its own. It is the causation of the hylic forms—i.e., those forms which perform their
function by means of the matter which they inform—which bestows
upon material bodies their natures and hence all their characteristics. A material thing, therefore, is the proper object of true
knowledge, according to this traditional model, only insofar as it
approximates the nature of its form. Matter, apart from form, is
absolutely unknowable and lacking in existence.

In positing the persistence of body which does not preserve
its shape apart from any formal causation, Gersonides is suggesting
a major modification of the prevailing ontology and epistemology of
his period. Though body which does not preserve its shape is formless, it is not absolute privation. It is intermediate between
existence and privation—it is something insofar as it is body
and it is nothing insofar as it is formless.[275] That he is serious
in asserting that its body renders it something other than absolute
potentiality is obvious from his subsequent discussions. That is,
he speaks of its magnitude, the likelihood of a remainder of it
persisting apart from the world after creation, and its persistence
after creation between the supralunar spheres, whose motions it
keeps unconfused. Most importantly, he insists that there is
significant distinction between Maimonides' theory of creation out
of absolute privation and his own theory of creation out of this
body. In Gersonides' terms, informed matter is that matter which
has actually definite dimensions. Formless matter has absolute
and only potentially definite dimensions.

Thus, there can be no question that he rejects the prevailing
hypothesis that formless matter is absolutely devoid of existence.
Though body which does not preserve its shape is formless, it has,
as he puts, a very weak degree of existence. Though it lacks a
nature which is bestowed upon matter by a form and though it consequently is not the proper subject of true conceptual knowledge,
it does have certain characteristics which persist in it apart
from formal causation—viz., the characteristics of a body which
lacks preservation of shape—and which render it the proper subject

of a very weak and tentative cognition, i.e., inferences which can
be made by analogy to the material world after creation.

   As is discussed briefly above in the summary of 6:1:17 in
Part III of this introduction and as is argued at length below in
note #49 of the commentary to 6:2:4, the most plausible hypothesis
to account for all of Gersonides' statements about body which does
not preserve its shape and about last form and prime matter in
6:1:17-28, 6:2:1-8, 5:2, 5:3, and in his Commentary to the Torah
is that he uses the term "body which does not preserve its shape"
to designate what Averroes had called, in his Sermo De Substantia
Orbis, "body with indefinite dimensions" (merḥaqim ha-biltiy
mugbalim)—i.e., body which is dimensional in that it has mass and
has potentially definite dimensions, but which has no actually
definite dimensions. It can be called nothing in that its formlessness gives its dimensions no definition, but it can be called
something in that it is dimensional, at least potentially. Thus,
unlike Maimonides, Gersonides would not agree that the purely
potential receptacle of the divine nomos is absolutely nothing.
It is nothing in that its formlessness renders it close to privation without the existence which a thing has when it receives a
form and a definition. It is not absolutely nothing, however, in
that it is dimensional in some sense of that term. Unlike Averroes,
from whom he inherits the concept of absolute, indefinite dimensional body but who did not believe in the creation of the world at
a moment in time, Gersonides asserts that absolute dimensional
body persists apart from the formal causation of the divine nomos.
Its absolute dimensionality, according to Gersonides, does not
require the causation of corporeal form, as Averroes had posited.

   Thus, Gersonides' account of creation is that this absolute
dimensional body persisted prior to the moment of God's creative
will that the divine nomos and its hierarchy of forms should overflow from His self-conception and should be received by the material receptacle. At that moment, things proceeded as follows:
In the supralunar world, the separate intellects overflowed from
God and their respective single conceptions of perpetual circular
motion caused the formation, out of some of the body which does
not preserve its shape, of the supralunar spheres. In the sublunar
world, the body which does not preserve its shape—which is now
referred to as prime matter in that it receives the disposition
to receive the elemental forms simultaneously with its reception
of them—receives last form. Last form is nothing other than the
four elemental forms when they are considered in their common

respect of bestowing definite dimensions on the matter which
receives them. That is, prior to (but not temporally prior to)
the generation of the hierarchy of lower existent things which
occurs when the contrary qualities of the elements perform their
natural function of interacting to produce all composite things
under the influence of the divine nomos which overflows from the
radiations of the stars, what happened in the sublunar world is
that absolute dimensional body received the last form of definite
dimensionality simultaneously with its reception of the elemental
forms. It thus existed, at this prior stage, as body with the
definite dimensions of the four concentric layers of the elements.

     As noted above, the originality of this theory is that
Gersonides rejects the notion that there was ever a pure potentiality without the characteristic of potentially definite dimensions,
viz., something that could be called absolute potentiality or
absolutely nothing. The more common theory posited that at the
first stage of coming to be, there was pure potentiality, which
was often named "prime matter," and corporeal form, which gave pure
potentiality the characteristic of either potential dimensionality
or definite dimensionality or absolute dimensionality. This body,
the nature of which was subject to controversy, was often named
"absolute body," and was posited to be the substratum which received
the elemental forms.

     Gersonides omits the first stage in his account of creation
and thus rejects the notion that absolute dimensionality is a
characteristic which can be attributed to a form which is part of
the divine nomos. In his argument in 6:1, he rejects the view that
the causation of a separate intellect—i.e., God—could have been
realized without a material receptacle and that body could have
come to be out of absolutely nothing. Implicit in this argument
is the view that the substratum which serves as the matter for all
the forms of the divine nomos and which is the cause of generation
and corruption in the sublunar world does not come from God, who
is the principle of unity and goodness and perpetuity in the world.
Also implicit is that to posit that God is not the cause of matter
is to posit no deprivation in Him. He has no relation with matter.
He is perfect in Himself and would have lacked no perfection if
there had not been a material receptacle to receive the divine
nomos. At no point does He conceive of the hylic forms which
matter receives, insofar as they are hylic. He does not know the
forms in their hylic multiplicity but rather knows them in their
separate unity.

The problems which are entailed by Gersonides' original account
of creation have been discussed above, in our summary of 6:1:18 in
Part III of this introduction, and are dealt with again below, in
Part V of this introduction. In this place, however, let us note
that the criticism of Gersonides' view which assumes that his absolute dimensional body is formless and nothing, and is therefore not
the proper subject of conception and discussion, is blunted by the
fact that the absolute body of Avicenna, Ibn Daud and Averroes is
no less inconceivable. According to Avicenna and Ibn Daud, the
corporeal form which prime matter receives yields an absolute body
with an accidental predisposition for the assumption of tri-dimen-
sionality. According to Averroes, it yields a body with the
absolute dimensionality of Gersonides' body which does not preserve
its shape. In neither case can absolute body be said to be more
appropriate as an object of conception than is Gersonides' "body
which does not preserve its shape." Indeed, relatively speaking,
Gersonides' "body which does not preserve its shape" is more
appropriate as an object of discussion and conception than is the
"prime matter" of any of these predecessors. Gersonides' "body" has
absolute dimensionality, while their "prime matter" is pure potentiality and therefore absolute privation.

A further strength of Gersonides' theory is that it does not
attribute the privation of materiality to divine causation. God,
in his view, cannot cause anything to be potential, as would be the
case if He were posited to have created body out of absolutely
nothing. Thus absolute dimensional body, which is the potentiality
of body for definite dimensions, cannot, in his view, be called a
"form." It is presumably for this reason that he does not attribute absolute dimensionality to the causation of a "corporeal form"
as do his predecessors. All potentiality in the sublunar world is
a consequence of the absolute dimensional body which persists prior
to and apart from the causation of the divine nomos and is not an
effect of any form of the divine nomos.

A word of further introduction is necessary about Gersonides'
use of the terms "last form" and "prime matter," to which he takes
the Biblical terms, tohu and bohu, to refer. As mentioned above,
he refers to the body which does not preserve its shape as "prime
matter" when he discusses it with reference to the disposition
which part of it receives in order to receive the elemental forms
at the moment of creation. Thus, the two terms, "prime matter"
and "body which does not preserve its shape," are interchangeable
when they are said with reference to the sublunar world. The term

"prime matter," however, cannot refer to the material receptacle
which persisted prior to creation, nor to the body from which the
supralunar bodies came to be, nor to the body which persists between
the spheres, nor to the remainder of the body which may have persisted after creation apart from the world. This is because in
none of these cases does the body which does not preserve its
shape have the disposition to receive the hierarchy of the hylic
forms. Thus, in these cases that body is not "matter," which is
the name of the material receptacle which underlies the hylic forms,
and it is not "prime" in the sense that it is the first "principle"
of all material substrata.

    "Last form," as mentioned above, is a term which Gersonides
uses when he is discussing the elemental forms before they intermix to form the hierarchy of the composite hylic forms, i.e., at
the prior stage at which they exist motionless as four concentric
layers with the common characteristic of definite dimensionality.
In some places Gersonides identifies last form with the elemental
forms, and in others he speaks of it as the nature which prime
matter receives prior to its reception of the elemental forms.
This is because last form is the nature of definite dimensionality
which prime matter receives prior in order to but simultaneously
in time with its reception of the elemental forms. As he interprets the reference in Isaiah to tohu and bohu in 6:2:4, last form
is analogous to the dimensions which an architect creates by using
bricks which constitute those dimensions; it is that in which
(bo hu⁾) prime matter is, in that it is its dimensions. He
describes prime matter, last form and the elemental forms all as
close to privation, in that none of them actually exists apart
from composite existent things.[276]

F. The Narrative of Creation

    What follows is an attempt to present the seven days of the
creation narrative of Genesis as Gersonides reads them. Included
in parentheses are verse notations of the Genesis text. Also, at
certain points we have included in parentheses phrases from the
narrative to which he refers when their inclusion seemed necessary
for clarification.

    (1:1) Prior in cause and in nature to all other things
(be-reᵓshit)—prior to God's creation of the supralunar and the
sublunar worlds, (1:2) and prior to the state of affairs in the
sublunar world which existed when there was last form and prime
matter (tohu va-vohu) and the element earth (ḥoshekh) was next to

the lowest surface of the element water (ᶜal penei tehom) and
the elements air and fire (ruaḥ ʾelohim) rested next to the upper
surface of the water (meraḥefet ᶜal penei ha-mayim)²⁷⁷ — (1:3) God
willed the existence of the intelligible world of the separate
intellects (va-yoʾmer ʾelohim yehiy ʾor). (1:4) This state of
affairs was good, in that separate intellects existed in a mode of
perfection through which the purpose of creation could be accomplished (va-yarʾ ʾelohim ʾet ha-ʾor kiy ṭov), and it was the divine
will that there be a distinction between those separate intellects
with more venerable conceptions and those with less venerable
conceptions (va-yavdel ʾelohim bein ha-ʾor u-vein ha-ḥoshekh).
(1:5) This gradation in the degrees of venerability of the conceptions of the separate intellects was perpetually the divine will
(va-yiqraʾ ʾelohim la-ʾor yom ve-la-ḥoshekh qaraʾ laylah), and this
variation in degree was one in that the more venerable intellects
are the form and the perfection of the less venerable intellects
and in that all of their conceptions are united in the divine nomos
(va-yehiy ᶜerev va-yehiy voqer). This is the first level of natural priority (yom ʾeḥad).²⁷⁸

(1:6) It was the divine will that the spheres should come to
be in the midst of the body which does not preserve its shape from
which the supralunar world would come to be (va-yoʾmer ʾelohim
yehiy raqiᶜa be-tokh ha-mayim) and that those spheres would distinguish between the body which does not preserve its shape which persists between adjacent spheres, in order to prevent the confusion
of their respective motions (viyhiy mavdil bein mayim la-mayim).
(1:7) Thus, the spheres were generated by divine will (va-yaᶜas
ʾelohim ʾet ha-raqiᶜa) and the part of the body which does not
preserve its shape from which the sublunar world would come to be
was distinguished from the part of that body from which the supralunar world would come to be, i.e., by its reception of the nature
of definite dimensionality which it received prior to but temporally
simultaneously with its reception of the elemental forms. This
distinction was between the nature for coming to be and passing
away which the sublunar world has as a consequence of the contrary
qualities of the elemental forms which interact to cause coming to
be and passing away, and the nature of the celestial substance of
the spheres, which remains perpetually in its definition (va-yavdel
bein ha-mayim ʾasher mi-taḥat la-raqiᶜa u-vein ha-mayim ʾasher me-
ᶜal la-raqiᶜa). Thus it was so, i.e., at this prior stage, the
four elements existed in concentric layers as described above in

Gen 1:2 (va-yehiy khen). (1:8) It was divine will that the relationships between the axes of the spheres' rotations, and thus the
dimensions of the individual spheres and the distances between
them, should remain perpetually unchanging (va-yiqra⁾ ⁾elohim la-
raqi⁽a shamayim). The spheres and their motions, which began
instantaneously, were united with the elements as their form
and perfection, in that they would move the stars from which the
divine nomos would overflow to the sublunar world and would cause
the elements to intermix in ways that would dispose them to receive
the hierarchy of hylic forms in the divine nomos (va-yehiy ⁽erev
va-yehiy voqer). This is the second level of natural priority
(yom sheniy).[279]

Only in the description of the second level of natural priority does the narrative fail to say that it was good. This is
because neither the spheres nor the elemental forms were complete
at this stage. The spheres move for the sake of moving the stars,
the creation of which is not described until the fourth "day."
The elemental forms exist for the sake of the composite forms from
which they derive their perfection. The elemental forms are close
to privation in that they have no existence except in composition.[280] Another interpretation of the rabbis is that the second
level of natural priority is not called good because it includes
the elemental forms, which are the source of passing away and
privation.[281]

(1:9) It was the divine will that part of the element earth
should depart from its nature to remain below the element water
and that it should be elevated above the water as visible, dry
land (va-yo⁾mer ⁾elohim yiqavu ha-mayim mi-taḥat ha-shamayim ⁾el
maqom ⁾eḥad ve-tera-⁾eh ha-yabashah). The divine will in this
regard was actualized instantaneously (va-yehiy khen). (1:10) It
was the divine will that the earth should perpetually be elevated
above the seas in this way (va-yiqra⁾ ⁾elohim la-yabasha ⁾ereṣ
u-le-miqveh ha-mayim qara⁾ yamim). This state of affairs was good,
because the earth is elevated for the sake of the species which
live upon it (va-yar⁾ ⁾elohim kiy ṭov). (1:11) It was the divine
will that the plant species should sprout upon the elevated part
of the earth (va-yo⁾mer ⁾elohim tadshe⁾ ha-⁾areṣ deshe⁾). The
existence of both the less perfect plant species—viz., the herbs
which bear seed—and the more perfect trees, which produce their
seeds in their fruit, were willed (⁽esev mazriy⁽a zera⁽ ⁽eṣ periy
⁽oseh periy le-miyno ⁾asher zar⁽o vo). The divine will that the

earth should be disposed to bring forth plants was actualized
instantaneously (va-yehiy khen). (1:12) Thus, it was as if seeds
were planted in the earth, which brought forth these plant species,
though the indirect description of their generation (va-toṣeh
ha-ꜣareṣ deshe ꜣ), which does not attribute their coming to be
directly to God, indicates that the plant species did not blossom
fully until some time after the moment of creation, as is described
in Gen 2:5. It may also indicate that the degree of existence of
the plant species, the soul of which contains only the nutritive
faculty and not the additional faculties possessed by the animal
soul, does not require the reception from the forms of the divine
nomos of any principle in addition to the principles possessed by
the earth and the seas. This state of affairs was good, because
the plant species exist for the sake of the sublunar species which
are posterior in order to them, and ultimately for the perfection
of the human species (va-yarꜣ ꜣelohim kiy ṭov). (1:13) The elevated
part of the earth was united with the plant species, for the sake
of which the earth was elevated. Similarly, all of the plant
species, in their varying degrees of perfection, were united in
the hierarchy of hylic forms, in which the plant species proceed,
degree by degree, from greater privation to greater perfection, and
the more perfect species are the form and perfection of those species which are hylically prior to them (va-yehiy ᶜerev va-yehiy
voqer). This is the third level of natural priority (yom
sheliyshiy). [282]

(1:14) It was the divine will that there be stars in the
supralunar spheres (va-yomerꜣ ꜣelohim yehiy meꜣorot birqiᶜa ha-
shamayim). These stars were willed for three purposes: to cause
the generation, in the sublunar world, of things from the contrary
qualities of the elements, the strength of which varies with the
variation in the intensity of the influence of each of the stars
(le-havdil bein ha-yom u-vein ha-laylah); to influence the sublunar
world in a variety of different ways through the influences of the
actions of each of the stars, each of which serves as a sign of
its individual influence, which varies over different periods of
time (ve-hayu le-ꜣotot u-le-moᶜadim u-le-yamim ve-shanim); (1:15)
and to illuminate the sublunar world, since the preservation of the
sublunar animal species in general requires that they exercise
their natural function of sight, and the ultimate perfection of
the human species—viz., conception—requires the prior visual
perception of the material embodiments of hylic forms, from which

actual conceptions can be abstracted (ve-hayu lim³orot birqi^ca
ha-shamayim le-ha³ir ^cal ha-³areṣ). The divine will in this respect
was actualized instantaneously (va-yehiy khen). That is, the
diverse states of affairs of the heavenly bodies, in all their
characteristics, came to be in the most perfect possible way for
the benefit of the sublunar world, which receives the divine nomos
which overflows from the supralunar world. (1:16) Thus, the two
great luminaries came to be—viz., the sun and the moon (va-ya^cas
³elohim ³et shenei ha-me³orot ha-gedolim). These two heavenly
bodies are mentioned specifically because their respective magni-
tudes and illuminations each produce an influence on the sublunar
world which is much stronger than the influences of other stars.
Thus, when the influence of the sun or of the moon reaches its
peak, its influence predominates over the influences of all the
rest of the stars (³et ha-ma³or ha-gadol le-memshelet ha-yom ve-
³et ha-ma³or ha-qoton le-memshelet ha-laylah). Also, the rest of
the stars came to be (ve-³et ha-kokhavim). (1:17) The heavenly
bodies were suspended in the spheres (va-yiten ³otam ³elohim
birqi^ca ha-shamayim) for the three purposes mentioned above: to
illuminate the sublunar world (le-ha³ir ^cal ha-³areṣ); (1:18) to
influence the contrary qualities of the sublunar world to act in a
variety of ways, each of which is caused by one of the stars and
each of which predominates when its star is most dominant in its
influence (ve-limshol ba-yom u-va-laylah); and to vary the influence
of the actions of the contrary qualities in the sublunar world in a
way that correlates with the periods of greater and lesser dominance of each star (u-le-havdil bein ha-³or u-vein ha-ḥoshekh).
This state of affairs was good. That is, the diversity and variations in the supralunar world exists neither accidentally, since
accidents occur only infrequently and for short durations while the
states of affairs of the supralunar world are perpetual, nor necessarily, since the characteristics of the heavens do not follow as
a necessary consequence of either the natures of the separate
intellects or the nature of the fifth body, viz., the substance of
the supralunar world. Thus, the stars and their diverse characteristics were created by divine will for the purpose of the perfection
which overflows from them to the sublunar world (va-yar³ ³elohim
kiy ṭov). (1:19) All of the stars and their diverse functions are
united as one in the divine nomos which is formed from those functions and which overflows from them (va-yehiy ^cerev va-yehiy voqer).
This is the fourth level of natural priority (yom reviy³iy).[283]

One should not think it problematic that the activities of the heavenly bodies function for the sake of the perfection of the sublunar world which is posterior to it in cause and in nature. In general, things of greater venerability always act for the sake of things of lesser venerability. They remain more venerable, however, because they derive no perfection from the less venerable things for the sake of which they act.[284]

The Torah describes the creation of the stars after it describes the creation of the visible part of the earth and plant species even though the former are prior in cause and in nature to the latter. It does so for pedagogical purposes, to cause the speculator to pause and to guide him to the realization of the following true conceptions: 1) The elevation of the visible part of the earth is not a necessary consequence of the influence of the divine nomos which overflows from the supralunar world. The nature which overflows in that nomos is that the element earth should be submerged beneath the element water. Rather, the earth was elevated by divine will for the purpose of the preservation of the species that live upon it. If the creation narrative had described the creation of the stars before the elevation of the earth, as would have been proper given the priority of the former to the latter, we might have concluded erroneously that the existence of dry land is a natural and necessary consequence of the activities of the supralunar world, as Aristotle and Averroes mistakenly believed. Since it thus described the elevation of the earth before its description of the creation of the stars, it also described the creation of the plant species, in order to indicate the purpose for which the earth was elevated, i.e., for the sake of the preservation of the species which live upon it. 2) The stars and their functions do not exist for the sake of the perfection of the spheres which move them. The spheres are perfect in themselves. The activities of the stars are rather for the sake of the perfection of the sublunar world. If the creation narrative had described the creation of the spheres, we might have been led to the erroneous conclusion that the spheres were not complete until the stars were created in them. The hiatus between the two descriptions serves to guide us to the true conception of this question.[285]

The Torah makes a special point of guiding us in these two respects because the true conception of these two questions is what constitutes a demonstration that the world must have come to be. That is, that demonstration is based on the observation that

both the heavenly bodies and the visible part of the earth possess
the characteristics of things which come to be: that they have a
final cause; that they have nonessential properties; and that they
act for the sake of some other thing. If we had not been warned,
by the disruption of the true order of things in the creation
narrative, against the misconception that the earth is elevated by
natural necessity and that the stars and their activities follow
necessarily from the nature of the supralunar world, then we might
have concluded that the heavenly bodies and the visible part of
the earth did not have the characteristics of things which come to
be, and that, as a consequence, the world as a whole was eternal.[286]

(1:20) It was the divine will that the fish species should
come to be in the waters and that bird species should come to be
and should fly around the sublunar world in the circular motion of
the supralunar world rather than in the rectilinear motion of the
elements (ᶜal penei reqiᶜa ha-shamayim). (1:21) All fish and bird
species which would subsequently come to be from members of their
own species (le-miynehem, le-miynehu) were thus created. This
state of affairs was good, in that these species serve the purpose
for the sake of which they were created, viz., the perfection of
the animal and the human species (va-yarᵓ ᵓelohim kiy ṭov). (1:22)
The preservation of these species requires divine providence over
the external factors which affect their reproductive processes,
because they reproduce by producing eggs outside of their bodies.
Thus, despite the dangers which they encounter in their reproduction, they can reproduce prolifically (va-yevarekh ᵓotam ᵓelohim
leᵓmor peru u-revu u-milᵓu ᵓet ha-mayim ba-yamin ve-ha-ᶜof yirev
ba-ᵓareṣ). (1:23) The less perfect fish species and the more perfect bird species are united in the hierarchy of the hylic forms
in which all things are one and the more perfect are the form and
the perfection of the more hylic, and particularly in the closeness
of the respective levels of natural priority of fish and birds
(va-yehiy ᶜerev va-yehiy voqer). This is the fifth level of
natural priority (yom ḥamiyshiy).[287]

(1:24) It was the divine will that there should come to be
the species of walking animals which would reproduce from their
own species (va-yoᵓmer ᵓelohim toṣeh ha-ᵓareṣ nefesh ḥayah le-
miynah...). The divine will in this respect was actualized instantaneously (va-yehiy khen). (1:25) Thus, the animal species were
created. This state of affairs was good, in that the animal

species function for the purpose of which they were created, viz.,
for the perfection of the human species (va-yar² ²elohim kiy ṭov).
(1:26) It was the divine will that the human species come to be
and that it be related both to the sublunar species of hylic forms
and to the separate intellects (va-yo²mer ²elohim naᶜaseh ²adam
be-ṣalmenu kidmutenu). It was also the divine will that the human
species be dominant over the lower sublunar species, because many
of the lower species are physically stronger than the human species
and, if the human species had not been given dominance over them,
those lower species could not have fulfilled their natural function,
viz., to act for the sake of the perfection of the human species
(ve-yirdu...). (1:27) Thus, the human species came to be with a
hylic intellect which can initially apprehend only hylic forms but
which has the disposition to acquire true conceptions by abstracting the definitions of things from the material embodiments of the
hylic forms. This true conception is thus separate and is related,
in some way, to the conception of the separate intellects
(va-yivra² ²elohim ²et ha-²adam be-ṣalmo be-ṣelem ²elohim bara²
²oto).

The Torah subsequently mentions (Gen 2:7) that the human soul
is immortal (nefesh ḥayah) and instructs us (Gen 2:19) that the
means of acquiring immortality is through the acquisition of true
conceptions of the definitions of things (in its description of
the way that Adam gave each species its true "name" or definition).
The human species also was generated male and female, for the sake
of the preservation of the species (zakhar u-neqevah bara² ²otam).

(1:28) It was not necessary, however, for human reproduction
to be governed by divine providence as was necessary for the
species of fish and birds which hazardously produce their eggs outside of their bodies. By contrast, the gestation of the human
fetus occurs within the womb. Rather, it was necessary to command
the human species to reproduce, because the human species alone has
the choice to procreate or not to procreate, by abstenance or by
birth control. Thus, the human species is commanded to exercise
its choice to procreate and to be prolific (va-yo²mer la-hem peru
u-revu). It was also the divine will that it be arranged providentially that the human species should inhabit all parts of the
earth and not be confined to a single location where a natural
disaster might render it extinct (va-yevarekh ²otam ²elohim va-
yo²mer la-hem...mil²u ²et ha-²areṣ). Thus, the human species was

created dominant over all other sublunar species so that these
other species can serve their natural end of service to the human
species.

(1:29) It was the divine will that the human species should
have the nature to benefit nutritionally from all plant species and
should have the power to cultivate its nutritional needs by means
of agriculture and to cook food so that it is digestible. (1:30)
It was also the divine will that the lower species have the nature
to eat all the plant species as food. These natures for nutrition
were actualized in these species instantaneously (va-yehiy khen).
(1:31) The state of affairs of all of creation was good, in that
all created things serve the natural functions for which they were
created in the most perfect possible way (va-yar> >elohim >et kol
>asher asah ve-hineh ṭov me>od). The narrative here is inclusive
(kol ^casher >asah) because it is referring to the perfection not
only of the sixth "day" but of the entire sublunar world, in which
all species function in the most perfect possible way for the sake
of one another. The narrative here is emphatic (ṭov me>od) because
the good which results from the natural functions of the lower
species is only truly realized when the perfection of the end of
all the lower species—viz., the perfection of the human species—
is realized. The animal species and the human species were united,
in that the animal species exist for the sake of the human species
and the human species is thus the form and the perfection of the
animal species (va-yehiy ^cerev va-yehiy voqer). Thus, we see that
the world is a macrocosm in which all parts are interrelated and
in which nothing is useless. This is the sixth level of natural
priority (yom shishiy).[288]

(2:1) After the moment of creation, in which all of the things
described in the narrative of the first six days (with the exception of the plant species, which matured at a later time) were
actualized instantaneously, viz., the intelligible, supralunar and
sublunar worlds. (2:2) After this initial moment of divine will,
God perpetually sustains the world, which would pass away if He
did not sustain it perpetually by causing it to function according
to the natural custom which He willed at the moment of creation.
This perpetual functioning by nature is the seventh level of natural priority (va-yekhal >elohim ba-yom ha-sheviy>iy melakhto
>asher ^casah). There are two ways to understand this statement
and the second is preferable. The first is that the narrative is
saying that, after the moment in which His will was actualized

instantaneously, God desires (va-yekhal) His creation. That is,
He can be said to desire the world insofar as He perpetually performs His single act of self-conception and in His self-conception
He conceives of the divine nomos which overflows from Him and
governs the world by natural custom. Because of His perpetual
self-conception, the separate intellects desire to approximate His
perfect conception and so move their spheres in accordance with the
divine nomos which is the end of their conception. From the rotations of the spheres, all other existent things are perpetually
sustained. This understanding of Gen 2:2 is possible, but it is
not preferred because to posit that God desires would seem to entail
the falsehood that He has an end which is His nature to perform.
The second way to understand Gen 2:3 is that, after the moment of
creation, God completed the work which He had willed (va-yekhal
ɔelohim...) by perpetually subjecting the separate movers to Him
through the profound perfection of His degree of existence, so
that they long for His perfect conception and consequently move
their spheres in accordance with His conception. In either case,
there is no suggestion of the cessation of divine work or of a
change in the single, perpetual divine activity of self-conception.
(2:3) Thus, when the Torah was revealed to Israel at Sinai, the
seventh day was declared blessed and sacred in order to teach us
about the way in which God perpetually sustains the world through
the natural custom with which the divine nomos governs as a consequence of His self-conception, so that the world cannot pass
away.[289]

PART FIVE

The Validity and Importance of
Gersonides' Account of Creation

The validity of Gersonides' account of creation may be
evaluated both in terms of his interpretation of the text of the
creation narrative in Genesis and in terms of the internal consistency of his theory of the creation of the world. His interpretation of the Torah is not open to question once we accept the
paradigm in which he proceeds, viz., that the Torah is a document
which was written by the greatest of all philosophers, Moses, and
which has as its providential purpose the guidance of the human
species towards its ultimate felicity of true conception. Throughout the text of 6:2:1-8, Gersonides holds fast to this underlying
assumption. In fact, he builds a reasonable case for his assertion
that the creation narrative of Genesis is meant to guide us to a
true conception of the way in which the world was created and the
order by which it is governed subsequently.

Given his belief that the purpose of the Torah is to guide
the speculator to the truth, his assertion that the inversion of
the description of creation on the third and fourth "days" is
designed to guide us to a speculative demonstration of the creation
of the world makes a great deal of sense. His view of the Torah's
purpose allows him to account for any apparent inconsistency as a
pedagogical device. The great lengths to which he must go to
explain Gen 1:1-2 as a parenthetical description of the creation
on the second "day" is perhaps farfetched, but one would be hard-
pressed to find an exegete—ancient, medieval or modern—who is
able to deal with this problematic passage in a way that is not
strained.

Perhaps the most obvious problem with Gersonides' interpretation of the Genesis narrative is his failure to find a reference
in it to the Active Intellect. This omission, however, can be
accounted for in a number of reasonable ways. For example, he may
be assuming the identification of the Active Intellect with God
when He is discussed in terms of the governance of the sublunar
world.

As argued above, in Part IV, section B, of this introduction,
and below, in note #1 of our commentary, it is not valid for us to
evaluate Gersonides' exegesis without reference to the assumptions
under which he proceeds. Given the radical way in which medieval

111

exegesis differs with the assumptions of modern Biblical scholarship, we may find his lack of regard for the "literal" meaning of
the text to be problematic. On the other hand, he would find
strange the prevailing modern assumption that the true meaning of
a divinely revealed text should be limited to the understanding
which the Israelites had of that text when it was first written.

The validity of Gersonides' theory of the creation of the
world may be properly evaluated for its internal consistency. In
general, his theory meets this criterion based, as it is, upon his
premises. That is, he believes that the existence of God is the
most perfect of all existence, so that no multiplicity in essence
or in action may be posited of Him. Thus, God is unchanging in
performing His single, perpetual action of self-conception, in
which He conceives of the divine nomos which governs the world in
its intelligible unity. His single act of will that the divine
nomos should overflow from His perpetual self-conception is nothing
other than His self-conception. Gersonides believes that God cannot do anything except what He does—cannot will except what He
wills—because His single, sublime activity is the most perfect of
all.

Given these premises about the nature of God, which eliminate
the possibility of a change in God's will, Gersonides' theory of
creation may be evaluated as consistent. That is, the "limitation"
which he seems to impose upon God's omnipotence, by requiring that
a material receptacle must have persisted prior to and apart from
God's will, is no limitation at all. Throughout The Wars he is
consistent in affirming that divine knowledge and governance of the
world does not entail divine knowledge of the material embodiments
of the forms which overflow from the divine nomos. In all of his
discussions, Gersonides consistently affirms the absolute perfection of God, by which he means that God perpetually conceives of
Himself in a simple and unchanging way. Thus, the knowledge which
a prophet receives in prophecy entails an actualization of the
potential conception of the prophet and not a change in God or in
the Active Intellect; the nature of divine providence is such that
it functions in proportion to the development of the human intellect and does not involve divine knowledge of particular, contingent things; and the generation of marvels occurs through the
natural governance of the divine nomos which perpetually overflows
from God in an unchanging way, and the marvelous character of these
occurrences are a function of the actualization of the intellect
of the prophet alone.

On the basis of the consistent way in which Gersonides
describes the nature of divine will and causation, his theory of
creation follows reasonably. God is no different before, during
or after the creation of the world. The divine nomos which overflows from His self-conception perpetually overflows from it. That
the material receptacle receives it at a given moment is a consequence of the characteristics of matter and not a consequence of a
change in the divine nature. That a relation between God and the
world is generated with the generation of the world does not entail
a change in Him. He remains unchanged, perfect in Himself, and He
derives no benefit from the world's existence. Thus, if there had
not been a material receptacle which was suitable to receive the
causal action of the forms of the divine nomos, the world would not
have been created and God would have been no worse for it. Thus,
Gersonides' theory of creation stands as a reasonable synthesis of
the Neoplatonic view of the nature of God and the Jewish view of
God as a Being who willfully creates and providentially governs.

There are at least two aspects of Gersonides' argument for
and account of the creation of the world the validity of which are
questionable in terms of internal consistency. In what follows,
these two issues will be presented and, in each case, it will be
argued that Gersonides' handling of them does, in fact, stand the
text of internal consistency.

The first issue is Gersonides' rejection of the possibility
of eternal emanation. His argument for the creation of the world
in 6:1 depends on this, though his discussion of the issue in
6:1:7 appears to be made as an aside. That is, his demonstration
that the world must have come to be in some manner is based upon
his observation that the supralunar world and the elevated part of
the earth have the properties of things which come to be, viz., a
final cause, nonessential properties and actions for the sake of
some other thing. These properties, however, only demonstrate that
the supralunar world and the elevated part of the earth, and hence
the world as a whole, are caused by will and not be necessity. The
demonstration of creation at a particular moment, therefore, rests
upon the assertion that it is impossible for the world to have been
caused perpetually by the perpetual will of God.

As is clear from our discussion immediately above, of
Gersonides' conception of God's nature, the impossibility of
eternal emanation does not derive from the divine nature. In fact,
the divine nomos, which overflows from God and which is the cause

of the creation and the preservation of the world, has always
overflowed from His perpetually unchanging self-conception.

Rather, Gersonides argues against the possibility of eternal
willful causation because he does not find the concept to be
intelligible. That is, he cannot conceive of what it means to
assert that God perpetually creates the world. The hypothesis
that God has multiple acts of will in which He wills identical
things at each moment, so that He perpetually recreates the world,
is intelligible, Gersonides argues, only if we also posit that the
world also passes away at every moment. Though this may be posited
by an Atomist, it is unacceptable in an Aristotelian universe in
which time and motion are continuous quantities. Furthermore,
Gersonides argues, the manifest teleological character of the
universe, which Aristotle himself acknowledges, cannot be accounted
for by positing natural and necessary causation by the First Cause.

To all of this it may be objected that our inability to conceive of the way in which God could have perpetually willed the
existence of the world from eternity does not constitute a valid
refutation of that possibility. In support of this objection,
one might cite Gersonides' own comments in 6:1:21 that the inability
of the human intellect to imagine a void "outside" of the world,
or a moment before which there is no time, does not entail that
such a void or such a moment does not exist.

Such an objection, however, does not recognize that Gersonides
is arguing from Aristotelian premises and that his argument in 6:1
is essentially that the createdness of the world is demonstrable
even from those premises. It is the latter assertion which enables
Gersonides to reject the possibility of infinite past time and
motion. Time and motion are infinitely numerable and infinitely
divisible only potentially, as he argues in the third treatise
and again in 6:1:10-12. The actual number to which any quantity
can be augmented and the actual number of parts into which any
continuous magnitude can be divided remains finite. Thus, given
the fact that the world can be shown to have been caused, it must
be posited to have first been caused at a specific moment in the
past which is an actual finite distance from the present.

The second issue is Gersonides' description of the absolute
dimensional body from which the world came to be. As discussed
above, in Parts III and IV of this introduction, he departs from
the prevailing ontological assumptions of his period by positing
that body persists with the characteristics of indefinite

dimensionality apart from the causation of form. He departs from
the prevailing epistemological assumptions by positing that even
though this body is formless, it is not absolute privation and has
existence, even if a very weak degree thereof. Thus, though it is
not the proper object of true conceptual knowledge, it is the
proper object of cautious assertions which make inferences about
it based upon the state of affairs of matter in the created world.

As noted above, he appears to base his account of creation
upon questionable ground when he rests it upon the discussion of
body which does not preserve its shape. Insofar as it is formless,
it is not knowable, since we can know a thing only insofar as we
know its form or definition. To base one's cosmology upon a body
which is formless and natureless would seem therefore to construct
a theory which is subject neither to verification nor to refutation.

Gersonides is not unaware of this problem. He prefaces his
discussion of this body by asserting that it is not knowable in
itself and that any knowledge of it can only be inferred from that
which can be known, viz., our observation of the state of affairs
of the world after the body has received the forms of the divine
nomos at creation. Nevertheless, he follows this cautious introduction by proceeding to propose views about the state of affairs
of the body which, if they do not claim to be knowledge of the
truth of this body, are not what one would expect to be able to
say about a formless, natureless body. Though he is careful to
preface all references to this body by affirming our necessary
uncertainty about it, it is unclear how his epistemology allows
for any assertion about the quantity, division, transparency or
any other characteristic of a body which is deprived of all nature.

Furthermore, it would seem fair enough to accuse Gersonides
of committing, with regard to absolute dimensional body, the error
for which he faults Maimonides, in the third treatise, with regard
to the latter's discussion of divine knowledge. That is, Gersonides
criticizes Maimonides' doctrine of absolute equivocation, in which
Maimonides affirms that knowledge, for example, can be attributed
to God only in a sense which is absolutely different from the way
that knowledge can be predicated of the human intellect. In
criticizing this view, Gersonides asserts that a doctrine of
absolute equivocation allows us to say anything at all about God,
since all attributes predicated of Him are said in an absolutely
different sense than they are normally said. On the basis of his
claim that Maimonides' approach is thus unintelligible, Gersonides

argues that attributes ought to be predicated by God by pros hen
equivocation (mah she-ne'emar be-qodem u-be-'iḥur). That is, God's
knowledge is the primary and perfect instance of which the term
"knowledge" is predicated. He knows things perfectly as their
cause. The term "knowledge" is predicated of all other instances
in a derivative, posterior way. Human beings, for example, know
things imperfectly by abstracting their true conceptions from their
material embodiments. The term, therefore, when predicated of
imperfect human cognition, refers to the primary and perfect
instance of divine knowledge of which it is most properly predicated and which is the cause of all other knowledge.[290]

Based upon his criticism of Maimonides' doctrine of absolute
equivocation, in which he objects strongly to our consequent
inability to predicate anything meaningful of God, Gersonides may
be subjected to the same criticism concerning his discussion of
body which does not preserve its shape. That is, if formless body
is not the proper object of knowledge, then it would seem to be
the case that anything at all can be said about it. Thus, Gersonides' attempts in 6:1:17-28 and in 6:2:4, 7 & 8 below to describe
its characteristics and to determine which principles of nature
apply to it are not the proper subject of verification or refutation. To the extent that this criticism is valid, Gersonides'
account of the creation of the world demonstrates nothing and may
be categorized as trivial.

Though this criticism may, in the end, be judged to be
inescapable, there is much to be said in Gersonides' defense.
First, it must be noted that Gersonides describes absolute dimensional body not as absolute privation but rather as something
which is intermediate between existence and privation: it is something in that it has the potentially definite dimensions of absolute body while it is nothing in that it is formless. Though he
would concede that its formlessness renders this body inappropriate
as an object of true conception, we may choose to emphasize this
concession alone only by disregarding his apparent conviction that
absolute dimensional body is, in some sense, something, and is, in
some sense, a proper subject for discussion—as it persisted prior
to creation, as it persists between the spheres, and as a remainder
of it may persist outside of the outermost sphere.

It is important to recall that the distinctive feature of
Gersonides' theory of creation is his view that matter cannot have
been caused by God. The divine nomos which overflows from God's

self-conception is the cause of the intelligible world of forms
and, as such, is the cause of goodness, order and the preservation
of things in the world. Matter, which underlies and receives this
formal causation, and which, after its reception of the elemental
forms and their contrary qualities, is the cause of evil, chaos
and passing away in the sublunar world, properly can be said to be
in no way related to God. God neither creates it nor does He know
it. The providential governance of the divine nomos which overflows from Him acts providentially for the human species only to
the extent that the human intellect separates its conception from
the world of hylic forms, and for the lower sublunar species only
insofar as it preserves the species, i.e., the form.

It is therefore incumbent upon us to consider seriously the
consequences of this view for Gersonides' epistemology. Maimonides,
who rejected the possibility of the persistence of formless body
prior to creation, and Aristotle, who asserted that matter has
served eternally as the substratum of the forms, could both agree
that there is no prime matter which exists in a formless state and
consequently that matter is not the proper object of conception.
Avicenna and Averroes could both discuss corporeal form as potential or absolute dimensional body, because neither affirmed the
creation of the world at a moment prior to which absolute body
was not informed by actually existent forms. Gersonides' distinctive view of creation, therefore, may be said to have required
that he depart from the prevailing epistemology and affirm the
possibility of a kind of perception which, though it is not knowledge, is nevertheless properly related to formless body.

In fact, it can be argued that Gersonides approaches absolute
dimensional body in a way that is completely consistent with his
approach to divine predication. His use of pros hen equivocation
is founded upon the following assumption: Although the knowledge
which we acquire by abstracting true conceptions from the hylic
forms of this world cannot be applied to the knowledge of God in
a univocal way, our knowledge can be applied to Him by inferring,
from empirical observation, that He is the cause of all the definitions which we conceive. We cannot have direct knowledge of the
divine nature because of our distance from His degree of perfect
existence. He knows all intelligible things in a single act of
self-conception; we know in multiple and progressive acts of
intellectual abstraction. Rather, what we can know and thus
intelligibly predicate of God is that which we can infer from the
effects of His causation.

Gersonides may be said to adopt the same approach with regard to absolute dimensional body. As he rejects Maimonides' assertion that God is absolutely beyond human conception, he similarly rejects Maimonides' view that the process of creation is utterly inaccessible to human conception. As we cannot properly be said to know anything about the divine nature, he would assert, similarly we cannot properly be said to know anything about absolute dimensional body. But as we can legitimately make inferences about the divine nature based upon our knowledge of this world, similarly we can make inferences on the same basis about the body which does not preserve its shape.

To adopt such an approach, Gersonides must assume in his discussion that the body about which he is making inferences is not absolute privation. Though it is absolutely unknowable in itself because of its formlessness, it is not absolutely nothing. As we argue below in notes #49 and #51 of our commentary, and in Part IV of the introduction above, he is referring to a body which Averroes had described as having absolute dimensions, i.e., a body with potentially definite but no actually definite dimensions, which Gersonides compares to water. He is asserting that the material receptacle, which exists prior to and apart from the divine nomos, and which is therefore formless, has absolute dimensionality without the causation of any form.

We may assume that he would respond to the above criticism by asserting that the human soul has many other faculties in addition to conception—perception, imagination, recollection, memory, etc. It is possible for a human being to perceive and to form a view concerning something about which he has no true conception. Though that person cannot be said to have true knowledge of that thing, a situation is conceivable in which that person could be reasonably certain that his view is more likely than other views.

As an example, let us take Gersonides' view of spontaneously generated species and homogeneous parts. He mentions these at the beginning of 6:2:8 by way of explaining that their creation is not attributed to the divine will because their generation occurs apart from the causal action of the forms of the divine nomos. We may infer from this statement that Gersonides would say that these things are not knowable. If we posit, however, a situation in which Gersonides happened upon a spontaneously generated organism with which he had no prior familiarity, it is likely that he would

insist that, although he could not form a true conception about
this organism, he could infer nevertheless, from its surrounding
environment and from other knowable phenomena, certain likely
views about its characteristics. He would furthermore assert that
some views about this spontaneously generated species would be
more reasonable than others. For example, if this organism had
been found in a cold pond, it would be less reasonable to assert
the view that it is related to fire than that it is related to
water, though no true knowledge of this organism could ever be
acquired.

Of course, this example only functions analogously. That is,
a more correct view about a spontaneously generated organism would
be based upon true conceptions about a variety of existent,
informed things associated with that organism. By contrast,
prior to the creation of the world, according to Gersonides, the
divine nomos which overflowed perpetually from God's self-conception
was not yet related to this unknowable formless body. Thus, this
formless body is not, in itself, the proper object of knowledge
of the divine nomos and, it would seem, our knowledge of the divine
nomos gives us no knowledge about it.

The critical judgment which one must make about the intelli-
gibility or triviality of Gersonides' account of creation turns
upon one's evaluation of his use of the term, "body which does not
preserve its shape." If one assumes that its formlessness renders
it absolutely unintelligible, then Gersonides' entire account is
unintelligible and cannot be said to differ significantly from
Maimonides' account of creation ex nihilo or from any other account
of creation out of nothing. Gersonides' central claim is that his
theory does differ significantly from that of Maimonides and that
his own view is philosophically demonstrable while creation
ex nihilo is neither demonstrable nor defensible. That claim rests
upon his argument that we can infer, from our knowledge of the
nature of the causation of separate intellects and from our knowledge of the material substrata underlying hylic forms, that a form
cannot be posited to have created a body out of absolutely nothing
but rather can only be posited to work its causal action upon a
material receptacle which is disposed to receive its causal action.
Though that material receptacle, viz., absolute dimensional body,
is therefore formless and cannot be known, the assumption of its
persistence can be reasonably inferred from what we know about
formal causation. And though, prior to creation, this body was
formless and unknowable, the divine nature and the divine nomos

which overflows from it may reasonably be posited to have been
exactly as they are now, after creation. It is from our knowledge
of them that we can make reasonable inferences about the material
receptacle.

As suggested above, it may be argued that this inference
about absolute dimensional body is similar to the inferences we
make about the divine nature if we employ Gersonides' approach of
pros hen equivocation. As the persistence and characteristics of
absolute dimensional body are inferred from an analogy with the
state of affairs of the divine nomos in this world, similarly what
we predicate of God is also based upon our inferences about Him
based upon the causation of the divine nomos in this world.

When Gersonides' discussions of "body which does not preserve
its shape" and "prime matter" are considered in this light, it is
clear that he is asserting that absolute dimensional body is like
sublunar matter and that absolute dimensionality is like a form.
At the end of 6:1:17, he states that it is proper for us to posit
a single material receptacle which underlies all body, since we
affirm the existence of God who is absolutely separate from all
hylic embodiments and in whom all forms are one. We cannot know
the matter which underlies all hylic forms in the sublunar world.
Rather, we make inferences about it from our observations of the
way in which hylic forms act upon it. Similarly we cannot know
formless body but rather make inferences about it from our observation of the formal causation of separate intellects in this world.
The absolute dimensional body which persisted without form prior
to creation is ontologically identical to the matter which underlies all hylic forms. In neither case is it knowable in itself.
By empirical observation, however, we can know that the state of
affairs of the sublunar world in which matter and hylic forms do
not exist separate from each other is not universally applicable.
This state of affairs exists in the sublunar world because, at the
moment of creation, prime matter received the nature of definite
dimensionality from last form simultaneously with its reception
of the elemental forms, and the contrary qualities of the elemental
forms, under the influence of the actions of the stars, interact
in such a way that matter is always informed. That this state of
affairs does not exist as a consequence of the inherent characteristics of form or of matter is clear from our conception of the
separate forms of the intelligible world and from our observation
of separate body—viz., absolute dimensional body—which persists
between the spheres of the supralunar world.

Thus, the body which does not preserve its shape which persisted prior to creation is ontologically one with the matter which underlies the hylic forms. It differs from the latter insofar as, lacking the definite dimensionality of last form, the contrary qualities of the elemental forms, and the causal influence of the actions of the stars, it does not receive the causal action of the forms of the divine nomos which perpetually overflows from God's self-conception. Nevertheless, it is possible to discuss this formless body inasmuch as it is like sublunar matter in a manner that parallels the pros hen equivocal statements which Gersonides makes about God's knowledge in the third treatise.

It is also clear that Gersonides considers absolute dimensionality to be a characteristic that is like a form. As mentioned above, he states on a number of occasions the body which does not preserve its shape is not absolute privation but is rather intermediate between something and nothing, or between existence and privation. It is something, he states, in that it is body, from which we can infer that he means to suggest that the absolute dimensionality of formless body renders absolute potentiality or privation into something that, in some very weak sense, has existence. He refers to prime matter and to last form as being "very weak in existence" in the course of referring to them as the first principles of existence. In these statements, it is clear that he does not mean to suggest that the formlessness of absolute dimensional body renders it as absolute privation. Insofar as it is something, in one sense, and as it is close to privation but has very weak existence, and as it can be called a "first principle" of existent things, absolute dimensionality can be said in a pros hen equivocal sense to be like a form.

If this interpretation is correct, then Gersonides' understanding of what constitutes "being" or "existence" is indeed a significant departure from the prevailing model of his time. Pros hen equivocation is based on the assumption that the primary and perfect instance of a predicate, from which all other instances of that predicate derive, is the cause of those derivative instances—viz., God's knowledge is the cause of our knowledge, God's being is the cause of our being, etc. Therefore, the logical extension of Gersonides' discussion, as it is presented above, is that our knowledge of material bodies which are informed by hylic forms in the sublunar world is a derivative knowledge which refers primarily to formless body. Body which lacks preservation of

shape—i.e., formless body—is the "cause" of all material
embodiments and their material properties. Insofar as the matter
of a thing predominates over its form, that thing lacks preservation
of shape and is subject to generation and corruption. Thus, as
Gersonides notes at the end of 6:1:17, inferior species, such as
plants, preserve their shape less than do superior species, such
as animals, and the heavenly bodies, whose forms are separate and
not hylic, preserve their shape perpetually. God is the cause of
order, goodness and unity. Body which does not preserve its shape,
which is itself uncaused and is unrelated to the divine nomos, is
the "cause" of disorder, corruption and multiplicity. It has less
being than anything else; it is not, however, absolute privation
and is not, therefore, absolutely beyond human conception.

The validity of Gersonides' account of creation is thus only
partially vulnerable to the criticism discussed above. That is,
his theory of creation is founded upon views which are not true
conceptual knowledge and are, at best, more probable than alternate
views. Given his premises, however, about the relationship between
formless body and informed material bodies, he cannot be faulted
for speaking nonsensically about formless body unless he is
faulted similarly for speaking nonsensically about the divine
nature. All of his assertions about formless body are based upon
inferences from true conceptions of the nature of God, of divine
causation, and of the created world. His doctrine of pros hen
equivocation, though it allows for no direct knowledge of God,
offers us a way of tentatively making reasonable assertions about
Him. Similarly, his discussion of the material receptacle offers
us no true knowledge of absolute dimensional body but it does offer
us a way of making reasonable assertions about creation.

Whether or not Gersonides' account of creation is evaluated
as internally consistent, the importance of his view is indisputable. This importance may be discussed in terms of his contributions
to the medieval philosophical discussion about the physical principles which underlie the material world and in terms of his contribution to the attempts of medieval Jewish philosophers to formulate
a conception of the world which is true both to the premises of
Neoplatonic and Aristotelian Physics and to the Jewish tradition.

The philosophical discussion of the origins of the matter
which serves as the substratum of all hylic forms is an extended
one and a complete review of it falls beyond the scope of this
summary. Our discussion here thus will be confined to a consideration of Averroes and his dispute with Alghazali and Avicenna about

the nature of absolute body, as that dispute is discussed below in note #49 of our commentary. All three of these philosophers were agreed that prime matter was absolute, nondimensional potentiality and that, in order for matter to become the absolute body which receives and serves as the substratum of hylic forms, prime matter first received corporeal form which bestowed upon it the dimensionality of absolute body. Their dispute involved the nature of the dimensionality of absolute body. Avicenna held the view that absolute body had potential dimensionality. Alghazali held the view that absolute body had definite dimensionality. Averroes held the view that absolute body had absolute dimensionality—i.e., that it was dimensional body but that it had no actual definite dimensions.

For Avicenna and Averroes, neither of whom believed that God had created the world at a moment prior to which the world had not existed, this discussion did not concern a temporal sequence of events. Insofar as they held the view that the existence of the world had been perpetually caused by God without a temporal beginning, their discussions of prime matter were explanations of the perpetual state of matter as it progresses in ontological priority from privation to existence. They did not believe, therefore, that there had ever been a state of affairs in which prime matter had persisted in a formless state or in which absolute body had existed without hylic forms.

For reasons discussed above, in Parts III and IV of this introduction, Gersonides rejects the possibility that this world could have been caused perpetually and without temporal beginning. He also rejects Maimonides' suggestion that God could have created this material world out of absolutely nothing and, in so doing, is unable to utilize Alghazali's account of creation as proceeding from the absolute potentiality of prime matter to the definite dimensionality of absolute body. Thus, Gersonides found it necessary to engage in a discussion of the first principles of material existence and to determine which characteristics of the material world could and could not be attributed to divine causation. Concluding that there must have been a material receptacle upon which divine causation acted, he was obliged to account for the sequence of events which led to the state of affairs in which the material receptacle was disposed at the moment of creation to receive the formal causation of a divine nomos which overflows perpetually from the self-conception of God.

In so accounting for the creation of the world, Gersonides
might have adopted the view that what had persisted prior to
creation was prime matter, as that term had been defined by his
predecessors—viz., absolute, nondimensional potentiality—and
that last form—viz., the form which absolutely potential prime
matter had first received and which gave it the disposition to
receive all the other hylic forms by means of the interaction of
the elemental forms—had been corporeal form. Ibn Daud sets a
precedent for such an account. That Gersonides does not do so, and
that he instead asserts that the body which persisted prior to
creation was absolute dimensional body, is indicative of his contribution to the discussion of the first principles of the material
world. As noted above, it is basic to his view that God has nothing
to do with the creation of body, so that what others call "corporeal form" cannot be a form. Rather, the dimensionality which others
attribute to corporeal form, and thus to divine causation, is, in
Gersonides' view, a characteristic of the material receptacle
which persists—or which exists in a very weak state of existence—
prior to and apart from the causation of the divine nomos. He is
able to maintain, therefore, that the potentiality of and the
process of generation and corruption in the sublunar world is in
no sense attributable to the will of God.

Furthermore, it may be noted that, in eliminating the first
stage of material coming to be and in asserting that prime matter
is absolute dimensional body apart from any formal causation,
Gersonides is able to adapt the discussion of Avicenna and Averroes
of the first principles of the material world to an account of
creation in a coherent way. That is, Avicenna and Averroes, in
their views of the beginningless causation of the world, were able
to assert that nondimensional prime matter had perpetually received
the dimensionality of corporeal form. They had no need to explain
a sequence in which prime matter received the disposition to receive
corporeal form subsequent to its lack of such a disposition. Given
the view that the creation of the world has a temporal beginning,
however, such an explanation is required. Thus, the philosopher
who asserts that, at the moment of creation, nondimensional prime
matter received the disposition to receive the dimensionality of
absolute body must assert not only that the potentiality of absolute body is an effect of divine causation. He must also assert
that the causation of the divine nomos must have first disposed
absolutely potential prime matter to receive the absolute

dimensionality of absolute body. In making the latter assertion, such a philosopher becomes vulnerable to the charge, articulated by Gersonides in his summary of the Aristotelian arguments for eternity in 6:1:3, that an infinite regress is being posited. That is, prime matter must have been disposed to be disposed to receive the disposition to receive corporeal form, ad infinitum.

Inasmuch as, in an Aristotelian universe, potential dispositions cannot be distinguished ontologically from one another, we can begin to understand the philosophical problems which Gersonides attempts to resolve with his account of creation. That is, in order to avoid the possibility of an infinite regress, it was necessary for him to assert that prime matter received the actual and definite dimensionality of last form, which is the nature or the disposition to receive the elemental forms, simultaneously with its reception of the elemental forms. If instead he had asserted that a nondimensional, absolutely potential prime matter had, at the moment of creation, received the disposition to receive the potential for definite dimensionality—viz., to become absolute body—he would have been compelled to make a gratuitous distinction between the potentiality of prime matter prior to its reception of corporeal form and the potentiality of absolute body thereafter. The importance of his account of creation, in this regard, lies in his original suggestion that the problem of an infinite regress of the dispositions of matter to receive the causation of form can be resolved by positing that prime matter has absolute dimensionality apart from formal causation.

Gersonides' account of creation is also important as a contribution to the formulation of a conception of the world which is true both to the premises of Neoplatonic and Aristotelian Physics and to the Jewish tradition. The distinctiveness of his theory in this regard lies in its underlying assumptions. He rejects the possibility that the world could have been created out of absolutely nothing because of his conviction that God cannot be posited to do the impossible and the causation of the divine nomos which perpetually overflows from His perpetually unchanging conception could not have brought body into existence.

As discussed above in Part IV of this introduction, his theory of creation shares the assumption of all of his views: that God cannot be posited to do anything aside from His perfect single action of perpetual self-conception and that, with regard to the material world, the governance of the natural law of the divine

nomos remains perpetually unchanged in all situations. The divine
nomos remains unchanged in the sublunar world, in which marvels are
generated within the natural custom of the divine nomos and in
which divine providence governs through the governance of that
nomos. The same divine nomos which governs the sublunar world
also governs the supralunar world, so that the laws which govern
the supralunar world are sufficiently conceivable by the human
intellect—contrary to Maimonides' view—to the extent that a
true speculative demonstration of creation can be founded upon
them. The perpetual overflow of the divine nomos also applies to
God, who in His single act of self-conception can only be imperfectly conceived by the human intellect but whose knowledge differs
from ours only in the degree of its unity and perfection and not in
definition. And the state of affairs of the divine nomos applies
to the state of affairs which persisted prior to the creation of
the world. That is, God necessarily wills what He wills according
to His perfect nature. The world and its nature follow necessarily
from His perpetually unchanging will. The imperfections and the
necessarily generated state of the world is not a consequence of
the divine nature but rather of the material receptacle which
receives His causation. Without the material receptacle, God could
not have willed the creation of the world as He cannot will any
other naturally or logically impossible state of affairs. The fact
that God does not relate to the material world, insofar as it is
material, is not an imperfection in Him. It is rather the consequence of His perfection.

Thus, Gersonides presents us with a view of the world which
accepts the prevailing premises of the scientific and philosophic
views of his age but which nevertheless also incorporates, in
reinterpreted form, an intelligible system of Jewish belief: an
anthropology which allows for the immortality of the soul and
prophecy; a metaphysics which affirms God's perfect knowledge of
and providence over creation; and a cosmology which offers us a
world which in all its aspects testifies to its own creation by
divine will and grace, and to the perfection of the governing
divine nomos.

The strength of Gersonides' account of creation may be located
in his consistent refusal to concede that anything at all is absolutely beyond human conception—not even the formless material
receptacle—even as he humbly maintains the relative ignorance
which even the most highly developed human intellects necessarily

have with regard to such issues as the divine nature, the
intelligible and supralunar worlds, creation, and even the state
of affairs of the sublunar world. As a consequence, he is able to
present us with a world which is a conceivable macrocosm of interrelated species united in the divine nomos, all of whom—intelligible, supralunar and sublunar—act according to their natures for
the sake of the ultimate felicity of the human species—true conception. On the one hand, Gersonides' theory of creation may be
said to limit God's omnipotence by affirming a material receptacle
which is independent of Him. That is, given Gersonides' conception
of God and of the way in which He relates to the world, our access
to God is limited to the actualization of the conceptions of our
intellects. This limitation disputes such traditional Jewish
notions as that God knows and cares about the accidental characteristics of one's personality and circumstances insofar as they are
accidental and particular, and that one's prayers represent a significant form of communication with a God who hears one's prayers.
On the other hand, Gersonides' account of creation may be said to
bring us closer to God and thus to be a better approximation of
the traditional Jewish view than the position of Maimonides.
Gersonides' world is anthropocentric. All things must, to some
extent, be conceivable for the human intellect, Gersonides would
assert, because all things act for the sake of the promotion of
the most perfect possible human conception of existence. Neither
our conception of God nor of creation is absolutely equivocal. And
the knowledge that the material receptacle underlies both the
supralunar and sublunar worlds, both of which are governed by the
same divine nomos, leads us, he asserts, to a conception of the
unity and perfection of this divinely governed world.

NOTES

¹For a complete discussion of his life and works, see Charles Touati, La pensée philosophique et théologique de Gersonide (Paris, 1973).

²See his concluding note to the first part of the sixth treatise of The Wars of the Lord, 6:1:29, p. 417. (All page citations of Milḥamot Ha-Shem [hereafter MH] refer to the Leipzig, 1866 edition. See below, note #2 of the commentary, for an explanation of the system of the transliteration of Hebrew terms followed.)

³Though this characterization permeates all of Wolfson's monumental corpus, perhaps the clearest statement of his view can be found in H. A. Wolfson, Philo: Foundations of Religious Philosophy in Judaism, Christianity and Islam, 2 vols. (Cambridge, Mass., 1948), 2:446ff. Reprinted in From Philo to Spinoza (New York, 1977), pp. 24ff.

⁴Charles Touati, translator, Les Guerres du Seigneur: Livres III et IV (Paris, 1968), p. 33. Cf. Touati, pp. 31ff. for a more complete discussion of the existent manuscript witnesses.

⁵MH 1:12.

⁶Topica 1.11.104b14ff.

⁷Guide 2:15.

⁸For Aristotle's discussion of this view, which he attributes to Empedocles and to Heraclitus, see De Caelo 1.10. Maimonides treats this as a view of some of the rabbis, based upon Gen. Rab. 3:7 & 9:2 (Guide 2:30). For Averroes' discussion of this view, see the references in H. A. Wolfson, The Philosophy of the Kalam (Cambridge, Mass., 1976), p. 401.

⁹Plato's discussion of the generation of the world is found in Timaeus 48e-53c and is reported by Aristotle in Physica 4.2.209b10ff., and De Caelo 1.10.279b32ff., and by Maimonides in Guide 2:13.

¹⁰Maimonides presents the Kalam view in Guide 1:73 & 74. For an exhaustive discussion of the Kalam arguments for creation, see Wolfson, The Philosophy of the Kalam, pp. 355-465.

¹¹Gersonides cites Averroes' commentary to the Metaphysica as his source for Philoponus' view (Long Commentary on the Metaphysica XII, Comm. 41). For a citation and translation of the passage as well as other related passages from Averroes' works, see Wolfson, The Philosophy of the Kalam, pp. 376ff. Philoponus makes the argument in De Aeternitate Mundi, edited by H. Rabe (Leipzig, 1899), pp. 7ff. Also note Maimonides' reference to Philoponus, Guide 1:71. For a discussion of Philoponus' argument, see our summary below, in this section of our introduction, of 6:1:14.

¹²Guide 2:13-30.

129

[13]Gersonides is careful not to label creation ex nihilo
either as an early or a unanimous view of the rabbis. Instead,
he states that some of them follow the Kalam view. For a review
of the midrashic discussions of the question, see E. E. Urbach,
The Sages: Their Concepts and Beliefs, translated by Israel
Abrahams (Jerusalem, 1975), Chapter 9. In general, Gersonides
uses the disagreements of the rabbis as a rationale for disregarding their views when he thinks that they are incorrect (see,
for example, his statement in his Commentary to the Torah [Venice,
1547] [hereafter CT], p. 12d, ll.35-37). In this particular case,
several additional factors may be operating. First, he may want
to indicate here that the rabbis did not deal with the question as
philosophers so that their views need not be considered as a part
of this philosophical discussion. Second, in choosing the term
natu, he may want to imply that both Maimonides and the rabbis
were inclined to this view but that they did not hold it as a
demonstrated truth. This would follow Maimonides' statement in
the Guide that the Platonic view can be reconciled with both the
text and the teachings of the Torah and that creation ex nihilo
cannot be demonstrated (2:25).

[14]Physica 8.1-10; De Caelo 1.10-12; Metaphysica 12.6-10.
Cf. Guide 2:13.

[15]Guide 2:25.

[16]Guide 2:25.

[17]On the infinite succession of motion, cf. Physica 8.2.252b9-
12. On its application by analogy to the world as a whole, cf.
De Caelo 1.10.279b20. For a discussion of how the argument from
analogy of Plato (Timaeus 28A) was used by the Kalam, cf. Wolfson,
The Philosophy of the Kalam, pp. 382ff. and Guide 1:74. Both Plato
and the Kalam, however, use the argument to establish a single
creation.

[18]Aristotle raises the problem in Physica 8.1.252a14ff. and
in De Caelo 1.12.283a11ff. Cf. Averroes, Tahafut al-Tahafut,
translated by Simon Van Den Bergh as The Incoherence of the Incoherence (London, 1969), The First Discussion, pp. 1-69. Gersonides
resolves the problem in a different way in 6:1:18.

[19]This is the first part of the first argument listed below
in this chapter in support of Aristotle's view of the world's
eternity. It is loosely based upon Physica 4.12.221a26ff.

[20]This is a variation of the second argument listed below in
this chapter in support of Aristotle's view of the world's eternity,
which is based on the definition of the "now" as that which divides
the before and the after. The argument here is based upon the
definition of the "now" as the moment in which future, potential
time is actualized. As he explains later (6:1:10, p. 330f.),
time is potential with regard to the future and is actual with
regard to the past. It is actualized in the present—the "now"
which measures time but which is not a part of time (cf. Physica
4.10.218a6ff.). Thus, we must assume that what he means to suggest
here is that if time had a beginning, its first moment could never
have been potential in the sense of having once been the unactualized future. Cf. his response below, MH 6:1:21.

[21]Physica 8.2.252b9ff.; 6.10.241a7.

[22]Physica 4.7.214a13; De Generatione et Corruptione 2.1.329a25.
For a discussion of Aristotle's view of prime matter, see W. Charlton, Aristotle's Physics: Books I and II (Oxford, 1970), pp. 129-
145.

[23]Physica 1.8.191a30ff.; 5.2.226a10; De Generatione et
Corruptione 1.1.314b27; Metaphysica 12.2.

[24]De Caelo 1.9-12.

[25]Physica 8.10.266a12-25.

[26]De Caelo 1.5-7.

[27]De Caelo 1.12.281b18-25; 282a21-25.

[28]De Caelo 1.12.282b2.

[29]See above, note #11, for the reference.

[30]Timaeus 28a, 30a; cf. De Caelo 1.10.280a5f.

[31]Physica 1.7.190b9-10; 8.2.252b9-10.

[32]Physica 6.10.241a7; 8.2.252b9ff.

[33]Timaeus 31b; cf. De Caelo 1.10.280a29ff.; Guide 2:27.

[34]Cf. De Caelo 1.3.270a13ff.; Metaphysica 8.5. In making a
similar argument in support of Aristotle later in this chapter,
Gersonides refers to the actions of the contrary qualities of the
elements upon one another as the cause of passing away. The heavens are made of the fifth body which has no contraries.

[35]Later in the treatise, Gersonides explains that it is
inconceivable that the heavens could exist without the existence
of the sublunar world, because the motions of the heavens are not
for their own sake but rather for the benefit of lower existent
things. If the sublunar world passed away, therefore, the motions
of the heavenly bodies would be in vain and the possibility of
sublunar existence would remain unactualized for an infinite time
(6:1:5, 7-9).

[36]De Caelo 1.12.282b5ff.

[37]See especially MH 1:11.

[38]MH 6:1:16.

[39]In structure, the argument resembles the Kalam argument
from analogy which Averroes discusses in his Long Commentary on the
Physica (cf. Wolfson, The Philosophy of the Kalam, p. 384). Gersonides' definition of "nothing," however, is based on Aristotelian
and not Atomistic physics.

[40]Physica 1.7-9.

[41]Guide 2:25. Maimonides only states that the Platonic view
has not been demonstrated. Gersonides offers his opinion that
Maimonides rejected the view because of the difficulties listed
here.

[42] He discusses this point at length in MH 6:1:27. Cf. De Caelo 1.12.281b20-25; 283a25-29; Physica 3.4.203b29.

[43] De Caelo 3.2.300b17ff.

[44] Guide 1:73-74; cf. Wolfson, The Philosophy of the Kalam, Chapters 5 & 6, especially pp. 386-410.

[45] He elaborates on this criticism of continuous causation or emanation in 6:1:7.

[46] This argument is based upon Physica 4.12.221a26ff.; 4.13. 222b17.

[47] Physica 4.10-14, especially 219a9ff.; 223a33. Cf. Guide 2, Introduction, Premise 15.

[48] Physica 3.1.

[49] On circular locomotion as the only perpetual, eternal, motion, cf. Physica 6.10.241b19ff.; 8.1.251b20ff.; 8.6.259b28ff.; 8.8.261b27ff., 264b8; Metaphysica 12.6.1071b5ff.; Guide 2, Introduction, Premises 13, 26.

[50] Physica 8.1.251b19f.

[51] Physica 8.1.251b19-27.

[52] Physica 8.1.251b10ff.

[53] Physica 8.7.260a26ff.; cf. 4.1.208a32; 4.4.211a12ff.; Guide 2, Introduction, Premise 14; 2:14, method 1.

[54] Physica 8.2.252b9ff.; cf. 7.1.242a16ff. This first motion, according to Aristotle, is the perpetual circular motion of the heavens. Hence, Gersonides proceeds to posit the coming to be of the heavens.

[55] Physica 3.4-8; 8.1.251a18ff. Though Aristotle does admit the existence of the potential infinite in the sense of infinite augmentation of number and the infinite divisibility of continuous magnitude (Physica 3.4), and though he does believe that time and motion are eternal in the sense that they are infinitely divisible and augmentable (Physica 3.6-8), he does not admit the possibility of an infinite series of movers, because in an infinite series there is no first and hence no final cause (Physica 8.5.256a18f.; Metaphysica 2.2.994a18f.). It is for this reason that Aristotle posits a first mover and a first moved object. To reproduce Aristotle's argument properly, therefore, Gersonides should have argued from the impossibility of an infinite series of movers rather than from the impossibility of an infinite number of bodies. Though Aristotle rejects the possibility of an infinite number of simultaneously existing bodies, he does not reject the possibility of an infinite series of causally related bodies with a first mover—a series that is infinite by potential augmentation.

[56] Physica 7.1.242a16ff.; 8.2.252b35; 8.9.266a6ff.

[57] De Generatione et Corruptione 1.3.317b16ff. Cf. Guide 2, Introduction, Premise 5; 2:14, method 4.

[58]Physica 8.4; cf. Physica 4.4-5 for a discussion of natural motion.

[59]Physica 4.8.215a1ff.

[60]Physica 8.1.251a27.

[61]Physica 6.6.237b18ff. On the issue of whether a change must be posited of an agent which causes after not causing, cf. De Caelo 1.12.283b11-14; Physica 3.2.202a2ff. Gersonides discusses the issue in depth in MH 6:1:18, 9th doubt.

[62]Physica 8.1.251b5ff.; 250a10ff.

[63]Cf. Guide 2:14, method 2.

[64]De Caelo 3.3.302a1ff.

[65]Physica 1.7-9; 5.2.226a10; De Generatione et Corruptione 1.1.314b27; Metaphysica 2.4.999b6ff.

[66]De Generatione et Corruptione 1.3; cf. Metaphysica 7.7. 1032a20.

[67]Physica 4.7.214a13; De Generatione et Corruptione 2.1.329a25.

[68]Cf. Guide 2:14, method 3.

[69]Physica 1.7-9; 8.7.261a23f.; De Caelo 1.2-4; De Generatione et Corruptione 1.3; 2.1.329a24ff.

[70]De Caelo 1.12.282b7.

[71]De Caelo 1.10-12.

[72]De Caelo 2.1.

[73]De Caelo 1.9.279a14; cf. Physica 4.7.213b32.

[74]Physica 4.8-9; De Caelo 1.9.279a12ff.

[75]Physica 8.6; cf. Guide 2:14, method 5. This consideration is not meant to be an additional argument in support of Aristotle. Rather, he is emphasizing part of the fifth Aristotelian argument above, to which he responds below in 6:1:4, 6:1:18 (9th doubt) and in 6:1:24.

[76]Topica 1.11.104b15ff.; Physica 8.1.251b15ff.; De Caelo 1.10.279b4ff.; 2.1.283b30ff. Cf. Guide 1:71; 2:15, 22; Averroes' Epitome and Middle Commentary on Topica at 1.11.104b13ff. (I am indebted to Touati for the references to Averroes.) Both Maimonides and Averroes attribute this to Alexander. For the reference to Alexander's statement, see Touati, La pensée, p. 197, n. 14.

[77]For Aristotle's arguments against an infinite succession of worlds, see De Caelo 1.10. For his refutations of Plato, see the references above in the discussion of both versions of the second view that the world came to be. It is likely, however, that Gersonides is referring here to the arguments which he has listed in support of the Aristotelian view which are all, in fact, refutations of the hypothesis that the world could have come to be, the basic assertion common to all three of the other views.

[78]Cf. MH 5:3:11, where he attributes this consideration to Averroes whom he says was led by it to affirm that God is the mover of the sphere of the fixed stars.

[79]MH 5:3:11. He is arguing here against Averroes' indentification of God with the First Mover and his argument for eternity. Cf. H. A. Wolfson, "Averroes' Lost Treatise on the Prime Mover," Hebrew Union College Annual, 23(1950-1951):683-710; reprinted in Studies in the History of Philosophy and Religion, edited by Isadore Twersky and G. H. Williams (Cambridge, Mass., 1973), 1:402-429. Gersonides reports Averroes' disagreement with Avicenna, who believed that God was not the mover of the first sphere, in MH 5:3:11. He refers Averroes' view to his commentary on the Metaphysica where he says that he attributes it to Aristotle (cf. Guide 1:69).

[80]MH 1:6, p. 37, l. 6f; p. 40, ll. 27ff.

[81]Guide 2:17.

[82]Cf. Guide 2:17 for Maimonides' use of a similar example.

[83]He refers here to De Anima 2.4.

[84]He refers here to Physica 8.1.251a18.

[85]He refers here to De Partibus Animalium 2.1.646a25ff.; cf. De Generatione Animalium 1.2.716a2ff.

[86]De Caelo 1.4.271a33.

[87]De Caelo 1.5-7; Physica 8.2.; cf. Guide 1:74, argument 4.

[88]Physica 8.1; cf. Metaphysica 12.6.

[89]Physica 2.2.

[90]Cf. Physica 2.8.198b17ff.; 2.5.196b10ff.; Guide 2:20.

[91]He refers here to Aristotle's discussion of chance. Cf. Physica 2.3-6. On Aristotle's view that eternal things cannot be contingent (except with regard to place—cf. Metaphysica 12.2. 1069b25ff.; 12.7.1072b4ff.), see Metaphysica 9.9.1050b8; De Generatione et Corruptione 2.11.337b35ff. On Aristotle's confusion of logical and ontological necessity—which Gersonides follows here— cf. Van Den Bergh, The Incoherence of the Incoherence, note 4 to p. 163.

[92]Touati, La pensée, p. 182, n. 36, assigns the source of this criterion to Alghazali as he is discussed by Averroes in the fifteenth discussion of Tahafut Al-Tahafut. Cf. The Incoherence of the Incoherence, pp. 293-300.

[93]MH 5:2, especially 5:2:9.

[94]Physica 2.4.196a25ff.; cf. 2.6.198a10ff.

[95]La pensée, p. 178. Although this view was used by the Kalam to argue for creation, Gersonides notes in 6:1:3 that the continuous creation of the world precludes its generation in time.

[96]De Generatione et Corruptione 2.11.338a3ff. Though
Gersonides is attacking the Atomist view of continuous re-creation,
we may presume that he is attributing that view not only to Aristotle but also to Avicenna. The latter, who held the view of
necessary causation, is a likely candidate for one of the followers
of Aristotle to whom Gersonides refers. For Averroes' (and
Alghazali's) critique of Avicenna, see The Incoherence of the Incoherence 3:165f., pp. 98ff. and Van Den Bergh's note 1 to page 99.
For Maimonides' discussion of this view, see Guide 2:21.

[97]Cf. his discussions in his supercommentaries, quoted in
H. A. Wolfson, Crescas' Critique of Aristotle (Cambridge, Mass.,
1929), p. 556f. Also cf. Guide 2:21 for Maimonides' critique of
Avicenna's view of causality.

[98]I am indebted to Seymour Feldman for his analysis of this
passage. See "Gersonides' Proofs for the Creation of the Universe,"
Proceedings of the American Academy for Jewish Research, 35(1967):
121ff.

[99]For Aristotle's definition of continuous existence, see
Physica 5.4.

[100]Physica 4.10.218a6ff; 6.3.234a1ff.

[101]Insofar as motion is the actualization of the potential
(Physica 3.1) and there is no motion in a "now" (Physica 6.3.
234a1ff.), that which only exists in a "now" can exist only
potentially.

[102]Physica 8.8.

[103]Physica 6.3.234a1ff.

[104]Gersonides demonstrates in the following chapter that
every differentiated characteristic of every heavenly body is
nonessential. For the accidental nature of celestial motion, cf.
Metaphysica 12.7; Physica 8.5.256b3ff.

[105]See De Caelo 1.4 for a discussion of the relation between
circular and rectilinear motion.

[106]De Caelo 1.3-4.

[107]Cf. Guide 2:19 for a similar argument, i.e., that the
diversity in the sublunar world must be the effect of purposeful
causation and not of necessity.

[108]De Anima 3.7.

[109]De Anima 2.1-4; Metaphysica 9.8.1050b24ff.; cf. The
Incoherence of the Incoherence, p. 294.

[110]Touati, La pensée, p. 183, n. 39, refers this argument to
Averroes' Epitome of the Metaphysica. Note that while Gersonides'
discussion here may appear to confuse the conception of the spheres'
separate movers with the conception of the spheres, it is clear
from his discussion in MH 5:3:6 that when he speaks of a sphere's
conception he means to refer to the separate conception of its
mover. Unlike Maimonides (cf. Guide 2:4, 10), he does not distinguish between the intellect of a sphere and the intellect of its
mover.

[111] Physica 7.3.247b9ff. Touati, La pensée, p. 183, n. 40,
refers this to Averroes' discussion in his Middle Commentary to
the Physica.

[112] Physica 7.3.248a1ff.

[113] De Caelo 2.5.288a6ff.; cf. De Partibus Animalium
3.9.671b30ff.; De Incessu Animalium 4.705b19ff., 706a27-b2. Also
cf. Averroes, The Incoherence of the Incoherence, 15th Discussion,
pp. 296ff.

[114] De Caelo 2.10, 12.

[115] De Caelo 2.12. Cf. Guide 2:19 for Maimonides' discussion
of the nonessential characteristics of the heavens and his argument against Aristotle's claim that the heavens' properties are
necessary. He argues there that we must posit a particularizer
who creates the heavens by will, not by necessity.

[116] Physica 2.8.

[117] He cites Maimonides as his source here. Cf. Guide 2:19-21.

[118] Given Gersonides' assumptions, one cannot argue that,
after a universal flood in which all land species were destroyed,
there would remain the possibility of a re-creation of those
species by the divine nomos which overflows from the heavens. All
individuals of sublunar species come to be, after the initial
creation of the species, from members of their own species. (The
exception is those species which are generated spontaneously.)
Thus, the creation of the species required a single divine act of
willful generation at the moment of the creation of the world as
a whole, a generation which is different from the natural generation of the parts of the world after creation. Thus, a re-creation
of sublunar species would require us to posit a second act of divine
will, and this is something which is inappropriate to posit of a
God whose will is unchanging and whose perfect wisdom would not
allow His creation to be flawed in this way.

[119] Cf. Meteorologica 2.3, where Aristotle correlates the
eternity of the Sea with the eternity of the world. For a list of
authors who deal with the problem of the earth's elevation above
the water, see Touati, La pensée, p. 185, nn. 51 & 52.

[120] Cf. MH 5:2 for his discussion of the ways in which the
stars influence the earth, to which he refers the reader here.
Note that his argument here presumes that these are transmitted to
the earth physically through their illuminations. He also seems
to lapse in places when he confuses the earth's visibility in the
sense that it is elevated with the earth's visibility in the sense
that it can be seen during the day.

[121] Meteorologica 2.4-5.

[122] Touati, La pensée, p. 186, n. 56, cites Averroes' Epitome
of the Meteorologica.

[123] De Generatione et Corruptione 2.3.

[124] Categoriae 6.6a27ff.

[125] *Categoriae* 6.5b26; cf. *Physica* 5.3.227a27ff.

[126] *Categoriae* 6.5a26ff.

[127] *Physica* 4.13.222a10ff.; 6.3.234a1ff.

[128] *Physica* 4.10.218a6.

[129] *Physica* 4.14.223b1.

[130] For example, a man who travels from New York to Chicago would both be in New York and not be in New York. If time were totally separate, there would be no way for the contraries to exist because we could not distinguish them from each other in temporal terms.

[131] *Physica* 4.11.219b10.

[132] *Physica* 4.10-14.

[133] *Physica* 3.2.

[134] *De Caelo* 1.12.283b13.

[135] *Physica* 3.1.200b32; 4.10.218b10ff.

[136] *Physica* 4.10.217b30ff.

[137] *Physica* 4.10.218b13.

[138] *Physica* 3.4; 1.4.187b7.

[139] *Physica* 3.4-8; *De Caelo* 1.7.

[140] *De Caelo* 1.5.272b17.

[141] *Physica* 3.6.206a16.

[142] *Physica* 3.5.204b7.

[143] *Physica* 3.6-7.

[144] *Physica* 3.5.204b7. See the discussion of Israel I. Efros, *The Problem of Space in Jewish Mediaeval Philosophy* (New York, 1917), pp. 98ff.

[145] *Physica* 8.8; *De Caelo* 1.6.273a7ff.

[146] *Physica* 3.5.204a20ff.; *De Caelo* 1.7.275b13ff.; cf. *De Caelo* 1.12. Also see the discussions of Averroes, *The Incoherence of the Incoherence*, pp. 8ff. and his *Long Commentary* to the *Physica*, which Wolfson, *The Philosophy of the Kalam*, p. 414, n. 31a, cites as III *Physica*, Comm. 37.

[147] Maimonides reports a similar Kalam argument for creation, *Guide* 1:74, 7th argument.

[148] *De Caelo* 2.6.288b6-30. Cf. Averroes, *The Incoherence of the Incoherence*, pp. 29ff.

[149]This argument resembles the argument of Philoponus and of the Kalam for the creation of the world based upon the impossibility of an infinite by succession. Cf. Wolfson, The Philosophy of the Kalam, pp. 410ff.

[150]Physica 3.6.

[151]Physica 5.3.227a3ff.

[152]Cf. Physica 8.8.263b9-264a6; 5.3.226b24ff.

[153]Guide 1:73, Premise 11; Averroes, The Incoherence of the Incoherence, pp. 14ff.

[154]Physica 8.10.266a24f.

[155]De Caelo 1.5.271b27ff.

[156]Physica 8.10.266a12f.

[157]For a discussion of the history of the transmission of this argument, see Wolfson, The Philosophy of the Kalam, pp. 374-382; Wolfson, Crescas' Critique of Aristotle, pp. 104-113; Herbert Davidson, "John Philoponus as a Source of Medieval Islamic and Jewish Proofs of Creation," Journal of the American Oriental Society, 89(1969):357-391; Shlomo Pines, "An Arabic Summary of a Lost Work of John Philoponus," Israel Oriental Studies, 2(1972): 320-352; Muhsin Mahdi, "Alfarabi Against Philoponus," Journal of Near Eastern Studies, 26(1967):233-260. Philoponus' refutation of Aristotle's arguments for the eternity of the world in his Contra Aristotelem has not survived and is known chiefly through the citations of Simplicius. His work, De Aeternitate Mundi Contra Proclum survives (edited by H. Rabe, Leipzig, 1909) and contains the argument cited here by Gersonides. Wolfson, The Philosophy of the Kalam, p. 374, cites as Gersonides' source the discussion of Averroes in his Long Commentary to the Metaphysica XII, Comm. 41.

[158]Cf. Physica 4.5.212b8ff.; 6.10.240b7ff.; 8.6-7.

[159]De Caelo 1.2.269b6ff. Cf. Wolfson, Crescas' Critique of Aristotle, pp. 551-561.

[160]De Caelo 2.12.292b27ff.

[161]Physica 1.4.187b7.

[162]MH 1:12.

[163]CT 2a, 9a, 12b, 12d.

[164]De Interpretatione 2.

[165]Meteorologica 4.1; De Generatione et Corruptione 1.3, 2.1. Cf. MH 4:3, p. 160f.

[166]De Caelo 1.3.

[167]Guide 2:27.

[168]And it is necessary for Him to create, given a receptacle which can receive His will.

[169] Timaeus 30a; De Caelo 1.10.280a5ff.

[170] Metaphysica 1.3.984a21ff.; Physica 3.2.202a9f.; cf. Wolfson, Crescas' Critique of Aristotle, p. 672f.

[171] De Caelo 1.2.268b15ff.

[172] De Caelo 3.2.300b16ff.; Physica 3.5.204b13ff.

[173] De Caelo 1.4.271a33; 2.5.287b24.

[174] Metaphysica 7.7.1032b30.

[175] Physica 4:6-9; De Caelo 3.2.302a1ff.; cf. Averroes, The Incoherence of the Incoherence, p. 52.

[176] De Caelo 1.9.279a14.

[177] Physica 4.8.214b35; 3.4.203b27ff.

[178] Physica 4.8.215a1ff.

[179] Cf. Physica 4.2, especially 209a26f.

[180] Categoriae 7.7a15ff.; Metaphysica 5.15.

[181] Guide 2:17.

[182] Guide 2:25.

[183] He expands on this point in MH 6:2:1, translated below.

[184] See MH 6:2:5 and 6:2:8, p. 429, ll. 1ff., translated below.

[185] Guide 2:19.

[186] Guide 2:25.

[187] Guide 2:19. See Guide 2:29 for Maimonides' view of wonders. For Gersonides' discussion of wonders, see MH 6:2:9-12. For a summary of his view and for the relationship of his view of wonders and of creation, see note #4 of the commentary below.

[188] Guide 2:25. For a discussion of Gersonides' view of the relationship between reason and revelation, see below, note #1 of the commentary, and Part IV, section B, of this introduction.

[189] For a complete discussion of his conception of formless body, see note #49 in the commentary below.

[190] His detailed description of this entire process constitutes MH 6:2:8, translated below.

[191] Cf. De Generatione Animalium 3.2.762a17 where, in discussing natural generation, Aristotle remarks that "nothing comes to be out of the whole of anything." Aristotle claims elsewhere (De Caelo 1.9.278b4ff.) that there is no matter outside the world.

[192] For a similar argument made by the Church Fathers in their refutation of the view that the world was generated from eternal, uncreated matter, see H.A. Wolfson, "Plato's Pre-existent Matter

in Patristic Philosophy," in The Classical Tradition, edited by
L. Wallach (Ithaca, 1966), pp. 409-420. Reprinted in Studies in
the History of Philosophy and Religion, edited by Isadore Twersky
and G. H. Williams (Cambridge, Mass., 1973)1:170-181, especially
Origen's argument cited on p. 180.

[193]Wolfson, "Plato's Pre-existent Matter," pp. 176ff., traces
the identification of eternity with divinity to Philo Judaeus,
De virtutibus 39,214. Cf. H. A. Wolfson, Philo (Cambridge, Mass.,
1947), 1:171-2, 200-217. Also see the comments of Saadia in his
discussion of creation, The Book of Beliefs and Opinions 1:2,
translated by Samuel Rosenblatt (New Haven, 1948), p. 48. For
Maimonides' dismissal of this identification, see Guide 2:13, 2nd
opinion.

[194]Rest occurs in the sublunar world when an existent thing
either reaches the natural place for the elements of which it is
composed or is obstructed from reaching its natural place. Anything which has a natural place or which is obstructed from reaching
that place must have a nature which it receives from its form. Cf.
Physica 5.2.226b10ff.; 5.6.229b23ff.

[195]Physica 1.6-9; 4.7.214a13; De Caelo 1.3-5; De Generatione
et Corruptione 2.1.329a25.

[196]De Caelo 3.2.301a6ff.

[197]Physica 8.1.251b1ff.

[198]Physica 4.1.; De Caelo 1.8-9. See discussion of Efros,
Problem of Space, pp. 66, 80.

[199]De Caelo 1.12.283a11ff.; Physica 8.1.252a14ff.; 8.6.
258b20ff. Cf. Averroes, The Incoherence of the Incoherence, 1st
discussion; Guide 2:12, 2:14, 2:18. Also see Wolfson's review of
the Kalam discussion of this problem, The Philosophy of the Kalam,
pp. 435ff.

[200]Cf. Metaphysica 7.10.1036a9. As Gersonides states (MH
6:2:5, p. 422), the form renders a thing intelligible.

[201]See MH 3:3. Cf. Norbert M. Samuelson, Gersonides. The
Wars of the Lord. Treatise Three: On God's Knowledge (Toronto,
1977), pp. 24-53, 182-224. Cf. also H. A. Wolfson, "Maimonides
and Gersonides on Divine Attributes as Ambiguous Terms," Mordecai
M. Kaplan Jubilee Volume (New York, 1953), pp. 515-530. Reprinted
in Studies in the History of Philosophy and Religion, edited by
Isadore Twersky and G. H. Williams (Cambridge, Mass., 1977) 2:231-
246.

[202]In positing the possibility and the likelihood of a
remainder, Gersonides is disagreeing with both Plato (Timaeus 32c)
and Aristotle (De Caelo 1.9.278a26ff.), both of whom assert that
there is no other matter outside of this world.

[203]On matter as the source of evil, see Metaphysica 1.6.988a
14f. Cf. Gen. Rab. 51:3 and Tanḥuma Va-Yeraᵓ 18, which he cites
here to support this view.

[204]Physica 5.6.

[205]Cf. Physica 5.2.226b10ff.; Metaphysica 4.2.1004a9ff.;
Categoriae 10.12a25ff.

[206]Physica 4.12.221b20ff.

[207]MH 5:2:2, p. 193f. Cf. Averroes, The Incoherence of the
Incoherence, p. 160f. Also see Wolfson, Crescas' Critique of
Aristotle, pp. 594ff., and note #242 of the commentary below.

[208]Seymour Feldman, "Platonic Themes in Gersonides'
Cosmology," Salo Wittmayer Baron Jubilee Volume (Jerusalem, 1975),
p. 395, n. 47, suggests that this argument seems to be based upon
Maimonides' second proof for the existence of a first unmoved
mover (Guide 2:1).

[209]So that to say it is deprived of its nature is a category
mistake parallel to saying that it is at rest, as he explains above
in his response to the 4th doubt.

[210]This latter observation seems to miss the point of the
objection. That is, when the cells of the human body are no longer
a part of it, they are not without nature. Rather, through a
process of alteration or generation they receive a different nature.

[211]As will be discussed below in note #49 of the commentary,
Gersonides' descriptions of the body which does not preserve its
shape lead to questions such as those raised by the 8th doubt here.
This is because he intends the body to have dimensionality without
actual, definite dimensions—what Averroes calls absolute dimensionality (cf. Wolfson, Crescas' Critique of Aristotle, pp. 101,
582-589). The distinction he attempts to make in his response to
the 8th doubt is that the existence of indefinite dimensional
body—body which in some sense can have a size (godel) and a quantity (shicur) and which in some way can prevent the motions of the
spheres from confusing one another—does not entail the existence
of form and nature. Absolute dimensional body is independent of
the divine nomos and persists prior to the overflow of the forms
from God's conception at the moment of creation.

[212]Cf. Guide 2:18, second method.

[213]Cf. his response to the 2nd doubt above, in this chapter.

[214]For a similar argument by Alghazali and its refutation by
Averroes, see The Incoherence of the Incoherence, pp. 18ff.
Gersonides would respond by asserting that the question is unintelligible, because the term "moment" is said equivocally of the
moment of creation and of all other moments.

[215]Cf. Guide 2:13, 2:19, 3:15; Averroes, The Incoherence of
the Incoherence, pp. 52ff. and Van Den Bergh's note #1 to p. 53.

[216]Cf. Guide 2:12.

[217]For a precedent in the procedure of concluding one's
demonstration of creation with a demonstration of the impossibility
of multiple worlds, see the end of Saadia's first proof for creation (from finitudes), The Book of Beliefs and Opinions 1:1, p. 41f.
of Rosenblatt translation. Cf. De Caelo 1.8.

[218]Physica 2.5.196b10ff.

[219]See the analysis of Efros, Problem of Space, pp. 75-77. Efros labels Gersonides' argument here as circular, because he assumes the impossibility of the void and uses that assumption to argue against the possibility of the void between parts of formless body.

[220]Cf. De Caelo 1.8.

[221]Physica 8.6.

[222]Physica 8.1.251b14.

[223]Physica 5.1.225a10-29.

[224]Physica 6.5.235b7ff. De Generatione et Corruptione 1.4.319b10ff. See Wolfson, Crescas' Critique of Aristotle, pp. 241-249, 503f., 540-550. Also see Feldman's discussion of the issue, "Gersonides' Proofs," p. 133f.

[225]De Caelo 1.9; Physica 4.5.212b16.

[226]Physica 4.11.219a30ff.

[227]Physica 4.11.219b1.

[228]Physica 4.11.219a21ff. Cf. Wolfson, Crescas' Critique of Aristotle, pp. 651-660.

[229]Physica 4.13.222a10ff.

[230]Physica 3.1.301a23ff. See Wolfson Crescas' Critique of Aristotle, pp. 526-529, for a discussion of the history of this issue.

[231]Metaphysica 9.8.1050a30ff.

[232]Metaphysica 12.7.1072b3ff.; cf. Guide 2:12, 18.

[233]For a general discussion of the Aristotelian argument, see Feldman, "Platonic Themes," pp. 398ff.

[234]De Caelo 1.12.283a20ff., 283b7ff.

[235]De Caelo 1.12.281b33-282a13; 282b13-283a3.

[236]De Caelo 1.12.283a6ff.

[237]De Caelo 1.12.283a11ff.

[238]De Caelo 1.12.283a18ff.

[239]De Generatione et Corruptione 2.11.

[240]See below commentary notes, #1, #5, #6 and #20. Also see Gersonides' discussions of Maimonides' position in 6:1:3 and 6:1:17, summarized above in this introduction.

[241]See above for a summary of 6:1:6-9, 13.

[242]Guide 2:13.

[243]See below, commentary notes #6, #20, #226, #234, #240, #253, #324, #332, #520, #521 and #525. Also see his discussion in 6:1:18, summarized above in this introduction.

[244]See 6:1:4 and 6:1:18, summarized above in this introduction.

[245]See Guide 2:26.

[246]See below, commentary notes #227, #230, #232, #283, #348, #362, #404 and #419. Also see his discussion of the supralunar world above, 6:1:7-9, summarized above in this introduction.

[247]See below, commentary notes #215, #216, #310, #362, #397, #398, #400, #402, #408, #409, #414, #433, #451, #465, #466, #476, and #478.

[248]See below, commentary notes #4, #5, #8, #20, #229, #283, and #313.

[249]This section is based primarily on commentary note #1 below.

[250]See below, commentary notes #1, #6, #17, #25, #37, #408, #409, #460, #489, #509, #544, and #545.

[251]See below, commentary notes #264, #338, #359, #408, #455, #456, #484, #486, #487, #491, #492, #499, #502, and #504.

[252]See below, commentary notes #1, #3, #232, #310, #407, #436, #456 and #491.

[253]See below, commentary notes #407-#411 and #418-#421.

[254]See below, commentary notes #1, #6, #295, #300-#302, #315, #362, #440, #460, #468, #489, #497 and #542-#544.

[255]See below, commentary notes #2, #195 and #248.

[256]See below, commentary notes #155, #178, #180, #191, #194, #195, #203, #222, #225, #227, #271, #273, #319, #321 and #322.

[257]See below, commentary notes #43, #64, #65, #141, #186, #188 and #263.

[258]See below, commentary notes #27, #33, #37, #145, #214, #235, #238, #300-#302 and #396.

[259]See below, commentary notes #48, #49, #50, #53 and #55.

[260]See below, commentary notes #64-#67, #70, #72, #93, #99, #242 and #334.

[261]See below, commentary notes #78, #79 and #92.

[262]See below, commentary notes #112, #115, #117, #122, #124, #126 and #127.

[263]See below, commentary notes #136, #143, #147, #154, #159, #175, #179, #180, #254-#257, #263 and #264.

^{264}See 6:1:10, 11, 17, 18, 20, and 24 and the summary above in this introduction.

^{265}See below, commentary notes #211, #212, #218, #222, #225, #226, #240, #288, #315, #319, #323, #324, #332, #362, #471 and #511.

^{266}See below, commentary notes #214, #235 and #242.

^{267}See below, commentary notes #27, #214, #215, #217, #235, #242, #269, #310, #340, #444, #445, #447, #451, #460, and #478.

^{268}See below, commentary notes #134, #297, #309, #315, #340 and #414.

^{269}See below, commentary notes #348, #350, #352, #355, #356 and #373.

^{270}See below, commentary notes #215, #217, #444, #445, #447 and #460.

^{271}See below, commentary notes #215-#217, #310, #409, #451, #465, #466, #476 and #478.

^{272}See below, commentary notes #27, #215, #269, #297, #309, #315, #362, #397, #398, #400-#405, #408, #414, #418, #433 and #476.

^{273}See below, commentary notes #245, #265, #266, #308-#310, #389, #439 and #477.

^{274}See below, commentary notes #228, #229, #232, #298 and #431.

^{275}See 6:1:17 and the summary above in this introduction.

^{276}The preceding section is based on the following commentary notes: #3, #48, #49, #51, #52, #56, #59, #147, #152, #173, #182, #191, #215, #232, #235, #236, #256, #269, #271, #297, #349 and #424.

^{277}See his discussion of the terms of Gen 1:2 in 6:2:3-6 and the summary above in this introduction.

^{278}See below, commentary notes #99, #215, #224, #242, #244-#246, #251, #335, #336, #338, #397, #501, #515, #518 and #536.

^{279}See below, commentary notes #49, #136, #141, #143, #191, #194, #215, #232, #235, #236, #241, #242, #251, #254, #256, #264, #269, #271, #277, #279, #283, #297, #344, #349, #361, #417-#420 and #424.

^{280}See below, commentary notes #232, #235, #268, #269, #297, #418-#420 and #424.

^{281}See below, commentary notes #270-#272.

^{282}See below, commentary notes #134, #215, #285, #289, #291, #297, #309, #313, #315, #319, #323-#325, #332, #340-#342, #392, #411 and #414. On the visible part of the earth, see also 6:1:13 and the summary of it above in this introduction.

^{283}See below, commentary notes #136, #152, #182, #184, #188, #197, #223, #225, #227, #230, #232, #234, #251, #266, #346, #348-

#350, #352, #355, #356, #362, #366, #373, #388, #390, #404, #405, #418-#420. For his discussion of the diverse characteristics of the heavenly bodies and the nomos which overflows from them to the sublunar world, see also 6:1:7-9 and the summary of that discussion above in this introduction.

[284] See the discussion above in this introduction, for a clarification of this point. Also see below, commentary notes #397-#405.

[285] See below, commentary notes #394-#421.

[286] Cf. 6:1:6-9, 13 and the summary of these chapters above in this introduction.

[287] See below, commentary notes #140, #429-#447, #460, #465, #466, #476 and #524.

[288] See below, commentary notes #264, #289, #310, #324, #335, #338, #359, #408, #409, #442, #444, #445, #447, #451, #455, #456, #460, #462, #465, #466, #468, #472, #476, #478, #484, #486, #487, #491, #492, #499, #501, #502, #504, #507, #524 and #531.

[289] See below, commentary notes #510-#540.

[290] See Wolfson, "Maimonides and Gersonides on Divine Attributes as Ambiguous Terms," pp. 515-530; N. M. Samuelson, Gersonides. On God's Knowledge. See also, Joseph Owens, The Doctrine of Being in the Aristotelian 'Metaphysics', Third Edition (Toronto: Pontifical Institute of Mediaeval Studies, 1978), pp. 116-121, 265-274.

THE TRANSLATION OF AND COMMENTARY TO
THE WARS OF THE LORD 6:2:1-8

TREATISE SIX, PART TWO: INTRODUCTION

Translation

   Part Two, in which we shall explain that that to which
speculation has led us is the view of our Torah,[1] and that
which is discussed of the account of creation[2] will be
explained here.   Next, in this Part we shall raise two
religious questions and we shall investigate them as far as
speculation and the Torah will allow us.[3]   They are: (a) in
what way signs and wonders[4] are possible, how they come to
be, by means of whom they come to be, and who is their cause,
and (b) how a prophet is tested.[5]

147

1) The purpose of this second part of the sixth treatise is
thus the proper reading of the creation narrative in Genesis so
that there will be no discrepancy between what the Torah teaches
us about creation and what has just been demonstrated by means of
speculation in the first part of the sixth treatise. Gersonides'
arguments and conclusions in 6:1 about the way in which the world
came to be have been summarized above in Part III of the introduction.

This enterprise to which 6:2 is devoted is not confined to it.
Rather, it can be said to be central to the purpose of all sections
of The Wars of the Lord. In his Introduction to the entire work,
Gersonides explains the very title he has chosen by saying, "Everything which is explained to us by way of speculation is the view of
the Torah" (p. 6, 1. 27f. All page citations to The Wars of the
Lord [hereafter MH] refer to the Leipzig, 1866 edition.). That is,
he believes that the value inherent in examining the issues with
which he deals in this work, and in reaching true and demonstrable
conclusions about these issues, derives from the fact that there
is only one truth: a truth which is revealed by the Torah when we
are able to read it properly, and which can be demonstrated, to
some extent at least, by means of speculation. Since there is
only one truth, and since the ultimate purpose of human beings is
to conceive of as much of that truth as they can, any work which
demonstrates the true conception of any issue is fighting the
Lord's "wars."

We may infer that Gersonides is convinced of this unitary
view of the truth on the basis of the following:

a) He repeatedly cites the precedent set by Maimonides in
The Guide of the Perplexed (hereafter referred to as Guide. Page
references are to the translation of Shlomo Pines [Chicago,
1963].). That is, Maimonides states explicitly with regard to the
issues of the corporeality of God and the creation of the world
that it is proper to believe that which speculation demonstrates
to be true, and that in cases in which there is an apparent
discrepancy between the apparent meaning of the Torah and the
demonstrated conclusions of speculation, the Torah should be
interpreted in a way that agrees with the demonstrated truth
(Guide, Introduction to Part 1; 1:55; 2:25. For Gersonides'
discussions of Maimonides' view, see MH Introduction p. 6f.;
6:1:17, p. 367, ll. 7ff.; 6:2:1, p. 419, ll. 10-15).

b) Gersonides' understanding of the nature and purpose of the
Torah leads him to this view. That is, he believes that the Torah

is the revelation of the divine wisdom which overflows from God
through the separate intellects and governs the sublunar world.
He also believes that the true and ultimate function of the human
species is the realization of true conceptions. As he explains in
the first treatise, the more an individual conceives of the divine
nomos which governs the world, the closer that person approximates
the separate conception of the Active Intellect. (David Blumenthal, in his article, "On the Intellect and the Rational Soul,"
Journal of the History of Philosophy 15 (1977): 207, argues that
the term sekhel ha-poᶜel ought to be translated as "Agent Intelli-
gence." Seymour Feldman adopts the term "Agent Intellect" in his
article, "Gersonides on the Possibility of Conjunction with the
Agent Intellect," AJS Review 3 (1978): 99-120. Our use of the
traditional term "Active Intellect" is not based on a judgment of
the relative merits of alternate translations but on its widespread
and traditional usage.) As a consequence, that person is overseen
to a greater extent by the providence which governs the world
through the divine nomos (as he explains in the fourth treatise),
and that person achieves a greater degree of immortality for his
acquired intellect.

In line with all of this, Gersonides believes that the Torah's
function is to guide us to our ultimate end, i.e., the most perfect
possible actualization of our intellect's conception. The Torah is
the revelation of the perfect divine nomos which governs the world
and, as such, it leads us to follow it by its self-evident and
therefore compelling truth. This is the way that it functions as
part of the divine providence; it is a gift which directs us to
our ultimate felicity (see MH, Introduction p. 6; The Commentary to
the Torah [hereafter CT] 2a, 2b, 2c, 9a, 16c. [All page citations
of the Commentary refer to the Venice, 1547 edition.]). Consequently, the Torah is not a coercive nomos which compels us to
adopt false views. To do so would contradict its purpose, which
is to guide us to the truth, and would undermine its authority,
which derives from its self-evident perfection which leads men to
desire that they conduct themselves in accordance with it (MH,
Introduction, p. 7; 6:2:1, p. 419, ll. 16ff.).

c) Gersonides' understanding of the nature of prophecy and
the process of revelation also leads him to this view. As he
explains in the second treatise, a prophet reaches the level of
prophecy if and only if he has attained a level of profound wisdom
and possesses true conceptions of the nature of existent things
(cf. 6:2:10, p. 446, l. 30f.). Thus, the contents of prophetic
revelation are known to the prophet insofar as he is profoundly

developed in the area of speculation, so that the identity of the
conclusions of speculation and of the teachings of prophecy is to
be expected (cf. MH, Introduction, p. 4f.). Specifically with
reference to the Torah, this principle leads him to the conclusion
that the teachings of the Torah revealed to Moses are inclusive of
all the truths which were partially revealed to other prophets.
Because the perfection of Moses' conception of the truth was so
exceedingly profound, he was able to conceive the truth of the
divine nomos in a more perfect way than has occurred through the
conception of any other human being. Thus, nothing revealed to
any other prophet was not revealed to Moses (CT 12b, ll. 36ff.;
12d, ll. 25ff.).

Given this view of the unitary nature of the truth, Gersonides
may appear to be primarily devoted to the pursuit of speculative
truth and may seem, in his interpretation of the creation story in
Genesis as well as elsewhere, to be insensitively manipulating the
literal meaning of Scripture to force it to conform to his philosophical conclusions. Indeed, the methodology he outlines in his
introduction to this work (MH, Introduction, p. 7) would seem to
confirm this view. That is, with regard to each of the issues
which he investigates in The Wars, he begins by determining the
truth that can be demonstrated by means of speculation and then he
approaches the interpretation of the Torah with the assumption that
the teachings of the Torah cannot, by definition, contain anything
that conflicts with the truth. It may reasonably appear, therefore,
to the modern student that Gersonides is being less than honest in
his claims that the Torah agrees with his views about such issues
as the immortality of the soul, the nature of prophecy and providence, God's knowledge of particular things, the nature of angels,
as well as the way in which the world was created.

Before we can defend Gersonides' intellectual integrity,
however, it is important to note that this problem is one instance
of the general and widespread difficulty which modern students of
medieval philosophy have encountered in their attempts to understand the medieval philosopher. This difficulty may be epitomized
in two, paradoxically opposite, questions which may occur to the
modern student. How could the medieval philosopher have believed
that he was being rational if he consciously and explicitly used
philosophy as a "handmaiden" of Scripture, using rational arguments
only in support of traditional doctrines which were assumed, in
advance, to be true? How, on the other hand, could the medieval
philosopher have believed that he was accurately interpreting the
literal meaning of Scripture when he was so obviously reading

Neoplatonic and Aristotelian concepts into texts, the apparent
meaning of which is totally foreign to the Greek philosophical
tradition?

Less sympathetic observers have often chosen to omit from the
study of philosophy those Jewish, Christian and Muslim thinkers
who lived after Philo Judaeus and before Spinoza. Scholars of
medieval philosophy such as Wolfson and Gilson often find it
necessary to begin their studies by responding to this unsympathetic view. (See, e.g., Etienne Gilson, Reason and Revelation in
the Middle Ages [New York, 1938], p. 3f.; H. A. Wolfson, "What's
New in Philo?", in From Philo to Spinoza: Two Studies in Religious
Philosophy [New York, 1977], p. 17.) The problem, however, is not
simply a question of sympathy. Every time we characterize medieval
philosophy as an enterprise in the "reconciliation" or "harmonization" of revealed and rational truth, we are faced with the
questions mentioned above.

It is for this reason that it is important, for an
understanding of Gersonides, to stress his unitary view of the
truth. From his perspective, he was not engaged in an enterprise
of reconciliation or harmonization. Those terms arise out of the
modern, post-Spinozan (according to Wolfson) view of the nature of
the truth. Insofar as we read the Torah as the product of an
historical context which reflects the insights of the Israelites
to whom it was revealed, and insofar as we view the philosophical
treatises of the medievals as the culmination of the transmission
and development of the Greek philosophical tradition, we cannot
avoid the view that Gersonides, for example, was a man faced with
reconciling conflicting truth claims. Gersonides, however, did
not believe that the Torah was a product of an historical context
and he did not believe the conclusions which he reached by means
of speculation were a function of the philosophical and scientific
tools to which he had access.

Rather, as explained above, Gersonides believed that the
Torah was the repository of the infinite wisdom of God. As such,
it was not a document which could be easily understood or could be
understood at all without extensive preparation. Its layers of
meaning were many and profound and the wisdom with which it guided
human beings to their ultimate felicity was only vaguely comprehensible to the human mind. It came as no surprise to him, therefore, that all preceding interpretations of the creation narrative
in Genesis had misunderstood its intention. Similarly, he did not
regard his philosophical investigations as a secular enterprise.
The study of the divine nomos which governs all existent things

was, for him, the most exalted of all religious activities. This
was because, as explained above, he believed that such things as
true knowledge of God and His purposes, prophecy, providence and
immortality of the soul were all the consequences of the attainment
of true philosophic knowledge.

Thus, Gersonides did not believe he was reconciling
conflicting truths. He believed rather that the ability to read
the text of the Torah properly was to be developed through the
actualization of one's intellectual conception. The study of
philosophy and the sciences was nothing other than a preparation
for the understanding of revelation. For him, there were not two
truths; there was one truth which could be reached by the proper
exercise of one's intellect and/or the accurate reading of revealed
Scripture. (For a complete exposition of this approach, which
applies generally to medieval philosophers, see Wolfson's description of the synthetic medieval philosopher in Philo: Foundations
of Religious Philosophy in Judaism, Christianity and Islam
[Cambridge, Mass., 1948], 2:446ff., reprinted in From Philo to
Spinoza, pp. 24ff.)

With this understanding, we can approach the specific features
which characterize Gersonides' view of the relationship between
reason and revelation. First, we note his view of the limitations
of human knowledge. Contrary to what may be presumed on the basis
of some of the more unorthodox and original conclusions which he
reaches, Gersonides was not a radical rationalist who believed that
the philosopher could actually discover the truth, with or without
the aid of revelation. He introduces The Wars with a recognition
of the difficulty of the issues to be discussed and with an admission of the limitations of human knowledge of such things as God,
the supralunar world and the perfect divine nomos which governs
the sublunar world (MH, Introduction, p. 6; cf. 1:12). In the
first treatise, he concludes that the conjunction of the human
intellect with the Active Intellect is not possible because we can
never know things as they are known by their cause. In the introduction to his commentary on the Torah, he states that the speculator would encounter insurmountable difficulties in his pursuit
of the truth without the aid and guidance of revelation (CT 2c. Cf.
the parallel view of Saadia in his Introductory Treatise to his
Kitab al-ᵓAmanat wal-Iᶜtiḳadat, translated as The Book of Beliefs
and Opinions by Samuel Rosenblatt [New Haven, 1948], and its
analysis by H. A. Wolfson, "The Double Faith Theory in Saadia,
Averroes and St. Thomas," Jewish Quarterly Review, n.s., 33 [1942]:
231-264.). Specifically with reference to creation, we note that

he begins the sixth treatise by devoting an entire chapter to a
discussion of the difficulties of the investigation (6:1:1) and,
when he finally presents his own view of the way in which the world
came to be, he again concedes our inability to know the body from
which the world was generated (6:1:18). As he states in his commentary (CT 16c, 11. 25ff.), given that the development of the
human intellect requires human choice, the guidance of the Torah is
needed to help us to choose correctly.

Second, the case of creation is unique in that Gersonides does
not merely claim that the Torah can be reinterpreted to agree with
the demonstrated conclusions of speculation. He makes the stronger
claim that the text of the creation narrative in Genesis actually
guided him to reach the conclusions he reaches (MH, Introduction,
p. 7; 6:1:29, p. 417, 1. 15f.; 6:2:1, p. 429, 11. 16ff.). This is
no empty claim. Throughout his discussion of the Genesis text
below, he repeatedly cites terms, phrases and other techniques
which the Torah employs to guide us to the truth of the investigation. For example, the days on which the various existent things
are created are taken to indicate their relative priority to one
another. The apparent inconsistency which he notes in the Torah's
description of the generation of the stars after the generation of
the earth and the plant species is interpreted as a meaningful
pedagogical device used by Moses to teach us significant truths
about the relationship of the stars to the spheres and of the
visible part of the earth to the supralunar world (6:2:8, p. 434,
11. 30ff. For a similar view of the pedagogic function of the
Qurᶜan, see the discussion of Averroes, Kitāb fasl al-maqāl, 8:11-
12, translated as On the Harmony of Religion and Philosophy by
George F. Hourani [London, 1961], p. 51.). The examples of this
phenomenon can be multiplied. Gersonides uses the same term—
haᶜarah (stimulation)—to refer both to the way in which the manifest order of existent things stimulates us to an awareness of and
a longing for a conception of the divine nomos (CT 15c, 11. 16ff.)
and to the way the Torah stimulates us to the truth of things by
its presentation of the creation of the world (6:2:8, p. 435, 11.
23, 25; p. 436, 1. 9; p. 438, 1. 27). That is, the Torah must be
consulted lest we draw hasty conclusions from our observations.

Third, lest we conclude that Gersonides was so devoted to the
discovery of the truth that he had no concern about the damage his
conclusions might inflict upon the faith of the simple folk, we
ought to note his statement that one should not resort to reading
the Torah metaphorically unless it is absolutely necessary in order
to make sense out of the text (CT 16d, 1. 10). As his concluding

chapter to the first treatise makes clear (1:14, p. 91), he is not
engaged in an iconoclastic disruption of traditional tenets of
faith. His work is intended to aid those who are interested in the
pursuit of the truth. Not everyone, however, is suited to engage
in this enterprise. To the reader whose faith is shaken by the
conclusions reached in The Wars, Gersonides advises a rejection of
the conclusions reached by speculation: "The following of speculation is not permitted when it departs from faith" (1:14, p. 91,
1. 16f.).

Finally, when Gersonides states that his exegesis yields the
literal meaning of the text (CT 2c) or when he concludes his
presentation of creation by asserting that the text of the Torah
undoubtedly testifies to the truth of his conclusions (6:2:8,
p. 441, 1. 14f.; cf. CT 11a, 11. 1ff.), it would be incorrect for
us to infer that he believes that anyone who opens the Book of
Genesis will arrive at conclusions identical to his own. In his
mind, there is no equation between literal meaning (peshat) and
obvious meaning. The literal meaning of revelation, as explained
above, is not obvious but rather requires a lifetime of preparation
if it is to be understood correctly.

2) Ma^{c}aseh be-re$^{\circ}$shit. The system of transliteration of Hebrew
terms into English letters which is used here is that suggested by
the AJS Review 3 (1978):vii-xi, which is the following:

Consonants

א ꜝ		ל l
quiescent א not transliterated		מ m
ב b		נ n
ב v		ס s
ג,ג g		ע c
ד,ד d		פ p
ה h		פ f
ו v (where not a vowel)		צ s
ז z		ק q
ח h		ר r
ט t		שׁ sh
י y		שׂ s
כ k		ת,ת t
כ kh		

Vowels

	short			
⟨ָ⟩	a	⟨ֱ⟩	e
⟨ַ⟩	a	⟨ִ⟩	i
⟨ֳ⟩, ֹו	o	⟨ֵ⟩	e
⟨ֻ⟩, וּ	u	⟨ֶ⟩	e
short ⟨ָ⟩	o	⟨ָ⟩	o
	ei	⟨ֲ⟩	a

vocal sheva   e

silent sheva not transliterated

Ma^caseh be-re^shit is a technical term in rabbinic literature designating the esoteric study of the origins of the world, most often based on the interpretation of the first chapters of Genesis (cf. m. Ḥag. 2:1; b. Ḥag. 12a-16a). This area of study was considered dangerous for the unprepared mind and consequently there was a prohibition against public instruction. Maimonides' definition of the term included not only the investigation of the beginning of creation but also the natural sciences (cf. Guide I, Introduction, p. 6f.; 1:17, p. 42f.; Commentary to Mishnah Ḥagigah 2:1). As a result, Maimonides displays great caution throughout the Guide and is concerned that its true meanings reach only those who are adequately prepared in their prior devotion to the Torah, education and moral training. He explicitly writes that his way of dealing with this problem is to make the Guide unintelligible to the vulgar, making nothing explicit and no explanation exhaustive, deliberately contradicting himself, and revealing the truth only in "flashes and indications" which can be immediately glimpsed by the proper reader (Guide, Epistle Dedicatory p. 3f.; Introduction, pp. 5, 6f., 17-19; 1:33, p. 72; 2:29, p. 347).

In his use of the term, Gersonides does not indicate similar concerns. It appears in our text only here, in the Introduction to 6:2:8, p. 427; 6:2:8, p. 441, l. 8; and, in a quotation from the Midrash, 6:2:10, p. 447, l. 35. He uses the term to designate the exposition of the first seven days of creation in the Genesis text. He displays no concern that his interpretation be kept from those who might misunderstand it. In fact, in the Introduction to The Wars (p. 8), he criticizes Maimonides for deliberately confusing the reader. He believes that his own purpose is to clarify, as far as that is possible, since the difficulty of the subject matter is sufficiently great that it need not be compounded with confused language and disorderly discussion.

Like Maimonides, he believes that the reader of this work must have prior training in mathematics, natural sciences and

metaphysics (Introduction, p. 3, l. 8f.), but he is confident that
the absence of such training will render this work unintelligible.
When he speaks of the "secrets of the order of existence" (Introduction, p. 4, l. 28; cf. 6:2:8, p. 435, l. 22f.), or a "hidden"
point (6:2:8, p. 439, l. 23), his intention is not to hide but
rather to clarify what heretofore has been misunderstood on account
of imprecise reasoning or incomplete knowledge. Only in the concluding chapter of the first treatise (1:14, p. 91) does he reveal
a concern about the potential damage which his conclusions may
inflict upon the faith of a reader who is unprepared to understand
them properly—a concern which approximates that of Maimonides in
the Guide and Averroes in Kitab fasl al-maqāl. In that chapter,
he advises the reader who finds his faith shaken by the conclusions
of speculation to reject the latter and to affirm his faith and his
former understanding of its teachings.

    3) As a careful thinker, Gersonides always remains aware of
the intrinsic limitations of human knowledge, especially with
regard to the complex metaphysical problems discussed in The Wars.
Humans know imperfectly because of the multiplicity of our knowledge (3:5; cf. Guide 1:68). That is, we conceive of the true form
of a thing by abstracting it from our perceptions of the material
instantiations of that form. These material things, however, are
rough approximations of the form itself (cf. 5:3:12, p. 279). For
example, our conception of health is inductively reached from our
observations of healthy people who are each only relatively healthy.
It is therefore impossible for us to conceive of the science of
existent things either with perfection or completeness (cf. 1:12,
pp. 85ff.; 6:2:10, p. 449, l. 1f.; CT 2a). In addition, our knowledge both of God and the heavens is very weak because of our
physical distance from the heavens and because we know the separate
intellects of the heavens and God only as an effect can know its
cause (Introduction, p. 2; 1:7, p. 49; 1:12, p. 85f.; 5:2:1, p.
294). Thus, our knowledge of the divine wisdom inherent in the
Torah is also very weak (CT 2a, 2c, 9a). Consequently, one
involved in speculation must be on guard against the pitfall of
pursuing a problem which is beyond his capacities. With regard to
understanding the body from which the world came to be, for example,
he states: "It is proper that one who investigates a given science
should know what is possible to be explained by that science and
what is impossible" (6:1:18, p. 371, l. 15f.). Investigations of
irresolvable aspects of problems are futile. Thus, he introduces
this section with an admission of his limitations.

4) This is the only instance in this section in which the
Biblical idiom ha-ʾotot ve-ha-moftim is used. The translation here
seeks to reproduce that idiom. Elsewhere, the term ʾot is used to
designate a "sign," either in the sense of a piece of evidence for
an argument (6:2:5, p. 422, ll. 24, 26) or of a symbol representing
something else (6:2:8, p. 433, l.8; p. 434, ll. 14, 16). The term
mofet occasionally has the sense of a (speculative or concrete)
"demonstration" (6:2:7, p. 425, l. 14; 6:2:8, p. 436, l. 11;
p. 441, l. 11; 6:2:9, p. 441, l. 32; p. 442, l. 9; 6:2:10, p. 445,
l. 32; 6:2:11, p. 453, l. 18; p. 454, l. 2). Its primary use in
our text is in the sense of a "wonder" and in this sense it appears
to be a synonym for niflaʾ, which is translated here as "marvel."
The identity of the meaning of mofet and niflaʾ becomes most
obvious when they are used in quick succession to refer to a single
phenomenon (Cf., for example, 6:2:10, p. 446, ll. 16, 17; p. 447,
ll. 2 and 3; p. 449, ll. 32, 34 and 35; p. 452, ll. 2 and 3, 5
and 7; p. 452, l. 34 and p. 453, l. 4; 6:2:11, p. 453, l. 19;
6:2:12, p. 456, ll. 8 and 9). The dual meaning of mofet is highlighted in 6:2:11, p. 453, ll. 18 and 19, where each of its two
occurrences has a different meaning. We have thus chosen to translate it with two different English terms—"demonstration" and
"wonder."

Our translation of niflaʾ, the most frequently used term in
the text, as "marvel" reflects Gersonides' use of other terms
deriving from the root plʾ. When he uses the phrase derekh peleʾ
("by way of marvel") he means something extraordinary, which does
not occur as things customarily do in nature, e.g., that things
come to be from something other than their species (6:2:8, p. 428,
l. 24), that the Lord gave the earth the power to bring forth
vegetation without it having been seeded (6:2:8, p. 431, l. 29),
that a star be generated in the heavens after the creation of the
world was completed (6:2:10, p. 446, l. 1), or that it rain at
some past moment after it had already not rained at that moment
(6:2:12, p. 456, ll. 1,3). Note that the former two instances can
and have occurred while the latter two are impossible because they
contradict natural and logical necessity respectively.

When he uses the phrase mah niflaʾ ba-zeh ("how marvelous
this is") he is commenting on the extraordinary accuracy of a
rabbinic interpretation of a Biblical text (6:2:4, p. 421, l. 19;
6:2:5, p. 423, l. 26).

His use of the adjective and adverb, niflaʾ and bifliyah,
again denotes something uncommon. It is his way of expressing
surprise or amazement, as at the marvelous error of his

predecessors (6:2:8, p. 439, l. 25), or at the marvelous ease with
which a person can be made to blush (6:2:10, p. 446, l. 25); of
describing the extraordinary, as the extraordinary distinction
between the marvels associated with Moses and those of other
prophets (6:2:10, p. 447, l. 1), the extraordinary preconditions
for prophecy (6:2:10, p. 446, l. 30), the extraordinary destruction
that would occur were there to be a change in the heavenly bodies
(6:2:12, p. 456, l. 13), or the extraordinary length of time it
takes for a staff to become a serpent (6:2:12, p. 459, l. 8); of
denoting the superlative, as the marvelous perfection of animal
biology (6:2:10, p. 444, l. 7), the marvelousness of providence
(6:2:10, p. 453, l. 20), or the marvelous benefit of wonders
(6:2:10, p. 448, l. 11).   On occasion, it can denote the impossible
(cf. 6:2:12, p. 454, .l. 18) but the primary meaning of these terms
remains clearly within the scope of things whose occurrence may be
uncommon for a variety of reasons but the occurrence of which does
not violate natural law.

It is for this reason that niflaᵓ has been translated as
"marvel" and not as "miracle."   That is, Gersonides' understanding
of the nature of marvels does not coincide with the contemporary
supernatural connotation of "miracle."   Note, for example, the
definition of The Compact Edition of the Oxford English Dictionary
(Oxford, 1977) 1:1806:

> A marvelous event occurring within human experience,
> which cannot have been brought about by human power or
> by the operation of any natural agency, and must there-
> fore be ascribed to the special intervention of the
> Deity or of some supernatural being.

Gersonides, by contrast, argues that wonders cannot change
nature from natural custom.   Something is generated by way of a
wonder only by natural custom over a length of time (6:2:12,
p. 459, ll. 31ff.).   In no way can a marvel contradict natural or
logical necessity: it cannot persist perpetually because that
would imply that the order of the heavens, set by the Lord at
creation, is deficient (6:2:12, p. 454, ll. 16ff.), nor can it be
generated in self-contradictions (6:2:12, p. 455, ll. 24ff.),
mathematical definitions (6:2:12, p. 455, ll. 29ff.), or past
events (6:2:12, p. 455, ll. 33ff.), all of which would contradict
logical necessity, nor can it be generated in the heavens (6:2:12,
p. 456, ll. 8ff.), whose states of affairs are everlasting and
unchangeable, i.e., naturally necessary.

All of this is so because Gersonides believes that marvels
are caused by the Active Intellect (6:2:10, p. 450, ll. 30ff.),

as are all sublunar phenomena, and, as such, do not depart from the
definition of the nomos ordered by the Lord for lower existent
things (6:2:10, p. 450, l. 18f.). Their causation can be attributed
neither to the Lord, except insofar as He created this nomos, nor to
the heavenly bodies, whose motions and functions are perpetual and
unchanging and from which the customary order of nature overflows.
Additionally, none of the separate movers of the spheres conceives
of the entire nomos which overflows to the sublunar world. Each
conceives only of the motion of its sphere (5:3:9, p. 274 f.).
The Active Intellect, on the other hand, knows the complete nomos
which overflows from the combination of all the motions of the
spheres and stars. It is the cause of marvels as part of its
function of providence, discussed in the fourth treatise. That is,
as the Active Intellect overflows providentially to individuals in
proportion to the degree to which their intellects approximate the
Active Intellect, similarly the level of the intellect of a
prophet—and all prophets have highly developed intellects—
determines the extent and degree to which that prophet can be
involved in the generation of a marvel (6:2:10, p. 451, ll. 14ff.).
Thus, the marvels of Moses are far more inclusive and of significantly longer duration than those of the other prophets (6:2:12,
p. 455, ll. 3ff.).

We must not conclude, however, that either the Active
Intellect or the prophet causes something to occur supernaturally.
As stated above, all marvels are included within the natural nomos
of sublunar existent things which overflows from the Active Intellect. Thus, the swallowing of Korah and his band by the earth
(Num 16) was not a deviation from natural law, but was rather the
coincidental culmination of a long volcanic process (6:2:12,
p. 459, ll. 15ff.). Similarly, the transformation of Moses' rod
into a serpent (Exod 4:3) was the natural culmination of an extraordinarily long process in which the form of the one replaced the
form of the other (6:2:12, p. 459, l. 29f.).

Gersonides admits that the generation of marvels differs from
other instances of generation in that the former is not generated
from something limited or defined (6:2:10, p. 448, l. 28; p. 452,
l. 17f.). That is, there is no way to account, for example, for
the generation of a serpent from a particular rod, or from a rod
at all. In his system, however, the existence of this distinction
can be explained by the fact that the laws of existent things
customarily overflow from the functions of the heavenly bodies
while marvels overflow directly from the Active Intellect (6:2:10,
p. 452, ll. 26ff.; 6:2:11, p. 453, ll. 27ff.). They occur

providentially, but the good they cause is a temporary and hence
accidental good which is occasionally needed to supplement that
which is lacking from the essential good of the nomos which overflows from the motions of the heavenly bodies (6:2:12, p. 455, ll.
6ff.; 6;2:10, p. 451, ll. 28ff.).

Thus, in Gersonides' view, a marvel is an extraordinary
phenomenon in that it is not the result of the order which overflows from the heavens, but it is not supernatural insofar as it
is contained within the nomos which the Active Intellect conceives
and requires no intervention from or generation of will in a
separate intellect. The marvel occurs not in a breach of natural
custom but rather from the degree of perfection of the intellect
of the prophet. The prophet can predict or associate himself with
a naturally occurring marvel insofar as his conception has developed and approximates the Active Intellect. We can infer that it
was because Moses' knowledge approximated that of the Active Intellect that he could anticipate the opening of the earth in the time
and place in which it occurred. The marvel did not occur by
necessity, for it depended on Moses' ability and inclination to
perfect his intellect. This seems to be the most sense that can
be made out of Gersonides' assertion that marvels occur because of
the overflow of providence from the Active Intellect to the prophet
in proportion to the perfection of his intellect. That Moses'
marvels are greater than others' is a consequence of his more
perfect knowledge.

The ambiguity which occurs in Gersonides' explanation of
Biblical accounts of marvels which occur in the sublunar world
results from the fact that he wants to affirm both that they
actually did occur in some extraordinary way and that their
generation does not involve an act of will or intervention from a
separate intellect. Thus, he chooses to correlate their occurrence
with the intellect of a prophet. We must assume, therefore, that
the earth would have opened, for example, even if Moses had not
chosen to develop his intellect but that, without his presence, it
would not have been a marvel because it would have had no providential aspect. In some sense, then, a marvel is an unusual
natural occurrence which derives its marvelous character from the
ability of the prophet to utilize it for providential ends.

With regard to Biblical accounts of marvels which are related
to the supralunar world, there is no such ambiguity. This is
because Gersonides denies that there is a possibility of change—
marvelous or otherwise—in the natural order of the heavens,
because it is the Active Intellect which causes marvels and the

heavens are not subject to its influence, and because any change
in the motions or functions of the heavens would cause the whole
of the sublunar world, which overflows from the heavens, to pass
away (6:2:12, p. 456, ll. 8ff.). As a result, Gersonides explains
all Biblical accounts of marvels in the supralunar world as
accounts of extraordinary human perception of natural and regular
celestial motion. Note, for example, his discussion of the sun
standing still for Joshua (6:2:12, p. 456, ll. 14ff.) and of the
lengthening of the shadow for Hezekiah (6:2:12, p. 458, ll. 26ff.).
In the former case, the sun continued its regular motion and the
marvel was in the speed of the Israelites' victory and Joshua's
foreknowledge of it. In the latter case, the marvel was in the
prophet's ability to predict the motions of clouds through his
expert knowledge of meteorology. Thus, while in the case of sublunar marvels Gersonides is willing to admit that something extraordinary, though natural, does occur, in cases involving the
supralunar world he makes no such admission. In both cases, however, the marvel depends on the perfection of the prophet's
intellect to predict it and/or to interpret and utilize it for
providential ends.

5) In the Introduction to The Wars (p. 3, ll. 3ff.),
Gersonides mentions that he will deal with these two religious
questions because they are very unclear. There as here he does
not explicitly discuss why they are examined immediately after the
question of the creation of the world. Below, however, in 6:2:9,
he places the question of marvels in the context of the distinctions he has drawn in this treatise between natural and volitional
coming to be. His analysis of marvels thus depends on his discussion of coming to be as well as on his prior discussions of the
natures of Active Intellect, providence and the heavens. In addition, the question of marvels becomes intertwined with that of the
generation of the world because of Maimonides' assertion, cited by
Gersonides in 6:2:1 below, that one's belief in marvels depends on
one's belief in creation ex nihilo (Guide 2:25). Once he has
argued speculatively for an alternative version of the generation
of the world and has demonstrated that this alternative is the
view of the Torah, he will then discuss marvels in a way that
implicitly shows that belief in them is not undercut by a rejection
of creation ex nihilo. He will seek to show that it is the
Aristotelian view that the world is eternal and proceeds from God
necessarily and not purposefully that eliminates the possibility
of marvels (cf. Guide 2:19). The generation of marvels does not

presuppose creation <u>ex nihilo</u>. Rather, it presupposes a
teleologically ordered universe in which part of the purpose of the
Creator is the preservation of sublunar species and the creation of
the possibility of the human achievement of immortality through
true conception. Both of these occur through the providence which
overflows from the Active Intellect, and marvels are caused by the
Active Intellect as part of its function of providence. All of
this depends on creation and not upon creation <u>ex nihilo</u>.

His discussion of the testing of a prophet clearly depends on
his understanding of marvels because he will examine in 6:2:13 the
relationship of accurate predictions of marvels and true prophecy.

Chapter One, in which we shall explain that it does not
necessarily follow from what is discussed in the Torah
and the Prophets that the world came to be from absolutely nothing.[6]

Summary

In this chapter, Gersonides asserts that the view that the
world came to be out of absolutely nothing does not necessarily
follow from the text and the principles of the Torah. In support
of this assertion, he argues as follows: a) All marvels described
in the Torah came to be from something. b) In principle, the Torah
is the repository of the truth and so cannot coerce us to believe
that which is false. c) Thus, as Maimonides asserts, the text of
the Torah must be interpreted to agree with the conclusive findings
of speculation.

Gersonides then asserts that, with regard to the issue of
creation, it was the text of the creation narrative in Genesis
which led him to the true conclusions which he reaches in Treatise
Six, Part One, by means of speculation.

He concludes with the observation that Maimonides is not
correct when he asserts that we must affirm the creation of the
world out of absolutely nothing in order to believe in the generation of marvels.

Translation

69aa
418

It is clearly obvious that in respect to the principles
of the Torah it does not necessarily follow that the world
came to be[7] something from nothing. The reason for this is
that we find that all the marvels were something from something, such as the coming to be of blood from water,[8] of
lice from dust,[9] and of a serpent from the rod.[10] Similarly,
the swallowing of the other rods by Aaron's rod[11] is not a
passing away to nothing.[12] Similarly, it is not necessary

419 that the wonder of the oil that was made by / Elisha[13] was
something from nothing. The reason for this is that, it is,
in our opinion, similar to the transformation of the rod into
a serpent,[14] for the air which entered the vessel when he
emptied it was transformed into oil.

In general, the Torah is not a coercive nomos which
compels us to believe things that are incorrect, or to do

things which have no benefit, as the multitude thinks.

1. 5   Rather, it is a perfect nomos of absolute perfection, as is
made clear in our commentary to the Torah,[15] so that the
perfection in it will lead men to desire that they conduct
themselves according to this perfect nomos. This is in
accordance with the definition of a perfect nomos, as the
Philosopher[16] explained.[17]

        This being the case, it is clear that there is nothing
in the Torah which leads us to believe that which is false,
for that which is false would not in itself lead to a belief

1. 10   in it and that which follows from it. It is therefore proper
that we posit what is in the Torah in a way that is suitable
to speculation.

        It is for this reason that the Master the Guide[18]
explained everything that is in the Torah which would lead
one to think that God, may He be blessed, is corporeal in a
way that does not contradict that which is made clear by way
of speculation.[19] Also, for this reason he said that if it
were clear by way of speculation that the eternity of
the world was necessarily true, then he would have been compelled to interpret that in the Torah which apparently

1. 15   differs with this view in a way that was suitable to speculation.[20]

        It is proper that you know that the opposite of this
notion occurred to us concerning that which is mentioned in
the Torah with regard to the generation of the world. That
is, we did not need to force ourselves to explain what is in
the Torah concerning this matter in a way that was suitable
to speculation. Rather, what is in the Torah was the cause
in some way of the truth reaching us by way of speculation.

1. 20   For what stimulated us to find the truth of this investigation was what was explained to us by the explanation in it
concerning the generation of the world. For its discussion
of the notion is done in a way that very much directs the
investigator in this investigation to find the truth in it,
as is explained in our explanation of the passage in which
the notion of the generation of the world is discussed.[21]
And it is appropriate that this should be the case with the
Torah, because the Torah is a nomos by which man is guided

1. 25   to the acquisition of his final perfection, as we have
explained in our commentary to the Torah.[22] Therefore, the
Torah must necessarily direct man to the realization of the
truth of deep problems, the realization of which is very

difficult. The reason for this is that, when the truth of
these problems is revealed by way of the tradition and
direction, together with this knowledge, in some way, of
those things which conduct man to the truth of the problems,
then much of the difficulty of their realization will be
removed.

1. 30   Prior to our explanation of the words of the Torah
concerning the generation of the world, we wanted first to
introduce the fact that it does not necessarily follow from
marvels that the world came to be something from nothing.
For the Master the Guide explained that it is this that compels us to believe in the generation of the world—for if it
were not necessary to believe in marvels, it would be easy
for us to explain that which is in the Torah about the generation of the world in a way that is suitable to the view of
1. 35   the Philosopher.[23]   Now, how marvels are possible, who is
their cause, from which things they are possible, and what
420   is their purpose / —these are among the things that we shall
investigate after we complete an explanation of that which is
in the Torah concerning the notion of the generation of the
world.[24]

6) The phrase yesh me-ʾayin be-muḥlat ("something from
absolutely nothing") is a reference back to Part One of this treatise, discussed above in the introduction. Briefly, he considers
there the position that absolutely nothing preceded the existence
of this world—a position which he attributes to John Philoponus,
the later Kalam, Maimonides and many of the sages of the Torah—and
finds it untenable for several reasons (cf. 6:1:17, pp. 364ff.).
As an alternative, he proposes that the world came to be from body
which does not preserve its shape. This body is something in the
sense that it is a body, and is nothing in that it has no form
(6:1:17, p. 367f.). Thus, he uses the word "absolutely" to designate the incorrect position and to distinguish it from his own.
He is less precise in the chapter below (p. 418, l. 2), where he
omits this word.

His purpose in this chapter is to show that there is nothing
in Scripture which contradicts the position he offers in Part One.
He will do so as follows:

a) He will demonstrate with Biblical examples that the Bible's
accounts of marvels neither assert nor entail that any of them
came to be out of nothing. The relationship between the generation
of the world and the generation of marvels is explained above, note
#5;

b) He will assert that, in any case, the Torah cannot compel
us to believe what is incorrect. As explained above, note #1, the
Torah is a perfect nomos, the primary function of which is to guide
men to the truth;

c) He will claim that, in this case of the generation of the
world, the meaning of the Scriptural text obviously accords with
speculation and indeed directed Gersonides to reach the speculative
conclusions he reaches; and

d) He will deny the correlation which Maimonides makes between
belief in creation ex nihilo and belief in marvels.

7) A careful and exhaustive examination of Gersonides' usage
of the words based on the roots, hvh and ḥdsh, in both parts of
this treatise reveals that he uses them interchangeably and with
nearly equal frequency. The possible exception is that he is more
inclined to use ḥdsh with regard to things whose existence is
accidental, e.g., time and motion (cf. 6:1:10-12). One hesitates,
however, to conclude that this is because the root hvh has the
connotation of "being," because he is more apt to speak of
ḥidush ha-ʿolam than of havayat ha-ʿolam. We have nevertheless
preserved the distinction by translating havayah as "coming to be,"

following the traditional Hebrew translation of Aristotle's De
Generatione et Corruptione as ha-havayah ve-ha-hefsed, and ḥidush
as "generation."

Note that Pines, in his translation of The Guide, uses the
phrase "produced in time" as an equivalent of Ibn Tibbon's ḥdsh.
Given Gersonides' argument above (6:1:7) that everything which is
generated must have a temporal beginning and that continuous
emanation is a logical and ontological impossibility, there are no
grounds to assume that he uses different terms to distinguish
between temporal and atemporal generation.

8) Exod 7:20. Note that this example and those which follow
below are instances of marvels which Maimonides cites in his discussion of this issue (Guide 2:29). Maimonides' view is that these
marvels were not permanent and therefore should not be assumed to
have involved an alteration in the nature of the object. Rather,
they occur through a temporary suspension of nature which God
willed in advance at creation (cf. his Commentary to Mishnah ʾAvot
5:6; Shemonah Peraqim, end). In his presentation here, Gersonides
is implicitly disagreeing with Maimonides' view. That is, he is
presuming in his discussion of these marvels that they come to be
in accordance with natural law. He will make this implicit pre-
sumption explicit in his discussion below, 6:2:9-12 (see above,
note #4).

9) Exod 8:12.

10) Exod 4:3.

11) Exod 7:12.

12) Aristotle's argument for the eternity of the world (his
eighth argument, as Gersonides lists them in 6:1:3) based on his
assertion that everything which comes to be must pass away is
discussed at length in the first part of this treatise (6:1:3,
p. 300, ll. 31ff.; 6:1:27, pp. 403ff.; cf. De Generatione et
Corruptione 1.3.317a32ff.). Gersonides argues that though the
world comes to be, it does not pass away (6:1:14,16). His argument
is based in part on the distinction he draws between natural and
willful coming to be and passing away. Thus, the significance of
his observation here that marvels also do not pass away to nothing
is related to his assertion that the world neither has natural nor
volitional causes for passing away. Since he will assert below
that the generation of marvels resembles both natural and volitional coming to be in different respects (6:2:10, p. 452, ll.
14ff.), the fact that marvels in the Torah do not pass away to

nothing is a Scriptural corroboration of his position concerning
the world as a whole.

In addition, the connection noted above (note #5) which
Maimonides makes between belief in marvels and in the creation of
the world out of absolutely nothing compels Gersonides to make this
observation in order to show that such a connection is not necessary.

13) 2 Kgs 4:2ff.

14) For a more detailed discussion of the nature of the
marvelous transformation of the rod into the serpent, see below,
6:2:12, p. 459, ll. 28ff. Elisha's wonder resembles it in that
they are both substantial marvels (6:2:9, p. 442, l. 13).

15) CT 2a and 2c. See note #1 above for a discussion of his
conception of the Torah and its relationship to speculation.

16) "The Philosopher" is the way that Gersonides refers to
Aristotle.

17) Cf. Rhetorica 1.15.1375a22ff., where Aristotle
distinguishes the written, mutable law from the unwritten, eternal,
immutable law. The latter accords with nature and it is its jus-
tice which persuades men to follow it. Note Gersonides' discussion
below (6:2:8, p. 439, ll. 34ff.) of the way in which the perfect
nomos of the Lord causes the supralunar movers to desire to be
subjected to it.

The belief that it is the perfection of the divine nomos
which persuades people to follow it in a compelling manner forms,
in part, the rationale for all of his speculative investigations.
In his Commentary to the Torah (9a), he rejects the claim that
following the commandments should precede study of the science of
existent things. He does so because he believes that we must first
conceive that there exists a First Cause which is to be feared and
served. Such a conception guides us to the conclusion that we
should fear and serve Him. This is consistent with his claim
(CT 2b and 2c) that both the second part—political science—and
the third part—the science of existent things—of the nomos of
the Torah are for the purpose of promoting its first part—the
obedience of the commandments. They promote such obedience by
leading, respectively, to the perfection of human virtues and the
human intellect. It is for this reason, he states, that the Torah
begins with the complex matter of creation (CT 9a). It does so
because an understanding of the marvelous nomos which governs this
world compels subservience to its Creator.

18) Maimonides.

19) Guide 1:55.

20) Guide 2:25. In rejecting Maimonides' argument for the
creation of the world out of nothing (6:1:17, p. 366f.), Gersonides
uses this statement both to undercut Maimonides and to support his
own assertion that his own view does not contradict the view of the
Torah. Maimonides states that the texts of the Torah which imply
the creation of the world in time could be interpreted figuratively
if he had wished to affirm the eternity of the world. As Gersonides presents it, Maimonides does not do so because of the following: a) The arguments in support of Aristotle's position are not
compelling because they incorrectly disregard the distinction
between the nature of a thing after it has been produced in time
and its nature prior to its actualization (Guide 2:17.). b) Since
speculation does not require the affirmation of the eternity of the
world, Aristotle's position should not be adopted because it entails
that the world exists by necessity, with no possibility that natural
custom can be altered. This consequence makes impossible the belief
both in the Law and its promises of reward and punishment, and in
miracles (Guide 2:25).

In the first part of this treatise (6:1:17, p. 366, ll. 10ff.),
Gersonides disputes the use which Maimonides makes of the distinction between the nature of a thing after it has been produced in
time and its nature prior to its actualization. He states that the
valid conclusion to be drawn from this distinction is not that no
inference is possible from the nature of the existent world to that
which preceded it. Rather, we cannot assume that what existed
prior to the creation of the world possessed those characteristics
which this world possesses by virtue of its having come to be.
Other characteristics, however, which are not the result of its
coming to be, can be attributed to the world at the moment of its
coming to be. For example, the preservation of its shape cannot
be attributed to it prior to its coming to be because this is an
effect of the Lord's creative agency. The existence of a body which
does not preserve its shape, on the other hand, is not to be dis-
counted, because such a body would not be the effect of an agent.

Having shown that Maimonides is incorrect in his dismissal of
speculation as a means of determining the origins of the world,
Gersonides will now attempt to show that one need not believe in
the creation of the world out of nothing in order to believe in
the Torah and its marvels. Though he agrees that if the world
were eternal there could be no marvels (CT 9a), there is no need

to believe in creation out of absolutely nothing. In the discussion of marvels below, he will argue that, given his own view of the coming to be of the world, marvels can still occur and the following of the Torah still produces beneficial effects (rewards).

21) 6:2:8 below. See note #1 above for a discussion of his assertion that the literal meaning of Genesis agrees with the views he has reached speculatively.

22) CT 2a.

23) Guide 2:25. See note #20 above.

24) See below, 6:2:9-12.

Chapter Two, in which the different ways in which
reꞋshit is said in our language will be discussed.

Summary

Gersonides begins by asserting that an understanding of the
creation narrative of Genesis requires a prior understanding of the
terms used in that narrative. He then proceeds to discuss the
different senses of priority which are referred to by the Torah's
use of the term reꞋshit. He concludes that the term, as it functions in Gen 1:1, refers to priority in cause and in nature.

Translation

69aa
420

It is appropriate that we first explain the terms which
the Torah uses in its discussion of the generation of the
world before we explain the words of the Torah concerning

1. 5 this,[25] for an understanding of the simple expression is
necessarily prior to an understanding of the composite
expression.[26]

We assert that, in our language, the intention of
reꞋshit is "that part of a thing which is prior to the rest
of its parts," in whatever priority of the priorities.[27]

It can mean temporal priority, as in: "In the beginning
(reꞋshit) of the reign of Jehoiakim."[28] That is to say, in
the earliest part of the time in which Jehoiakim reigned.
Similarly: "Of the first (reꞋshit) of your dough (you shall

1. 10 set aside a cake)."[29] That is to say, the part of the dough
which they shall set aside first in time. Similarly: "The
first (reꞋshit) shearing of your sheep."[30] And there are
many such examples.

Or it can mean priority in order, as it says "They shall
not exchange nor pass along the first (reꞋshit) portion of
the land, for it is holy to the Lord."[31] That is to say, the
part which is prior in order, referring to one of the spatial
dimensions discussed above it.[32] And it is also possible
that this is its meaning when it says, "The beginning
(reꞋshit) of his kingdom was Babel."[33] And this is the
meaning when it says, "The beginning (reꞋshit) of wisdom is

1. 15 the fear of the Lord,"[34] for the fear of the Lord is wisdom,"[35] as it is written, "Behold, the fear of the Lord, that
is wisdom."[36] And therefore it says that the prior part /

171

69ab   of wisdom is the wisdom through which one is directed to the
       fear of the Lord.   This is political philosophy, for the
       perfection of the virtues is necessarily prior in order to
       intellectual perfection.   And this is one of the things that
       requires no explanation for the speculator in this book.[37]

            Or it can mean priority in degree, as in: "(Israel is)
1. 20 the Lord's hallowed portion, the first (re$^{?}$shit) of His
       produce."[38]   That is to say, this is the part of the species
       which is separated for the service of the Lord more than the
       rest of the species, and this is priority in degree.

            Or it can mean priority in cause and in nature, as in:
       "The Lord made me (in wisdom) as the beginning (re$^{?}$shit) of
       His way."[39]   For the intelligible order is prior in cause
       and in nature to the activity[40] which is generated from it.
       And it is with this last intention that it is said: "In the
       beginning (be-re$^{?}$shit) God created,"[41] as will be explained
       below.[42]

25) This is the method he follows in his <u>Commentary to the Torah</u>. That is, he begins with an explanation of the words of a Biblical passage (bi'ur ha-millot) and then proceeds to an explanation of the contents of that passage (bi'ur divrei ha-parashah). This is in accordance with his comment above (6:2:1, p. 419, ll. 27ff.) that the truth of difficult problems is realized through a combination of the guidance of the Torah and one's speculative knowledge. His assumption is that one can benefit from the Torah's guidance only if one possesses the required knowledge of the terms and concepts of which the Torah speaks.

In the following chapters (6:2:2-7) he will explain the meaning of those terms used in the Genesis narrative of creation which he believes must be understood properly if one is to understand the Torah's view of the creation of the world.

26) Cf. <u>Categoriae</u> 2.1a16ff.

27) Cf. <u>Guide</u> 2:30, where Maimonides distinguishes between that which is temporally prior (ri'shon) and that which is the principle of a thing (re'shit).

In the <u>Categoriae</u> 12.14a25ff., Aristotle lists five senses of the term "prior." They are: a) Temporal priority. b) The priority of x to y when the existence of y is dependent upon the existence of x and the converse is not true. For example, Aristotle says that one is prior to two because the existence of two entails the existence of one. J. L. Ackrill refers to this as the priority of "what does not reciprocate as to implication of existence" (<u>Aristotle's Categories and De Interpretatione</u> [Oxford, 1963], p. 39). c) Priority in order, as the elements of a geometrical demonstration are prior to its propositions, or as the letters are prior to syllables in grammar. d) The priority of that which is better and more honorable, as when we refer to those whom we love and honor as 'prior.' (Aristotle regards this sense as most far-fetched.) e) Priority in nature, as when x is prior to y if the existence of each implies the existence of the other but when the existence of x may be said to be the cause of the existence of y and the existence of y is not the cause of the existence of x. For example, the existence of a man and the truth of the proposition that he exists each imply the existence of the other. While the existence of the man is the cause of the truth of the proposition, the truth of the proposition is not the cause of his existence.

The way in which the fifth sense, priority in nature, differs from the second sense, priority in existence, is made clearer in

the discussion which follows in the Categoriae 13.14b24ff., where
Aristotle discusses simultaneity. Two things are simultaneous by
nature if they "reciprocate as to implication of existence" but
each does not cause the existence of the other. For example, a
double and a half are simultaneous by nature, implying each other's
existence but not causing each other's existence. By contrast, the
fifth sense of priority includes reciprocal implication of existence
but there is a priority in the cause of existence. In the second
sense of priority, there is neither reciprocal implication of
existence nor causation of existence. Though the existence of two
depends on the existence of one, so that one is prior to two, one
does not cause the existence of two as the existence of man causes
the existence of the proposition asserting his existence. Thus,
that which is prior in cause and in nature (fifth sense) exists
simultaneously with that which is posterior to it while that which
is prior in the second sense does not necessarily exist simultaneously with that which is posterior to it.

In the Metaphysica 5.11.1018b8-1019a14, Aristotle provides us
with another discussion of the uses of the term priority. Though
Gersonides seems to be following the discussion in the Categoriae,
the discussion in the Metaphysica is helpful in clarifying the
intentions of both Aristotle and Gersonides. In the Metaphysica,
Aristotle lists the following uses of the term priority:

a) The priority of a thing which is nearer to some natural or
conventional beginning. For example, a thing is prior in place
when it is nearer to a given place. A thing is prior in time when
it is nearer to a given moment. It is prior in movement when it
is nearer to a given first mover. It is prior in power when it
causes the posterior to move. It is prior in arrangement when it
is nearer with reference to something arranged according to a rule.

b) Priority in knowledge. With regard to priority in formula
or definition, universals are prior in knowledge to individuals.
With regard to priority in sensation or perception, individuals
are prior in knowledge to universals. That is, universals which
are prior in the "order of being" may be known by humans after
they know sensible individual objects (cf. Analytica Posteriora
1.2.71b33-72a5). For example, though the universal "musical" is
prior in definition to individual instances of musical persons, we
come to know musical individuals prior to our knowing the universal
"musical." We induce the latter from our knowledge of individuals
(cf. Topica 6.4.141b6ff.). (Note that priority in knowledge is not
presented here as a distinct sense of priority. Rather, Aristotle
is explaining that, with reference to our knowledge, we use the

term in two different senses: 1) the sense in which the universal
is prior to its particular instantiations, i.e., priority in nature;
and 2) the sense in which the particular is prior to the universal
it approximates, i.e., priority in order.)

c) The attributes of a prior thing are called prior. Thus
straightness, an attribute of a line, is prior to smoothness, an
attribute of a surface, because a line is prior to a surface.
(Note that this is not a distinct sense of priority but is rather
a rule for applying the term to attributes.)

d) Priority in respect of nature and substance, which refers
to the priority of those things which can be without posterior
things while those posterior things cannot be without them. Here,
Aristotle appears to be combining the second and fifth senses of
priority as he enumerates them in the Categoriae. The above
definition does not speak of reciprocal implication of existence
and so appears to be his second sense of priority in the Categoriae.
On the other hand, he refers this sense of priority to Plato.
W. D. Ross's note to his translation in the Oxford edition cites
the following passage from the Timaeus 34b-c. The translation
which follows is that of Benjamin Jowett (The Collected Dialogues
of Plato, edited by Edith Hamilton and Huntington Cairns, [Prince-
ton, 1961]):

> Now God did not make the soul after the body,...for
> when he put them together he would never have allowed
> that the elder should be ruled by the younger...
> Whereas he made the soul in origin and excellence prior
> to and older than the body, to be the ruler and mistress,
> of whom the body was to be the subject.

In this sense, Aristotle explains, that which is prior is prior
with respect to actuality. Though an individual approximation of
a definition is prior in the accidental sense of being, the definition is prior in the essential sense of being (cf. Metaphysica
5.7.1017a8-1017b9). The definition or the universal or the nature
is what the thing actually is. An individual instance of that
definition is potentially that definition. Elsewhere, he writes
that "what is posterior in the order of becoming is prior in the
order of nature" (Physica 8.7.261a13, Oxford translation), and
that (De Generatione Animalium 2.6.742a20, Oxford translation):

> There is a difference between the end or final cause
> and that which exists for the sake of it; the latter
> is prior in order of development, the former is prior
> in reality.

All of this appears to correspond to the fifth sense in the
Categoriae, priority in nature. The combination of these two

senses here may indicate their interrelatedness and may help to
explain why Gersonides, as will be discussed below in this note,
seems to omit the second sense of the term.

Thus, the first sense of priority, in the Categoriae,
temporal priority, is presented in the Metaphysica as an instance
of a class of prior things all of which are prior in the sense of
their proximity to a natural or conventional beginning. The
second sense in the Categoriae, priority where there is no reciprocal implication of existence, is omitted from the discussion in
the Metaphysica, except in Aristotle's allusion to it under the
category of priority in nature and substance. The third sense,
priority in order, is presented in the Metaphysica as one of the
senses of priority of our knowledge. The particular, sensible
thing is prior to its universal definition. The fourth sense,
priority in honor or good is omitted from the Metaphysica. The
fifth sense, priority in nature, corresponds to the fourth sense
in the Metaphysica, priority in nature and substance, and to one
of the senses of priority of knowledge—the priority of the universal definition to its particular instances.

With this as background, we can approach Gersonides' list.
His first sense of temporal priority corresponds to the first
sense of priority in the Categoriae, and to the temporal subdivision
of the first sense of priority in the Metaphysica.

With regard to Gersonides' second sense, priority in order,
only his third example clearly reveals his intended meaning. He
says that the perfection of the virtues is prior in order to
intellectual perfection. This corresponds to Aristotle's third
sense in the Categoriae and to his discussion in the Metaphysica
of the priority in our knowledge of the particular to the universal
definition. As the elements of a geometrical demonstration are
prior in order to its propositions, as the introduction of a speech
is prior in order to its exposition, or as our knowledge of particulars is prior in knowledge to our knowledge of their universal
definition, so the perfection of one's virtues is prior to the
perfection of one's intellect. As discussed below, note #37, the
perfection of the virtues is for the sake of the end or final cause
of intellectual perfection. It is prior in order and in coming to
be, though it is posterior in nature or reality. (Cf. De Generatione Animalium 2.2.742a20, quoted above in this note.)

Gersonides' two other examples of priority in order are
ambiguous and his intentions in citing them need to be read in
light of his third example. That is, he cannot mean that the
"first portion of the land" is prior in order because "it is holy

to the Lord" (Ezek 48:14), because priority with reference to the
sanctity of being devoted to the Lord is discussed explicitly in
his discussion of his third sense, priority in degree. Similarly,
if we assume that he is being consistent in his examples of priority in order, then he must mean that Nimrod's acquisition of Babel
as a portion of his kingdom was prior in order to his acquisition
of the entirety of his kingdom and was a necessary prerequisite for
the entirety of his kingdom, but that Babel was posterior in nature
to his entire kingdom as a whole in that it was for the sake of his
whole kingdom.

   Note that when he speaks below of hylic priority (6:2:8,
p. 427, l. 31; cf. note #215), he is referring to what he here
calls priority in order. The heavenly bodies, for example, are
hylically prior to their separate forms (6:2:8, p. 429, l. 4) from
which they proceed and which are their final cause and end. That
is, they are prior in coming to be but posterior in nature. They
are the corporeal approximations of the separate forms.

   Gersonides' third sense, priority in degree, corresponds to
Aristotle's fourth sense in the Categoriae, priority of that which
is better and more honorable. The service of the Lord is the most
honorable human activity. It is, in a sense, morally prior.

   Gersonides' fourth sense, priority in cause and in nature,
corresponds to Aristotle's fifth sense in the Categoriae, priority
in nature, and to Aristotle's fourth sense in the Metaphysica,
priority in nature and in substance. The example he provides is
the priority of the intelligible order. On the meaning of "nature"
with regard to the intelligible order, see below, note #214. The
nature of a thing is its form or definition. It is what that thing
truly is. The intelligible world is prior in nature to the material world, because matter receives the forms contained in the
nomos of the intelligible world (6:2:4, p. 421, ll. 3-18; cf.
below, notes #49 and #51) and is clothed by those forms. The form
is the nature of the material object of which it is the form. In
Aristotle's terms, the existence of the intelligible world and of
the material world imply the existence of the other. The existence
of the intelligible world can be said to be the cause of the world
of material things, while the converse is not true.

   Thus, Gersonides' list corresponds to Aristotle's list in the
Categoriae, but does not include the second of the five senses of
priority in the Categoriae, i.e., the priority of a to b when there
is no reciprocal implication of existence but where b cannot exist
unless a exists. As discussed above in this note, Aristotle himself had combined the second and the fifth senses of the Categoriae

in his discussion of priority in nature and substance in the
Metaphysica. On the basis of Gersonides' discussion below
(6:2:8, p. 434, ll. 30ff.; cf. below, notes #396, #397, #400-#402,
#404), we may infer that he omits the second sense of priority of
the Categoriae because he does not believe that there can be nonreciprocal implication of existence. In a teleologically ordered
universe, if the existence of a implies the existence of b, then a
cannot exist without b and b cannot exist without a. That is,
there is reciprocal implication of existence in all cases because
a cause cannot fulfill its function without the existence of its
effect. This view becomes explicit in his discussion of the
heavens' relation to the sublunar world. Though the heavens are
prior in cause and in existence to the sublunar world, they cannot
exist without the sublunar world. Thus the existence of the
heavens implies the existence of the sublunar world as its effect
and the existence of the sublunar world entails the existence of
the heavens as its cause. Much of Gersonides' argument for creation in the first part of this treatise depends on this view.

28) Jer 27:1.

29) Num 15:20; cf. 15:21.

30) Deut 18:4.

31) Ezek 48:14.

32) Ezek 48:8ff. The priority in order here refers to the
land which is to be set aside for the priests and which is thus
sacred. On the meaning of "priority in order," see above, note #27.

33) Gen 10:10. Gersonides is tentative here because of the
ambiguity of the text, which can be taken to mean temporal priority,
i.e., that Babel was Nimrod's first conquest. The meaning of
re'shit here seems to be that Babel and the other listed states
were most prominent parts of Nimrod's kingdom. The new translation
of the Jewish Publication Society (Philadelphia, 1962) translates
the term as "mainstays." On the meaning of "priority in order" in
this verse, see above, note #27.

34) Ps 111:10.

35) Job 28:28.

36) Ibid.

37) See his discussion in the introduction to his Commentary
to the Torah (2a-c), where he identifies political science
(ha-ḥakhmah ha-medinit) as that part of the nomos of the Torah

which leads to the perfection of virtues and dispositions. This "welfare of the body" (<u>tiqqun ha-guf</u>) leads to observance of the commandments as does the "welfare of the soul" (<u>tiqqun ha-nefesh</u>) which is promoted by the study of the science of existent things. It is not itself commanded by the Torah, because it would be extremely difficult to comply with a commandment to react emotionally in a precise way. Rather, the Torah arouses us to the perfection of our virtues by telling stories which can serve as positive and negative examples. See note #17 above for a discussion of his belief in the priority of speculation.

His statement here that "the perfection of the virtues is necessarily prior in order to intellectual perfection" is in accordance with the view of Maimonides, who in turn is influenced in this respect by Alfarabi (cf. the introductory essay of Shlomo Pines to <u>The Guide of the Perplexed</u> [Chicago, 1963], pp. lxxxvi-xcii; Leo Strauss, <u>Persecution and the Art of Writing</u> [Glencoe, Illinois, 1952], pp. 9-21). In the <u>Guide</u> (3:27, 54), Maimonides asserts that intellectual perfection (the welfare of the soul) is the end of man and is the means "through which the ultimate perfection is achieved" (3:27, p. 511 of Pines' translation; cf. 3:54, p. 634f.). It is thus far more important than the perfection of the moral virtues (the welfare of the body) but the latter is nevertheless prior in order (see above, note #27, for a discussion of priority in order). Maimonides writes (3:27, Pines' translation, p. 510):

> Know that as between these two aims, one is undubitably greater in nobility, namely, the welfare of the soul-I mean the procuring of correct opinions-while the second aim-I mean the welfare of the body-is prior in nature and in time. The latter aim consists in the governance of the city and the well-being of the states of all its people according to their capacity. This second aim is the more certain one, and it is the one regarding which every effort has been made precisely to expound it and all its particulars. For the first aim can only be achieved after achieving this second one.

Though Maimonides states here that the welfare of the body is prior to the welfare of the soul in nature and in time, his disagreement with Gersonides appears to be one of terminology and not of substance. While Maimonides does distinguish between temporal and natural priority (cf. above, note #27), in this passage he fails to distinguish priority in order and in degree in relation to temporal and natural priority. Thus, when he states here that the welfare of the body is prior in nature to the welfare of the soul, it is clear from the larger context that he is talking about what

Gersonides would call priority in order. Gersonides appears to
be following Aristotle, who states, "What is posterior in the
order of becoming is prior in the order of nature" (Physica 8.7.
261a13, Oxford translation.) As Gersonides writes in his
Commentary to the Torah (9a, ll. 19ff.):

> The part (of the Torah's intentions) which encompasses
> the science of existent things proceeds in the path of
> perfection and form for the other parts (i.e., the per-
> formance of the commandments and political science).
> Thus it is proper for us to posit first that it is (the
> science of existent things) which was the (primary)
> intention of the Torah.

38) Jer 2:3.

39) Both the printed editions and the manuscripts consulted
add "in wisdom" (be-ḥakhmah) to this quotation from Prov 8:22,
perhaps conflating it with Prov 3:19.

40) The letters pᶜl can be read as poᶜel ("cause" or "agent")
or as poᶜal ("activity"). In the present context both readings
are appropriate because, as he makes clear in chapter eight below
(p. 427, ll. 27ff.), the intelligible order of the movers of the
heavenly bodies are prior in cause and in nature both to the
heavenly bodies and to the lower existent world which overflows
from the heavenly bodies. Since the heavenly bodies and their
activity are themselves the cause of lower existence, the reference
here remains ambiguous.

41) Gen 1:1.

42) 6:2:8, p. 427, ll. 27ff.

TREATISE SIX, PART TWO: CHAPTER THREE

THE MEANING OF ᵓEREṢ (EARTH)

Chapter Three, in which the different ways in which
ᵓereṣ is said in our language will be explained.

Summary

Gersonides discusses the different senses of the term ᵓereṣ
in the Torah and concludes that the term in Gen 1:1 and 1:2 refers
to the sublunar world.

Translation

1. 25
69ab
420

ᵓereṣ is an equivocal[43] term which is said in particular
with reference to the earthly element, and numerous instances
of this can be found.[44] It is used in general to refer to
all the elements. This is so because the earthly element is
in a lowly place, and the elements in general are below the
heaven. Therefore, this usage is frequent when the word is
used with the word "heaven," as it says, "What god is there
in the heaven or on the earth (ᵓereṣ) that equals Your works
and mighty acts,"[45] and as in: "In the beginning God created

421   the heaven and / the earth (ha-ᵓareṣ)."[46] Numerous instances
of this can also be found. And it is in this sense that it
is said: "And the earth (ve-ha-ᵓareṣ) was unformed and void
(tohu va-vohu)," for this is the same sense of "earth" that
was mentioned in the preceding verse.[47]

43) __mishtatef__. His use of the term here follows the definition
given by Aristotle in the __Categoriae__ 1.1a1 (Oxford translation):

> Things are said to be named 'equivocally' when, though
> they have a common name, the definition corresponding
> with the name differs for each.

For a more complete discussion of his understanding of equivocation, see MH 3:2, and the notes to it by Norbert M. Samuelson,
__Gersonides: On God's Knowledge__ (Toronto, 1977), pp. 134ff.

44) In the Torah. His discussion of the senses of this term
follows that of Maimonides, __Guide__ 2:30.

45) Deut 3:24.

46) Gen 1:1.

47) In Gen 1:1, where the heaven and the earth are mentioned
together.

TREATISE SIX, PART TWO: CHAPTER FOUR
THE MEANING OF TOHU AND BOHU
(LAST FORM AND PRIME MATTER)

Chapter Four, in which it will be explained what is
intended in the Torah by tohu and bohu.

Summary

Gersonides explains the meaning of the terms tohu and bohu
in Gen 1:2 as "last form" and "prime matter" by referring to the
use of those terms in Isa 34:11, to the discussion of those terms
by Abraham bar Ḥiyya and to a rabbinic discussion of the terms.

Translation

69ab
421

Tohu and bohu are used in our language to refer to
"the matter most distant from (a given) existent thing[48]
and to its last form which is prior in order."[49] As it
1. 5   says, "And he shall stretch over it a line of tohu and a
stone of bohu."[50] This is the dwelling place of those
animals which he mentions in the place of destruction. He
means by it that they will dwell there until they prepare
that place for them, as if prime matter[51] and last form
would be stretched out there for them for the construction
of what they need, for they are the elements of the thing
and its foundations. The point of this example is that one
who wants to build a house must first draw an image of the
1. 10 lower area of the house in the magnitude that he wishes and
in the image that he wishes—whether rectangular or
circular—and afterwards he brings the stones which are the
elements of the walls and their foundations.

The relation of the form to tohu—that is, the line
which they will first stretch out for the construction—is
like the relation of the matter to bohu—that is, the
stones—for the matter is the substratum of the form, as if
to say "it is in it (bo huᵓ)."[52] Rabbi Abraham bar Ḥiyya
the Prince discusses this sense of the term bohu in the
1. 15 book, The Form of the Earth.[53] The form is prior to the
matter since the matter is for the sake of the form. And
it is in this way that it says: "The earth was tohu and
bohu" (Gen 1:2), that is to say, last form and prime matter.
This form is the elemental forms, by means of which prime
matter is prepared to receive the rest of the forms.[54]

183

How marvelous is the explanation of this of our rabbis,
may their memories be for a blessing. They said that <u>tohu</u>
l. 20 is "a green line which encompasses the world," and <u>bohu</u> are
"slimy stones."[55] The reason for this is that these forms
are contrary, and elements are elements for things in
respect of their mixture which is an intermediate thing.[56]
So they took an instance of a thing which is an intermediate
between the contraries—the green. They took the intermediate color[57] because it is more generally recognized[58]
than the intermediate between the rest of the contraries.

l. 25 And their term "slimy" (<u>mefullamot</u>) has the sense of "so-and-
so" (<u>peloniy</u>), for its intention is that which is completely
hidden and concealed. Therefore, it was composed of so-and-
so (<u>peloniy</u>), and so-and-so (<u>ᶜalmoniy</u>), for they are two
expressions which indicate the hidden and the concealed.
And you, the speculator, already know what there is of the
hidden in the state of affairs of prime matter as well as
the deficiency in its apprehension in its respect.[59]

48) The text is awkward here: <u>ha-ḥomer ha-raḥoq la-nimṣaʾ ha-</u>
<u>huʾ</u>. He uses the term "distant" (<u>reḥoqah</u>) below (6:2:5, p. 423,
1. 7) to describe the element earth, which is lowest in the
hierarchy of elements and "is more lacking in form and goodness
than any of the other elements" (1. 9f.). In speaking here of
the material body which is most lacking in existence, he is referring to what he will call <u>ḥomer rishon</u> ("prime matter"). For a
discussion of what he means by "lacking in existence," see below,
notes #51 and #215.

Because of the ambiguous way in which he uses this term, as
discussed below, note #51, it is not possible to determine with
certainty from the context here whether he means to refer here to
an absolutely potential, formless prime matter, or to a prime
matter which is informed by a form of corporeality which prepares
it to receive the forms of the elements, or if he does not make
such a distinction (also see note #49). If we assume that by "last
form" (<u>ṣurah aḥaronah</u>) he is referring to the form of tridimensionality which is prior to the elemental forms and which is the form
of what functions as matter for the elemental forms, it follows
that the matter to which he is referring here is prime matter
informed by the form of tridimensionality. (See below, note #49,
for an explanation of this.)

49) The Leipzig edition of the text designates the preceding
as a quotation, but I have been unable to locate the reference.
As in a similar instance above (6:2:2, p. 420, 1. 6f.), Gersonides
is defining the terms under discussion.

Determining the referent of the term "last form" (<u>ṣurah</u>
<u>aḥaronah</u>) is something of a problem. Presumably he calls it "last"
because it is the lowest in the hierarchy of forms, in which God
is the first form. It is last among the forms when they are
discussed in terms of priority in cause and in nature (cf. above,
6:2:2, p. 420, 11. 21-24, and note #27). As such, it corresponds
to the matter which is most lacking in existence (see notes #48
and #51).

The problem is that he makes no mention of "last form" either
in the first part of this treatise or in 6:2:7 and 8 below—the
two places where he makes a comprehensive presentation of his view
of the process of the coming to be of the world. In those places,
he speaks only of the elemental forms (<u>ṣurot yesodiyot</u>) and he
gives the impression that he does not recognize a prior stage in
which last form informs prime matter. He writes in the first part
of this treatise (6:1:17, p. 367, 11. 32-35):

> (The Lord) set in some of (the body which does not
> preserve its shape) a nature so that it has the
> possibility to receive all the forms. This is the
> lower matter, because of the elemental forms which
> He created in it and (because of) the power which
> He gave the elements to change into one another and
> to intermix with one another. In this way lower
> matter is prepared to receive all the forms.

Elsewhere, he writes (6:1:18, p. 374, ll. 16-24):

> It is impossible that matter exist without form in
> these (lower) existent things. Thus, all these
> things are clothed with primary qualities which are
> the forms of the elements. It is impossible for
> them to be absolutely abstracted from (these forms).
> Rather, they are changed from contrary to contrary
> and they necessarily acquire from the forms what is
> fitting for them with respect to the degree they are
> in—from these qualities and their mixtures. All of
> this is clear to one who speculates in Physics. This
> is the nature which the Lord, may He be blessed, gave
> them in lower matter to receive all the forms by
> means of one another through these elemental forms
> which He first gave them and through the possibility
> which He gave them to change from contrary to con-
> trary of these qualities.

In a third place he speaks of "the nature" to receive forms which
"was generated in prime matter with the generation of the elemental forms in it" (6:1:25, p. 402, l. 6f.). Thus, on every
occasion in the first part of this treatise in which he has
occasion to discuss the process by which the sublunar world of
lower existent things came to be, he chooses to speak only of a
nature which the Lord gave prime matter to receive all of the
forms by means of the elemental forms. He makes no use of the
term "last form."

There is nothing in his discussions of this process in 6:2:7
and 8 below which departs from his discussion in the first part
of this treatise. With regard to the first "day" of creation, he
writes (6:2:8, p. 428, ll. 33-35):

> He created the first principles of the lower matter,
> which are prime matter and the forms which are primary
> to it in order—that is, the elemental forms. For it
> is through (the elemental forms) that (prime matter)
> is prepared to receive all the forms so that all the
> elements are in a way that the element earth is in the
> lowest area of the element water, and that the fire and
> the air are upon the highest area of the water.

With regard to the second day, he writes (6:2:7, p. 427, ll. 3-6):

> The lower waters—that is, the lower matter—is
> distinguished from the upper waters by the elemental
> forms which the Lord, may He be blessed, placed in
> it. It is through (the elemental forms) that (the

lower matter) has the power to receive all the forms.
In these elemental forms, there exists two active
powers, the hot and the cold, and through them they
act upon one another.

Also, with regard to the second day, he writes (6:2:8, p. 429,
ll. 20-24):

> The Lord, may He be blessed, said that there be a
> heavenly body from some of the body which does not
> preserve its shape, and that a nature be created
> which would distinguish it from the part of this
> body which does not preserve its shape which is
> below the raqiᶜa. This nature which divides between
> them is the creation of the elemental forms in this
> lower part of this body, through which it is pre-
> pared to receive all of the forms.

Also cf. 6:2:8, p. 428, l. 25f.; p. 430, ll. 2-4, 6f.; p. 436,
l. 13.

All of this may reasonably be taken as evidence that he means
what he says later in this chapter (6:2:4, p. 421, l. 17f.) when
he writes:

> This (last) form is the elemental forms, by means of
> which prime matter is prepared to receive the rest of
> the forms.

That is, in all of the places just cited, he seems to make no
distinction between "last form" and "the elemental forms" and
indeed identifies the two on at least this one occasion. On the
basis of this evidence alone, it would be proper to assume that
he conceives of the process of the coming to be of lower existent
things as follows: When God began to create the world out of body
which does not preserve its shape (see below, notes #51 and #152,
for a discussion of this term), He willed that the part of it
from which the sublunar world would come to be should have the
nature of the elemental forms which prepares it to receive all the
other forms. The elemental forms prepare it by causing the existence of the four elements (which at this prior stage exist separately in concentric layers). These elements possess the primary
active qualities of the hot and the cold which are contraries and
which interact under the influence of the supralunar motions, to
produce the respective mixtures of the elements and the qualities
which each species of lower existent things has as its nature.
Thus, the "last form" to which he refers here can be presumed to
be, on the basis of the evidence presented thus far, a superfluous
term which is nothing other than the elemental forms when they are
discussed in terms of the hierarchy of forms.

It is not possible, however, to leave this subject in this
way because of the following considerations: First, if indeed
this is what Gersonides intends to say, then he would seem to be
making a significant departure from the way in which the first
principles of the process of coming to be were traditionally
discussed in medieval philosophy. The following summary of this
traditional position relies upon the discussion of H. A. Wolfson
in his work, Crescas' Critique of Aristotle (Cambridge, Mass.,
1929), pp. 99-104, 577-594. This position distinguished two
successive stages in the process. At the first stage, there were
prime matter and corporeal form (ṣurah gashmit, also called ṣurah
ri'shonah, "first form"). Neither of the two had actual existence
in itself. Prime matter was pure potentiality and corporeal form
was that form which gave prime matter the form of tridimensionality or body. The conjunction of the two yielded body (geshem,
or geshem meshullaḥ, "absolute body"). Whether this body had
actual tridimensionality or merely had a predisposition for tridimensionality was a subject of some dispute, as will be discussed
below in this note. In either case, it was this body—prime matter
informed by corporeal form—which was thought to serve as the matter
or the substratum of the four elemental forms, which yielded the
first actually existent things, i.e., the elements.

We need not be compelled to read Gersonides in a way that
conforms to the way others discussed this subject. He was an
original and independent thinker who clearly proposed new solutions
to other issues which he investigated. Indeed, that he boldly
proposes that the world was not created out of nothing but rather
out of body which does not preserve its shape might lead us to
expect that he will also present a different view of the process
of coming to be. Nevertheless, we are obliged to determine the
extent to which he followed and departed from the traditional
model and to explore the possible motives he had for his departures
from it. His very use of the term "last form" raises the question
of whether he intended it to refer to what others called "first
form" or "corporeal form."

The second consideration which calls for further investigation
is his statement here that last form is prior in order to the
matter most distant from existence. In his discussion of priority
in order above (6:2:2, p. 420, ll. 11-19; cf. note #27), he
implies that something which is prior in order is a component of
or is a means to that which is posterior to it in order but which
is prior to it in cause and in nature. (Thus, the perfection of

the virtues is prior in order to intellectual perfection, as
discussed above, note #37, or in Aristotle's terms, discussed above,
note #27, the elements of a geometrical demonstration are prior in
order to its propositions.) If he is using priority in order in
this way, it seems plausible that he is saying that last form,
i.e., corporeal form, is prior in order to the body which is the
substratum of the elemental forms. This corporeal form would be
prior in order because it is the informing of prime matter by
corporeal form which yields that tridimensional substratum. It is
difficult, on the other hand, to make sense out of this statement
if we assume that he means to refer to the elemental forms with
the term "last form." The elemental forms are neither prior in
order to the first material principle which is informed by corporeal form nor to the body which serves as their matter or substratum. The priority of the elemental forms to these is priority in
cause and in nature.

It would seem, therefore, that the form which he says here is
prior in order to the matter which is most distant from existence
cannot be the elemental forms. Consequently, this statement can
be taken as evidence that he does make a distinction between the
elemental forms and a form of a prior stage which he is designating
as "last form." This piece of evidence, however, is weakened by
his statement below, in 6:2:8 (p. 428, l. 32f., quoted above in
this note), in which he identifies the first principles of lower
matter as prime matter and the elemental forms and states that the
elemental forms are primary in order to prime matter. He does not
say that they are prior in order to prime matter but rather that
they are primary (ri'shonot lo) in order. This probably indicates
that he does not intend to refer to priority in order as he has
discussed it in 6:2:2. (See below, note #235, for a discussion of
this phrase, which seems to mean that the elemental forms are first
in the order of hylic forms.)

The third consideration which raises doubts about the
identification of last form with the elemental forms is the most
persuasive one. That is, in the two places where he does choose
to use the term "last form"—in this chapter and in his Commentary
to the Torah—he seems to make a distinction between it and the
elemental forms. As was just mentioned, to state that last form
is prior in order to the matter most distant from existence is,
in itself, to imply that last form is a component of the matter
under discussion. This is not true of the elemental forms. In
his commentary, he describes last form as follows (CT 9c, ll.
28-32):

> Tohu and bohu are the matter and form which are the
> principles of coming to be as explained in the Physica.
> They are prime matter and last form. That is, the form
> which prime matter first receives prior to its reception
> of the other forms, i.e., the elemental forms.

It seems clear in this passage that he is assuming a distinction
between last form and the elemental forms and that he is saying
that prime matter receives last form prior to its reception of the
elemental forms. His commentary continues (CT 9c, ll. 35-37):

> Because the part of existence which these principles
> have is so weak that their nature is close to the
> nature of privation, it is generally recognized in the
> words of our rabbis that the passing away of this world
> is expressed as its return to tohu and bohu.

Again, it is clear that he cannot be referring here to the
elemental forms, because they are not lacking in existence.
Rather, they bestow existence upon their tridimensional substratum.
It is a prior form (i.e., the form of corporeality or tridimensionality, according to the traditional model) that can be properly
described as being extremely lacking in existence. This is because
it does not itself have an actual existence and its informing of
prime matter yields the tridimensional substratum of the elemental
forms, and that substratum is itself potential and not actual.
Finally, he writes the following in his commentary (CT 10d, ll.
14-17):

> A nature was created to distinguish between the part
> of (body which does not preserve its shape) below the
> raqiᶜa and the part above the raqiᶜa. This is the
> nature which is the disposition and potential which
> the Lord, may He be exalted, gave at the moment of
> creation to the lower part to receive the elemental
> forms for which they have the potential.

Though he does not use the term "last form" here, he does
distinguish between the elemental forms which lower matter has the
potential to receive and a prior nature which is the disposition
which lower matter is first given to receive the elemental forms.
Such a disposition would be a form of a sort, and we might reasonably identify it with his last form. (Cf. Guide 2:12 for Maimonides' discussion of the requisite preparation of matter.)

Thus, though he gives little, if any, indication in the first
part of this treatise and in chapters 7 and 8 below that he wishes
to distinguish between the elemental forms and a prior form, there
are some indications of such a distinction in those places where
he uses the term "last form." We must therefore consider the

possibility that he recognized such a distinction but that there
were reasons which caused him to omit the mention of it. (Note
that his omission of a prior form at a prior stage need not be
taken as his rejection of the existence of that prior stage.
Everyone agrees that the actual existence of lower existent things
begins with the elemental forms. What is at issue is whether
prime matter was the substratum of the elemental forms or if prime
matter needed prior preparation, i.e., the form of tridimensionality
which all four elements have in common.) These reasons will be
explored below, in this note. We must first inquire whether there
are any indications that, when he does make this distinction, he
intends to say that the prior form was the form of corporeality or
tridimensionality.

There are at least three pieces of evidence that he intended
this prior stage of preparation of prime matter for the elemental
forms to be a form of tridimensionality. It should be noted,
however, that each of the three pieces of evidence is dependent
upon the imaginative exegesis of his writing. Nowhere does he use
the term "corporeal form" or "tridimensionality." When they are
considered together, they form a plausible but weak case that he
intended last form to be what others called "corporeal form."
Even if we accept this to be the case, however, we must still
account for the reasons which caused him to be so very abstruse
on this issue.

First, note that in his only description of the relationship
between prime matter and last form, which follows immediately
below (ll. 4-13), he uses the passage from Isaiah to compare last
form to the measurements which an architect takes of a house to
be constructed. Prime matter is the stones which compose those
measurements. A simple reading of the literal meaning of this
description seems to indicate that he is describing last form as
the measurements of tridimensionality.

Second, in the first part of this treatise, he describes the
body which does not preserve its shape from which the world came
to be as follows (6:1:17, p. 368, l. 20f.):

We intend that it is deprived of the nature from which
preservation of shape follows for a body.

An attempt will be made, in note #51 below, to show that he uses
the terms "body which does not preserve its shape" and "prime
matter" (in its sense of the first material principle which is
informed by last form to yield the tridimensional substratum of
the elemental forms, and not in its sense of the tridimensional

substratum of the elemental forms, assuming that he intends to
make such a distinction) synonymously. Assuming this identity,
this comment distinguishes between two types of "body": a) the
"body" of body which does not preserve its shape or of prime matter;
and b) the "body" which preserves its shape. Given that the term
"body" is traditionally used to refer to something which is tridimensional (cf. Physica 3.5.204b5, 4.5.212a32ff., where Aristotle
defines "body" as being bounded by a surface, i.e., with definite
dimensionality), it is reasonable to infer that this statement is
intended to distinguish between nondimensional or inextended "body"
(what others refer to as "body" or "absolute body") and dimensional
body. This inference is by no means certain and depends entirely
upon what is meant by "preservation of shape." (See below in this
note for a discussion of this problem.) Assuming this inference,
however, and assuming that this "nature" is the "nature" to which
he refers in his commentary (CT 10d, ll. 14-17, quoted above in
this note) which is the disposition which enables the lower part
of body which does not preserve its shape (i.e., prime matter) to
receive the elemental forms, then he may be implying that prime
matter first receives a form or a nature of corporeality or tridimensionality which enables it to become the corporeal substratum
underlying the elemental forms.

     Third, in 6:2:7 below, he states that the term raqiᶜa refers
"to anything which is stretched out and which preserves its shape"
(p. 424, l. 19). The examples he gives there are stretched out
plates of gold, the visible part of the earth which is higher than
the water, and the sky. (It is likely that he understands the
word "sky" here to refer to the lowest of the heavenly spheres
which encompasses the sublunar world. See, for example, his statement in the first part of this treatise [6:1:17, p. 368, ll. 1-5]
that it is the heavenly bodies which preserve their shape more than
anything else. Also see below, note #180, for the way in which the
spheres form the limit of the sublunar world.) All of these
instances refer to things which are extended, i.e., which have
dimensions. Thus, we can infer that body which does not preserve
its shape is neither extended nor tridimensional, and that the
nature which God gives it to receive the elemental forms is the
nature of extension or tridimensionality, i.e., what others call
"corporeal form."

     As stated above, these pieces of evidence only give tentative
support at most to the assertion that Gersonides wants to distinguish between the tridimensional body which receives the elemental

forms and the nondimensional prime matter which must first be
given the form of tridimensionality so that it can receive those
elemental forms. Indeed, the resolution of the issue may turn on
his discussion of the body which does not preserve its shape in
the first part of the Fifth Treatise, which is included neither in
the manuscripts nor in the published editions of the Wars of the
Lord (cf. below, notes #51 and #152). On the basis of the preceding evidence, however, we may now speculate about the reasons
which caused Gersonides either to ignore the traditional distinction between the elemental forms and prior corporeal form or to
make his references to that distinction extremely oblique.

It is possible that he rejects this distinction, at least in
part. As explained above in this note, he does not seem to use
the term "body" in the traditional way. Rather, he refers to the
body from which the world came to be and which precedes the world
as "body which does not preserve its shape." As will be discussed
more fully in note #51 below, he never makes it clear that this
body is nondimensional. Indeed, we would expect this to follow
from his descriptions of it as matter which persists without form,
which is motionless and therefore not subject to time, and which
is absolutely deprived of all goodness and perfection. What he
seems to be describing is pure potentiality—what is traditionally
called "prime matter." It seems to be a formless substratum which
serves as the receptacle for the divine will. In contrast to the
position espoused by Maimonides that the world was created out of
absolutely nothing, he seems to be proposing that the potentiality
for actualization was there before God willed its actualization.
Nevertheless, this potentiality, devoid as it is of all form, would
have no actual existence and would thus be "nothing" in itself,
if not "absolutely nothing." It certainly would not be expected
to be tridimensional body.

There are places, however, in which he seems to imply that
the body which does not preserve its shape has some kind of tridimensionality. For example, he says that it persists between the
spheres as an instrument which prevents the motions of the stars
of one sphere from reaching the motions of the stars of another
sphere (cf. 5:2:2, summarized below, note #152; 6:2:7, p. 425, l.
9f.; 6:1:7, p. 311, ll. 31-33; 6:1:17, p. 368, ll. 5-7). Such an
instrument would seem to be a tridimensional body of some kind,
unless he is referring to something analogous to the magnetic
fields which quantum physics tells us exist between celestial
bodies. He also spends some time in the first part of this

treatise addressing the question of whether a remainder of the body
which does not preserve its shape may persist after the world comes
to be from it. Although he concludes that we can infer from empirical observation that there was not enough of it to form another
universe, he does allow for the possibility that some remainder
persists and that we need not assume that it persisted in exactly
the proper "quantity" (kamut) required for the generation of this
world (6:1:18, p. 368, l. 25-p. 369, l. 35; p. 370, ll. 1-7; p. 371,
l. 12-p. 372, l. 13; p. 372, l. 30-p. 373, l. 15). He begins this
discussion with the disclaimer that we cannot know anything about
body which does not preserve its shape because it is not the effect
of the action of an agent, so that everything he says is said tentatively and inductively from empirical observation and not on the
basis of any true knowledge of its essence. Nevertheless, he seems
to assume some form of tridimensionality or quantity in his discussion of the issue of a remainder. If the body which does not preserve its shape is truly formless and thus absolute potentiality,
then it would make no sense to speak about quantities of it which
can be differentiated from one another. Potential things cannot
be distinguished from each other (cf. 6:1:25, p. 402, l. 1).

Insofar as there is evidence that he does not consider the
body which does not preserve its shape to be nondimensional, we
may speculate that he was not interested in making a distinction
between corporeal form and the elemental forms. Matter would
have already possessed extension, in some sense of the term.
Other thinkers who believe that prime matter is not extended are
required to posit a prior corporeal form which yields the tridimen-
sial body as the substratum of the forms of the elements. Gersonides, on the other hand, is not convinced, according to this theory,
that prime matter has no extension and thus does not speak of
corporeal form.

If this is what caused him to blur the distinction, it must
be considered a major defect in his theory of creation for the following reasons: First, it would be difficult to make intelligible
his assertion that body which does not preserve its shape is both
formless and nonexistent, and that it in some sense has quantity
or tridimensionality. Second, it would be difficult to distinguish
between his theory of this "pre-existent" body and the theory of
Plato that matter existed before creation in confused motion. All
the arguments which he advances in 6:1:17 to refute the Platonic
theory would apply equally to his own theory if he, in fact thought
that the body which does not preserve its shape had some sort of
corporeal form.

We may thus want to assume that he did not intend to attribute
extension to the body which does not preserve its shape and that
there are other ways to explain his intentions when he discusses
its function between the spheres and the possibility that a
remainder of it persists after creation. It is possible nevertheless that his confusion in this regard caused him to blur the
distinction between corporeal form and the elemental forms.

Another possible explanation for his virtual silence on the
issue of corporeal form is that he assumes this prior stage in the
process of coming to be. If he assumes that everyone knows that
matter must first become tridimensional before it can serve as the
substratum of the elemental forms, then there is no need for him to
clarify the issue. Thus, he speaks primarily of the elemental
forms, as that which causes the first existent sublunar things,
i.e., the elements, and his allusions to a prior stage are made in
passing. If this is the correct explanation, then he is proceeding
in a fashion which is consistent with his basic methodological
approach throughout The Wars of the Lord. That is, the work does
not deal with all the questions that were at issue in medieval
philosophy. It deals rather with only those issues which he
believes were resolved inadequately by Maimonides in The Guide of
the Perplexed. If his lack of clarity results from the fact that
he takes this prior stage for granted, then he can be faulted for
his imprecision but he cannot be charged with inconsistency.
Nowhere does he deny the prior stage of corporeal form. He would
be omitting it because he is discussing the beginning of existent
things and corporeal form cannot be said to exist in actuality.

A third possible explanation is related to the second. That
is, he may omit the prior stage of the informing of prime matter by
corporeal form for a reason other than lack of precision. The
omission may result from his understanding of the nature of corporeal form. This was a subject of some controversy in medieval
philosophy. As Wolfson presents it (Crescas' Critique of Aristotle,
pp. 101, 582-589), Avicenna, Alghazali and Averroes held different
views about the nature of corporeal form. Avicenna believed that
though prime matter is incorporeal, it has a predisposition for
the assumption of tridimensionality. This predisposition is corporeal form, which is itself an accident which falls under the
category of quantity. It is not identical with cohesion.
Alghazali differed with Avicenna and asserted that corporeal form
is the cohesiveness or massiveness of matter in which tridimensionality may be posited. Averroes asserted that corporeal form is

absolute dimensionality, i.e., dimensionality which is indeterminate
and unlimited (merḥaqim ha-biltiy muḡbalim). It is not merely the
predisposition for cohesion nor is it cohesion itself. Though
determinate dimensions are transformable in that the particular
dimensions of a body may be altered, the fact that body is dimensional is not altered by addition and division. This "absolute
dimensionality" is corporeal form, which causes something nondimensional to become dimensional. This description is to be contrasted
with Avicenna's assertion that corporeal form is prime matter's
predisposition for tridimensionality (see the discussion of Léon
Gauthier, Ibn Rochd [Paris, 1948], pp. 68-75). Avicenna is saying
that the informing of prime matter by corporeal form yields nothing
actual but rather yields a potentially tridimensional body which
becomes tridimensional when informed by the elemental forms.
Averroes, on the other hand, asserts that corporeal form is indeterminate dimensionality. That is, the informing of prime matter by
corporeal form yields a body which is dimensional, though its
determinate dimensions are potentials to be actualized in its
reception of particular forms. Alghazali would also say that the
conjunction of prime matter and corporeal form yields dimensional
body, but, as Wolfson presents him, he did not make the distinction
between determinate and indeterminate dimensionality.

There was thus some question among Gersonides' predecessors
about whether corporeal form endowed prime matter (Avicenna) with
a potential disposition for dimensionality (in which case the body
which serves as the substratum for the elemental forms is only
potentially existent), or with an actual dimensionality—(Alghazali) determinate (yielding a body with definite dimensions), or
(Averroes) indeterminate (yielding a body with dimensions which
are actually indefinite but potentially definite).

Those thinkers who accepted Alghazali's view that corporeal
form is identical with tridimensional body itself (Wolfson identifies Ibn Daud as one such thinker, p. 587) would be likely to
clearly distinguish between the prior stage, in which prime matter
and corporeal form are potential existents, and the subsequent
stage in which their conjunction yields a corporeal substratum with
dimensions. We may assume that Gersonides did not accept Alghazali's
position but rather accepted Averroes' assertion that the informing
of prime matter by corporeal form yields a body with potentially
definite dimensions. Though its actual dimensions are indefinite,
it may be called a body because it possesses indeterminate dimensionality. In another sense, however, it cannot be said to

actually exist because its definite dimensions are potential and
are actualized only after it receives a determinate form. If we
assume that this is Gersonides' position, then we can explain why
he alludes to a prior stage of dimensionality without ever explicitly stating that it actually exists and why he omits any reference
to that prior stage in most of his discussions of the process of
the coming to be of lower existence. His vague allusions to dimensionality assume the potential that matter has for definite tridimensionality but assume that this potential is not actualized until
matter receives the elemental forms. It is then that matter exists
in actuality. Similarly, his omission of this prior stage assumes
that body with definite dimensions does not become actual until it
receives the elemental forms.

An intriguing possibility is that Gersonides thinks of "body
which does not preserve its shape" as prime matter when it is
informed by corporeal form—that is, in fact, as a body. If he is
following Averroes, then this body would have absolute dimensionality, i.e., it would be tridimensional but would have no actual
definite dimensions. It would be posterior to "prime matter," when
he uses that term to designate the first material principle which
is wholly potential and nonextended. If this is correct, then
absolute dimensional body—and corporeal form—is not a result of
divine creation. It rather persists prior to the actions resulting
from the divine will. This interpretation solves a number of problems but also creates others.

In support of this interpretation is the following:
a) Gersonides states that lack of preservation of shape is analogous
to water and that preservation of shape is analogous to "stretched
out plates," to the visible part of the earth, to the sky (i.e.,
the lowest sphere) and to the congealing of water (see below,
6:2:7). If we take him at his word, then we may observe that, of
all actually existent bodies, water is most like absolute dimensional body in its failure to maintain definite dimensions. The
congealing of water and all of the other contrasting examples are
bodies with definite dimensions.
b) This interpretation would make sense out of his statements
concerning the body which does not preserve its shape which is
between the spheres, and the remainder of this body which may
persist outside of the world after its creation. In both cases,
absolute dimensional body with no actual definite dimensions fits
the context better than absolute, nonextended potentiality.

c) Absolute dimensional body would have no motion, because it
would not be a body with actual dimensions. The persistence of
this body prior to the creation of the world thus would not be
subject to the refutations which he makes of Plato's pre-existent
matter which has confused motion.

d) Absolute dimensional body would have no actual existence and
might be said to be deprived of all form, since the "form" of
absolute dimensionality which it has differs from all other forms
in that it is not a part of the divine nomos. As he states in his
commentary (quoted above in this note), both prime matter and last
form are so lacking in existence that their nature is close to the
nature of privation. We could interpret this to refer to the nonextended material principle and the "form" of absolute dimensionality which are characteristics of body which does not preserve
its shape.

e) The term "last form" is used only in conjunction with "prime
matter" and never with "body which does not preserve its shape."
As will be shown below, note #51, he does use the term "prime
matter" to refer to the (presumably dimensional) substratum of the
elemental forms. Thus, in his discussions of tohu and bohu in
this chapter and in his commentary, and in his identification of
them as last form and prime matter, he may be speaking of the components of body which does not preserve its shape. As will be
shown below, note #235, he regards tohu and bohu to be part of a
parenthetical statement. They are not, in his view, created on
the first "day." He may therefore be reading Gen 1:2 as follows:
"The sublunar world (ha-ʾareṣ) was, at the moment of creation,
composed of body which does not preserve its shape, i.e., the
absolute dimensional body which is formed from last form (tohu)
and prime matter (bohu)."

f) His failure to clearly define "last form" as the form of
dimensionality would result from the fact that it is not truly a
form and thus is not knowable, except by inductive inference from
existent things.

g) His omission of this prior stage in all places in which he is
not discussing tohu and bohu is due to the fact that, in his view,
the creation of the sublunar world does not begin with the formation of tridimensional body. That body already persisted. It is
what he calls "body which does not preserve its shape." Creation
rather begins with the informing of absolute dimensional body by
the elemental forms which give it actual definite dimensions.
When he speaks of the "nature" which God gives this body to

receive the rest of the forms through the creation of the elemental
forms (6:1:17, p. 367, ll. 32-35; CT 10d, ll. 14-17) he would not
be referring to the nature of corporeality, but rather to the
nature of actual definite dimensionality and subjection to change
which matter acquires from the elemental forms.

h) This interpretation gives substance to the distinction he makes
between Maimonides' theory of creation out of absolutely nothing
and his own theory of creation out of nothing (cf. above, note #6).
Though absolute dimensional body is "nothing" it is not "absolutely
nothing."

There are several problems, however, which occur when we
assume that body which does not preserve its shape is absolute
dimensional body:

a) He states here that last form is prior in order to the matter
most distant from existence. If tohu and bohu refer to the nonextended material principle (prime matter) and to the "form" of
absolute dimensionality (last form), then last form is not prior
in order to prime matter, as explained above in this note. It
would rather be posterior in order. We may assume, however, that
he means to say that last form is prior in order for prime matter,
to all of the other forms which are posterior to it in order in the
hierarchy of forms. (This solution also fits his statement below,
6:2:8, p. 428, l. 33, that the elemental forms are first in order
for prime matter. Cf. below, note #235.)

b) The assumption is based upon his obliqueness and virtual
silence. He never makes it clear that he means "body which does
not preserve its shape" to refer to absolute dimensional body.
This observation should be kept in mind, but it is counter-
balanced by all the problematic passages which this assumption
apparently resolves. His silence can be attributed either to his
conviction that absolute dimensional body is unknowable (his
insistence upon the unknowability of body which does preserve its
shape is a separate problem which is dealt with above in Part V
of the introduction), or it results from his assumption that all
readers of this work would be familiar with Averroes' understanding
of the nature of corporeal form ("All of this is clear to one who
speculates in Physics," 6:1:18, p. 374, l. 21).

c) Because he clearly states that body which does not preserve its
shape is deprived of all form (6:1:17, p. 367, ll. 19, 35ff.;
6:1:18, p. 374, l. 14f.), this theory seems to depend on our
assumption that last form is not properly a form because it is the
"form" of absolute dimensional body which persists prior to

creation. Yet it cannot be ignored that he does use the term "last
form", and never suggests that he is using it equivocally. Thus,
not only does he call it a "form", but his term "last" implies some
kind of connection with the hierarchy of forms. Insofar as "last
form" is his own term, it would seem that his choice of the term
refutes the possibility that body which does not preserve its shape
has last form, because he states that it has no form. He was not
limited in his choice of terms. For example, he could have called
the disposition for absolute dimensional body, "last disposition"
(tekhunah aḥaronah) or "first disposition" (tekhunah riʾshonah).
d) He states below in this chapter that last form is the elemental
forms (p. 421, l. 17). This could not be true in any sense if last
form is a disposition which belongs to body which does not preserve
its shape, because in no sense can the elemental forms be connected
to body which does not preserve its shape. Such a connection would
lead to all the absurdities which he attributes to Plato's theory
in 6:1:17.

Problems (c) and (d), which occur when we assume that "body
which does not preserve its shape" is absolute dimensional body and
"last form" is the "form" of absolute dimensionality, can be resolved
if we assume that his term for absolute dimensionality is "lack of
preservation of shape." Problem (c) thus is resolved because he
never speaks of "lack of preservation of shape" as a form. Problem (d) is resolved because it avoids the assumption that the term
"last form" is connected to body which does not preserve its shape.

The resolution of these problems thus depends upon our assumption, after all, that "last form" is identical with "the elemental
forms" and that he is being quite precise when he makes that identification below in this chapter (p. 421, l. 17). That is, "last
form" is the elemental forms when they are considered with respect
to their imparting of definite dimensionality to absolute dimensional body. He only uses the term "last form" as an interpretation
of the word tohu in Gen 1:2, so that it is reasonable to assume
that it is a term which he uses to describe the position of the
elemental forms at the bottom of the hierarchy of forms. He would
be reading the verse as follows: "the sublunar world (ha-ʾareṣ)
was (on the second day--see note #235 for an explanation of his
parenthetical reading) composed of last form (tohu, i.e., the definite dimensionality of the elemental forms) and the matter most
distant from existence (bohu, i.e., absolute dimensional body).
Thus, the element earth (ḥoshekh) was next to the lowest area of
the element water (ʿal penei tehom) and the elements air and fire

(ruaḥ ᵓelohim) were resting (meraḥefet) next to the highest area
of the element water (ᶜal penei ha-mayim)."

In support of the identification of "last form" with "the
elemental forms" is the following:
a) He never associates "last form" with the form of absolute dimensionality. The three pieces of evidence which were listed above
in this note in support of this association can be explained as
follows:

1) His analogy between last form and prime matter and the
measurements made for building blocks can be read as implying not
that last form gives prime matter absolute dimensionality but that
it rather gives it definite dimensions. If last form is the elemental forms, then it does in fact give body its first definite
dimensions, i.e., the dimensions of the concentric layers of the
elements, which are the first actually existent things.

2) When he refers to the "nature" which is lacking in body
which does not preserve its shape, from which preservation of
shape follows for a body (6:1:17, p. 368, l. 20f.) and which is the
disposition which enables it to receive the elemental forms
(CT 10d, ll. 14-17), it reasonably may be assumed that he is referring to the nature or disposition for definite dimensions which
absolute dimensional body which does not preserve its shape receives
in its reception of the elemental forms. If body which does not
preserve its shape has absolute dimensionality, then it does not
need to receive a form of corporeality for the sublunar world to
be created from it. Last form, i.e., the elemental forms, would
rather give it definite dimensions.

3) It has already been explained that preservation of shape,
which he compares to the congealing of water, etc., is better understood as definite dimensionality rather than absolute dimensionality.
b) He never distinguishes between "last form" and "the elemental
forms." The evidence presented above in support of such a distinction can be explained as follows:

1) The priority in order which he attributes to last form is
a priority to the rest of the forms which are posterior to the
elemental forms in the hierarchy of forms. As he states in his
commentary, the elemental forms are "first hylic form," i.e., the
first form which informs matter (CT 10a, l. 17f.). (This depends
upon the interpretation of "prime matter" not as the first nonextended material principle but rather as absolute dimensional body,
i.e., body which does not preserve its shape. This will be

discussed immediately below in argument (c).)

2) His description in his commentary of the principles of
coming to be is ambiguous (CT 9c ll. 30-32):

> They are prime matter and last form. That is, the
> form which prime matter first receives prior to its
> reception of the other forms, i.e., the elemental
> forms.

The ambiguity derives from the fact that he may be making an identification of last form with the elemental forms but that we are
led to believe that it is the other forms which he is identifying
with the elemental forms because the term "forms" is plural in
these cases and singular in the case of "last form." Nevertheless,
the syntax of this passage can be read as an identification of last
form with the elemental forms, i.e., as follows: "(Last form is)
the form, i.e., the elemental forms, which prime matter first
receives prior to its reception of the other (composite) forms."

3) When he states in his commentary (CT 9c, ll. 35-37) that
prime matter and last form are so weak in existence that they
approach the nature of privation, we are admittedly led to believe
that he is referring to the first nonextended material principle
and the form of dimensionality which is prior to the elemental
forms. This is because these first principles do not have actual
existence, as explained above. He may be referring, however, to
absolute dimensional body and to the elemental forms. The former
clearly is close to nonexistence because he states this clearly
with reference to body which does not preserve its shape which is,
we are assuming, absolute dimensional body. The elemental forms
may also be described as lacking in existence because, although
they are the forms of the first actually existent things, i.e.,
the elements, the elements do not continue to exist as pure elements. They rather exist as components of composite things which
have other forms. Thus, none of the elemental forms exists in a
pure noncomposite state in the sublunar world after the moment of
creation. As he consistently describes them, they are the means
by which matter receives the other forms. Also note his description of the element earth as "absolutely absent of form" (6:2:5,
p. 422, l. 15: cf. his Commentary to Job, which he cites there),
and his insistence on the distinction between elemental air and
fire and their perceptible manifestations in the sublunar world
(6:2:6, p. 424, ll. 5f., 13ff.).

4) The mention (CT 10d, ll. 14-17) of the creation of a nature
which is the disposition to receive the elemental forms may be

interpreted, as mentioned above, not as the nature for absolute,
indefinite dimensionality but rather as the nature for definite
dimensions.
c) As mentioned above, the identification of last form and the
elemental forms requires that he use the term "prime matter" to
refer exclusively to absolute dimensional body and not to a first
nonextended material principle. Prime matter would thus be another
term for body which does not preserve its shape. As we will show
below, note #51, there is nothing in his writings that requires or
even suggests that prime matter is a first, nonextended material
principle, i.e., what others call "prime matter." All interpretations of his use of this term as a nonextended principle depend
upon the assumptions that last form is the form of dimensionality
and that body which does not preserve its shape is not extended.
d) As will be discussed in note #56 below, the problems which his
statement that last form is an intermediate between contraries
(6:2:4, p. 421, ll. 19-24) have raised can be dealt with as follows:
If we assume that last form is a form of dimensionality which is
prior to the elemental forms, then it is an intermediate in that
it has no contraries. It is the elements which have contrary
qualities, and last form is at a stage prior to the elements. If
we assume, however, that "last form" is a term which describes the
aspect of the elemental forms which causes absolute dimensional
body to acquire definite dimensions, then last form is again an
intermediate in that it is what all the elemental forms have in
common--definite dimensionality. It is not to be associated with
the contrary qualities which they possess.
    The following is a summary of the possible interpretations of
this issue which we have discussed above:
    1) Gersonides rejects the distinction between nondimensional
body which does not preserve its shape and the dimensional substratum of the elemental forms, because he is confused about the nature
of the body which does not preserve its shape. On the one hand,
he intends it to be formless and thus nondimensional, but on the
other hand, he chooses to call it "body" and to speak about it in
places as if it were dimensional. Because he is unclear about
the exact nature of its dimensionality, he often chooses to ignore
the stage at which the nonextended material principle receives the
form of dimensionality which it needs to serve as the substratum
of the elemental forms. He betrays his confusion, however, when
he does make a distinction between the elemental forms and a prior
nature which matter receives and when he uses the term "last form"

to refer vaguely to dimensionality. This confusion threatens to undercut his theory of creation because he seems not to account for the fact that he sometimes considers body which does not preserve its shape to have a form of dimensionality, so that it is not nothing but something. His theory is thus vulnerable to the refutations which he makes of Plato's theory of pre-existent matter.

2) Gersonides assumes a distinction between nondimensional prime matter and prime matter after it has received dimensionality from last form. He uses the same term to denote both stages and often ignores the prior stage of nondimensionality because he takes for granted that all of his readers are aware of this prior stage. His apparent assumption that body which does not preserve its shape is, in some sense, dimensional can be accounted for in other ways. That "body" is nondimensional and is identical to "prime matter" when this term is used to denote the first nonextended material principle.

3) Gersonides follows Averroes and assumes that corporeal form is the form of absolute dimensionality. Thus, the body which serves as the substratum for the elemental forms is dimensional but only has the potential for definite dimensions. It has no actual definite dimensions. Thus, Gersonides makes vague allusions to a prior nature of dimensionality and occasionally refers to last form, which is corporeal form. He ignores this stage in most places, however, because it is not an actual stage. Corporeal form yields a dimensional body with only potentially definite dimensions--dimensions which are only actualized by the elemental forms. It is for this reason that he does not use two different terms for the nonextended material principle and absolute dimensional body. That is, he considers both to be potential existents and thus designates both with the term prime matter. Body which does not preserve its shape is the first nonextended material principle and its apparent dimensionality in some contexts can be explained in other ways.

4) Gersonides follows Averroes and uses the term "body which does not preserve its shape" to refer to absolute dimensional body. He thus uses the term "body" intentionally and meaningfully and believes that absolute dimensional body persists prior to the creation of the world and does not follow from the divine nomos. He uses the terms "prime matter" and "last form" only when he is discussing tohu and bohu. His reading of the second verse of Genesis is that it is parenthetical and that it describes the first

components of body which does not preserve its shape. Thus, in
these contexts, "prime matter" is nondimensional, absolute potentiality and "last form" is corporeal form which causes absolute
dimensionality. Absolute dimensional body, however, was not created but rather persisted prior to creation. Its components are
described only parenthetically. In other contexts, "prime matter"
designates the absolute dimensional body which is the substratum
of the elemental forms. He does not mention a prior stage in the
process of creation because absolute dimensionality persists prior
to the process itself. Thus, he indeed intends to imply that body
which does not preserve its shape is dimensional, in the sense of
absolute dimensionality. It can be said to be formless because
corporeal "form" is not related to the divine nomos as are all
other forms. It can be said to be nothing because it has no actually definite dimensions. It thus is not an actual body and has
no motion, unlike Plato's pre-existent matter. It is not, however,
"absolutely nothing" as Maimonides asserts.

5) Gersonides follows Averroes and uses the term "body which
does not preserve its shape" to refer to absolute dimensional
body. He uses the term "body" intentionally and meaningfully and
believes that absolute dimensional body persists prior to the
creation of the world and does not follow from the divine nomos.
Thus, there is no inconsistency in his discussion of this body
between the spheres or in his discussion of its possible remainder
after creation. His term for absolute dimensionality is "lack of
preservation of shape" and his term for definite dimensionality is
"preservation of shape." He does not refer to absolute dimensional
body as having a form. He considers it close to privation because
it has no form which follows from the divine nomos. As in interpretation (4) above, this is clearly distinct from the theories of
Maimonides and Plato. Unlike interpretation (4), however, "last
form" is another term for the elemental forms, which refers to their
lowest place in the hierarchy of forms and which is used to discuss
them with respect to the aspect of definite dimensionality which
they all bestow upon absolute dimensional body. He reads tohu and
bohu in the second verse of Genesis as a parenthetical description
not of the principles of absolute dimensional body (i.e., body
which does not preserve its shape) but rather of the things created
on the second "day." Tohu is last form (i.e., the definite dimensionality of elemental forms) and bohu is prime matter (i.e.,
absolute dimensional body). The verse continues with an enumeration
of the four pure elements which tohu includes. "Prime matter,"

in this context and in all contexts, is absolute dimensional body
and is ontologically identical to "body which does not preserve
its shape." "Prime matter" is the term he uses to refer to the
part of that body which serves as the substratum of the sublunar
world. The creation of the sublunar world begins with the informing of absolute dimensional body by the elemental forms simultaneous
with its reception of the prior nature of definite dimensionality.
No prior stage is ever mentioned because there is no prior stage.

Both of the first two interpretations assume that Gersonides
was confused about the issue of corporeal form and fail to explain
his discussions of body which does not preserve its shape which
imply that it is dimensional. To accept either of them is to
assume that his theory of creation is inconsistent and unviable.
The third interpretation makes more sense out of the apparent
inconsistency of his distinctions, but it also does not explain
adequately his notion of lack of preservation of shape. It thus
seems that we must adopt either the fourth or the fifth interpretation if we want to assume he had a viable and consistent theory
of creation. The fifth is preferable to the fourth because it
assumes that his terminology is more consistent, i.e., that he
means what he says when he asserts that body which does not preserve
its shape is deprived of all form, including "last form," and when
he says that last form is the elemental forms.

As mentioned at the outset, his theory that the world comes
to be out of a body which persists prior to creation is singular
and might reasonably be expected to be based upon an equally singular account of the first principles of the process of coming to be.
If the fifth interpretation is correct, this is undoubtedly the
case, because he is using the term "prime matter" in a way which
departs from all of his predecessors and because, unlike them, he
does not include corporeal form in the process of creation.

50) Isa 34:11. His reading of the passage (34:1ff.) is that
when the Lord avenges Himself on the nations, they will be
reduced to the first components of lower existence which existed
at the moment of the generation of the world, prior to the coming
to be of composite material things. From bohu and tohu, it will
be possible at that time for things to be generated again as they
were at creation. See above, note #49, for a discussion of his
understanding of the meaning of bohu and tohu. The meaning of the
present passage, however, remains the same no matter how these
terms are understood. That is, in all cases he is referring here
to the reduction of the world of composite things back to its first

component parts. Also note his statement in his commentary
(CT 9c, 11. 35-37, quoted above in note #49) that the principles
designated by the terms tohu and bohu are close to nonexistence
and to the nature of privation.

        51) Our understanding of his use of the term "prime matter,"
and of the term "body which does not preserve its shape," will
depend upon our interpretation of the distinction which he makes
or does not make between "last form" and "the elemental forms"
(see above, note #49). According to the first and fifth interpretations discussed in note #49, both of which assume that "last
form" is synonymous with "the elemental forms," he uses "prime
matter" to designate the (absolute) dimensional substratum of the
elemental forms. According to the second, third and fourth interpretations, which assume a distinction in which last form bestows
upon the first nonextended material principle the form of either
actual (second interpretation), or absolute (third interpretation),
or definite (fourth interpretation) dimensionality, the term
"prime matter" will refer to nonextended, absolute potentiality
when it is used in conjunction with "last form" and will refer to
(some kind of) dimensional body when it is used in conjunction with
"the elemental forms." According to the first three interpretations, which assume that "body which does not preserve its shape"
is nondimensional, that term will be synonymous with "prime matter"
when the latter is used to designate nondimensional, absolute
potentiality. According to the fourth and fifth interpretations,
"body which does not preserve its shape" always refers to absolute
dimensional body and never to a nondimensional, absolute potentiality.

        Gersonides concludes in the first part of this treatise that
prior (in a nontemporal sense) to the creation of the world, body
which does not preserve its shape (geshem biltiy shomer temunato)
persisted. He reaches this conclusion after determining that the
world is not eternal and that it is philosophically untenable to
assert either that the world came to be out of actually existent
matter or out of absolutely nothing. (See his proofs for the
createdness of the world in 6:1:5-15, and his rejection of the
latter two alternative descriptions of creation in 6:1:17.) Thus,
he concludes that the world was created out of body which does not
preserve its shape, which is something in one respect—in that it
is a "body"—and is nothing in another respect—in that it is a
"body" deprived of all form. Since it is formless, it has no
motion, because matter does not move itself, and is not subject

to time, because time is the measure of motion. It is rather the
substratum or receptacle which receives God's will (6:1:17, p. 367,
ll. 16-26; p. 367, l. 35-p. 368, l. 21; 6:1:18, p. 373, l. 14;
p. 374, ll. 12-32). Because it has no form, it is more distant
than anything from perfection and can be described as privation,
though not as absolute privation because it is an intermediate
between existence and privation (6:1:18, p. 372, ll. 16-19; p. 373,
ll. 23-29). It is the single principle of all matter and, as pure
substratum, it is totally potential and in no way actual (6:1:17,
p. 368, l. 13f.; 6:1:25, p. 401, l. 30-p. 402, l. 4). No true
knowledge of it is possible because it is not from the action of
an agent and has no final cause or purpose. (We can have knowledge
of a thing insofar as we know its form, and body which does not
preserve its shape is formless.) Thus, unlike things with form
which exist for a benefit (to^{c}elet) and cannot exist accidentally
for no purpose except for very short periods of time and infrequently, body which does not preserve its shape may be for no
benefit. If there had not been a sufficient "quantity" of it, the
world might not have come to be. If there happened to be more of
it than was needed for the world to come to be, as Gersonides
tentatively thinks is likely, then there may be a useless remainder
of it persisting outside of the world (6:1:18, p. 371, l. 12-p.
373, l. 15).

As discussed above, note #49, there are two ways to understand
the nature of this "body." We may assume that its formlessness
entails the privation of the form of corporeality so that it is
nondimensional and is pure potentiality. This interpretation leads
to a number of problems:
1) Gersonides would be hard-pressed to explain the distinction
which, he asserts, exists between his theory of creation out of
nothing and Maimonides' theory of creation out of absolutely
nothing. We may assume that Maimonides would agree that, in some
sense, prior to the creation of the world there was a potential
for the world to exist. Both of them reject the possibility of
the persistence of a vacuum or of absolute privation (see below,
note #178; cf. 6:1:17, p. 364, ll. 19-34; 6:2:7, p. 426, l. 15f.).
It is thus difficult to discern anything meaningful in Gersonides'
assertion that this body persists prior to creation if he intends
the body to denote pure potentiality. He would be speaking about
what others call "prime matter" (cf. above, note #49, for a summary
of Wolfson's history of the discussions of this term), i.e., a
nondimensional, potentially existent material principle. Since

there is no time prior to creation, Gersonides' assertion that
this principle persists "prior" to creation would not differ from
the priority which others attribute to "prime matter" at creation.
2) In at least two contexts, Gersonides discusses body which does
not preserve its shape in ways that seem to imply that it is
dimensional in some sense. He says that it persists between the
spheres to prevent the motions of the stars from reaching one
another and becoming confused, and he discusses the question of
the possibility that a remainder exists of this body after creation
(see above, note #49, for a more complete discussion of this problem). To assume that he intends it to be nondimensional in some
places and dimensional in others is unlikely, as discussed above
in note #49.
3) In both of his discussions of the process of creation, he states
that the creation of the sublunar world occurred when the body
which does not preserve its shape was given the nature to be lower
matter and that that nature is its reception of the elemental forms
(6:1:17, p. 367, ll. 27-36, partially quoted above, note #49;
6:2:8, p. 429, ll. 21-24, quoted above, note #49; CT 10d, ll.
12-17, partially quoted above, note #49). As discussed in note
#49, it is possible to interpret these passages as vaguely alluding
to a prior stage in which this nondimensional body is given the
dimensionality it needs to serve as the substratum of the elemental
forms. These passages, however, can be read more easily as assuming that this body is that dimensional substratum.

Thus, the second way to interpret this body is to assume that
he meant it to be dimensional in some sense. It is unlikely that
it had actual, definite dimensions, because this would require this
formless body to have form and because this would imply that this
body, which is close to privation, had actual existence. It is
more likely that he meant to assert that this body had absolute
dimensionality but had no actual definite dimensions.

According to those interpretations which assume that this
body was absolutely nonextended, it is necessary to posit that the
first stage of the creation of the sublunar world was the reception
by part of this body of a corporeal form so that it could serve as
the dimensional substratum of the elemental forms. Thus, these
interpretations must understand "last form" and the "nature" which
he states that "prime matter" or "body which does not preserve its
shape" receives to be the form of dimensionality. It is necessary,
therefore to assume that he uses the term "prime matter" to refer
to two different things: nondimensional, absolute potentiality,

in which case it is synonymous with "body which does not preserve
its shape" and which is its meaning when it is used in conjunction
with "last form;" and the dimensional substratum of the elemental
forms, which is its meaning when it is used in conjunction with
"the elemental forms" and when there is no mention of a prior
nature.

    According to those interpretations which assume that this
body is absolute dimensional body, "prime matter" is used as a
synonym for "body which does not preserve its shape" in all cases
(fifth interpretation), or in all cases except where it is used in
conjunction with the term "last form" (fourth interpretation), in
which case, it is nondimensional, absolute potentiality which is
prior to absolute dimensional body which does not preserve its
shape.

    In support of the reading of "prime matter" as nondimensional,
absolute potentiality is his reference to "the privation of the
forms which inhere in" prime matter and his statement that the
element earth is compared to prime matter because it is "ultimately
deprived of form" (6:2:5, p. 422, ll. 11f., 14f.). He also refers
there (1. 12) to his commentary to the Book of Job, where he states
that prime matter is the source of all privation (Commentary to
Job, the Explanation of the Discourse of Chapters 27-28, in Rabbinic
Bibles (Miqra³ot Gedolot), quoted below, note #70). Also relevant
here is the statement in his commentary (CT 9c, ll. 28-32, quoted
above in note #49) that prime matter is so weak in existence that
its nature is close to the nature of privation. All of these
instances, however, suggest only that prime matter is as close to
the nature of privation as is body which does not preserve its
shape, which is described in similar terms. What all interpretations must agree upon, therefore, is that at least one sense of
"prime matter" is synonymous with "body which does not preserve its
shape." Either they are both nondimensional or they are both dimensional in one of the senses of that term. Also in support of the
claim that they are synonymous are his references to body which
does not preserve its shape as "matter," and specifically his
description of it as a single matter which is the principle of all
matter (6:1:17, p. 368, l. 13f.; cf. 6:1:18, p. 370, l. 35; p. 375,
l. 17). But whereas the two terms are synonymous in all cases
according to the (first and fifth) interpretations which identify
last form with the elemental forms, the other interpretations

must assume that they are synonymous only when the term occurs in
conjunction with "last form" and not with "the elemental forms."

Our interpretation of the present text will thus depend upon
our view of his entire theory of creation. "Prime matter" either
refers to the nondimensional material principle or to the absolute
dimensional substratum of the elemental forms. If it refers to the
former, then "last form" designates that form which gives the nondimensional material principle either actual dimensions, or absolute
dimensions or definite dimensions. If it refers to the latter,
then "last form" designates that form which gives absolute dimensional body the forms of the elements themselves with their definite
dimensionality. For reasons explained in note #49 above, the last
alternative is most plausible.

52) That is, prime matter "is in" last form. Note that this is
not to be taken literally. The matter of a given tree, for example,
cannot be properly said to be in the form of that tree, as if the
form of the tree was a mold filled with matter. The analogy is
somewhat more apt, however, if he is using "last form" to refer to
corporeal form or to the form of definite dimensionality. If so,
the form is in fact providing the matter either with absolute or
definite dimensionality.

53) The reference is to the first part of the work, Sefer
Ṣurat Ha-ʔareṣ Ve-tavnit Ha-shamayim, edited by M. Jaffe and Jonathan ben Joseph (Offenbach, 1720). In his introduction to his
translation of Abraham bar Ḥayya's The Meditation of the Sad Soul
(New York, 1968), p. 5, Geoffrey Wigoder writes that the work was
"the first exposition of the Ptolemaic system in Hebrew" which
"became the chief source of geographical knowledge in Jewish literature." His influence on Gersonides in the field of astronomy is
clear in Treatise Five, Part One of The Wars of the Lord (cf.
Bernard R. Goldstein, "Preliminary Remarks on Levi Ben Gerson's
Contributions to Astronomy," Proceedings of the Israel Academy of
Sciences and Humanities 3.9[1969]:243).

I have not been able to find the view which Gersonides
attributes here to Bar Ḥiyya in the Offenbach, 1720 edition.
Charles Touati, La pensée philosophique et théologique de Gersonide
(Paris, 1973), p. 271, n. 12, says that he was not able to find it
in Vallicrosa's modern translation, La obra Forma de la Tierra
(Madrid, 1956). Bar Ḥiyya also deals with the creation of the
world, however, in the first section of Hegyon Ha-nefesh Ha-ᶜaṣuvah

(edited by E. Freimann, Leipzig, 1860; reprinted Jerusalem, 1967).
Bar Ḥiyya there identifies tohu with hyle (i.e. formless matter)
and bohu with the form which covers and sustains the tohu (2b, 3a).
Thus, though Gersonides borrows his analysis of the word bohu, he
does not follow his understanding of the passage in Isaiah.

54) See note #49 above for a discussion of the relationship
between last form and the elemental forms.

55) b. Ḥag. 12a. The complete passage reads as follows
(translation taken from the Soncino edition, [London, 1938]):

> It is taught: Tohu is a green line that encompasses
> the whole world, out of which darkness proceeds, for
> it is said: "He made darkness His hiding-place round
> about Him" (Ps 18:12). Bohu, this means the slimy
> stones that are sunk in the deep, out of which the
> waters proceed, for it is said: "And he shall stretch
> over it the line of confusion (Tohu) and the plummet
> of emptiness (Bohu)" (Isa 34:11).

56) As mentioned above, note #49, there are two ways to understand his intention here. If last form is the form of (absolute)
dimensionality which nonextended prime matter receives so that it
can serve as the substratum of the elemental forms, then last form
is an intermediate between the contrary qualities of the elements
because it exists at a prior stage at which the elements, and hence
their qualities, have not yet come to be. If "last form" is a
term which denotes that aspect of definite dimensionality which
absolute dimensional prime matter receives from all four of the
elemental forms, then last form is intermediate between the contrary qualities of the elements because it is their aspect of
definite dimensionality, which is shared by all of them. Aristotle's definition of an intermediate is something between contraries
which is neither extreme (Categoriae 5.2b23) and which is composed
of these contraries (Metaphysica 1057a18ff.; cf. Physica 5.3.
226b24f., 227a7). Though both interpretations of last form assume
that it has neither extreme of the primary qualities of the elements, only the second interpretation assumes that it is composed
of these contraries. This is yet another piece of evidence in
support of the fifth interpretation of his theory of creation discussed above, note #49.

The contraries to which he is referring are the qualities
which the elements possess (see De Generatione et Corruptione
2.3-4). For example, fire is composed of the hot and the dry
(De Generatione et Corruptione 2.2.329b18ff.).

57) Ṣevaᶜ. Cf. the parallel passage in his Commentary to the Torah (CT 9c, l. 43), where he uses the word marᵓeh. On green as the intermediate color, cf. Categoriae 10.12a17.

58) Mefursam. Gersonides uses this term to designate that which is true by consensus. For example, that a wonder should be generated without the presence of a prophet is contrary to that which is generally recognized to be true (6:2:10, p. 448, l. 4); that the Torah is of divine origin is generally recognized by all men today (CT 2a); and a study of marvels should begin with those aspects of marvels which have been made known to all (nitfarsem) by Biblical narratives (6:2:9, p. 441, l. 23). See H. A. Wolfson, "The Double Faith Theory in Saadia, Averroes and St. Thomas," Jewish Quarterly Review, n.s. 33 (1942):238, for a discussion of Saadia's concept of generally recognized notions.

59) In the first part of this treatise (6:1:18, p. 371, ll. 13ff.), he asserts the limited nature of our knowledge of body which does not preserve its shape which preceded the generation of the world. Our knowledge is limited because that body is not the effect of an agent and therefore has no final cause which is the proper object of knowledge. The tentative conclusions he does make the concerning that body are reached inductively from his observation of the world after its generation.

His choice of words here, mi-ṣado ("in its respect"), is a reference back to the first part of this treatise (6:1:19, p. 378, ll. 6ff.) where he states that any investigation of the body in respect to itself is beyond us. It is rather in respect to the cause of generation that any inferences about the generation of the world can be drawn.

Cf. above, note #51, for a discussion of the relationship between the terms "body which does not preserve its shape" and "prime matter."

TREATISE SIX, PART TWO: CHAPTER FIVE

THE MEANING OF ᵓOR AND ḤOSHEKH (LIGHT AND DARKNESS)

Chapter Five, in which the number of ways in which
light and darkness are said will be explained.

Summary

Gersonides discusses the different senses of the terms "light"
and "darkness." He takes the term "light" in Gen 1:3 to refer to
the perfect conception of the intelligible world of the separate
intellects, and the term "darkness" in Gen 1:2 to refer to the
element earth. Incidentally, he asserts that the term tehom in
Gen 1:2 refers to the element water. Also, he cites a rabbinic
discussion to support his assertion that the term ᶜal need not mean
"on" but often means "next to," so that the element earth was next
to the element water.

He then engages in a lengthy refutation of the exegesis of
Maimonides, who identifies the term "darkness" with the element
fire. He concludes by citing the rabbis to support his own view
that the term "light" refers to the intelligible world.

Translation

69ab
421   Light and darkness are equivocal terms. The reason for
this is that light is first said of perceptible light, and
darkness of the privation of perceptible light. There are

422   many instances of this: "the light of the sun,"[60] / "for
light by day."[61] The case is similar with darkness: "The
sun shall be dark when it rises,"[62] "At Tehaphnehes also the
day shall be dark."[63] And there are many instances of this.
And from this sense, it says, a bit analogously, "Their
faces are darker than soot."[64]

Next, light said metaphorically for eyes which see with
perfection, as it says, "how my eyes have been brightened."[65]
Similarly, darkness is used metaphorically for eyes that can-

1. 5   not see, as it says, "And those that look through the windows
shall be darkened."[66] This is the case because the perception of visible things cannot be perfected in darkness.

And because the form resembles light—in that it is the
perfection of the thing of which it is the form, just as
light is the perfection of a transparent body insofar as it
is transparent,[67] and furthermore, in that it renders intelligible those things which have form, for it is in this
respect alone that they are intelligible, just as (light)

215

69ba
1. 10   renders visible those things / which one perceives—form is
therefore metaphorically represented by light, and matter by
darkness and gloom.[68] Thus it says, "The stones of gloom
and deep darkness,"[69] with reference to prime matter, in
respect to the privation of the forms which inhere in it, as
we have explained in our commentary to the Book of Job.[70]
And it is in this sense that it says, "And darkness was upon
the face of the deep,"[71] that is to say, the element earth,
which is absolutely deprived[72] of form and good, in addition
to its being the least of all existent things. And because

1. 15   it is ultimately deprived of form it is compared to prime
matter. As it says, "For you are dust, and to dust you
shall return,"[73] for man will return to his dust, as he once
was.[74] Therefore, it says that (darkness) is "ᶜal the face
of the deep,"[75] for the deep is the lowest place of the water.
This is clear from its context. Therefore, the face of the
deep is the lowliest area of the water. The explanation of
"(ᶜal) the face of the deep"[76] is that which is next to the
lowest area of the water, for the word "upon" (ᶜal) is said

1. 20   with this intention. As it says, "next to him (ve-ᶜalav) is
the tribe of Manasseh,"[77] and as it says, "And you shall put
pure frankincense ᶜal each row,"[78] for its explanation is
"next to" the row, as is explained in Menahot.[79]

        But the Master the Guide asserted that the intention of
the word "darkness" is the element fire.[80] He brought proof
from what the Torah says: "When you heard the voice out of
the midst of the darkness."[81] And in another place it says,
"You heard His words out of the midst of the fire."[82] This

1. 25   is a sign that fire is called darkness. Similarly, it says,
"All darkness is laid up for His treasures, a fire not blown
upon (shall consume him)."[83] This is also a sign that darkness is fire. According to what Maimonides believes, elemental fire is called darkness because it does not shine, as
is explained in Physics, and light occurs to it when it is
interwoven in bodies.[84]

        In our opinion this notion is not adequate. The reason
for this is that it does not necessarily follow from its

1. 30   saying in one place, "Out of the midst of the fire"[85] and in
another place "Out of the midst of darkness,"[86] that darkness
is fire. Rather, the darkness was the dark cloud there from
which the fire went out, for the cloud whose way this is is

very dark. Therefore, it says, "The Lord spoke these words
to your whole congregation, at the mountain out of the midst
of the fire and the dense clouds."[87] It has already been
explained to you[88] that they heard His words out of the
midst of the fire and out of the midst of the dense clouds

l. 35 which are darkness. Therefore, it is clear that from its
saying, "When you heard the voice out of the midst of the

423   darkness,"[89] it does not / necessarily follow that its intention is "Out of the midst of the fire." Similarly, when it
says, "All darkness is laid up for his treasures,"[90] if we
admit that (darkness) alludes to the fire that is mentioned
in this verse, then (the fire) returns to the cloud from
which the flames and the things which cause passing away come,
for most of the time it is very dark.[91]

Furthermore, it is a difficult question for Maimonides
l. 5   why it relates the place of the fire to the lowliest area of
the water, for it would be proper to relate it to the face of
the wind (and) not to the face of the water. How much the
more so is it improper to relate it to the lowliest area of
the water. And this is very clear.[92]

Furthermore, the earth is more distant from light than
the rest of the elements, for it is a very dark material
body. Therefore, it necessarily follows that it be described
by the term "darkness" rather than any of the other elements.
l. 10 Additionally, it is more deprived of form and goodness than
any of the other elements.[93] Therefore, it is proper that
it be called "darkness," as we have explained.[94]

The term "darkness" is said metaphorically with reference
to one who cannot conceive the intelligibles, which are the
forms, just as the term "darkness" is metaphorically said
with reference to the privation of the forms. As it says,
"The fool walks in darkness."[95] For this reason light is
metaphorically used to refer to one who conceives with a
perfect conception.[96] As it says of the Lord, may He be
blessed, "And the light dwells with Him."[97] It is in this
l. 15 sense that it says, "You wrap Yourself with light as with a
garment."[98] This light is the separate intellects which are
the movers of the heavenly bodies. It is in this sense that
it says, "Let there be light."[99]

Our rabbis, may their memories be for a blessing,
commented on this notion in the Midrash:[100]

"God saw that the light was good."[101] R. Judah
bar Simon said: The Holy One, blessed be He, set
apart the light for Himself. It is to be compared
to a king who saw a nice portion and said, "This
1. 20   is for me." Similarly, when the Holy One, blessed
be He, created it, He said, "No creature may use
it. Only Me." Thus it is written, "And the light
dwells with Him."[102]

R. Abbin the Levite said: The Holy One, blessed
be He, took it and wrapped Himself in it, as in
a tallit[103] and shined forth[104] His world with
His splendor. Thus it is written, "You wrap Yourself with light as with a garment."[105]

And the rabbis said: He shined it forth[106] to give
it to the righteous in the world to come. It is to
be compared to a king who saw a nice portion and
said, "This is for my son." Thus it is written,
"Light is sown for the righteous."[107]

1. 25   It is thus explained to you that all of them agreed that

this light is not perceptible light, but that, according to

them, it is intelligible light. How marvelous are their

statements with regard to this for one who reflects upon

them and who understands the way of the argument among them.

That is, R. Judah bar Simon believed that it is impossible

for the human intellect to conceive the separate intellects

in any respect of conception.[108] The sages believed that

some manner of their conception is possible for (the human

intellect) in that which overflows to it of (the separate

1. 30 intellects') light and splendor in a way that immortality

is perfected for it in this conception,[109] even though it

is impossible for it to conceive of them in a perfect manner,

as was explained in the first treatise of this book.[110] The

statement of R. Abbin the Levite is very wonderful for

69bb through it it is explained that this light is prior / in

cause to the rest of created things.[111] And through this

the sage asserted that the Lord, may He be blessed, contem-

plates the world of the separate intellects, and that exist-

ence overflows from them.

60) Isa 30:26.

61) Isa 60:19 and Jer 31:35.

62) Isa 13:10.

63) Ezek 30:18.

64) Lam 4:8. Analogy (dimyon) is one of the terms which he uses to refer to equivocation. In that the text here is not talking about the absence of perceptible light itself, he says that it is speaking analogously (dimyon). Similarly, he says below that it is by analogy that the soul is called ruaḥ, the primary meaning of which is "wind," because its first instrument is wind (6:2:6, p. 424, 1. 2). Further on, he uses the term dimyon in conjunction with hemshel (similitude) to indicate that a rabbinic statement is "not truly so" (6:2:7, p. 426, 11. 27, 29, 35). In the last case, it is water which is said by way of analogy with the body which does not keep its shape. In all of these instances, analogy is said when two things are named equivocally and the second possesses some attribute but not all attributes of the first.

65) 1 Sam 14:29. He uses the term "metaphor" (hash³alah) only to refer to equivocation which relates to light and darkness. Here, light is metaphorically said of eyes which see perfectly in the physical sense of perception. (In the cited passage, Jonathan's eyes are brightened because he eats honey and his physical stamina is improved.) Later in this chapter, light is metaphorically said of form (p. 422, 1. 10), because form resembles light, and of one who conceives with a perfect conception (p. 423, 1. 13; cf. Topica 1.17.108a10, where Aristotle draws a likeness between sight in the eye and reason in the soul, using this as an example of things which belong to different genera and which are alike in relation. Also cf. Guide 1:47, where Maimonides allows for the figurative attribution of sight to God.) Gersonides asserts that light is also said of the separate intellects (p. 423, 1. 15f.). On the basis of this limited use of the term, it is difficult to generalize about its precise meaning. It is clear, however, that a metaphor (hash³alah) is less literal and more figurative than an analogy (dimyon).

66) Qoh 12:3. I.e., they shall not be able to see well.

67) That is, light enables a transparent thing to fulfill its function—to be transparent—just as the form of a thing enables

a body to perform its function by endowing it with the appropriate
nature. For an explanation of light's activity in transparent
bodies, see De Anima 2.7.418b4-13.

68) One knows a thing insofar as one knows the form or
definition of that thing. His discussion of human knowledge can
be found in the first treatise. Also cf. the third treatise, where
his arguments about God's knowledge turn on this premise.

The manuscripts consulted differ here with the printed editions
as follows: On p. 422, 1. 9, the manuscripts read kemo she-yasim
ha-ɔor for kemo she-yasim. On p. 422, 1. 10, the manuscripts
read hineh hishɔil heᶜder ha-ṣurah le-ḥoshekh ve-ɔofel for hineh
hishɔil ha-ṣurah la-ɔor ve-ha-ḥomer le-ḥoshekh ve-ɔofel. If the
manuscripts are correct (Touati prefers them here to the printed
editions) then the translated text should read as follows:

> just as light renders visible those things which one
> perceives by means of light—the privation of form is
> therefore metaphorically represented by darkness and
> gloom.

The basic meaning of the text, however, remains unchanged.

69) Job 28:3.

70) Commentary to Job, The Explanation of the Discourse of
Chapters 27-28, in Rabbinic Bibles (Miqraɔot Gedolot). He states
there:

> "The stones of gloom and deep darkness" (28:3). That
> is the prime matter which all privations are with and
> which is the end of all things which come to be. Or,
> it called the element earth "the stones of gloom and
> deep darkness," because it is absolute privation in
> relation to the rest of sensible existent things.

For an alternate translation, see Abraham L. Lassen, translator,
The Commentary of Levi ben Gersom (Gersonides) on the Book of Job
(New York, 1946), p. 170.

71) Gen 1:2.

72) Note that he is exaggerating here. The element earth is
most devoid of form and good relative to the other elements and
to composite existent things (see below #93). It is the densest
and most material of the four elements and the elemental forms are
the lowest of the hylic forms (see above, note #49). The element
earth, however, is not absolutely devoid of form and good, because
it is informed by the elemental form of earth. This is more
properly said of prime matter and/or body which does not preserve

its shape (depending upon one's interpretation of his description
of the process of coming to be, as explained above, notes #49 and
#51). As another example of the loose and metaphorical usage which
can be applied to the terms "matter" and "form," cf. Meteorologica
4.1.379a16, where Aristotle states that earth, water and air are
all matter relatively to fire. See below in this chapter (p. 423,
l. 9) where Gersonides is more precise.

73) Gen 3:19.

74) This is a paraphrase of Qoh 12:7.

75) Gen 1:2.

76) Gen 1:2.

77) Num 2:20.

78) Lev 24:7. His interpretation of Gen 1:2 identifies darkness
as the element earth and places it in the lowest part of the water.
This is the natural position of the element earth at the point at
which matter had received only the elemental forms and the elements
had not yet intermixed under the influence of the motions of the
stars (see above, notes #49 and #51).

79) b. Menaḥ. 62a reads as follows (Soncino translation):

R. Ḥisda said to R. Hamnuna (others say, R. Hamnuna
said to R. Ḥisda), Rabbi follows his general view that
ᶜal means 'near to'; as it was taught: It is written,
"And thou shalt put pure frankincense ᶜal each row"
(Lev 24:7). Rabbi says, ᶜal means 'near to.' You say
that ᶜal means 'near to'; but perhaps it is not so but
rather it signifies literally 'upon'? Since it states,
"and thou shalt put a veil ᶜal the ark" (Exod 40:3),
conclude that ᶜal means 'near to'.

m. Menaḥ 11:5 reads as follows (Soncino translation):

Abba Saul says, There (i.e., between the shewbread) they
used to put the two dishes of frankincense pertaining to
the shewbread. They said to him, Is it not written,
"And thou shalt put pure frankincense upon (ᶜal) each
row?" (Lev 24:7) He replied, But is it not written, "And
next unto (ᶜal) him shall be the tribe of Manasseh"
(Num 2:20).

80) Guide 2:30.

81) Deut 5:20.

82) Deut 4:36.

83) Job 20:26.

84) Maimonides states only that elemental fire is transparent and does not shine. Gersonides adds the last explanatory phrase. Cf. De Generatione Animalium 3.2.761b18.

85) Deut 4:36.

86) Deut 5:20.

87) Deut 5:19.

88) In Deut 5:19. His argument here is that the darkness of 5:20 is a reference to the clouds of 5:19, and not to the fire of 4:36.

89) Deut 5:20.

90) Job 20:26.

91) So that darkness is a reference to the cloud rather than to the fire in it.

92) His argument here relies on his interpretation of the word ᶜal in the phrase, "ᶜal the face of the deep" (Gen 1:2), for which he cites b. Menaḥot above. He believes it means "next to the lowest part of the water." Maimonides also deals with the question of the natural position of the elements. (Guide, 2:30, Pines translation, p. 351):

> The elements are mentioned according to their natural position; namely first the earth, then the water that is above it, then the air that adheres to the water, then the fire that is above the air. For in view of the specification of the air as being "over the face of the waters" (Gen 1:2), "darkness" that is "upon the face of the deep" (Gen 1:2) is indubitably above the "spirit."

Maimonides reads the phrase ᶜal penei tehom in a way that supports his understanding of the term darkness.

93) In his Commentary to the Torah (9d, 1. 22) he adds that the degree of existence of the element earth is closest of all existent bodies to the degree of prime matter. Also note, for example, his statement in his commentary to Job, quoted above in note #70, that the element earth is "absolute privation" in relation to the rest of sensible existent things.

94) In this chapter, p. 422, ll. 12ff.

95) Qoh 2:14.

96) That is, a separate intellect.

97) Dan 2:22.

98) Ps 104:2.

99) Gen 1:3. That is, "Let there be the upper, intelligible world of separate intellects." Cf. 6:2:8, p. 429, l. 2 and CT 9d, l. 50, where he calls this light, "the world of the angels."

100) His quotation is close to the passage in Midr. Ps. 27 (edited by S. Buber [Vilna, 1891; reprinted Jerusalem, 1977], p. 111). Cf. Gen. Rab. 3:4, 6; Lev. Rab. 31:7; y. Ber. 8:6.

101) Gen 1:4. The verse continues, "and God pronounced a distinction (va-yavdel)" which is crucial to an understanding of the rabbinic interpretation in this passage. The discussion concerns the manner in which the distinction was pronounced.

102) Dan 2:22.

103) A prayer shawl.

104) hivriq. Literally, to brighten or flash. The parallel text in his Commentary to the Torah (10a, l. 3) has hidbiq, which might mean "caused (His light) to cleave (to the righteous)." Midr. Ps. 27 and Gen. Rab. 3:4 have hivhiq, to shine or be bright. The manuscripts consulted agree here with the printed editions.

105) Ps 104:2.

106) See above, note #104.

107) Ps 97:11.

108) Because God reserves the intelligible light for Himself.

109) Because God gives the intelligible light to the righteous in the world to come.

110) 1:12, pp. 85ff. At the conclusion of that chapter, (p. 88) he refers to this midrashic passage to show that the rabbis as well as the philosophers were divided on the question of whether the acquired intellect can ever achieve conjunction with the Active Intellect.

111) R. Abbin states that God creates the world out of His light. Gersonides, identifying this light with the separate intellects, identifies this as his own view that the sublunar world overflows from the activities of the heavenly bodies. These activities are caused by the longing of the separate intellects for God. Thus, these intellects are "prior in cause" to the rest of created things.

TREATISE SIX, PART TWO: CHAPTER SIX
THE MEANING OF RUAH

Chapter Six, in which many of the ways in which ruah
is said will be explained.

Summary

Gersonides discusses the different senses of the term ruah
and concludes that the phrase ruah ᵓelohim in Gen 1:2 refers to the
elements air and fire, and the term merahefet in Gen 1:2 means
"resting."

Translation

69bb
424
Ruah is an equivocal term which is said with reference
to the wind,[112] as in, "a very strong west wind."[113] There
are many such instances.[114] In this sense, by way of a
slight analogy, the soul is called ruah, because natural heat
is the first instrument of the soul, and its substratum is
the breath (ruah) which comes to be in the heart and which
comes to the organs by means of the veins which pulsate.[115]

1. 5   Ruah is (also) said with reference to elemental air.
It is in this sense that it says, "the ruah of God."[116] It
is placed in a construct state with "God" to indicate the
magnitude of its quantity, for the wind is small in quantity.[117] Since ruah is equivocal for elemental air and for
the wind, (the Torah) describes (elemental air) in terms of
magnitude to indicate about which of the senses of ruah it
is speaking. You find that this often occurs in our language.
That is, that one of the names of the Lord, may He be blessed,
is adjoined when one wants to emphasize the magnitude or
strength (of a word). As it says, "(Your righteousness is)

1. 10 like the mountains of ᵓEl,"[118] "the flame of the Yah,"[119]
"the arrows of Shadday,"[120] like the voice of Shadday."[121]
It is in this sense[122] that ruah is said to be "resting over
(merahefet) the face of the water."[123] That is, it was
resting upon the surface of the water,[124] as in, "(As an
eagle that rouses her nestlings) resting over (yerahef)
her young,"[125] where the intention is "resting."

The term ruah includes elemental air and elemental
fire,[126] because the Torah refused to call elemental fire
"fire" in order to indicate the distance between it and

1. 15 perceptible fire.[127] (Fire) is similar to air except that

225

it is dry and it is hotter than air.[128]   It is in this sense
that the sages[129] said that air has two[130] parts: the lower
part in which there is the heavy rain and the light rain and
the other usual kinds of things, which is hot and moist; and
the upper part, which is hot and dry.

112) <u>Ruaḥ ha-menashevet</u>. Literally, "blowing wind." In his
<u>Commentary to the Torah</u> (9d, l. 48f.), he calls it composite in
contrast to the simple nature of elemental air.

113) Exod 10:19.

114) In the Bible.

115) This follows Aristotle rather closely. The heart is the
body's central source of heat (<u>De Partibus Animalium</u> 3.7.670a24;
cf. <u>De Generatione Animalium</u> 4.1.766b1; <u>Problemata</u> 10.54.897a3)
and that heat is distributed through the veins (<u>De Spiritu</u>
5.483b19). The breath is distributed by the heart (<u>De Spiritu</u>
4.482b6) and respiration is a function of the soul which resides
in the air (<u>De Spiritu</u> 1.481a17, 4.482b22f., 5.483a26ff.).

116) Gen 1:2.

117) In contrast to the quantity of elemental air.

118) Ps 36:7.

119) Cant 8:6.

120) Job 6:4.

121) Ezek 1:24; cf. Ezek 10:5.

122) That is, the sense of elemental air. The preceding
discussion of the significance of God's names has been a digression,
and he now returns to his original thought at the beginning of the
paragraph.

123) Gen 1:2.

124) That is, the elements were pure and unmixed and elemental
air was "resting upon" the layer of elemental water below it.

125) Deut 32:11. The translation of <u>meraḥefet</u> and <u>yeraḥef</u> as
"resting" is singular among Jewish commentators on the Bible and
without apparent textual basis. Note that in his commentary on
Deut 32:11 (CT 242b) he first repeats this interpretation of the
term and then allows for the possibility that it may mean "flying."
There can be no possibility of motion in our verse, however,
because of his view that <u>ruaḥ</u> refers to elemental air and that this
stage, at which the elements were unmixed, was prior to subsequent
changes wrought by the actions of contraries under the influence
of the motions of the stars. Cf. <u>Topica</u> 4.5.127a4ff., where
Aristotle defines "wind" as "a movement of air."

126) Though he uses the phrase yesod ha-ʾavir here instead of
ha-ʾavir ha-yesodiy above (l. 5), it is clear that, with regard to
both air and fire, he is referring to the pure, unmixed states of
these elements. This is clear both from the contrast he is about
to make between elemental fire and perceptible fire and from his
understanding of the state of affairs which existed at the first
"day" of creation (see 6:2:8, p. 428, l. 31-p. 429, l. 18; cf.
above, notes #49 and #51). On the basis of his discussion below of
the first "day" of creation, we can assume that the term kolel
("includes") means not that ruaḥ is said of the conjunction of
elemental air and elemental fire, for their definitions preclude
the possibility of any intermixing between them (6:2:8, p. 428,
l. 35). Rather, the term ruaḥ means elemental air or elemental
fire. He makes this statement because his interpretation of the
passage is that, on the first day of creation, God placed the elemental forms in matter so that there existed four separate elemental
masses. He has already stated that "darkness" means earth (6:2:5,
p. 422, l. 13) and that "the deep" means the lowest part of the
water (6:2:5, p. 422, l. 18). Thus there remains only the ruaḥ
which rests above the water—one term to designate the two upper
elements.

127) Perceptible fire is composite whereas elemental fire is
simple. Cf. De Generatione Animalium 3.2.761b18ff. (Oxford translation):

> The form which fire assumes never appears to be peculiar
> to it, but it always exists in some other of the ele-
> ments, for that which is ignited appears to be either
> air or smoke or earth.

128) Cf. De Generatione et Corruptione 2.3.330b4 where Aristotle
designates Fire as hot and dry and Air as hot and moist. The
similarity to which Gersonides refers depends on both possessing
the elementary quality of heat. Cf. 6:1:8, p. 319, l. 26, where he
attributes the diversity of qualities that existent things possess
to the diverse degrees in which they possess heat, cold, moisture
and dryness.

129) Gersonides uses the term ḥakhamim ("sages") most
frequently to refer to the rabbis. There is evidence in rabbinic
literature of a familiarity with the notion of concentric layers
of the four elements. Note, for example, the following statement
from Num. Rab. 14:12 (Soncino translation, p. 623):

>...The four elements from which the Holy One, blessed
>be He, created the world, three of them being of a
>superior nature, one higher than the other, and the
>fourth the lowest, the heaviest of them all. They are
>as follows: The earth is the heaviest of all of them...
>The water is above the earth; the air, from which the
>wind is formed, is above the earth, and the fire is
>above the air, for fire is lighter than all the others,
>ascending right up to the sky... It has also been said
>that the fire surrounds the whole universe high up as
>far as the sky.

I have not been able to find, however, a passage in rabbinic
literature to which the following statement of Gersonides might
refer. Note, however, that the manuscripts consulted have yo$^{\circ}$mru
for $^{\circ}$amru. If they are correct, our text should be translated as,
"the sages say," and would not refer back to the rabbis necessarily.

130) The Riva di Trento edition (69bb, l. 21), the parallel
passage in his commentary (CT 9d, l. 46) and the manuscripts consulted have sheloshah (three) for the Leipzig's shenei (two). The
commentary and the manuscripts consulted also add the phrase
ve-ḥeleq ha-$^{\circ}$emṣa^{c}i (the intermediate part) before the words "which
is hot and moist" (below, l. 17). This phrase is omitted from both
the Leipzig and the Riva di Trento editions.

The latter additional phrase of the manuscripts and the
commentary indicates the source of confusion. If there are two
parts, they are: a) the lower part in which there is the heavy
rain and the light rain and the other usual kinds of things (which
is hot and moist); and b) the upper part (which is hot and dry).
If there are three parts, they are a) the lower part in which there
is the heavy rain and the light rain and the other usual kinds of
things; b) the intermediate part (which is hot and moist); and
c) the upper part (which is hot and dry).

Both interpretations are plausible. Respectively, the three
parts might designate a) perceptible air, i.e., the atmosphere
which is composite, b) elemental air, and c) elemental fire. This
is unlikely, however, because Gersonides gives no indication that
he thinks that the simple elements persist in their noncomposite
form after the first day of creation, so that there would be no
reason for him to retain a distinction between perceptible and
elemental air. Alternately, the three parts might designate a) the
lower part of the atmosphere in which clouds and rain are formed,
which is (relatively) cold and moist (cf. below, 6:2:7, p. 425,
l. 11f., where he refers to "the cold part of the air in which
clouds and rain come to be"), b) the intermediate part of the

atmosphere, which is hot and moist (the primary qualities of air)
and c) the upper part of the sublunar world, which is hot and dry
(the primary qualities of fire). The two part distinction would
ignore the lowest of these parts. It is the second interpretation
of the three part distinction which conforms most closely to
Aristotle's discussion of the question (Meteorologica 1.3.340b19ff.,
Oxford translation):

> So at the centre and round it we get earth and water,
> the heaviest and the coldest elements, by themselves;
> round them and contiguous with them, air and what we
> commonly call fire.
>
> It is not really fire, for fire is an excess of heat
> and a sort of ebulition; but in reality, of what we
> call air, the part surrounding the earth is moist and
> warm, because it contains both vapour and dry exhala-
> tion from the earth. But the next part, above that,
> is warm and dry. For vapour is naturally moist and
> cold, but the exhalation warm and dry; and vapour is
> potentially like water, the exhalation potentially
> like fire. So we must take the reason why clouds are
> not formed in the upper region to be this: that it is
> filled not with mere air but rather with a sort of
> fire.

Cf. Meteorologica 1.8.345b32.

TREATISE SIX, PART TWO: CHAPTER SEVEN
THE MEANING OF RAQI^CA, MAYIM ^CELYONIM (UPPER WATERS)
MAYIM TAḤTONIM (LOWER WATERS)

Chapter Seven, in which what is intended in the Torah
by the terms raqi^ca, "lower waters" and "upper waters"
will be explained.

Summary

Gersonides discusses the different senses of the terms raqi^ca,
"lower waters" and "upper waters" which occur in the Genesis narrative's account of the second "day" of creation. He concludes that
the term raqi^ca is used there to refer to the supralunar spheres.
He takes the "waters" to refer to body which does not preserve its
shape which persisted prior to the creation of the world. "Lower
waters" refers to the part of that body out of which the sublunar
world came to be, and "upper waters" refers to the part of that
body out of which the supralunar world came to be.

He then argues with Maimonides' understanding that the term
raqi^ca refers to a part of the sublunar atmosphere and cites
several rabbinic texts in support of his own view.

Translation

69bb
424   The notion of raqi^ca is said with reference to anything
which is stretched out and which preserves its shape, as it
says, "They stretched out (va-yeraqe^cu) the plates of
gold,"[131] and as in, "stretched out plates (requ^cei),"[132]
and as in "To Him who stretched out (le-roqa^c) the earth
over the water."[133] That is, He stretched out a part of
(the earth) higher than the elemental water, and that is
the height which is the visible part of the earth, which is
the only instrument by means of which this enlarged part is
perfected, as we explained above.[134] It is in this sense
that it says, "Can you stretch out (tarqi^ca) the sky with
Him?"[135]

         You will find that, in our language, the term raqi^ca
1. 25 refers specifically to the heavenly body.[136] As it says,
"Let there be lights in the raqi^ca of the heavens,"[137] "And
(God) set them in the raqi^ca of the heavens."[138] It is in
this sense that it says, "(and birds that fly above the
earth) on the face of the raqi^ca of the heavens,"[139] for
birds fly above the earth alongside of the surface of the
water, which is spherical.[140] And in this motion, they do

231

not move in a straight motion down or up, as is the state of
affairs of the parts of the elements.[141]   It is in this sense
that it says, "Let there be a raqiᶜa in the midst of the
425   waters,"[142] that is, the spheres.[143]   / The movers of the
heavenly bodies were created[144] first in cause and in nature,
for they are the cause and the form and the perfection of
them, and the form is prior in existence, even if it is
posterior in coming to be.[145]

It says, "in the midst of the waters,"[146] because,
as has already been explained,[147] there was a body which
does not preserve its shape, from which the upper and the
1. 5   lower (waters) came to be, and, in our language, the notion
of not persisting in a single disposition is related to
water. As it says, "like water spilled (on the ground),"[148]
and as in, "the hearts of the people melted and became like
water."[149]   Their hearts are related to water because of its
softness and the ease with which it is influenced. It is in
this sense that the body which does not have the nature to
preserve its shape is related to water. This is what David
referred to when he said, "Praise Him, you (highest)[150]
heavens, and you waters above the heavens."[151]   That is, the
1. 10   body which does not preserve its shape which is in the spheres
so that all the motions do not reach each other.[152]

The Master the Guide understood the term raqiᶜa to
refer to the cold part of the air in which clouds and rain
come to be.[153]   What brought him to this conclusion was that
it seemed strange to him that there should be water in the
heavenly body.[154]   It is proper, however, that you should
know that not only is it the case that the true notion in
this is what we have explained, according to what was
1. 15   explained in the preceding demonstration. It is furthermore
the view of all the preceding sages of the Torah who said
something about the explanation of this verse.[155]   This is
made clear to you from their statements. They said in
Genesis Rabbah:[156]

> When the Holy One, blessed be He, said, "Let
> there be a raqiᶜa in the midst of the waters,"[157]
> the middle layer of the water solidified, and
> the lower heavens and the highest heavens were
> made.... The heavens[158] were in fluid form on
> the first day, and on the second day they
> congealed.[159] "Let there be raqiᶜa"[160] means

1. 20   "Let the raqi^{c}a be strengthened." R. Judah
b. R. Simon (said): "Let a lining be made for
the raqi^{c}a." As it says, "They stretched out
(va-yeraqe^{c}u) the plate of gold."[161] R. Ḥanina
said: A fire went forth from above and dried
up the face of the raqi^{c}a.... R. Pinḥas said in
the name of (R.) Hoshayah: As there is an
empty space between the raqi^{c}a and the earth,
so there is one between the raqi^{c}a and the
upper waters. As it is written, "Let there be a
raqi^{c}a in the midst of the waters,"[162] that is,

70aa   between them. / R. Tanḥuma said: I will state
1. 25   the proof. If it had said, "God made the raqi^{c}a,"
and divided between the waters that were upon
(^{c}al) the raqi^{c}a," I would have said that the
waters were placed upon the raqi^{c}a itself. Since,
however, it says, "between the waters which are
above (me-^{c}al) the raqi^{c}a,"[163] the upper waters
were suspended by (God's) word.

In this statement you have proofs that they understood

the raqi^{c}a to be the heavenly body. The first (proof) is

1. 30 that he[164] said: "the lower heavens and the highest heavens

were made." This would not be proper to say of a cloud nor

of a place in which (a cloud) comes to be.[165]

The second (proof) is that (R. Ḥanina) said: "A fire

went forth from above and dried up the face of the raqi^{c}a."

This would not be proper to say of a cloud,[166] for its

condensation is moistening, and it is disposed to water, not

to the dry. Its active agent is the cold, which is in that

part of the air, and not the fire, as is explained in the

1. 35 Meteorologica.[167] How much more so is it improper to say

this with reference to the cold part of the air in which the

cloud comes to be.

426   What is marvelous / is that he says, "a fire from

above." The reason for this is that we reckon that a thing

will only acquire the preservation of shape in respect to

the dry,[168] and it is the fire which dries and causes evapo-

ration,[169] so that this activity is related to fire. To

indicate that the nature of this is not like the nature of

elemental fire,[170] he says, "a fire from above." It is in

1. 5 this way that you find them saying in many places that the

heavens came to be from fire and water.[171] That is, that

they have two natures in them—a nature which preserves its

shape, and a nature which does not preserve its shape.[172]

God forbid that this sage should intend that God, may He be

blessed, made the heavens by means of an instrument, whether

fire or something related to fire.[173] Rather, he intends

by this that God, may He be blessed, bestowed this nature to
it through which it would preserve its shape.

The third proof is that (R. Pinḥas) said:

l. 10   As there is an empty space between the raqiᶜa
             and the earth, so there is one between the
             raqiᶜa and the upper waters.

If the raqiᶜa were the cloud or the place of the cloud, the
upper waters also would be there potentially. They would
not be above it.[174] But when this is understood according
to the way in which we have related it,[175] this statement is
suitable. For you find (the rabbis) saying that the thickness of the raqiᶜa is a certain measure between the earth
and the raqiᶜa.[176] Similarly, according to them, there is a
measure between raqiᶜa and raqiᶜa, and it is there that the
l. 15 body which does not preserve its shape—which has been
explained to be between them—is located,[177] for it is false
that there should be a vacuum.[178] The reason for this is
that they said in Genesis Rabbah:[179]

             From the earth to the raqiᶜa is a journey of
             five hundred years (and from the first raqiᶜa
             to the next raqiᶜa is a journey of five hundred
             years).[180]

The statement of R. Tanḥuma[181] that "the upper waters
were suspended by (God's) word" is very marvelous. The
reason for this is that he would say that the nature of the
upper waters is not like the nature of the lower waters
l. 20 which are heavy and which the earth bears. Rather, "(the
upper waters) are suspended by (God's) word." That is, they
have nothing which bears them, for they are neither light
nor heavy.[182] Therefore, he is precise and he says that if
it had been written,

             'And He divided between the waters that were on
             (ᶜal) the raqiᶜa,' I would have said that the
             waters were placed on the body of the raqiᶜa.

That is, that they were upon it and it bears them. But it
says that they are "above (me-ᶜal) the raqiᶜa,"[183] and it
does not describe them as being upon the raqiᶜa, so that
they were self-supporting. The precision of this comment
l. 25 is very wonderful.[184]

They have indicated to us that the statement that the
heavens are fire and water[185] is said by way of the

analogy,[186] and that it is not truly so, in their statement
in Genesis Rabbah:[187]

> "The heavens (shamayim)." (They are so called)
> because people wonder (mishtomemim) at them,
> saying: "...Are they made of water? Are they
> made of fire?"

In this statement they indicated that this is said only by
l. 30 way of analogy and similitude.[188]   Therefore, R. Aqiba
said, in the chapter ᵓEin Dorshin:[189]

> When you arrive at the stones of pure marble, do
> not say, "Water, water." For it is written:
> "He who speaks falsehoods shall not be established
> before My eyes."[190]

This sage called the heavenly bodies "stones of pure marble."
He called them this because they are transparent and are
free of all density and thickness.[191] He said this to indicate that what is called "water" is the body which does not
preserve its shape. ("Water") is the term (which is used)
l. 35 with respect to analogy and similitude. It does not have
the nature of elemental water.[192]

427   / The statement of Ben Zoma, in the chapter ᵓEin Dorshin,[193]
that "there is only two[194] fingers' (breadth) between the
upper waters and the lower waters," is very marvelous.[195]
The reason for this is that the lower waters—that is, the
lower matter—is distinguished from the upper waters by the
elemental forms which the Lord, may He be blessed, placed in
it. It is through (the elemental forms) that (the lower
l. 5 matter) has the power to receive all the forms. In these
elemental forms, there exists two active powers, the hot and
the cold, and through them they act upon one another.[196]
This is something that does not exist in the upper waters.[197]
And you know that "finger" is said in our language with
reference to the active power. As it says, "The finger of
God,"[198] and as in, "The finger of God...engraved upon the
tablets."[199] This is the case because the hand is a wonderful instrument with which one can do everything, and this is
l. 10 done by means of the fingers which are created in it. This
is clear from its context.

Furthermore, you will find a statement of our rabbis,
70ab   may their memories be for a blessing, / which indicates without a doubt that this raqiᶜa is the heavenly body. They said

in <u>Genesis Rabbah</u>[200] in the exposition of the verse, "These
are the generations of the heavens and the earth:"[201]

> R. Azaryah (said) in the name of Rabbi: This
> was said with reference to the One above.[202]
> Everything that you see are the generations of
> the heavens and the earth,[203] as it says,
> "In the beginning God created the heavens
> and the earth."[204] On the second day, He created
> things of the upper (world), as it says, "God
> said: Let there be a <u>raqiᶜa</u>."[205] On the third
> day, He created things of the lower (world), as
> it says, "God said: Let the earth put forth
> grass."[206] On the fourth day, He created things
> of the upper (world), as it says, "God said: Let
> there be luminaries in the <u>raqiᶜa</u> of the heavens."[207]
> etc.

l. 15

It is made clear to you in this statement that this sage
l. 20 believed that the <u>raqiᶜa</u> which was created on the second
day was of the heavenly bodies.

131) Exod 39:3. As discussed above, notes #49 and #51, it is
likely that he intends to refer to absolute dimensionality with
the phrase "lack of preservation of shape" and to definite dimensionality with the term "preservation of shape."

132) Num 17:3.

133) Ps 136:6.

134) The manuscripts consulted have the more plausible reading
of ha-ḥeleq ha-higgalut for ha-ḥeleq ha-higgaldut at p. 424, l. 23,
so that the translation would read "this visible part" rather than
"this enlarged part." Nevertheless, we have retained the reading
of the printed text because it plausibly refers to the enlargement
of the earth in the sense that the earth is raised in elevation
above the water.

In the first part of this treatise, Gersonides investigates
the nature of those things whose existence is continuous: the
heavenly bodies, time, motion and the visible part of the earth.
(For his discussion of continuous existence, see 3:4.) One might
think, he says, that these things do not have a coming to be
because their existence is continuous (6:1:5, pp. 306ff.). His
method is to show that each of these must have come to be and that
consquently the world as a whole must have come to be.

In the chapter which demonstrates that the visible part of
the earth must have been generated (6:1:13), he shows it possesses
the three characteristics common to those things which come to be
(which he enumerates in 6:1:6). First, it has a purpose or a final
cause. That is, the purpose of its existence is to provide the
proper conditions for the preservation of lower existent things
which serves the final cause of the divine nomos. Their coming to
be could not have occurred if the earth were encompassed by water.
Second, it possesses characteristics which are not essential to
its nature. That is, the elevation of the earth is not determined
by the natures of the elements earth and water. By nature, water
should encompass the earth. It is also not determined by the
nature of that which overflows from the activities of the heavenly
bodies. (For an explanation of this, see 6:1:13, p. 350, l. 18-p.
351, l. 12.) Third, there is something in its essence that is for
the sake of something else, viz. that is for the benefit of lower
existent things.

In arguing that the earth's elevation, which makes the earth
visible, must have been generated by will and choice through the

action of an agent at the beginning of its existence, Gersonides
seeks to refute Aristotle's contention that the earth's elevation
occurs necessarily and naturally from the heat of the sun which
dries the water (Meteorologica 2.3.360a7, to which Gersonides
refers at 6:1:13, p. 351, ll. 24ff.). He refers here in our text
to the Lord's willful elevation of the part of the earth to create
dry land in order to serve as an "instrument" of the coming to be
and perfection of living things.

135) Job 37:18.

136) Ha-gerem ha-shemiymiy. "The heavenly body" is an inclusive term which he consistently uses to refer to all of the components of the heavens—the stars, the sphere of each star, and the
body which does not preserve its shape which is between the spheres
of one star and the spheres of the next star. This is most explicit
in Treatise Five (see, e.g., 5:2:2, p. 193, ll. 26ff.), but he
follows that usage in the text here. (Note that Aristotle also
uses the term "heaven" in several different senses. Cf. De Caelo
1.9.278a10ff. Also cf. Wolfson, Crescas' Critique of Aristotle,
p. 432.) He will occasionally use the word geshem instead of gerem
(e.g., 6:2:7, p. 425, l. 28), but in general he avoids the word
geshem because it is said equivocally of the fifth body of the
heavens and sublunar bodies (cf. 5:2:2, p. 193, l. 19f.). He
uses the plural form (ha-geramim ha-shemiymiyim), however, to refer
both to the world of the heavenly bodies and to all of its component parts in general, and specifically to the stars which are
fixed in the spheres or to the spheres themselves to the exclusion
of the stars.

Note, however, that when he says here that the raqiᶜa refers
specifically to the heavenly body, he means that it refers to that
part of the heavenly body which is stretched out, i.e., the celestial spheres. Thus, the luminaries of Gen 1:14 are fixed in the
raqiᶜa, i.e., the spheres. The raqiᶜa which is formed in the
midst of the waters (Gen 1:6), i.e., the body which does not
preserve its shape, is the spheres. Cf. below, note #143.

Also note that the term "stars" (kokhavim) includes the
planets, the sun and the moon, and those celestial bodies which
we too call "stars." Stars are those parts of the heavens which
emit and/or reflect light, in contrast to the spheres which are
transparent. Thus, when the Bible refers to lights or luminaries

(me'orot) in Gen 1:14-18, he will understand it to be referring
to all of the stars, including the planets (cf. 6:2:8, p. 433,
ll. 9ff.).

137) Gen 1:14. That is, "Let there be heavenly bodies (stars)
in the heavenly body." (See note #136.)

138) Gen 1:17.

139) Gen 1:20.

140) The manuscripts consulted have sheṭaḥ ha-shamayim for
sheṭaḥ ha-mayim at p. 424, l. 27, so that the translation would
read "the surface of the heavens" for "the surface of the water."
The manuscript reading is more plausible because the text which he
is paraphrasing is ᶜal penei reqiᶜa ha-shamayim (Gen 1:20). Nevertheless, he may have intended to say that birds fly next to the
surface of the water, in that the latter is spherical in the way
that it encompasses the earth. As mentioned immediately below in
note #141, it is possible that he interprets the text analogously
to imply that any circular motion is "heavenly."

141) The natural motions of the four elements of which the
sublunar world is composed are rectilinear—upwards and downwards.
For example, the natural motion of fire is upwards and the natural
motion of earth is downwards (Physica 8.4.254b12ff.). "All simple
motion, then, must be motion either away from or towards or about
the centre" (De Caelo, 1.2.268b23, Oxford translation).

By contrast, the motion of the heavenly body is circular.
Gersonides seems to understand Gen 1:20 as meaning that the motion
of birds is "heavenly" motion because it is circular, around the
spherical surface of the water. If the text of the printed
editions is correct (see above, note #140), then he does not
interpret the reference to "the face of the raqiᶜa (viz., the
spheres)" in a literal way. The term raqiᶜa would be said analogously of the heavenly spheres and of other things which also move
circularly. For a discussion of his use of the term "analogy,"
see above, note #64.

142) Gen 1:6.

143) It is explicit here that he understands the term raqiᶜa
to refer specifically to the celestial spheres and not to the
heavenly body in general, as might have been inferred from his
initial statement in this chapter (p. 424, l. 24; cf. note #136)

and from his discussion of Gen 1:6 in chapter eight below (p. 429,
l. 21). One must keep in mind, however, that the stars are not
created until the fourth "day" (6:2:8, p. 432, ll. 28ff.) so that
at this prior stage of creation the heavenly body is identical to
the spheres. In addition, he perhaps conceives of the creation of
the spheres as the creation of the heavenly body, because it is
the spheres which define and encompass the celestial world. Also,
in the creation of their perpetual nature, the heavens are distinguished from the sublunar world of the elements (cf. 6:2:8, p. 429,
ll. 22ff.).

144) nivreʾu. The terms baraʾ and beriʾat ha-ʿolam are synonymous with hoveh and havayat ha-ʿolam, and with ḥidesh and ḥidush
ha-ʿolam (see above, note #7). In general, he uses baraʾ when making
a Biblical allusion or reference, thus retaining the terminology of
the Bible.

145) For example, wisdom is prior in cause and in nature to
the coming to be of wisdom in Reuben, but it is temporally posterior
to Reuben's becoming wise. For his discussion of the different
senses of the term "prior," see above, 6:2:2. Cf. notes #27 and
#37, and Aristotle's discussion of this topic in the Metaphysica
5.11. Also note the following statement of Maimonides in his discussion of priority (Guide 2:30; Pines translation, p. 348):

> A principle exists in the thing whose principle it is
> or simultaneously with it, even if it does not precede
> it in time.

146) Gen 1:6.

147) 6:1:17, p. 367, where he writes (ll. 27-33):

> How this coming to be (of the world) should be
> apprehended is as follows: That is, the Lord, may
> He be blessed, made some of this (formless) body
> from which the world came to be into that which
> preserves its shape, i.e., the heavenly body. In it
> He created the stars and the spheres which move (the
> stars) in a way that there overflows from them what
> is needed to perfect lower existence. Some of it
> remained without preservation of shape, i.e., that
> which is between the spheres of one star and the
> spheres of the next star. To some of it He gave the
> nature which makes it possible for it to receive all
> the forms, i.e., lower matter (which can receive all
> the forms) because of the elemental forms which He
> created in it.

The creation of the world was precisely the move from lack of
preservation of shape to preservation of shape, which is itself

the motion from nonexistence or privation of nature (6:1:17, p. 368, 1. 20) to existence (cf. 6:1:18, p. 377, 1. 27f. For a discussion of the meaning of "preservation of shape," see above, notes #49 and #51). For a discussion of that part of the heavenly body which still does not preserve its shape, see below, note #152.

For his discussion of what was created on the second "day," see below, 6:2:8, p. 429, 11. 19ff. As will be explained there, his view is that on the second "day," two things were formed from the body which does not preserve its shape: a) the heavenly body which the Torah calls the raqiᶜa and which in this context denotes the spheres without the stars; and b) the four concentric layers of the elements which form the beginnings of the sublunar world.

148) 2 Sam 14:14.

149) Josh 7:5.

150) The printed text omits the word shemei, which is included in the manuscripts consulted.

151) Ps 148:4.

152) Cf. 5:2:2, p. 193, 11. 1ff.; 6:1:7, p. 311, 11. 30-33; 6:1:17, p. 367, 1. 30f., quoted above, note #147. On the meaning of this term, cf. above, note #51.

He first makes reference to the existence of the body which does not preserve its shape in his work on astronomy which composes the first part of Treatise Five. This is not published with the rest of The Wars of the Lord because of its length (136 chapters). Nor is it included in the manuscript version of the work. It exists in separate manuscript form and has been translated in part by Bernard R. Goldstein, The Astronomical Tables of Levi ben Gerson (Hamden, Connecticut, 1974). Se also Goldstein's article, "Preliminary Remarks on Levi ben Gerson's Contributions to Astronomy," pp. 239-254. Gersonides refers back to his discussion in 5:1 in several places (e.g., 5:2:3, p. 193, 1. 1f.; CT 10b, 1. 27). Charles Touati, La pensée philosophique et théologique de Gersonide (Paris, 1973), p. 255, n. 67, refers the discussion to 5:1:8. Maimonides cites a similar view which he attributed to Thābit Ibn Qurra (Guide 2:24, 3:14). Cf. Pierre Duhem, Le système du monde (Paris, 1954), volume 1, chapter 11.

In 5:2:2, Gersonides conducts an investigation of the essence of the body which does not preserve its shape which exists between the spheres of the stars. He states there "that it appears that

it does not have a form" (p. 193, l. 5). (Note the tentative form
of his statement, presumably due to the ultimate unknowability of
something which is not the effect of an agent, as we have discussed
above, note #59.) Though no sublunar body can exist without form,
he maintains that formless body is possible in the supralunar
world for the following reasons (p. 193, l. 16-p. 194, l. 20):
1) Since the term "body" is said equivocally of the supralunar
bodies and of lower existent things, no valid inference can be
made from an analogy between the two. 2) Sublunar bodies cannot
exist without form because the state of affairs of hylic forms
(i.e., forms which depend on matter to perform their functions;
cf. 6:2:8, p. 432, l. 16) is such that, in the process of changes
wrought by contraries, when one form leaves a material substratum,
it is replaced by another. Since the forms of the supralunar
bodies are not hylic and exist separately, this state of affairs
need not apply to them. 3) As some parts of sublunar bodies, such
as bones, are lifeless, similarly there are varying degrees of
life in the supralunar world. 4) A single subject receives contraries either at different times or in different parts. (For
example, it can rain in Jerusalem at one time and not rain at
another, or it can rain in one part of Jerusalem and not rain in a
different part. Cf. below, 6:2:12, p. 455, l. 24-p. 456, l. 7.)
Given that the preservation of shape is the contrary of the privation of the preservation of shape and that the heavenly body as a
whole cannot receive the privation of the preservation of shape
(because this quality entails nonexistence and the heavens cannot
pass away), it is possible that some parts of the heavenly body
receive the one contrary and other parts receive the other. 5)
As all parts of an animal—including lifeless bones—function
cooperatively to perfect its nature and functions, similarly, all
parts of the heavens function cooperatively to effect the proper
providence over lower existent things. (Cf. 6:1:7, p. 310, l.
22-p. 312, l. 14, where Gersonides argues that the slightest variation of any of the characteristics of any part of the heavens
would lead to the passing away of the sublunar world. Touati,
La pensée, p. 284, n. 82, states that this view is based upon
De Mundo 6.397b9, an apocryphal text of Aristotle, repeated often
by medieval Jewish thinkers, which is cited by Averroes in Tahafut
Al-Tahafut 3:152. Cf. p. 90 of the van den Bergh translation.)

    153) Guide 2:30, p. 352f. of Pines translation. Maimonides
states that the raqiᶜa is not the heaven. The latter is above the

raqiᶜa. The raqiᶜa itself was produced from water and it is that
part of the air where birds fly (Gen 1:24). He does not explicitly
speak about the cold part of the air in which clouds and rain come
to be, but he does refer the reader to the Meteorologica (1.9.
346b16ff., quoted below in note #167).

154) Maimonides does not take the term "water" to refer to
anything which does not persist in a single disposition, as
Gersonides has just done (1. 5). Thus, he reads the "upper waters"
and "lower waters" of Gen 1:6-7 as referring to the element water,
which cannot exist in the supralunar world. It is for this reason
that Maimonides must understand raqiᶜa, which divides between the
waters, as something within the sublunar world.

155) Cf. CT 10c, 1. 49f., where he concedes that there are a
few rabbis who agree with Maimonides' position (see Gen. Rab. 4:5,
for example).

Gersonides' purpose in citing rabbinic statements which support
his own interpretations of the Bible is an interesting subject for
further inquiry. In the present instance, his disagreement with
Maimonides is based exclusively on their respective interpretations
of the text. There is no issue of speculation involved. Thus, the
citation of rabbinic interpretations which support his claim lends
credibility to his own exegetical position. Note, for example,
the comment which concludes his discussion of the second day (on
which the raqiᶜa was created) in his Commentary to the Torah (11a,
11. 1-3):

> This is what we see in the explanation of this second
> passage (parashah). It is marvelous, as you can see,
> and it agrees with the words of our rabbis, may their
> memories be for a blessing, and with the truth in
> itself according to what we explained of the creation
> of the world in the book, The Wars of the Lord.
> (italics added)

In general, however, his purposes are not as clear. Elsewhere
in his commentary, he explicitly states that the opinions of the
rabbis are not binding, because the rabbis' statements often contradict one another (CT 12d, 11. 35-37). We may also note that
his citations of rabbinic views are obviously selective—he makes
no mention of statements which disagree with him. For example,
he cites b. Ḥagigah 12a to his own advantage on several occasions
(6:2:4, p. 421, 1. 19; 6:2:8, p. 427, 1. 23; p. 428, 1. 9), but
makes no reference to that text when it differs with him on the

interpretation of the term ruaḥ as "wind" (6:2:6; cf. note #125).
In the introduction to his Commentary to the Torah (2c, ll. 23ff.),
he states that he will not cite midrashic interpretations of the
rabbis because they are not literal explanations of the biblical
verses to which they are related. It would be difficult, however,
to determine the criteria he uses to judge which rabbinic statements are midrashic and which are literal. As explained above,
note #1, when he says that he is explaining the peshat (literal
meaning) of the text, he does not mean that his explanations are
the obvious ones which can be reached by anyone who reads the Torah.
Rather, he means that they are statements of the truth which the
revelation of the divine nomos is trying to teach us in guiding us
to our true and ultimate purpose—i.e., the most perfect possible
conception of the truth. This "literal" meaning of the text most
definitely is not its obvious sense—it takes the speculator a
lifetime of preparation before he can begin to apprehend it at all.
When he distinguishes between rabbinic interpretations which are
literal (peshat) and those which are midrashic, we are led to conclude, therefore, that the former are those which agree with the
conclusions of speculation and the latter are those which do not
do so. Thus, his statement at the end of the first part of this
treatise that not only does the Torah agree with his view of the
creation of the world but also the Tradition agrees with his view
of creation (6:1:29, p. 417, l. 15f.) cannot mean that he believes
that all rabbinic views agree with his exegesis but must mean that
many rabbinic statements agree with his view.

156) 4:2, 3. My translation.

157) Gen 1:6.

158) Ha-shamayim. Our text of Genesis Rabbah has maᶜaseihem
("their handiwork"), but the meaning remains the same with either
reading.

159) Here Gersonides inserts the following remark into the
text of Genesis Rabbah which he is quoting: "That is to say, He
gave them steadiness and duration." As he will explain below
(6:2:8, p. 429, ll. 19ff.), it was on the second "day" of creation
that the Lord willed that the heavenly body should come to be from
the body which does not preserve its shape. As the latter is
represented as "water," the coming to be of the heavenly body is
spoken of as the "congealing" of that water (see above, notes #49
and #51).

160) Gen 1:6.

161) Exod 39:3.

162) Gen 1:6.

163) Gen 1:7.

164) The reference is to the first part of the passage just
cited. Though he omits the name of the speaker, the text of
Genesis Rabbah begins as follows (my translation):

> Our rabbis said the following in the name of R. Ḥanina
> while R. Pinḥas and R. Jacob b. R. Avun said it in the
> name of R. Samuel b. Naḥman:

165) I.e., there are no clouds in the heavens, since clouds
are composed of the elements of the sublunar world.

166) As Maimonides claims.

167) 1.9.346b16ff., where Aristotle writes (Oxford translation):

> Let us go on to treat of the region which follows next
> in order after this and which immediately surrounds the
> earth. It is the region common to water and air, and
> the processes attending the formation of water above
> take place in it...

> The efficient and chief and first cause is the circle
> in which the sun moves. For the sun as it approaches
> or recedes obviously causes dissipation and condensation
> and so gives rise to generation and destruction. Now
> the earth remains but the moisture surrounding it is
> made to evaporate by the sun's rays and the other heat
> from above, and rises. But when the heat which was
> raising it leaves it, in part dispersing to the higher
> region, in part quenched through rising so far into the
> upper air, then the vapour cools because its heat is
> gone and because the place is cold, and condenses again
> and turns from air into water. And after the water has
> formed it falls down again to the earth.

> The exhalation of water is vapour: air condensing into
> water is cloud. Mist is what is left over when a cloud
> condenses into water, and is therefore rather a sign of
> fine weather than of rain.

The qualities of fire are heat and dryness (cf. De Generatione et
Corruptione 2.3.330b4) so that it can have nothing to do with the
formation of clouds, which occurs when rising vapor is cooled in
the lower part of the atmosphere and condenses into water.

168) Since we use "water" to refer to something which does not
preserve its shape.

169) Ha-meyavesh ve-ha-menagev. Both words denote the process
of drying. Though it is the element earth which is primarily dry

while fire is primarily hot (De Generatione et Corruptione
2.3.331a4-6; cf. De Sensu et Sensibili 4.441b11f.), fire is the
contrary of water (De Generatione et Corruptione 2.3.331a1; 2.8.
335a5) and as such is related to the activity of drying.

170) Elemental fire is part of the sublunar world. Cf. above,
notes #49, #126.

171) Gen. Rab. 4:7, cf. b. Ḥag. 12a; Num. Rab. 12:4.

172) Cf. above, note #152.

173) The force of his exclamation here is a further indication
that body which does not preserve its shape from which the world
came to be is next to privation, whether we think of it as nondimensional or as absolute dimensional body (cf. above, notes #49
and #51). It has no characteristics through which it could be
considered an "instrument." It is rather the receptacle upon
which God acts.

174) According to Maimonides' interpretation of raqiᶜa as the
place in the atmosphere in which clouds form, there would be no
space between the raqiᶜa and these "upper waters."

175) I.e., that the raqiᶜa is the celestial spheres, and that
the "upper waters" are that part of the body which does not preserve its shape from which the heavens came to be.

176) Cf. Gen. Rab. 4:5. Also see his expansion of this in his
Commentary to the Torah, quoted below, note #180.

177) For a discussion of the body which does not preserve its
shape which is between the spheres, cf. above, note #152. Here he
understands raqiᶜa to refer specifically to a single sphere, or
perhaps to all of the spheres of a single star, rather than to the
celestial spheres in general. This alternation parallels that
which occurs in his use of the term "heavenly bodies" (see above,
note #136).

178) I.e., since the existence of a vacuum is impossible,
R. Pinḥas cannot be referring to one in his use of the term ḥalal
("empty space"). Rather, he is referring to the body which does
not preserve its shape which exists between the spheres.

On the refutation of the arguments for the existence of a
vacuum, i.e., of place deprived of body which is potentially body,
cf. Physica 4.6-9; Guide 1:73, Premise Two. Also see the discussion of H. A. Wolfson, Crescas' Critique of Aristotle, pp. 54ff.

For Gersonides' own discussion of the impossibility of the
existence of a vacuum out of which the world came to be, see
6:1:17, p. 364, 1. 19-p. 366, 1. 3. One of the arguments reads as
follows: Divine action is realized in that which has the potential
to receive that action; it had to have been possible for the world
to come to be, and possibility requires a substratum; by definition,
however, a vacuum is void of body and body cannot come to be from
nothing. This consideration is part of what leads him to posit a
body of absolute dimensionality out of which the world came to be.

179) 6:6.

180) The addition in parentheses is part of the text of
Genesis Rabbah which Gersonides does not cite. In his Commentary
to the Torah, he cites the expanded quote and continues with the
following remarks (CT 10c, 11. 23-31):

> According to this statement, the measure of the lower
> waters—that is, the empty space between the raqi^{c}a
> and the earth, i.e., between the lower surface of the
> raqi^{c}a and the earth—is (equal to) the measure between
> the lower surface of the raqi^{c}a and the upper waters.
> Therefore, (the Torah) says, "Let there be a raqi^{c}a
> in the midst of the waters" (Gen 1:6), i.e., that the
> measures between them be equal. Thus, the measure of
> the thickness of the raqi^{c}a is (equal to) the measure
> of the lower waters, and the measure of the upper
> waters is also (equal to) this measure. The measure
> of the lower waters is an empty space between the
> raqi^{c}a and the earth. The measure of the raqi^{c}a is
> an empty space between the raqi^{c}a which is the lower
> surface of the sphere and the upper waters. In this
> way, the measure of each raqi^{c}a follows their (measure).

Given that he has identified the term "empty space" (ḥalal)
as the body which does not preserve its shape (cf. above, note
#178), in this passage he cannot be identifying the lower waters
with lower, sublunar matter as he does elsewhere (e.g., 6:2:7,
p. 427, 1. 3). He gives no indication that any part of the body
which does not preserve its shape persists in the sublunar world.
(Cf. above, note #152, for an exposition of 5:2:2, where he argues
that though such a body can persist in the supralunar world, it
cannot persist in the sublunar world, because sublunar matter can
never be formless due to the nature it has received from the contrary qualities of the elemental forms.) Indeed, the purpose of
his citation of these rabbinic statements and of this entire discussion is to refute the assertion of Maimonides that the raqi^{c}a
is a place within the sublunar world. It therefore seems probable

that he understands the term "earth" in these rabbinic passages
and in his explanation of them to refer to the entire sublunar
world (cf. 6:2:3, p. 420, l. 26, where he makes note of this
usage), so that the "empty space" is between the lowest raqi^{c}a
and the outermost part of the sublunar atmosphere. Thus, where
the term "lower waters" occurs in the context of the second day of
creation, prior to the completion of the world as it now exists,
he understands it to refer to the part of the body which does not
preserve its shape out of which sublunar matter came to be. In
the present passage in which he seems to be discussing the current
state of affairs of the world, he understands the term "lower
waters" to refer to the part of the body which does not preserve
its shape which persists in the part of the heavens closest to the
sublunar world.

Thus, the comments just quoted from the Commentary to the
Torah seem to have the following sense: The distance from the
outer limit of the sublunar world ("earth") to the lower edge of
the lowest sphere (raqi^{c}a) is equal in measure to the distance
between the lowest sphere and the sphere next to it. The area
between the sublunar world and the lowest sphere is filled with
the body which does not preserve its shape ("empty space") as is
the area between the lowest sphere and the sphere next to it.
This distance is also the distance between any two adjacent spheres
and the area between any two adjacent spheres is filled with the
body which does not preserve its shape.

In so interpreting these rabbinic statements, he is supporting
his claim that the rabbis speak of the raqi^{c}a as a celestial
phenomenon and not as a place in the atmosphere of the sublunar
world.

With regard to the extraordinarily large distance from the
sublunar world to the heavens and between each of the spheres, note
that Goldstein makes a similar observation in comparing his astronomical calculations with those of other medieval astronomers
("Preliminary Remarks," p. 251).

181) Gen. Rab. 4:3, quoted above in our text, p. 425, l. 27.

182) Heaviness and lightness are characteristics of sublunar
elements (cf. De Caelo 4.3). The body which does not preserve its
shape would not have these nor any other characteristics, since it
is formless. See above, notes #49 and #51, for a discussion of
the body which does not preserve its shape. It can be said to be

formless because that which lacks "preservation of shape" is
absolute dimensional body. Absolute dimensionality is not a form
but is rather a disposition of the body which persists prior to
creation and which is distinct from the hierarchy of forms in the
divine nomos. Though it has no actual existence as a body with
definite dimensions, it does have the disposition of absolute,
indefinite dimensionality, so that it does have indefinite place.

Nor would the heavenly bodies be heavy or light, because
heaviness and lightness are said of bodies whose natural tendency
is to move towards or away from the center of the earth (cf. De
Caelo 4.3.310a32ff.). The motion of the heavens is circular—
around the earth—and the heavens are thus neither heavy nor
light (cf. De Caelo 1.4.270b32ff.).

183) Gen 1:7.

184) The sense in which the upper waters, viz., supralunar
body, can be said to be self-supporting (nismakhim ᶜal ᶜaṣmam) is
related to his comment above on the absence of the characteristics
of heaviness and lightness in the supralunar world (see above,
note #182). That is, since heavenly matter is not subject to
weight, it cannot be said to rest on anything. Thus, the body which
does not preserve its shape which is between the spheres does not
rest on the spheres as sublunar water rests on the earth. Sublunar
water has a natural tendency to move towards the center of the
earth. The formless body between the spheres has no such nature.

His point, therefore, is that R. Tanḥuma's distinction between
the terms "ᶜal" ("on") and "me-ᶜal" ("above") is a distinction
which recognizes the difference between the natures of sublunar
and supralunar "water."

185) Gen. Rab. 4:7; cf. b. Ḥag. 12a; Num. Rab. 12:4. He has
already referred to this in this chapter (p. 426, l. 5) in the
course of demonstrating that R. Ḥanina did not mean "elemental
fire" when he spoke about "the fire from above." He was rather
using the term to refer to the nature of the preservation of shape
in the heavens, in contrast to "water" which refers to that which
does not preserve its shape.

186) On his use of the term "analogy" (dimyon), cf. above,
note #64.

187) 4:7. The printed editions begin the passage with the
word she-ᵓeino, which is not in the text of Genesis Rabbah, in

place of the word shamayim in Genesis Rabbah to which the
manuscripts consulted attest. The translation follows the text of
the midrash and of the manuscripts.

188) I.e., that the elements of water and fire are not in the
heavens.

Note that in his Commentary to the Torah (9c, 11. 10-16) he
adds the following interpretation of his own of the word
"shamayim":

> It is proper that you know that water is called mayim
> because it indicates the doubling of the world mah
> ("what"). This is in respect to the multiplicity of
> positions which the parts (of water) assume without
> limit. Similarly, the sphere is called shamayim to
> indicate the doubling of the word sham ("there") which
> indicates place. This is because of the multiplicity
> of positions which it has in a single place in itself
> and in its circular motion in which it does not change
> its place. Only its parts change accidentally.

189) b. Ḥag. 14b.

190) Ps 101:7.

191) ᶜakhirut ve-ᶜovi. The two terms are synonymous according
to Jacob Klatzkin, ꜣOṣar Ha-Munaḥim Ha-Filosofiyim Ve-ꜣAntologiyah
Filosofit 3 (New York, 1968):132. Wolfson, Crescas' Critique of
Aristotle, p. 579, n. 18 (cf. p. 587f.), relates the term ᶜovi,
which he translates as "mass" or "bulk," to the cohesion or dimensionality of matter. In the text here, then, Gersonides is commenting upon the lack of cohesion or dimensionality in the body which
does not preserve its shape which persists between the spheres
(see above, notes #49 and #51). This body is transparent because
it is natureless and thus cannot reflect light, as he explains
above in 6:1:19, in the course of arguing from empirical evidence
that there is only one world. Also note that he uses the term
"heavenly bodies" here to refer exclusively to the body which does
not preserve its shape which is between the spheres (see above,
note #136, for a discussion of the equivocal senses of the term
ha-geramim ha-shemiymiyim).

192) He understands R. Aqiba to be warning against the confusion
of the body which does not preserve its shape between the spheres
with the element water, which does not exist in the supralunar
world.

193) b. Ḥag. 15a.

194) <u>Shetei</u>. Our text of <u>b. Ḥagigah</u> 15a has <u>sheloshah</u>
("three"), but a parallel passage in <u>Genesis Rabbah</u> (2:4) has
<u>ki-shtayim ve-shalosh</u> ("two or three"). Gersonides clearly prefers
the reading of "two," because his interpretation of the passage
depends on it.

195) Note that he applauds Ben Zoma's statement even though,
in the context of the narrative of the Midrash, Ben Zoma's statement signals his demise—either in terms of his ability to function
within the rabbinic tradition (<u>b. Ḥag.</u> 15a—"Ben Zoma is still
outside") or in terms of his incipient death (<u>Tosefta Ḥag.</u> 2:5;
<u>Gen. Rab.</u> 2:4). Ben Zoma was one of those who entered the <u>Pardes</u>
with R. Aqiba (<u>b. Hag.</u> 14b) and who did not heed Aqiba's warning,
quoted above in our text (p. 426, l. 30f.). Gersonides' lack of
concern for the adverse effects on Ben Zoma of the study of <u>Maᶜaseh
Bereʾshit</u> (the account of creation) is yet another indication that
he does not consider the subject matter of this treatise to be
esoteric and dangerous (see above, note #2).

196) See above, notes #49 and #51, for a discussion of the
state of affairs of lower matter after its reception of the elemental forms but prior to the intermixing of the elements through
the actions of contrary powers. On the hot and the cold as the
active qualities, see <u>Meteorologica</u> 4.1.378b12ff., where Aristotle
states (ll. 28ff., Oxford translation):

> True becoming, that is, natural change, is always the
> work of these powers and so is the corresponding natural
> destruction.... True natural becoming is a change intro-
> duced by these powers into the matter underlying a given
> thing when they are in a certain ratio to that matter.

197) Cf. 6:2:8, p. 429, l. 24f., where he further explains that
the heavenly bodies do not have the nature to receive all of the
forms but rather remain perpetually in their definition. It is
this distinction in natures to which he believes Gen 1:6 is
referring.

198) Exod 8:15.

199) He is bringing together phrases from Exod 31:18 and 32:16.

200) 12:7, 8 (my translation). Cf. <u>Lev. Rab.</u> 9:9; <u>Tanḥuma
Bereʾshit</u> 15.

201) Gen 2:4.

202) This statement refers to what precedes it and is not
directly related to the following passage or to Gersonides' purpose
in quoting the passage, i.e., that the raqi^ca is part of the
celestial world. It is therefore unclear whether he had a purpose
in mind in quoting it or if it was simply part of the passage as
he remembered it. He reproduces it exactly in his Commentary to
the Torah (10b, ll. 33-39). What precedes this statement of R.
Azaryah in Genesis Rabbah and what he asserts "was said with reference to the One Above" is the following (Soncino translation):

> It was taught: Whatever has offspring dies, decays, is
> created, but cannot create; but what has no offspring
> neither dies nor decays, creates but is not created.

203) Our text and the manuscripts consulted omit the following
from the passage in Genesis Rabbah: "On the first day, He created
things of the upper (world) and of the lower (world)." It is
possible that he omits this intentionally, because he disagrees
with this omitted rabbinic statement. See notes #49 and #235 for
a discussion of this aspect of his interpretation of the first
"day." In his discussion of the first "day" (6:2:8, p. 428, l.
31-p. 429, l. 18), he treats Gen 1:1 as introductory and Gen 1:2
as parenthetical. The intelligible world ("light") was created on
the first "day." The sublunar world of lower matter and the elemental forms, as well as the supralunar spheres, were not created
until the second "day." Thus, he would assert that things of the
upper world alone were created on the first "day."

There is another problematic feature of Gersonides' citation
of this text. R. Azaryah also states that, on the second day,
(only) things in the upper world were created. Gersonides disagrees
with this also, since the elemental forms and sublunar matter were
also created, in his view, on the second "day." We must assume,
therefore, that he is citing this midrash only to support his
assertion that the rabbis agree with his view that the raqi^ca
refers to the heavenly body and do not agree with Maimonides that
the raqi^ca refers to a sublunar phenomenon. His citation of this
midrash is thus an excellent example of the problems involved by
his view of the value of rabbinic statements, as discussed above,
note #155. He has no problem citing a midrashic passage which
partly agrees with him and partly disagrees with him, apparently
because rabbinic statements are not binding, as explained above
(note #155). But though incorrect rabbinic statements can be
disregarded, rabbinic statements which confirm his own position are
nevertheless of some value in support of his own exegesis.

204) Gen 1:1.

205) Gen 1:6. Both the Riva di Trento and the Leipzig editions have "Let there be light" (Gen 1:3) here. The actual text of Genesis Rabbah, the parallel passage in his Commentary (CT 10b, 1. 37), and the manuscripts consulted all have "Let there be a raqiᶜa." The latter is undoubtedly what Gersonides intended to say, both because it was the raqiᶜa and not light which was created on the second "day" and because, in his discussion of this passage below, he refers to the raqiᶜa (p. 427, 1. 20).

206) Gen 1:11.

207) Gen 1:14. For his explanation of why the Torah relates things of the lower world to the third "day" and things of the upper world to the fourth "day" when it is the latter which are prior in cause and in nature to the former, see below, 6:2:8, pp. 434ff.

TREATISE SIX, PART TWO: CHAPTER EIGHT

THE MEANING OF THE CREATION NARRATIVE OF GENESIS

Chapter Eight, in which what is discussed in the Torah
of the account of creation[208] will be explained.

Summary

Gersonides begins by explaining that there was no time prior
to the creation of the world nor during the process of creation.
Thus, all things described in the first six days of the creation
narrative of Genesis came to be simultaneously as the instantaneous
actualization of the divine will at the moment of creation. Rather,
the "days" of the narrative indicate the priority of some things
to other things—priority in cause and in nature and hylic priority.

He also explains that the creation narrative of Genesis
attributes to the Lord only the creation of things which have
natures bestowed upon them from the hierarchy of the forms of the
divine nomos. Thus, the creation of homogeneous parts and of
things which are spontaneously generated are not described.

He then proceeds with his exegesis of the creation narrative
of Genesis. On the first "day," the intelligible world of the
separate intellects was created. They are mentioned first because
they are prior in cause and in nature to all other created things.
(The description of Gen 1:1-2 after the word be-re'shit is a parenthetical reference to things which came to be on the second "day.")
The Lord willed that the conceptions of these intellects should
vary in venerability, so that a single nomos would overflow from a
combination of their effects to the sublunar world.

On the second "day," the narrative describes the creation of
the supralunar spheres and the creation of the elemental forms,
which part of the body which does not preserve its shape received
when it received the nature of definite dimensionality. The supralunar and sublunar worlds were distinguished from each other by
the contrary qualities of the elements which cause the processes
of coming to be and passing away in the sublunar world but which
the perpetually unchanging supralunar world does not have. At this
stage, the sublunar world was composed of the four concentric layers
of the elements, because the interaction of the element's contrary
qualities is caused by the influences of the stars, the creation
of which has not yet been described. Since the spheres move
for the sake of moving the stars and the elemental forms exist for
the sake of composite forms, the description of neither is yet

complete and so the narrative does not say with regard to the
second day that it was "good." Gersonides also explains here why
the narrative cannot mean to imply a division in place with the
term mavdil.

On the third "day," the narrative describes the elevation of
the visible part of the earth above the waters. It also describes
the creation of the plant species and it indicates their relative
priority to one another.

Of all created things described in the narrative, only the
plant species did not come to be instantaneously. Rather they
sprouted only after the watering described in Gen 2:5-6. Because
of this, and because of the relatively low degree of existence of
the souls of plants, the narrative does not say that God made them.
It also does not say this of the separate intellects on the first
"day," but for a different reason, i.e., because separate forms do
not come to be in themselves.

On the fourth "day," the narrative describes the creation of
the stars and it describes the three functions which they serve:
a) to cause the generation, in the sublunar world, of things from
the contrary qualities of the elements, the strength of which vary
with the variation in the intensity of the influence of each of
the stars; b) to influence the sublunar world in a variety of different ways through the respective distinctive influences of the
actions of each of the stars; and c) to illuminate the earth. The
narrative comments on the relative strength of the influences upon
the sublunar world of the sun and the moon, in comparison with the
influences of the other stars. It also clarifies that the period
of influence of each star is not defined by twenty-four hour days.

All of the actions of the stars combine to form a single
nomos which overflows from them to govern the sublunar world in
the most perfect possible way. The doubt which is raised about the
actions of the more venerable stars being for the sake of the perfection of the less venerable sublunar world is groundless. More
venerable things always act for the sake of less venerable things.
This state of affairs does not diminish their venerability, because
the more venerable thing does not acquire its perfection from the
less venerable thing and because the less venerable thing is not
its final cause. Its final cause is the divine nomos which gives
it the nature which it strives to fulfill. By listing the benefits
which the supralunar world bestows upon the sublunar world, the

Torah leads us to the conclusion that the supralunar world, and
hence the world as a whole, must have come to be.

Similarly, the creation narrative of Genesis describes the
creation of the prior stars after it describes the posterior
visible part of the earth in order to provide us with the following
data which serve as demonstrations that the world must have come
to be: a) that the elevation of the earth is not a necessary consequence of the divine nomos which overflows from the stars but is
rather an effect of the divine will; and b) that the spheres are
perfect in themselves and do not derive any perfection from the
existence of the stars in them. The latter perform their functions
for the sake of the sublunar world.

On the fifth "day," the narrative describes the creation of
the fish and bird species. These species required a "blessing"
because of the precarious nature of their reproductive processes
in which they lay their eggs outside of their bodies. Thus, the
preservation of these species requires divine providence over
factors which are external to their natures.

On the sixth "day," the narrative describes the creation of
the animal species. It then describes the creation of the human
species and the fact of its rule over the lower sublunar species,
all of which exist for its sake. The human species is related to
the world of the separate intellects in that its form—the hylic
intellect—possesses the potential to acquire true, separate conceptions. The human species is commanded to be fruitful and
multiply because only the human species has a choice to refrain
from procreation by means of abstinence or birth control. It is
also blessed to fill the earth so that natural disasters do not
render it extinct. Furthermore, it is given the nature to cultivate and to cook foods for its nutritional needs.

The description of the creation of the human species
culminates with the statement that "all that He had made was very
good," because the good for the sake of which the lower species
are created is not realized until the human species benefits from
it.

The creation of the human species is described in the plural
form because, unlike the lower sublunar species, the human form is
not entirely hylic. That is, there is a part of the human intellect
in which true, separate conceptions are actualized. In the second
chapter of Genesis, the narrative elaborates upon the way in which

the human species acquires immortality, i.e., through the naming—
conceiving the true definitions—of all species. These true conceptions endure and give immortality to the human intellect which
acquires them. The Torah begins with an account of the way in
which we acquire spiritual immortality, because this is the purpose
of the entire Torah, viz., to guide us to true conceptions and to
the consequent immortality of our souls.

The narrative's description of the seventh "day" is a
discussion of the way in which the divine self-conception sustains
the world after the moment of creation. That is, God perpetually
performs His single action of self-conception. The separate intellects conceive of this most exalted and perfect of all conceptions
and, as a result of their desire to approximate the perfection of
the divine conception, they each conceive of the single, perpetual,
perfect circular motion of their respective spheres. The spheres
thus move their stars perpetually and from the combined actions
of the stars, the divine nomos overflows from them and governs the
sublunar world in the most perfect possible way. Thus, after the
single act of divine will at the moment of creation that the divine
nomos should overflow from Him and should be received by body which
does not preserve its shape, the world exists perpetually according
to the nature of the divine nomos which governs on account of His
perpetual self-conception.

Gersonides concludes this chapter by asserting that his
interpretation of the Genesis narrative is indisputable and should
be obvious to anyone engaged in speculation. He gives thanks to
the Lord for the providential gift of the creation narrative which
led him to reach the truth about the question of creation.

Translation

70ab

427

You already know from what preceded that the coming to
be of the world from the Lord, may He be blessed, was nontemporal[209] because it was from nothing to something.[210]
Our rabbis, may their memories be for a blessing, agreed that
the heavens and the earth were created together.[211] They
said, in the chapter ᵓEin Dorshin:[212]

> Both were created as one, as it says, "My hand
> laid the foundation of the earth, and My right
1. 25   hand spread out the heavens. When I call to
> them, they stand up together."

Therefore it is clear that what is attributed to this coming
to be—namely, that it was completed in six days—is not

(said) in a way that from the first to the second (measures) on day,[213] for example. Rather, this was said to indicate the priority of some existent things over others. For example, the movers of the heavenly bodies are prior in

1. 30 cause and in nature to the heavenly bodies, and the heavenly bodies are prior in cause and in nature to the elements and to that which is generated from them.[214] The elements are prior to that which is generated from them in a hylic priority.[215] Also, in that which is composite there are some things which are prior to others in this (hylic) manner of

428 priority. For example, the plant is / prior to the perfect animal,[216] and in this way the water animal is prior to the flying (animal), and the flying (animal) to the walking (animal), and the walking (animal) to the rational (animal). The reason for this is the the water animal produces an imperfect egg, and the flying (animal) produces a perfect egg, and the walking animal produces the animal in its body. For this reason, it is explained in De Generatione Animalium

1. 5 that the flying (animal) is more perfect than the water (animal), and that the walking (animal) is more perfect than the flying (animal).[217] And there is no doubt that the human being is more perfect than the rest of the walking animals.

From this standpoint[218] the doubt raised by some of our preceding rabbis, may their memories be for a blessing, is removed. For they raised the question: How was the (time of the) first day and the second day and the third day reckoned when the luminaries did not exist until the fourth day?[219] This is the sense in which they, may their memories be for a blessing, said in the solution of this doubt:[220]

1. 10
> It (i.e., the light created on the first day) is identical with the luminaries which were created on the first day. But He did not suspend them until the fourth day.

That is, He did not suspend their coming to be at a time prior to the fourth day. They existed, however, on the first day, for everything was created together at the will of the Lord, may He be blessed.[221] There is no doubt that it is impossible for the sense of their statement that "He did not suspend them until the fourth day" to be understood in any other way than the one we have discussed.[222] For it

l. 15 is impossible for us to say that the stars[223] were created separate[224] on the first day, and afterwards, on the fourth day, He suspended them in the raqiᶜa, for they are not suspended in it, but are rather in the depth of the raqiᶜa.[225] Also, it is clearly absurd that He would have placed them in it.[226] Therefore, it is clear that the intention of "He (did not) suspend them" is that of "relation," for in our language the term "suspension" is often said with this intention.[227]

l. 20 It is proper that you know that in this marvelous story the creation of everything whose generation in nature is possible, according to the nature given to it by the Lord,[228] may He be blessed, is not attributed to the Lord, may He be blessed, for He produces this by means of nature. Therefore the coming to be of the plants and the animals, which come to be from the mould or from something other than their species, is not attributed to the Lord, may He be blessed.[229] Rather, what is attributed to the Lord, may He be blessed, is the creation of only that which comes to be from its species by natural custom,[230] for the creation of something not from its species was in a marvelous way.[231] Therefore,

l. 25 the coming to be of homogenous parts is not attributed to the Lord, may He be blessed.[232] The reason for this is that in the motions of the heavenly bodies together with the power that the lower matter has to receive all of the forms by means of the elemental forms which He created in (the lower matter) there are sufficient means for the homogeneous parts and for these species of plants and animals which are born of the mould to come to be from the lower matter. And this is clear to one who speculates in this book. This is what we saw fit to explain before we explained the words of this

l. 30 section in which the generation of the world is discussed.[233] For it is beneficial that we begin with its explanation.[234]

It says that "In the beginning"[235] of creation, when the Lord created the heavens and that which is beneath them, He created the first principles of the lower matter, which are prime matter and the forms which are primary to it in order[236]—that is, the elemental forms. For it is through (the elemental forms) that (prime matter) is prepared to receive all the forms so that all of the elements are in a

l. 35 way that the element earth is in the lowest area of the
      element water, and that the fire and the air are upon the
      highest areas of the water.[237]

429   / "In the beginning"[238] of all of this creation the Lord, may
      He be blessed, said that the world of light should exist—

70ba that is, the world of angels / who are the movers of the
      heavenly bodies.[239] And as soon as He willed this it was.
      No action was required.[240] The Lord, may He be blessed,
      divided between this light, which is that venerable world,
      and between that which proceeds from it in the hylic degree.

l. 5 That is, the heavenly body,[241] which is the darkness in this
      similitude.[242] The two of them[243] were a single thing, for
      these forms[244] are the perfection of the heavenly bodies.
      And in this way the "evening" and the "morning"[245] of these
      existent things were a single degree of the degrees of exist-
      ent things, for the form united with that to which it is the
      form, as is explained in the Metaphysica in connection with
      the investigation of the notion of definitions.[246] The
      light and the darkness are called "evening" and "morning"[247]

l. 10 in order to add to the hiddenness of this wonderful simili-
      tude,[248] as the notion of unity is explained by it, for from
      day and night there is one day.

          It is possible for us to say that the intention of
      this[249] is that within this light[250] some degrees are dif-
      ferent than others, some being more venerable than others,
      and the degree of the form of some of them goes to others
      of them, as we explained in the fifth treatise of this
      book.[251] Therefore, some of them are dark in relation to
      what proceeds to them by way of the form. But all of them

l. 15 would be united in a way that a nomos, which was one in
      number, would overflow from all of them, as was explained in
      what preceded.[252]

          With regard to this creation it is mentioned that it
      was generated when the Lord, may He be blessed, said so.
      This is to indicate that it was done by will, for the Lord,
      may He be blessed, does not make statements composed of
      letters and voice, as the Master the Guide explained.[253]

          After it relates the manner of the creation of this first

l. 20 degree of existent things, it begins to relate the manner of
      the creation of the second degree. It says that the Lord,

may he blessed, said that the heavenly body come to be
from some of the body which does not preserve its shape,[254]
and that a nature be created which would distinguish it from
the part of this body which does not preserve its shape which
is below the raqi^{c}a.[255] This nature which distinguishes
between them is the creation of the elemental forms in this
lower part of this body, through which it is prepared to
1. 25 receive all of the forms.[256] In the upper part of this
body, however, this nature does not exist. Rather, it perpetually remains in its definition.[257] In this way, the
lower matter is "so"[258]—that is, what we see of its state
of affairs of the existence in it of the elemental forms.
Or, its saying, "it was so"[259] returns to that which was discussed in the first passage of the state of affairs of the
existence in it of the elemental forms. Thus, its saying,
"and it was so"[260] indicates that in this way the lower
matter was in the mode first mentioned in the verse, "And
1. 30 the earth was tohu and bohu."[261] The Torah did not want to
go back and mention it again, in order that there not be
superfluous words.[262]

        Because raqi^{c}a is an equivocal term for everything that
is stretched out,[263] the Lord, may He be blessed, called
this raqi^{c}a by its specific name, the heavens.[264] And the
"evening" and the "morning"[265] of this degree of existent
things were also a single thing. The reason for this is
that the spheres proceed in the course of the form and the
perfection of the elements, and in this way they are
united.[266]

1. 35   It is not said of that which was created on the second
day "that it was good."[267] The reason for this is that the
430 spheres which were created on it / were not yet completed
and would not be until the mention of the creation of the
stars. This is mentioned on the fourth day and it is then
said "that it was good."[268] Also, the elemental forms of
the lower matter which were created on it were not in a
complete state. The reason for this is that these (elemental)
forms were created in (the lower matter) for the sake of the
rest of the forms which the lower matter has the power to
receive.[269]

        This is the context of (the rabbis') statements in
1. 5 Genesis Rabbah[270] regarding the question: Why is it not

written on the second day "that it was good?" Some of them
said that this is because hell (Geihinnom) was created on
it. They intended by this that passing away and privation
occur to lower existent things because of the power of lower
matter to receive all of the forms by means of the elemental
forms which were created in it.[271] Some of them said that
because of the separation—that is, because the contraries
were created in the lower matter—it is not proper to say of
it "that it was good." The reason for this is that because
of this (existence of contraries), they cause each other to

l. 10 pass away.[272] And some of them said that the reason for
this was because the work of the upper waters—that is, the
heavenly bodies—was not completed, nor was the work of the
lower waters—that is, the lower matter, as we have
explained.[273]

It is proper for you to know that it is impossible for
us to say that the division which is said in this passage[274]
is a division in place, for if this were so this statement

l. 15 would be superfluous. The reason for this is that the body
which is in the middle of the water undoubtedly divides what
is above it from what is below it. Therefore, its saying,
"and let it divide the waters from the waters"[275] would be
superfluous and unnecessary. Similarly, its saying that "He
divided the waters which were below the raqiᶜa from the
waters which were above the raqiᶜa"[276] would be superfluous.[277] Furthermore, according to this intention, its
saying, "and it was so"[278] would be completely strange, for

l. 20 after He made it there is no need to say that it was so.
This would have been needed if it had not mentioned that the
Lord, may He be blessed, made the raqiᶜa. This would have
been so if it had said, "God said: Let there be a raqiᶜa
in the midst of the waters and let it divide the waters from
the waters. And it was so."[279] This is very clear. Therefore it is clear that its saying, "and it was so"[280] is an
allusion to the coming to be which the Lord created in the

70bb lower matter—that is, the elemental forms / which are mentioned in the verse, "And the earth was tohu and bohu."[281]

l. 25   The Torah gave us a great benefit when it made known to
us that there is a unity of a sort of the lower matter and
the heavenly body.[282] The reason for this is that if there
were not a unity between them, it would necessarily follow

that there would be two divinities, one of which would
oversee and govern the matter of the spheres, and one of
which would oversee the lower matter. The error of those
who believe in two divinities derives from here.[283]

l. 30   After it completes relating this second degree of
creation, it relates the degree which follows it.[284] It
says that the Lord, may He be blessed, said that the waters,
which by nature encompass the earthly element, should be
gathered to one place in a way that dry land can be seen.[285]
And this necessarily was the point at which He created, in
this visible part of the earth, something which deviates from
its spherical shape and is a certain measure higher than
the watery element, as was explained above.[286] Therefore it
l. 35 says that the Lord, may He be blessed, stretched out the
earth over the water.[287] And as soon as the Lord, may He be
431 blessed, willed this state of affairs, it was / "so."[288]

The Lord, may He be blessed, called the dry land
"earth."[289] Even though "earth" is said in general with
reference to all of the elements in their totality, as was
explained above,[290] the term "earth" was specifically associated with this element. And the Lord, may He be blessed,
called the gathering of the waters "seas."[291] It says "seas"
and does not say "sea," because the nature of the sea varies
with the variety of the natures of the places on the earth
l. 5 through which its waters pass, as is explained in the
Meteorologica.[292] This is the intention of the statement
(of the rabbis), may their memories be for a blessing, in
Genesis Rabbah:

> Isn't there only one sea? Why then does the Torah
> say, "(He called the gathering of the waters)
> 'seas'?" This is because the taste of a fish
> caught at Acco is not similar to one caught at
> Sidon, nor to one caught at Aspamia.[293]

The Torah teaches us with this (expression)[294] that (the
seas) were the watery element, and the Philosopher explained
l. 10 this in Meteorologica.[295] Furthermore, it relates that the
Lord, may He be blessed, knew that what He had brought into
existence of this "was good."[296] The reason for this is that
from (the dry land) comes the benefit of the instances of
coming to be of those things which come to be on the visible
part of the earth, and He brought it into existence for the
sake of this purpose.[297]

Next, the Lord, may He be blessed, said that the earth
should bring forth its plants which come to be from their
species.[298] It first mentions the imperfect plant—that is,
the herb which bears seed—and it then mentions the perfect
plant—that is, the tree which produces the fruit, in which
the seed comes to be from its species.[299] The reason for

l. 15 this is that this is the proper order according to nature.[300]
Therefore, it says that the species of trees is more perfect
than that of the plants, and its functions are therefore more
perfect.[301] The reason for this is that we always take proof
from the functions, which are ordered from the forms, to the
forms, as the Philosopher discussed in De Anima.[302] And at
the time when the Lord, may He be blessed, said that these
plants should come to be from the earth, they did as He
willed.[303] That is, "The earth" brought forth "grass, herbs

l. 20 yielding seed,"[304] the species of which comes to be from the
seed, (and) "the trees which produce fruit,"[305] in which the
seed from which the species comes to be is in the fruit.
The Lord, may He be blessed, knew that what He had brought
into existence of this was "good."[306] And this coming to
be is related to the third day.[307]

The "evening" and the "morning"[308] of this degree of
creation were united. The significance of this is that the
appearance of the earth is for the sake of these instances
of coming to be.[309] Similarly, the imperfect and perfect
plants are united. The reason for this is that all forms

l. 25 which the lower matter has the power to receive are in the
degree of the form and the perfection to each other. In
this way they are all united and there is one coming to be
from them, as we discussed in the first treatise of this
book.[310]

It is possible for us to say that the intention of this
(passage) is that the Lord, may He be blessed, said that the
earth should then[311] have the potential to bring forth these
plants, "and it was so."[312] That is, the earth was given
this potential and this disposition in a marvelous way,[313]
and it then brought forth these plants which sprouted from

l. 30 it as if the seeds had been planted in the earth. Therefore,
these seeds[314] existed together at the moment of creation,
as was the case with the rest of the created things.[315]
It therefore says later[316] that

No shrub of the field was yet in the earth, and
no herb of the field had yet sprouted, for (the
Lord God) had not caused it to rain, etc.

It has already been explained that after this creation which
is mentioned[317] there was the sprouting (of the plants). [318]
This is the intention of the statement (of the rabbis) in
Genesis Rabbah:[319]

l. 35
'The earth brought forth,[320] (implies that) something was already deposited within it.

That is, it was like a deposit in it.[321] Furthermore, they
stated there:[322]

432
The generations / of the earth (were created) on
the first day,[323] according to Beit Hillel. It
waited three days—the first, second and third—
and brought forth three generations—trees,
grasses, and the Garden of Eden.

They explained to you (here) that the sprouting occurred some
time after the Lord, may He be blessed, placed this procrea-
tive potential in the earth.

The Lord, may He be blessed, knew that these plants
which He brought into existence were good.[324] For this
l. 5 reason,[325] it does not say, "God created the grass, herbs,
etc.," as it says this about the rest of the created things.
That is, it says, "God made the raqiᶜa,"[326] "God made the
two luminaries,"[327] "God created the great sea monsters,"[328]
"God made the beast of the earth,"[329] and "God created
man."[330] But it says, "The earth brought forth (grass)"[331]
in order to indicate that the plants which the Lord, may He
l. 10 be blessed, created were not in a complete state of sprouting, as was the state of affairs of the rest of the things
which He created. The reason for this is that He created the
7laa rest of the things / in a complete creation on the day on
which they were created.[332]

It is proper that you know that concerning what was
created on the first day it does not say, "God made the
light."[333] The reason for this is that the light is the
form of the heavenly body,[334] and the form does not have a
coming to be in itself. Rather, it comes to be in the coming
to be of that for which it is the perfection.[335] It is not
l. 15 proper for you to think that this form is not connected to
the heavenly body because it is posited to be separate.[336]

The reason for this is that we have explained[337] that when
we posit that it is separate we intend that it does not perform the function which is specific to it—that is, its
conception of itself—by means of an instrument which is a
material body, as in the state of affairs of the hylic
forms.[338]

Furthermore, it is possible for us to say that the
cause of its saying, "The earth brought forth (grass,
etc.)"[339] rather than saying, "God made grass, herbs" is
l. 20 because this species of living thing does not acquire a
different form for the purpose of the completion of its
coming to be, as is the state of affairs of animals. The
reason for this is that in an animal there first exists the
vegetative power until its coming to be is somewhat perfected,
at which point the animal soul is realized in it.[340] Therefore, it is necessary to introduce a different principle
other than the principle which the Lord, may He be blessed,
then placed in the waters and in the earth.[341] Therefore,
this creation[342] is attributed to the Lord, may He be blessed.
l. 25 The plants, however, do not require another principle other
than the principle which the Lord, may He be blessed, placed
in the earth to cause the sprouting of these plants, because
they do not have a form which is added to sprouting.

After (the Torah) completes relating this third degree
of creation it begins to relate the next degree of creation.[343] It says that the Lord, may He be blessed, said that
l. 30 there should be material bodies[344] which illuminate in the
raqi^ca of the heavens.[345] They are the sun, the moon and the
rest of the stars.[346] He willed their existence[347] in order
to distinguish day from night.[348] That is, that there be
generated from them in this lower matter things that are
opposites with respect to the day and the night which are
generated from (the heavenly bodies).[349] That is, in this
way the four seasons which vary from one another are generated
from (the heavens). This day and this night which are
l. 35 generated from them are generated from them from every one
of the species of rotations which exist in them. The day of
433   the star is when / its influence upon this visible part of
the earth is at its greatest degree of strength, and its
night is when (its influence) is at its weakest. For example,
just as the day of the sun is when it is above the horizon

and its night is when it is below (the horizon), similarly
the day of the sun is when it is among the northern constellations and its night is when it is among the southern con-
1. 5   stellations. In this way, the four seasons of the year,
which vary from one another, are generated from the sun.[350]
        Furthermore, it mentions that the Lord, may He be
blessed, willed their existence for a second benefit. That
is, that there be a variety of actions from (the heavenly
bodies) through which the stars would be individuated from
one another, so that the stars would be signs of these actions
through which they are individuated.[351] This occurs from
them for "set times, for years and days."[352] That is, in
this period of time that which is generated follows that
1. 10 which is decreed by this star, and in a second period of
time it follows that which is decreed by another star.
Thus, one would say that the ruler at this hour is Saturn,
and the ruler at a second hour is Jupiter; that the ruler
of this day is Saturn, and the ruler of a second day is the
sun. This state of affairs is similar with regard to years
and to the other periods of time which are larger than a
year and the rule of which is related to each star,[353]
according to what is clear from observation to one who
1. 15 employs Astrology.[354] And it is clear from what preceded in
the fifth treatise of this book that these two reasons[355]
which are mentioned with regard to the creation (of the stars)
are the cause of the perfection of the multitude of instances
of coming to be in this lower matter.
        Furthermore, it mentions that the Lord, may He be
blessed, willed their existence for a third benefit. That
is, that they should illuminate the earth,[356] for it is in
this way that the existence of the human being and the rest
1. 20 of the animals which have the sense of sight is perfected.[357]
This is very clear. The reason for this is that without light
the organ through which the animal sees its objects of perception would not perceive anything, and its seeing of the
objects of perception is very necessary to it, for it is one
of the greater causes of its fleeing from that which is harmful to that which is beneficial.[358] Together with this in
the human being (sight) is a major connection to his perfection of conceptions, for the conceptual principles are
acquired from the senses, and the sense through which

l. 25 (the objects of perception) appear to him in a major intro-
       duction (to conceptual perfection) is the sense of sight.[359]
       This is self-evident.

           Because the Lord, may He be blessed, willed the creation
       of the stars in order that these actions would be realized
       through them,[360] it is clear that this is the reason that He
       brought them into existence in the most perfect possible way,
       in terms of proximity and distance, of greatness and small-
       ness, of the diversity of the colors in their twinkling, of
       the large and small number of their motions, and of the
       rest of the things which exist in the heavenly bodies[361] for

l. 30 the sake of this purpose, so that these benefits would be
       realized from them in the most perfect possible way.[362]

           It mentions that as soon as the Lord, may He be blessed,
       willed this, it was.[363] It then returns to relate the manner
       of this creation. It says that the Lord, may He be blessed,
       made "the two great luminaries."[364] They are the sun and the

71ab   moon. / He made them larger than the rest of the stars
       because the need of the lower existent things for the sun and

l. 35 the moon is greater than their need for the rest of the
       stars.[365] Therefore, it was necessary that (the sun and the
       moon) be of greater magnitude in a way that, by means of
       (their magnitude), they would rule[366] over the rest of the

434   stars, / as was discussed above.[367] Because of this it says
       that He caused the sun "to rule the day" and the moon "to
       rule the night."[368] Their stars also rule, as was discussed
       above.[369]

           It mentions that He made[370] them in a way that these
       already-mentioned benefits would be perfected through them.
       That is: a) that they would illumine the earth[371] in order
       that the animal (species) would be able to see its objects

l. 5   of perception; b) that they would "rule the day and the
       night"[372] in a way that these diverse accidents, which are
       generated in the lower world, would be ordered by means of
       the ruling of this (star) at one time and another (star) at
       another time, as was discussed above;[373] and c) that they
       would "divide the light"[374] (of the star)—that is, the time
       when it is above the horizon—"from the darkness"[375] (of the
       star)—that is, the time when it is below the horizon.

           Similarly, the light and the darkness of the star are
       related to the four seasons which are generated from all of
       the species of rotations which exist in (the heavens), as

l. 10 was discussed above.[376] Therefore its says here, "to divide

the light from the darkness"[377] in apposition to what it
first says, "to divide the day from the night,"[378] in order
to add clarity to what it intended by this statement. The
reason for this is that it would have been possible to think
that the only thing intended by (the first statement) was
the daily period of time.[379] Therefore, it translated the
language[380] in this place to "the light" and "the darkness."[381] For this reason it says "to rule the day and the
night"[382] in apposition to its saying, "they shall serve as
l. 15 signs for the set times, for days and years,"[383] for this
(latter statement) adds clarity and perfection to what we
explained about this (earlier) statement—that is, its saying
"they shall serve as signs for the set times, for days and
years."[384] And it says next that the Lord, may He be blessed,
knew that what He had brought into existence of the stars
"was good."[385] He created them for this purpose,[386] for it
is false that this good[387] should be perfected from (the
stars) by accident.[388]

The "evening" and the "morning"[389] of this degree of
creation were united. The reason for this is that all of
l. 20 (the stars) cooperate when the nomos, order and rightness[390]
of these lower existent things overflow from them. The
evening and the morning in them occur in two respects.[391]
The first (respect) is (the unity of the state of affairs
in which) diverse relations with this visible part of the
earth are generated from each star, so that the morning is
the time at which this action which is realized from it on
the visible part of the earth is strong, and the evening
l. 25 is the time at which its action is weak.[392] This state of
affairs is united even though diverse actions are ordered
through it in some way. The second (respect) is that the
stars vary from one another in veneration[393] and lack of
veneration in relation to the degrees of the actions which
are ordered by each star. With all of this they are all
united so that this wonderful nomos, which exists in these
lower existent things, is perfected from (them all in) their
totality.

l. 30   There are two profound doubts here, and it is proper
that we endeavor to solve them. The first (doubt) is that
it has been explained from what we have said[394] that the
Lord, may He be blessed, brought these (supralunar) things
into existence for the sake of these lower existent things.

If this is so, the venerable would be for the sake of the
inferior, and this is a profound falsehood according to the
sages.[395] The second (doubt) is that it would have been
proper, according to this natural order, for this coming to
be (of the stars) to have been related to the third day,
l. 35 since the heavens and the stars are prior in cause and in
existence to the elements and to that which comes to be
from them.[396]

435   We say that in the solution of the first doubt / there
exists little difficulty, given the preceding (explanations)
of these things in this treatise.[397] The reason for this
is that one observes that that which is venerable always
perfects that which is lower through what overflows to it.
In this way, the Lord, may He be blessed, overflows[398] to
all existent things. Nevertheless, we do not say because of
this that the Lord, may He be blessed, is for the sake of
things which are lower than Him. We rather say that His
l. 5 existence has a mode of perfection such that He can overflow
from His perfection to all of the existent things, according
to what is possible for them to receive of it.[399] Indeed,
it is false that that which is venerable acquires its perfection from that which is inferior.[400] This being the case,
this doubt is removed as follows: The spheres and their
movers exist for the sake of themselves.[401] Nevertheless,
it is more venerable for that which has a body, insofar as
it has a body, to perform some actions than for it not to
l. 10 perform them, for actions are the vital power of bodies in
some way and without them they would be dead material bodies
placed in motion.[402] Because it is not proper that they
should perform a useless activity,[403] that is, that they
should move and that no benefit would be generated from their
motion, and because it was impossible for this benefit to be
generated for themselves, because they have no potentiality
in them, (for these reasons) these actions were placed in
them to perfect the rest of the existent things. For this
l. 15 reason the shape and number of the spheres, the twinkling of
the stars, and the rest of the states of affairs which exist
in the heavens are all in the most perfect possible way in
order to perfect these (lower) existent things.

        It is clear that this doubt cannot possibly be solved
unless the world is posited to be generated.[404] Therefore,

the generation of the world is made clear from it, as we made

<u>71ba</u>   clear in what / preceded.[405]

The second doubt[406] is very difficult, and it is proper

that we address its solution according to our shortcomings.[407]

l. 20   We say that the purpose of the intention of our perfect Torah

was to cause one who speculates in it and follows its path to

realize true success, as we explained in our commentary to the

Torah.[408]   (The Torah) therefore wanted to stimulate man in

respect to speculation about the secrets of existence with

this order which is found in its relating the description of

the creation of the world.[409]   It intended with this (order)

to stimulate him (to see) that in respect to speculation it

is necessarily the case that the world is generated. This

was done by (the Torah) by its setting before him something

l. 25   at which he would pause. The reason for this is that one who

walks on a path will not be diverted to an investigation of

that path when he walks on it if he is certain that there

are no obstacles on it. Sometimes this cause is what turns

him aside from its end in a way that is better than for him

to remain in his place, so that he perpetually goes far on

his path from the place to which he intends to come. When

there is an obstacle in (his path), he will emphasize the

investigation of it, and he will set his endeavors to remove

it, or he will turn aside from it to a path which will lead

l. 30   him to the place to which he intends to go. The state of

affairs of the Torah is similar, for if there were nothing

in it to cause man to pause, the speculator would not empha-

size the speculation about it, and this would be a cause of

the obstruction of (the Torah's) benefit.[410]

The change of the order of creation in this context is

for this reason in itself. The reason for this is that if

the notion of the creation of the stars had been discussed

prior to the appearance of the earth, it would have been

possible for the thinker to think erroneously that it was

l. 35   possible that the appearance of the earth was related to the

stars, as the Philosopher and his followers thought.[411]

436   / Therefore, the notion of the appearance of the earth is

discussed in the Torah first[412] before it discusses the crea-

tion of the stars.[413]   And because it discusses the appear-

ance of the earth, whose state of affairs is not intended

for the sake of itself but is rather intended for the sake of

the coming to be of those things which come to be on it,[414]
it was necessary for (the Torah) to discuss the coming to be
of the plants along with (its discussion) of the appearance
of the earth.[415] It was also necessary for this reason to
make known the notion of the evening and the morning in this
l. 5   coming to be, and (to make known) that they are united.[416]

Furthermore, if it had discussed the creation of the
stars (immediately) after the creation of the heavenly
body,[417] it would have been possible for the speculator to
think erroneously that the stars were in the spheres for
their own sake[418] and that the benefit which is realized
from them in these (lower) existent things came from them in
a secondary way.[419] Therefore, it interrupted between them
with the creation of the appearance of the earth and of the
plants, in order to stimulate us (to see) that the creation
l. 10 of the spheres was perfected without the stars, with reference to what they needed for themselves, and that the stars
are in them for the sake of those benefits which were mentioned.[420] The Torah directed us with this (order) to that
from which we can derive a demonstration of the generation
of the world.[421]

Furthermore, because along with (its discussion of) the
creation of the spheres[422] it discusses the creation in the
lower matter of the elemental forms through which it has the
power to receive all of the forms,[423] it was not proper for
it to interrupt the exposition of this lower matter before
l. 15 telling something about the perfection which it has the power
(to receive).[424] Therefore, it was necessary to mention the
coming to be of the plants.[425] And because of this it was
necessary to mention with it the creation of the appearance
of the earth, because (the elevated part of the earth) is in
some way the cause of the bringing into existence of these
instances of coming to be.[426] After this,[427] it completes
relating the creation of that which it had yet to complete
about the creation of the spheres, that is, the stars.[428]

After it completes relating this degree of creation, it
l. 20 begins to relate the next degree of creation in this lower
matter.[429] It says that the Lord, may He be blessed, said
that "the waters" should "swarm with...living creatures" and
that "birds that fly above the earth" should come to be in
the air, "on the face of the raqi^c a of the heavens."[430]

That is, the Lord, may He be blessed, created in this way all
the species of fish which procreate their species, to exist
in the waters, and all the species of birds which procreate
their species.[431] The Lord, may He be blessed, knew that
what He had brought into existence of (these species) was
l. 25 very "good"[432] for the sake of the purpose for which it had
been created.[433] He also created their creation in the most
perfect possible way, so that what we perceive of the goodness and the grace[434] which He brought into existence in their
their creation—which is very great, as is explained in the
science of physics in a discussion of the benefits of the
organs of the animal[435]—is but a trifle in comparison with
what exists of the good and the gracious in their nature.[436]
The Lord, may He be blessed, gave them the power to procreate
l. 30 their species and He blessed them so that the fish would be
fruitful and multiply and fill the waters[437] in the seas and
that the bird would be fruitful and multiply on the earth.[438]
The evening and the morning in this degree of creation were
united.[439] The evening is the animal which is more imperfect—that is, the fish, according to their degrees—and
the morning is the animal which is more perfect—that is,
the birds, according to their degrees.[440]
      These two classes of animals[441] needed the blessing that
l. 35 they be fruitful and multiply, whereas the perfect animal[442]
did not need it. The reason for this is that the procreation
437   of these classes is imperfect because they produce / either
a perfect or an imperfect egg in their body.[443] They therefore need additional divine providence over the procreation
71bb of their species in order for (their) / coming to be to be
completed and for their species to endure. They need this
more than the walking animal because the latter produces an
animal within its body. This providence is that the Lord,
may He be blessed, gave them an instrument by means of which
their imperfect procreation would be perfected.[444]
l. 5   The human being did not need the blessing to be fruitful
and multiply, because his procreation is perfect.[445] This
(blessing) was rather made[446] in respect to a commandment.
That is, the Lord, may He be blessed, commanded him to be
fruitful and multiply in order that his species not be
destroyed. We explained this beyond a doubt in our commentary to the Torah,[447] and this is not the place for this
investigation.

After it completes this degree of creation, it begins
1. 10 to relate the next degree.[448] It says that the Lord, may He
be blessed, said that there should be every species of large
walking animals which procreates its species. That is to
say, the Lord, may He be blessed, made every species of non-
speaking walking animal in this way.[449] The Lord, may He be
blessed, knew that what He had brought into existence of
these things was "good."[450] He brought them into existence
in the most perfect possible way, for He placed His nature
1. 15 (in them) in the most venerable way possible, according to
what He intended.[451]

Next, the Lord, may He be blessed, said to the upper
and lower (beings) that there should be made from them a
human being with an intellect.[452] The Lord, may He be
blessed, also said that this human being be created in a
manner so that its individuals would rule over every living
thing which exists in the world of coming to be and passing
away.[453] And it was so.[454] That is, the Lord, may He be
blessed, created in this way the human being in the human
form ascribed to him—that is, the hylic intellect.[455]
1. 20 Therefore, He created him in the image of the upper (beings)
in some way, for they have intellects and the human intellect
is related in some way to the intellects of the upper
(beings).[456]

He created them male and female,[457] for without this
procreation could not have been completed. It is proper for
us to understand that the state of affairs in which the Lord,
may He be blessed, created (the human species) was (different)
than the rest of the animals. The Lord, may He be blessed,
blessed them with providence over their endurance and their
preservation. And He said to them that they should be fruit-
1. 25 ful and multiply and fill the earth and be strong[458] over
it,[459] for this is necessary for the preservation of the
human species.[460] The reason for this is that if the human
species was entirely in a specific part of the earth,[461]
this species would pass away when some passing away would
occur to that part, as was explained in the preceding part
of this treatise.[462] It is for this reason that it was
necessary that the languages by diversified, as we explained
in our commentary to the Torah.[463]

On the day of their creation, He also gave them the
power to rule over "the fish of the sea, the birds of the
l. 30 heavens, and every living thing that creeps upon the
earth."[464] The reason for this is that because all of them
are for the sake of man,[465] it is necessary for man to have
rulership over them. If this were not the case, the end for
the sake of which (these lower species) exist would not
reach man.[466]

Next, it relates that the Lord, may He be blessed,
said, "I am giving you the nature and the power so that every
seed-bearing herb and the seed-bearing fruit of every tree
will be beneficial to you as food."[467] This was the point
l. 35 at which He placed the power in man to alter those things
which he eats and to transform them into the substance of
438 the one who eats.[468] Similarly, He gave[469] / the power and
nature to all the classes of animals on the earth so that
they would have this food as a benefit, together with "every
green herb."[470] That is, the leaves of plants and trees are
also beneficial food for them. And when the Lord, may He be
blessed, willed this to be so, it was as He willed it.[471]
It discusses this creation[472] here, for it is through it
that these species endure and their existence is preserved
l. 5   for the time that is possible.[473]

The Lord, may He be blessed, knew that everything that
He made was very good according to what He intended,[474]
and He therefore brought it into existence in the most perfect possible way. (The Torah) generalizes in this statement,
saying, "all that He has made,"[475] because those things which
He made in the lower world are for the sake of one another.
The good is not perfected until it reaches the end for the
sake of which what was prior to the end existed.[476] Simi-
l. 10 larly, the perfect good is not perfected in the world as a
whole until it is in its perfection and totality. The evening
and the morning[477] of this degree of creation were united.
That is, the non-speaking animal and the speaking animal
(were united) because some walk the path of perfection for
others.[478] In this way, it is made clear that all parts of
the world are united, and in this unity, the world as a
whole is like a single individual. Through this wonderful
story, (the Torah) informs us of one principle upon which

l. 15 the whole science of Physics is constructed. That is, there
is nothing among the natural existent things which is useless. This is what it informs us (in its saying that) everything that the Lord, may He be blessed, made of these existent
things is "very good."[479]

It is proper for you to know that it says regarding
man, "Let us make man"[480] in the plural form, while it does
not say so with regard to the rest of the instances of coming
to be. It rather says, "Let the earth sprout,"[481] and "Let
the waters swarm,"[482] and "Let the earth bring forth."[483]

l. 20 The reason for this is that in the other things which came
to be the only form which exists is hylic.[484] It therefore
attributes their coming to be to the elements together with
the power which He then marvelously gave them so that these
instances of coming to be would come from them.[485] But
because in some respects form exists in man which is not

72aa hylic,[486] his coming to be is not attributed / to the elements
alone. Rather, the coming to be of his matter is attributed
to the elements, and the coming to be of his form, which is
separate in some way, (is attributed to) the upper (beings),

l. 25 as we explained the verse, "And the ruaḥ returns to God who
gave it."[487] Therefore, you find that (the rabbis), may
their memories be for a blessing, said in many places that
man is created from the upper (beings) and from the lower
(beings).[488] All of this is to stimulate[489] us (to see)
that man has an intellect through which he is in some way
related to the upper (beings). Because it discusses the
creation of man here in summary form in order to complete
the story of the creation of the world, it later returns to
relate the secrets of the creation of man.[490] It completes
(the discussion there about) what the Lord, may He be

l. 30 blessed, gave (man) to cause him to realize his spiritual
success, as we explained in our commentary to the Torah
regarding the passage about Adam and Eve and the serpent and
the Garden of Eden and the cherubim and the fiery ever-
turning sword.[491] This is not the place for this investigation, for the intention here is to explain what the Torah
related about the description of the creation of the world.

It is proper that you should know that the Torah
discusses an explanation in this story that the acquired
l. 35 intellect[492] is everlasting. The reason for this is that it

says that man "became a living soul (nefesh ḥayah)."[493]

439   That is, / a distinction exists between his soul and the
souls of the rest of the animals, because the soul of man
has the power to be living and to endure in itself[494]—
something that is not so for the rest of the animals.[495]
With the exception of man you do not find the soul described
as living. The reason for this is that when it says, "Let
the earth bring forth the soul of the beast (nefesh ḥayah)
according to its species,"[496] the word ḥayah is not an

l. 5   adjective describing "soul" (nefesh). It is rather the name
of a class of animals—the beasts. This is self-evident.[497]
In general, its statement that man "became a living soul"[498]
is necessarily (made) to inform us of the uniqueness of this
soul among all the other souls of animals, and to indicate
this uniqueness it also says that man was created in the
image of the upper (beings).[499]

        Afterwards, the Torah explains the manner in which it
is possible for the human soul to endure in itself. It

l. 10   relates that it was in the nature of man to name all of the
animals.[500] That is, (he called them) the names which indicate their essence.[501] It is this which indicates the
definition (of the animal) and that which is willed for it,
for man has the power to conceive the essence of these
things.[502] It says that for everything which man named in
this way, its name was a living soul.[503] That is, the conception of that essence is an intellect which endures in
itself.

        See how the Torah explains that the acquired intellect

l. 15   is everlasting, and how (the Torah) also testifies that
(human) success occurs through apprehension. It is not in
the verification of the truth insofar as it is verifiable,
but it rather occurs with respect to apprehension, as we
explained in the first treatise of this book.[504] Consequently, it testifies to us that the calling of names to
things is an act of apprehension, not one of verification.
This is very clear. To make this point the Torah uses the
classes of the animals from among the other natural things,[505]

l. 20   such as the elements, the homogeneous parts,[506] and the
plants. The success that reaches man in his conception of
more venerable notions is more profound, as was explained in
the first treatise of this book.[507]

See how the Torah explained this notion in clear
language. This point was hidden from those who preceded us
only because of the blindness which was placed in their eyes
because of the views of the philosophers about the immortality
of the soul.[508] Therefore, those who say that the Torah does

l. 25 not comment about the notion of spiritual success make a
marvelous error. Rather, the Torah is prefaced by its discussion, for without it there would be no benefit in the
state of the perfection of the soul by speculation, whose
purpose is conception alone—that is, the state to which the
Torah is directed. This endeavoring on (the Torah's) account
would be useless. Therefore, it was necessary that the
Torah be prefaced by information about the notion of spiritual immortality, because it is the purpose for the sake of
which it is proper for everyone to endeavor to acquire the
perfection of the soul.[509]

l. 30   We shall complete here the explanation of the story of
the degrees of creation at the time of the generation of the
world. The seventh degree[510] relates the Lord, may He be
blessed, to the creation of the world in that it is His
preservation of it perpetually in the way in which it is.[511]
This action is not in the degree of work which is done in
craftsmanship and which does not need the cause after its
completion.[512] Rather, (the world) needs its cause perpet-

l. 35 ually. This occurs when it perpetually has the wonderful
desire for this most venerable conception.[513] Because of

440 the wonderful desire[514] / which exists in the nature of this
venerable conception, the movers of the heavenly bodies
desire that there perpetually overflow from them that which
overflows to these (lower) existent things. The reason for
this is that part of the desire which (the movers) have is
this wonderful desire in respect to the imperfect nomos
which is in their souls. But they necessarily have this
wonderful desire in respect to their conception that this

l. 5 imperfect nomos which is in their souls is part of the perfect nomos which the Lord, may He be blessed, has.[515]
Because of this, they subject their desire to the nomos
which is in the soul of the Lord,[516] may He be blessed, so
that they perpetually move their spheres in a way that the
nomos of these (lower) existent things overflows from them.

72ab / And if it is imagined that their subjection to the Lord,

may He be blessed, in this state of affairs were to cease
for one moment, all of these (lower) existent things would
pass away, for this subjection is what causes the motions of

l. 10 the spheres to be perpetually the way they are.[517] Furthermore, when (the movers) apprehend their own state of affairs—
that their existence, as well as the existence of the spheres
and the stars to which they cleave in this wonderful way,
overflow from the Lord, may He be blessed—they desire to
resemble the Lord, may He be blessed, insofar as it is possible. It is in this way that they desire to overflow to what
is below them in order to complete the divine intention for
the sake of which He created them in this marvelous way.[518]

l. 15   Therefore, it relates and says that the creation of the
heaven and the earth and everything of the other existent
things that are in them was completed[519] and that the seventh
degree of creation was that the Lord, may He be blessed,
desired "the work which He had done."[520] That is, (He
desired) the conception of the work which is the nomos, order
and rightness of the existent things.[521] In this way the
Lord, may He be blessed, caused existence to continue.[522]
In the way that He is, it is not necessary (for Him) to do
anything (with His desire), as is the case with these (other)
existences[523] in which the movers of the heavenly bodies

l. 20 perpetually possess the desire to be subjected to the Lord,
may He be blessed, and so to move their spheres in the way
through which the nomos of these (lower) existent things is
perfected. For this reason (the Torah says that) the Lord,
may He be blessed, blessed the seventh day and made it sacred
at the time that He gave the Torah to Israel[524] in order to
comment about the notion of the generation of the world. The
reason for this is that in this seventh degree of creation
the Lord rested from doing the kind of actions which he
caused at the time of His generation of the world. This is

l. 25 the work which the Lord, may He be blessed, created to cause
existence perpetually according to the nature which He gave
it at the time of creation.[525]

        We have interpreted "God finished (va-yekhal)"[526] in
the sense of desire, as in the case of "David yearned."[527]
One may object and say that if the matter were so, the word
"soul" is lacking, for this verb is always connected with
"soul." As it says, "My soul longs and yearns,"[528] and as

in, "David yearned,"[529] the sense of which is "David's soul
yearned."[530] We respond to this objection as follows: This

l. 30 is possible when the one who desires is composed of a body
and a soul, as is man. The reason for this is that it is
proper for this desire to be attributed to the soul, which
is the part of him to which it is possible to attribute
desire and longing.[531] But there is no part of the Lord,
may He be blessed, to which desire can be exclusively attributed, because He is not composite. Therefore, the desire
which He desired is attributed to Him in Himself, not to a
part of Him.[532]

It is possible for us to say that the intention of its
saying, "On the seventh day God finished (va-yekhal) the

l. 35 work which He had done"[533] is that, in this seventh degree,
He completed "the work which He had done"[534] through the

441   subjection to Him which He perpetually sets / in the movers
of the heavenly bodies.[535] He does so with respect to the
high degree of his existence which causes the movers of the
heavenly bodies to be differentiated before Him[536] perpetually and consequently to move their spheres in the way
through which the nomos of these (lower) existent things is
perfected. The sense (of the verse) is one no matter which
of these interpretations is employed,[537] but, in our opinion,

l. 5   the last explanation is most adequate.[538] This seventh
degree is perpetual; it can neither be destroyed nor can it
cease,[539] as we explained above concerning the notion that
it is impossible for the world to pass away.[540]

This is the lesson which we see in this place of the
account of creation.[541] It is, in itself, that to which
speculation brought us concerning the notion of the genera-

l. 10 tion of the world.[542] It is proper that it should be so, for
it is impossible that the Torah should establish a false
view for us. Therefore, it was necessary that the Torah
agree with that which is explained to be necessary by demonstration.[543]

You, O speculator, see how distinctive our explanation
of this section of the Torah has been among (the explanations
of) all those who preceded us, so that in no respect is it
possible that its explanation be other than in the way in
which we have discussed it. The speculator cannot be
ignorant of this with regard to our words. The reason for

this if that this section of the Torah testifies to the fact
that ours is undoubtedly its explanation—either with respect

1. 15 to its language or with respect to its order. We do not
intend to extend this treatise in order to refute the explanations of those who preceded us.[544] In our view this is
superfluous after the revelation of the truth and the suggestion of the section of the Torah itself that this is
undoubtedly its explanation. The belief of (one's) opponent
does not require witnesses.[545]

It is proper that we give wonderful thanks to the
Lord, may He be blessed, that He brought this wonderful

1. 20 story into existence for us. It stimulates our eyes (to see
the truth)[546] and it is the cause of our finding the truth
in this investigation through this wonderful guidance[547]
to the (truth) which it contains, as has been made clear by
our words.

208) Ma^caseh be-re^ɔshit. For an explanation of this term,
see above, note #2.

209) Be-zulat zeman, literally: "without time." In the first
part of this treatise he explains that time is that which numbers
motion (6:1:10, p. 329, ll. 33-35, where he refers the reader to
the Physica 4.11.219b2; cf. 4.11.220a24). As a result, the existence of time presupposes the existence of a moved object which time
can measure in respect to the before and the after (6:1:11, p. 345,
l. 30). But body which does not preserve its shape out of which
the world came to be has no motion, because it is formless and
matter needs form to move it (6:1:17, p. 364, ll. 1-3; p. 367, l.
23f.; cf. above, note #51). Thus he concludes (6:1:18, p. 374, ll.
7-9; the reference is to the Physica 4.1.218b21ff.):

> Prior to the creation of the world there was no time at
> all, for there was neither motion nor rest, and that
> which neither moves nor is at rest is not clothed in
> time at all, as is explained in the Physica.

Note also his argument above (6:1:20) that there was no time
involved in the process of the world's coming to be prior to its
completion. He distinguishes there between alteration, locomotion
and quantitative change, all of which occur in time, and absolute
generation from nonbeing to being. In the latter case, the generated thing, prior to its complete generation, does not yet exist
and thus has no motion. In the case of the generation of the
world, body which does not preserve its shape and which does not
exist in actuality prior to creation receives the disposition (i.e.,
last form) to receive the hierarchy of forms which overflows from
the divine nomos simultaneously with its reception of the forms
themselves (6:1:24). Thus, there is no time prior to the moment
of creation and at the moment of creation all the species of existent things come to be simultaneously.

210) He designates the body out of which the world came to be
as nothing because it is nonexistent and devoid of all form (see
above, notes #49, #51, #147, and #152). His position that the
world came to be "from nothing" is distinct from the position of
Maimonides and others which he designates as "from absolutely
nothing" (see above, note #6).

211) Note that the position that the heavens and the earth
were created together is distinct from and is not entailed by the
position that there was no time prior to the creation of the world.

In the first sentence of this chapter, he refers to what he has
previously explained, i.e., that time does not precede creation.
Beginning with this second sentence he proceeds to argue that the
details of creation that are described in Genesis, chs. 1 and 2,
are not intended to imply that there was a temporal sequence of six
days in which various parts of the world were created in succession.

212) b. Ḥag. 12a. The text cited in the passage is from Isa
48:13. Note that though he describes this as the view of the
rabbis, the quotation is extracted from a series of views about the
issue, all of which conflict with one another. Cf. his Commentary
to the Torah (9b, ll. 10-12), where he also cites Gen 2:4 ("These
are the generations of the heaven and the earth when they were
created on the day that the Lord God made the earth and the
heaven.") as evidence for the simultaneous creation of the heaven
and the earth.

213) The manuscripts consulted read ha-ʾeḥad qodem la-sheniy
for ha-ʾeḥad la-sheniy at p. 427, l. 27. This clarifies but does
not alter the meaning of our text, which would be translated as:
"in a way that the first precedes the second by one day."

214) On priority in cause and in nature, cf. above, 6:2:2, p.
420, ll. 21ff. and note #27. The movers (which he calls "separate
intellects" in the parallel passage of his Commentary to the Torah
[9b, l. 34]) are prior in cause and in nature to the heavenly
bodies because they are the forms of those bodies (cf. below
6:2:8, p. 429, l. 6 and note #242) and because it is they who cause
the motions of the heavenly bodies as a result of their longing
for the divine nomos (6:2:8, p. 439, ll. 30ff.). The heavenly
bodies are prior in cause and in nature to the sublunar world
because it is the combination of all of their activities which
produces the nomos which rules lower existent things. In the
absence of any single characteristic of the heavens, the whole of
the sublunar world would pass away (6:1:7, p. 310, l. 24f. Cf.
above, note #152.). This fits Aristotle's fifth sense of the term
"prior" in the Categoriae 12, in that the existence of the heavens
and the existence of the sublunar world reciprocally imply each
other and in that the heavens are the cause of the sublunar world
(see above, note #27).

Note that in describing this priority in his Commentary, he
uses the term "essence" in place of "nature" in one place (CT 9b,
l. 17) and the term "existence" in place of "nature" in another

place (CT 9c, ll. 1, 2; cf. 6:2:8, p. 434, l. 35). His apparent
ambivalence about using the term "nature" to refer to the supralunar world and to the world of the separate intellects may be due
to his belief that "nature" refers to the sublunar laws of the
elemental motion and not to the motions of the heavenly bodies.
Cf. 5:3:6, p. 259, ll. 27ff., where he distinguishes between the
natural law of the elements, which is to be at rest by nature and
to move by accident, and the law of heavenly motion, which is to
move by nature. (On the term "nature," cf. below, note #228.) It
may be inferred, therefore, that while the nature of a sublunar
thing is identical to its essence, this is not the case in the
supralunar world. In all cases, however, he retains the term
"priority in cause" and appears to be speaking about Aristotle's
fifth and his own fourth sense of the term "prior."

215) He views the variety of species in the sublunar world as
a hierarchy which proceeds from that which has more privation to
that which has more existence. For example, he begins his
Commentary to the Torah (2a, ll. 3-6) as follows:

> Praised be the Creator who, in His desire to improve
> existent things and to bring them from existence which
> is lacking to perfect existence, oversaw these lower
> existent things and raised their existence, degree by
> degree, until they reached human existence.

When he speaks in our text of hylic priority, he is referring to
the priority of a thing which is more material and hence less
perfect in its approximation of the perfection of the existence of
a separate form. The latter's perfection consists in the fact that
it is not dependent upon material bodies to conceive (cf. 6:2:8,
p. 432, ll. 14ff.) and that, as a consequence, it is better able to
conceive of the divine nomos. Its knowledge is not multiple, as
is human conception, which acquires its knowledge inductively from
the multiplicity of material existent things (see above, note #3).
It rather longs for the divine nomos, which it imperfectly conceives, conceives of itself and of the single, simple motion of the
sphere of which it is the form (6:2:8, p. 439, ll. 30ff.; 5:3:9,
p. 274f.; cf. below, note #251).

To the extent that the form of a species predominates over its
matter, the purpose of the existence of that species is apparent
to us. For example, we know that the ultimate end of human existence is the attainment of the most perfect possible conception
because the form of the human species is more predominant over its

matter than is the case with lower species. Nevertheless, as he
argues in the first treatise, insofar as a human being is material,
he can never become identical with his definition, i.e., he can
never achieve perfect conception. The latter is possible only for
a noncorporeal, separate form. A lower species is hylically prior
to a higher one in that it is more material. Its greater degree
of corporeality makes it more potential and less actual (since matter is the source of potentiality) and it thus is less able to
actualize its definition or nature. (For a discussion of the term
"nature," see below, note #228.) Note, for example, the following
comment of Aristotle (Meteorologica 4.12.390a3ff., Oxford translation):

> For the end is least obvious there where matter
> predominates most. If you take the extremes, matter is
> pure matter and the essence is pure definition; but the
> bodies intermediate between the two are matter or defini-
> tion in proportion as they are near to either.

When Gersonides speaks of the priority of the thing which is
more material to the thing which is more able to approximate perfect conception, he is referring to the extent to which more perfect species, and man in particular, depend upon lower species for
their welfare. In the first part of this treatise, he states
(6:1:27, p. 405, l. 4f.):

> That which receives privation is prior in nature to
> that which comes to be and passes away in the priority
> of the animal to man. When the prior is removed, the
> posterior is removed.

Cf. below in this chapter (p. 438, l. 12), where he states that
the lower animals "walk the path of perfection" for human beings
(cf. above, 1:6, p. 37, ll. 28ff.; p. 40, ll. 20ff.). This sense
of priority corresponds to the second sense which he lists above,
priority in order (cf. above, note #27).

    One of his most complete descriptions of hylic priority occurs
in the first treatise, from which we quote here at length (1:12,
p. 86, ll. 8-24).

> The elements are absolutely in the hylic degree of the
> the minerals. They are (also) in the hylic degree of
> one another, i.e., the earth is in the hylic degree of
> the water and the water is in hylic degree of the ele-
> ment air and the element air is in the hylic degree of
> the element fire. The minerals are in the hylic degree
> of the plants and the plants are in the hylic degree of
> animals. It also appears that the forms of the minerals
> are also in the hylic degree of one another, so that the

state of affairs is realized that is like an intermediate between the plant and that which is inanimate,
i.e., coral. The case is similar with plants. That
is, some are in hylic degree of others, so that the
state of affairs is realized that is like an intermediate between the plant and the animal, i.e., the
water sponge and the species of shellfish. The case
is similar with animals, so that the end of the state
of affairs is completed with the human species....

Prime matter proceeds through these forms from
privation to existence. Therefore, all intermediate
forms are privation in a respect and existence in a
respect. That is, they are existent with respect to
those forms which are prior to them and the are privation with respect to those forms which are posterior
to them, just as parts of motion are actual with
respect to the past and potential with respect to the
future. Therefore, it is necessarily the case that
every one of the forms is in hylic degree of that
which is posterior to it, so that the whole state of
affairs ends with the human species.

(My thanks to Professor Seymour Feldman for his assistance in the
translation of this passage.) Though this passage deals with
"hylic degree" rather than "hylic priority," it is clear from it
that if a is in the hylic degree of b, i.e., if a is the species
just lower than b in the hierarchy of existence, than a is prior
to b. It is this which he is calling "hylic priority" (cf. 5:3:12,
p. 280).

Note that he switches from priority in cause and in nature to
hylic priority. The switch occurs in the move from the celestial
to the sublunar world. Whereas the order of the heavens is from
the more venerable to the less venerable, in the sublunar world of
matter the order is from the less perfect to the more perfect,
culminating with the human species. He has prepared us for this
in his discussion above of the different senses of the term "priority" (6:2:2). The priority which exists in the sublunar world is
priority in order. He could not have continued with priority in
cause and in nature, for though man is more perfect than lower
species, he is not prior to them in cause and in nature.

216) The manuscripts consulted read qodem la-ḥay ve-la-zeh
yihyeh ha-ḥay he-ḥaser qodem la-ḥay ha-shalem for qodem le-ḥay
ha-shalem at p. 428, l. 1. Thus, instead of the translated phrase,
"the plant is prior to the perfect animal," the text would be
translated as: "the plant is prior to the animal and in this way
the more deprived animal is prior to the more perfect animal."
The manuscript reading is to be preferred here for the following

reasons: a) The reading of the printed texts, taken literally,
implies that plant species are prior only to perfect animal
species and not to those which are less perfect. As noted above,
note #215, this is not the case. b) What follows immediately is
precisely an exposition of the instances which illustrate the
priority of less perfect animal species to more perfect animal
species. c) It is likely that the omitted phrase is due to a
scribal error.

217) De Generatione Animalium 1.8.718a35-1.11.719a30 and
passim. On his use of the term "perfect" here, see below, 6:2:8,
p. 436, l. 34 - p. 437, l. 3, where he explains that the procreation of fish and birds is imperfect because they produce eggs outside their bodies. By contrast, the survival of the species of
walking animals, which produce their babies within their bodies,
is less dependent upon the regulation of divine providence over
factors in existence which are external to the species' nature.
Thus, the degree of perfection of a class is related also to the
efficiency with which it reproduces.

218) I.e., that the description of the seven days of creation
in Genesis does not indicate a temporal sequence but rather indicates the priority of some things over other things.

219) Since the rotation of the sun is the measure of the day.

220) b. Ḥag. 12a.

221) Cf. above, 6:2:8, p. 427, l. 23, where he cites this
rabbinic view.

222) I.e., that the "days" do not denote temporal priority.

223) kokhavim. The term denotes all non-transparent bodies in
the supralunar world, including the sun, the moon, the planets and
the fixed stars.

224) nifradim. Clearly he does not mean "separate" in the
same sense as when he uses the term to refer to the incorporeal
nature of the separate intellects (e.g., 6:2:5, p. 423, ll. 15,
20; see below, 6:2:8, p. 432, ll. 15-18, for his explanation of
this other sense of "separate"). Here, he apparently means sepa-
rated, i.e., distinct from the rest of the heavens. Cf. 6:1:25,
p. 402, l. 1, where he uses the term to state that potentials cannot be distinguished from one another.

225) There are two interrelated points here. The first is that
the "days" do not denote temporal priority, so that the creation
of the stars is not temporally posterior to the creation of light
which is prior to them. The light of the first "day," as he will
explain below, p. 429, ll. 1ff., denotes the world of the separate
intellects and has nothing to do with the creation of visible
light, except insofar as the term "light" is used equivocally
(see above, 6:2:5).

His second point is that the rabbinic statement concerning the
suspension of the luminaries on the fourth day cannot be interpreted to imply that they meant to say that the stars were placed
in the spheres at a later time, after their initial creation. He
argues this point here by assuming that the Astronomy of the rabbis
was in agreement with his own. Given that assumption, he says here
that the stars are not "suspended" in the spheres. As he adds in
his commentary (discussed below, note #227), the motions of the
stars are related to the axes of their respective spheres. Assuming the rabbis' knowledge of this, he is saying that their use of
the term "suspension" must be figurative and cannot be taken to
imply that they believed either in temporal "days" of creation or
that the stars were hung in the sky.

226) God does not do anything in a physical or spatial sense.
Rather, He perpetually performs His single act of self-conception
from which the divine nomos overflows from Him, motivating the
separate intellects to move their spheres and giving the supralunar
bodies their perpetual natures. This overflow is what He refers
to as the divine will in his statement below: "As soon as He
willed this, it was. No action was required" (6:2:8, p. 429, l.
2f.; cf. p. 429, ll. 16-18; p. 430, l. 35f.; p. 433, l. 31; and
note #240 below).

227) The relation to which he is referring here is further
explained in the discussion of the term raqi^{c}a in his commentary
(CT 10d, ll. 27-32, quoted below, note #264). He speaks there of
the relation between the two axes upon which the celestial sphere
moves. The supralunar motion began immediately upon the creation
of the spheres on the second "day" (prior, but not temporally prior,
to the creation of the stars on the fourth "day"). As these
motions are perpetual and unchanging, so is this relation between
the axes.

Elsewhere, he describes the relations which exist among the positions and motions of the various stars which are fixed in the spheres. All of their activities are interrelated in such a way that what is needed for the existence of the sublunar world overflows from them (cf. 5:2:3, pp. 194-197; 6:1:7, p. 311f.). Thus, he understands this rabbinic statement to mean that God willed that the stars be interrelated on the fourth "day."

Note that once again he is assuming that the rabbis understand things as he does and are not capable of erring in matter of Astronomy or in anthropomorphic attributions to God (cf. above, notes #155, #178).

228) His use of the term, "nature" (teva^c) follows Aristotle's definition of it (Physica 2.1.193a30) as "the shape or form which is specified in the definition of the thing" (Oxford translation). It is through the divine nomos which overflows from the activities of the celestial world, or indirectly through God's will, that lower matter is endowed with the various natures or forms of lower existent things. Endowed with their nature, these things exist according to the definitions of what they are (cf. 5:3:6, p. 259). He is explaining here that the Genesis narrative only attributes to God the creation of those things which come to be according to the natures which overflow from the divine nomos. This is so because God created the world solely by willing that this nomos should overflow from Him in this way. He "works," in the sublunar world, through the principles of nature.

229) In the Historia Animalium (5.1.539a16-26), Aristotle writes (Oxford translation):

> Now there is one property that animals are found to have in common with plants. For some plants are generated from seed of plants, whilst other plants are self-generated through the formation of some elemental principle similar to a seed; and of these latter plants some derive their nutriment from the ground, whilst others grow inside other plants, as is mentioned, by the way, in my treatise on Botany. So with animals, some spring from parent animals according to their kind, whilst others grow spontaneously and not from kindred stock; and of these instances of spontaneous generation some come from putrefying earth or vegetable matter, as is the case with a number of insects, while others are spontaneously generated in the inside of animals out of the secretions of their several organs.

Throughout this work, Aristotle speaks of the spontaneous generation of a variety of creatures out of decaying mud, dung, excrements,

sand, soil or slime. (See, for example, 5.19.551al-10; 5.11.
543b18, 547b18, 548a15.) Gersonides seems to include all of these
environments within his term "mould" (ᶜipush), the root of which
means "to decay."

230) I.e., in accordance with the principles of nature which
overflow from the divine nomos and in which it is the nature of
members of most species to reproduce themselves. Cf. above, note
#228.

231) In the Metaphysica (7.9.1034a33-1034b7), Aristotle
describes things which are spontaneously generated as follows
(Oxford translation):

> Things which are formed by nature are in the same case
> as these products of art. For the seed produces them
> as the artist produces the works of art; for it has the
> form potentially, and that from which the seed comes has
> in a sense the same name as the offspring; only in a
> sense, for we must not expect all cases to have exactly
> the same name, as in the production of 'human being'
> from 'human being'...; we must expect this only if the
> offspring is not an imperfect form. The natural things
> which (like some artificial objects) can be produced
> spontaneously are those whose matter can be moved even
> by itself in the way in which the seed usually moves
> it; but those things which have not such matter cannot
> be produced except by parents.

Thus, those things which are spontaneously generated are imperfect
forms of life whose matter can move itself and need not be moved
by a form.

It is in this sense, I believe, that Gersonides uses the term
"marvelous" here. As he will explain below (6:2:9-12), marvels do
not depart from the nomos of existent things (as spontaneously
generated hermit crabs do not depart from it). They do not, however,
come to be from that which overflows from the heavenly bodies
(which he designates here as "natural custom"). As a result, they
can be distinguished from other customary things in that they do
not come to be from something defined. (For a discussion of these
aspects of marvels, see above, note #4.) Inasmuch as the definition of a thing is its nature and its form (see above, note #228),
a thing which is spontaneously generated comes to be "in a marvelous way," because, as Aristotle explains in the Metaphysica, its
formal causation is very weak.

232) The homogeneous parts of animals and plants are those
simple parts which divide into parts identical to themselves.
Examples which Aristotle gives of them include blood, flesh, bone,

skin, marrow and sperm (cf. Historia Animalium 1.1.486a5; De
Partibus Animalium 1.1.640b19ff.). All the works of nature are
composed of homogeneous bodies or parts as their matter (cf.
Meteorologica 4.12.389b27). These homogeneous parts themselves
are composed of varying degrees of water and earth (cf. Meteorologica 4.8.384b31). They have no life or soul, as heterogeneous
parts (organs) do, and are formed by heat and cold and not by
their own nature (cf. De Generatione Animalium 2.1.734b20ff.;
2.6.743a5). This is because matter is most predominant in them;
so predominant, in fact, that one cannot state their forms accurately (cf. Meteorologica 4.12.390a4ff.). Though they are geneti-
cally posterior to the elements, they are prior to the heterogeneous parts (organs) because (De Partibus Animalium 2.1.646b8-10,
Oxford translation):

> These heterogeneous parts have reached the end and
> goal, having the third degree of composition, in
> which degree generation or development often attains
> its final term.

(Cf. the note of William Ogle to his translation of this passage
[Oxford, 1911].) Homogeneous parts, by contrast, do not attain
this degree of development.

Because they do not come to be by their own nature and because
their nature is so imperfect that it cannot be conceived by us,
Gersonides is saying that the Bible does not attribute their
creation to those forms which overflow from the divine nomos.
Though both they and species which are spontaneously generated
do not depart from this nomos of existent things, the degree of
their formal causation is so weak that their creation is not
directly attributed to God.

Note that in the parallel passage of his commentary (CT 10d,
ll. 9-11) he also includes the elements in this category. He
states:

> Therefore, it does not attribute the coming to be of
> the elements of the Lord, may He be exalted, because
> their coming to be is adequately (accounted for) by
> means of the elemental forms, as is clear to anyone
> who speculates in Physics.

That is, the creation of the elements is mentioned by the creation
narrative of Genesis only in the indirect use of the term mavdil
(Gen 1:6), which refers to the distinction between supralunar
body and sublunar matter which is consequent upon the contrary
qualities of the elemental forms in the latter (6:2:8, p. 429, ll.
19ff.; see below, notes #256-#257), and in the parenthetical

description of Gen 1:2, which describes the state of the sublunar
world after the elements were formed in concentric layers but
before they began, through the influence of the actions of the
heavenly bodies, to interact to form composite material things
(6:2:8, p. 428, ll. 37ff.; see below, note #235). No direct
statement about the creation of the elements can be found in
Genesis.

This view—viz., that the elements are so lacking in existence
that they are not directly attributed in the Torah to the creation
which occurs through the overflow of the divine nomos—is relevant
to the discussion above, note #49, about Gersonides' description
of the first principles of coming to be. When he says elsewhere
in his commentary that the first principles of coming to be—prime
matter and last form—are so weak in existence that their natures
are close to the nature of privation (CT 9c, l. 35f.), we need
not infer that last form must therefore be something other than
the elemental forms. From the statement quoted above in this note,
it is clear that he would say that the natures of the elemental
forms are also close to the nature of privation. They cause the
elements on the second "day," prior to the formation of the overflow
of the nomos from the actions of the heavenly bodies on the fourth
"day." Thus, no existent thing comes to be from them—only the
four concentric elemental layers. Though they are the formal
causes of the elements, the degree of their formal causation is
so weak that the coming to be of their effects—the elements—is
not directly attributed to God. Thus the fifth, and our preferred,
view discussed in note #49 above, which identifies last form with
the elemental forms in their common characteristic of definite
dimensionality, is supported by the passage from the commentary
quoted in this note.

233) His explanation is what follows immediately. It is the
subject of the rest of chapter 8.

234) To summarize, Gersonides explains in this introductory
paragraph what the Torah means when it says that God creates or
that God says something should come to be. As explained above,
note #226, God creates in the sense that it is His will that things
in existence should come to be from the causal action of the
divine nomos which He wills to overflow from Him. He has no need
of them but rather wills out of the goodness and grace which He
wishes to bestow upon existent things (cf. 6:1:18, p. 377, ll. 3-7;

6:2:8, p. 435, ll. 1-7). He therefore wills the existence of the
separate intellects on the first "day," and from their conceptions
there follows the formation of the heavenly body on the second
"day," as well as the formation of the four elements which are
caused by the elemental forms which overflow from the heavenly
spheres. The elevation of the earth on the third "day" is not,
in some sense, caused by the heavenly overflow, but on the fourth
"day," the stars are created, and from the nomos formed from their
combined activities, the forms of all the other species of lower
existent things overflow (cf. Guide 2:4). Thus, God wills that
there should be the most perfect possible conditions for the perpetuation of the sublunar species. He does not "create" them
Himself. Rather, he bestows matter with the ability to benefit
from the forms in the nomos which overflows from the activities of
the heavenly bodies, which in turn are moved by the desire of the
separate intellects to approximate the divine nomos as far as that
is possible (6:2:8, p. 438, l. 34 - p. 439, l. 14). The initial
volition of God is an instance of volitional coming to be. All
subsequent instances of coming to be, however, whether volitional
or natural, proceed according to the natural custom which perpetually overflows from His will (6:2:8, p. 440, l.33 - p. 441, l. 7;
cf. 6:2:10, p. 452, ll. 5-19).

Those existent things which are not attributed directly to
God—i.e., species which are spontaneously generated and homogeneous parts—correspond to the nomos of existent things insofar
as they come to be as a result of the potentials with which sublunar matter is endowed and of the sublunar conditions created by
celestial activities. They do not possess, however, a sufficiently
perfected nature which would allow us to attribute a formal cause
to their coming to be. As a consequence, the Bible does not
include them in its list of those species of existent things which
come to be as a result of the natural laws which overflow from the
divine nomos.

235) Gen 1:1. Note that he states above (6:2:3, p. 420, l. 4)
that the term re^{c}shit in Gen 1:1 is used in the sense of priority
in cause and in nature. (For a discussion of the meaning of this
phrase, see above, note #27.) What is created on the first "day"
which is prior in cause and in nature is the intelligible world.
Thus, he will refer the creation of the intelligible world to the
word re^{c}shit (p. 429, l. 1).

What follows immediately, however, is not a description of
the separate intellects but is rather a description of the first
principles of sublunar matter. It can be assumed, therefore,
that he does not intend to say that God created the first principles of sublunar matter (which he here calls prime matter and the
elemental forms) on the first "day," because they are not prior in
cause and in nature to the rest of creation, and because the
elemental forms are created on the second "day" (p. 429, ll. 21-24).
What follows (p. 428, ll. 31-35) should be read as a parenthetical
aside. That is: "At the stage of creation which is most prior in
cause and in nature (be-re⁾shit ha-beri⁾ah), (The Lord was about
to create [on the second day] the heavens and what is below them.
The sublunar world [ha-⁾areṣ] consisted at that point of last
form [tohu] and prime matter [bohu]. The Lord would [on the
second day] create in sublunar matter its first principles, i.e.,
prime matter and the elemental forms, so that the element earth
[ḥoshekh] would be next to [ᶜal] the lowest part of the element
water [penei tehom] and the elements air and fire [ruaḥ ⁾elohim]
would rest [meraḥefet] next to the highest part of the element
water [ᶜal penei ha-mayim].), He willed the existence of the intelligible world of light." (For his discussion of each of these
translations of the terms of Gen 1:2, cf. above, 6:2:2-6.)

It is interesting to note that this reading is caused by the
difficult syntax of Gen 1:1-2 and that Gersonides' parenthetical
reading of verse 2 foreshadows the conclusions of may modern
scholars. (Cf. the new translation of the Jewish Publication
Society of America [Philadelphia, 1962] which reads:

> When God began to create the heaven and the earth - the
> earth being unformed and void with darkness over the
> surface of the deep and a wind from God sweeping over
> the water - God said, "Let there be light.")

Rashi had already interpreted these verses in this way and Gersonides follows him by referring the creation of light alone to the
first "day" and referring verse 2 to the second "day."

Our understanding of the meaning of the parenthetical statement depends in part upon the way in which we understand his use
of the terms "prime matter" and "the elemental forms" in this
passage (cf. above, notes #49 and #51). He states here (l. 32f.)
that the elemental forms are "primary in order" to prime matter
(ri⁾shonot lo be-seder) rather than prior in order to it (qodmot
lo be-seder). In the parallel passage in his commentary (CT 10a,

1. 18f.), he speaks instead of ha-ṣurah ha-hiyulaᵓnit ha-riᵓshonah
("the prime hylic form"). If, in spite of his avoidance of the
term "priority" both here and in the commentary, we assume that
he intends to denote the priority in order of elemental forms to
prime matter, then we are faced with a number of difficult problems
(see above, note #49). The reason for this is that A is prior in
order to B if A is a means to or a component of B, in which case B
can be said to be prior to A in venerability and/or cause and
nature (cf. above, notes #27 and #37). But the elemental forms
are not prior in order to any of the possible understandings of
"prime matter" discussed above (notes #49 and #51) - neither to
nondimensional absolute potentiality, nor to an actually existent
dimensional substratum of the elemental forms, nor to an absolute
dimensional substratum. They are prior in order only to composite
existent things, because they are the forms of the components of
those things. "Prime matter," however, cannot refer to composite
matter here, because he describes it as a "first principle" of
lower matter, and not as lower matter itself. Thus, it is more
likely that he intends to say that the elemental forms are first
in order in the hierarchy of forms, in which they are the lowest.
His parenthetical remark (between be-reᵓshit ha-beriᵓah on p. 428,
1. 31 and hineh be-reᵓshit zoᵓt ha-beriᵓah on p. 429, 1. 1) would
include therefore a description of all things created on the
second "day," i.e., the heavenly body and the elements.

236) Ha-ṣurot ha-riᵓshonot lo be-seder. See above, note #235,
for a discussion of the meaning of this phrase.

237) See above, note #49 and #51, for a discussion of the
process he is describing here.

238) See above, note #235, for a discussion of his understanding of the term be-reᵓshit as a designation here for priority in
cause and in nature. Also note his additional comment in the
parallel passage of his commentary (CT 10a, 11. 41-46):

> It says that the Lord, may He be exalted, called the
> light "day" and called the darkness "night" in order
> to comment upon the perfection which is possible for
> each of these separate intellects on the day on which
> it was created. He established them so that they can
> acquire no additional perfection, as is possible for
> us, because our perfection is first in us potentially
> and not actually. The state of affairs is not like
> this with regard to these intellects. Rather, they
> remain perpetually in their definition.

On the priority of the actual to the potential, cf. Metaphysica
9.8.1049b4-1050b39, where Aristotle speaks of priority in formula,
time and substantiality.

239) For his identification of light with the intelligible
world, see above, 6:2:5.

240) His emphasis on the instantaneous actualization of that
which God wills serves two purposes. First, it is a reminder that
God does not perform an overt physical act when He creates (cf.
above, note #234). The unity of God requires that He can have one
and only one act, and that act is His willing. Additionally, it
is a reference back to his argument in the first part of this
treatise that the coming to be of the world was willful and not
natural. On this basis, he refutes many of the arguments for the
eternity of the world which rely on an analogy between the characteristics of instances of coming to be in this world and the
coming to be of the world as a whole. Whereas the former are
natural, the latter are the effect of a volitional agent (cf.
6:1:18, p. 377, ll. 5-7, 6:1:24, p. 395, l. 1-p. 396, l. 29).

241) Ha-gerem ha-shemiymiy. For a discussion of his use of
this term, see above, notes #136 and #143. In the present case,
the term refers to the spheres, because the stars are not created
until the fourth "day."

242) On the hylic degree, see above, note #215. In 6:2:5,
he identifies the darkness of Gen 1:2 with the element earth
(p. 422, l. 10 - p. 423, l. 11). He is speaking here of Gen 1:4,
"God pronounced a distinction (va-yavdel) between the light and the
darkness." In chapter five (p. 423, ll. 11-35), he discusses this
verse and identifies "light" as the perfect conception of the
separate intellects. He states that darkness is said metaphorically
of imperfect conception but does not explicitly refer it to the
heavenly body. Rather, he cites a midrash which speaks of the
imperfections of the human intellect.

Nevertheless, his identification of the "darkness" of Gen 1:4
with the heavenly body is consistent with his discussion of 6:2:5.
The separate intellects conceive with a relatively perfect conception and are therefore "light." The spheres (which is what the
heavenly body designates here, since the stars are not created
until the fourth "day," as he discusses in 6:2:7 [see above, note
#143]), are bodies formed out of body which does not preserve its

shape. Though they remain perpetually in their definition and are
not subject to change (except for their accidental motion) or to
coming to be and passing away as is sublunar matter, and though
they move with a perfect circular motion, they do not conceive
perfectly. Indeed, in themselves they do not conceive at all
since it is the separate intellects which are their principles of
life and conception (cf. 5:3:6, where he explains that their souls
are separate, and not hylic). The heavenly body can be said to
proceed from the separate intellects in the hylic degree in that
it is the embodiment of those intellects and is therefore of a
lower degree of existence. (Cf. above, 5:3:8, p. 269, ll. 7-9,
where he writes: "The conception of the effect proceeds in the
hylic degree from the conception of its cause.")

    For a description of the nature of the celestial substance,
see Wolfson, Crescas' Critique of Aristotle, pp. 104, 594-598.
Averroes states that the celestial substance has no opposite and
no substratum and is not composed of matter and form. It resembles
both matter and form, though it has a greater resemblance to matter
in its relation to the separate forms and insofar as it is perceptible, is something definite, is a body and has potentiality with
reference to place. It resembles form insofar as it is actual.
Thus, the heavenly body is hylic in relation to the separate
intellects, though its corporeality is not that of sublunar
matter.

    It would seem that Gersonides' motivation for identifying
"darkness" here with the heavenly body rather than with the sublunar world is that he is going to say that the distinction between
the celestial and sublunar worlds was pronounced on the second
"day" with the creation of the raqi^{c}a and the elemental forms.
Note, however, that in his discussion of Gen 1:4 in his Commentary
on the Torah, he first interprets this darkness as the sublunar
world and then offers the alternate interpretation that it refers
to the hylic forms of the sublunar world (10a, ll. 23-33):

> The Lord may He be exalted, distinguished between
> this venerable world and between this lower (world)
> which is absolute darkness. The distinction consists
> in the fact that this light cleaves to venerable light
> perpetually and is absolutely happy in its venerable
> conception. Lower existence is the opposite of this.
> The Lord, may He be exalted, compared this light to
> day because of the high level of its transparency and
> clarity. (He compared) darkness to night because of
> the high level of its mixture and density and the evil

of its order. It is possible for us to say that
the Lord, may He be exalted, distinguished between
this venerable world, which is like the form of
the intermediate world (i.e., the heavenly body),
and between the hylic forms in this lower world,
which are darkness in relation to this venerable
light (i.e., the separate intellects). He compared this light to day because of the high level
of its transparency and clarity and (He compared)
these hylic forms to night because of the privation of this light in them.

He continues in his commentary by saying that the most accurate
interpretation of light and darkness here is the one which follows
below in our text. That is, there are a variety of degrees of
existence among the separate intellects which are "light" and
"dark" in relation to one another. Cf. below, note #251.

His difficulty stems from the following: a) he has identified the "darkness" of Gen 1:2 with the element earth; and b) he
has interpreted all of Gen 1:1-2 after the word be-re'shit as a
parenthetical reference to the creation of the second "day" (cf.
above, note #235). He thus maintains that the only thing created
on the first "day" is the world of the separate intellects, which
is prior in cause and in nature to everything else in the universe.
He is correct, therefore, when he states in his commentary that
the most accurate interpretation of "light" and "darkness" in
Gen 1:4,5 is that it refers to the different degrees of existence
among the separate intellects. The other interpretations, which
suggest a distinction between the intelligible world and either
the heavenly body, or the hylic forms, or the sublunar world, all
ignore the fact that none of these had yet been created on the
first "day" and are only mentioned parenthetically in Gen 1:1,2.

243) I.e., the venerable world of the separate intellects
and the heavenly body.

244) I.e., the separate intellects. See the passage from
his Commentary to the Torah, quoted above, note #242, where he
speaks of them as the form of the heavenly body. The forms of
the spheres are called separate because, in contrast to the hylic
forms of the sublunar world, they do not perform their function
(self-conception) by means of an instrument which is a material
body (6:2:8, p. 432, ll. 14-18; cf. 1:2, p. 15, l. 10f.; 1:3, p. 25,
ll. 4ff.; 1:4, p. 31). They nevertheless are connected to the
heavenly bodies as their forms.

245) Gen 1:5. In his discussion of each of the "days" of
creation, Gersonides understands the phrase va-yehiy ᶜerev va-yehiy
voqer to refer to the unity of each "day" of creation. On the
second "day," the spheres are described as the form and perfection
of the elements and they are thus united (p. 429, ll. 32-34). On
the third "day," he states that the unity derives from the fact
that the visible part of the earth exists for the sake of the
species which live on it and that the various degrees of plants
are form and perfection to one another (p. 431, ll. 22-27). On
the fourth "day," the unity is in the cooperation of the diverse
activities of the heavenly bodies which form a single nomos which
overflows to the sublunar world (p. 434, ll. 18-20). On the fifth
"day," there is a unity of fish and birds in the variation in their
degrees of perfection (p. 436, ll. 31-33). On the sixth "day,"
there is a unity of animals and humans, since the former exist for
the sake of the perfection of the latter (p. 438, ll. 10-12). His
intention is made explicit there, when he states that all parts
of the world are united such that the world is a macrocosm (p. 438,
ll. 12-14; cf. Guide 1:72).

In the present case, the separate intellects are united with
the heavenly bodies of which they are the form (cf. Metaphysica
5.6.1016a33ff.). Note, however, that the spheres are not created
until the second "day" and the stars are created on the fourth
"day." See above, note #242, for a discussion of this problem.
Since the movers of the heavenly bodies are separate (cf. above,
note #244), they do exist distinct from and prior to the creation
of that of which they are the forms. It is difficult to understand, however, how their unity with the heavenly body can be
described prior to the existence of the heavenly body. Thus, his
alternate explanation that "evening" and "morning" refer to the
different degrees of existence within the intelligible world is
more consistent.

246) Metaphysica 8.6.1045a6-1045b25. In the case of the
heavenly bodies which have no differentia—i.e., there is only one
body to a species—there is absolute unity with the form of the
species, i.e., the mover of each sphere. Cf. above, (5:3:7,
p. 268, l. 9f.) where he describes the connection between each
separate intellect and its sphere as follows: "The conception,
conceiver and object of conception are one in number in the intellect." Also cf. 6:1:19, p. 380, ll. 11-17.

247) Gen 1:5.

248) On his use of the term "hiddenness" (he^clem), see above, note #2.

249) I.e., the unity implied by "evening" and "morning."

250) I.e., the intelligible world of the separate intellects, as he explains above, p. 429, l. 1f.

251) His discussion of the heavenly movers and their inter-relationships is the subject of the third part of Treatise Five. There is one separate intellect for each of the spheres, which number forty-eight or fifty-eight or sixty-four (5:3:6, p. 263, ll. 17-24). Each intellect is thus connected to a single simple motion (see above, note #246). All of these simple motions combine to form the unified nomos which overflows to lower existent things. None of the separate intellects, however, conceives of this composite nomos. Each conceives only of its single simple motion (5:3:9, p. 274f.). The entire nomos is conceived rather by a more elevated cause which oversees them and the nomos which is perfected from them (5:3:8, p. 273, l. 4f.), i.e., the Lord (5:3:11, pp. 276ff.), who is not Himself a mover of any of the spheres. The relative degree of venerability of each intellect is determined by the relative speed of its sphere's motion (slower is more venerable), by the number of the stars in its sphere (the sphere of the fixed stars is most venerable in this respect), and by the size of the star in its sphere (the sun and the moon are most venerable in this respect) (5:3:8, p. 273, l. 22f.). Thus, though the intellects vary in their degrees of venerability, so that some may be said to be "darker" than others (see 1:5, p. 36, l. 4f., where he speaks of the hylic priority of some to others), the combination of their respective particular conceptions is overseen by the Lord, who is the first cause, and results in the nomos which overflows from all of them (1:6, p. 37, ll. 28ff.).

Though it is the separate intellects which are properly the subject of his discussion here, since it is they of whom "light" is said, note that Gersonides also speaks of variation of perfection among the parts of the heavenly body (5:2:2, p. 193, l. 29— p. 194, l. 6):

> It is possible that there be different degrees in the
> heavenly bodies in this way, so that they have parts to
> which the most perfect possible life that exists in
> them cleaves, i.e., the stars. (It is the stars which

> are most perfect) because of the actions which over-
> flow from them—the heavenly bodies—are ordered from
> (the stars) and the motions of the spheres are for
> the sake (of the stars), as will be explained below.
> And there are (also) parts in them which are abso-
> lutely without life, i.e., these bodies between the
> spheres of one star and the spheres of the next star.
> The intermediate things between these two existences
> are the spheres, according to their degrees. That is,
> the spheres in which the stars are fixed are second
> in the degree of life. After them are the spheres
> which serve them in realizing the motion of the sphere
> in which the star is (fixed).

We may infer from this that there is an additional distinction
among the separate intellects. That is, the intellect of a sphere
which does not contain a star but which contributes to the motion
of a sphere which contains a star is less venerable than the intellect of a sphere which contains a star.

Wolfson mentions (Crescas' Critique of Aristotle, p. 108f.) a
disagreement between Avicenna and Averroes on the question of the
way in which the separate intellects are differentiated. Avicenna
believes that they evolve from one another by a process of emanation and are thus mutually interrelated as causes and effects.
Maimonides follows Avicenna on this issue. Averroes believes that
there is no such causal interrelation. Rather, they all proceed
directly and simultaneously from God and yet are distinguished from
one another in the different degrees of perfection of their
respective conceptions of the divine essence. On the basis of his
discussions above, 5:3:9 & 11, where he criticizes Averroes'
views on the first mover of the spheres, and on the basis of his
statement here that "the degree of the form of some goes to others
of them" (or: that "some of them proceed to others in a formal
degree"), we may infer that Gersonides would agree with Avicenna's
(and Maimonides') position (see below, note #515).

252) 5:3:5, p. 257f.; cf. 6:1:7, p. 311f.

253) Guide 1:67.

254) He reads all occurrences of the term "water" (mayim) in
Gen 1:6-8 as referring to body which does not preserve its shape
(cf. above, 6:2:7). This is because water is the sublunar substance which is most analogous to absolute dimensional body, which
has no actual definite dimensions (cf. above, note #49). The
"upper waters" (ha-mayim ᵓasher me-ᶜal la-raqiᶜa) are the part of
this body from which the heavenly body comes to be.

He is describing the formation of the supralunar world, which
in this context denotes the spheres, since the stars are not
created until the fourth "day." See above, note #136, for a discussion of his use of the term, ha-gerem ha-shemiymiy. For a
discussion of the body which does not preserve its shape, see
above, notes #49, #51, and #152.

The celestial spheres can be said to be "material" insofar as
they are formed from body which does not preserve its shape. Their
"matter," however, is not identical to the matter of the sublunar
world because sublunar matter does not exist without hylic form
while the forms of the "matter" of the celestial spheres are
separate (cf. above, note #242). They are not subject to the
process of coming to be and passing away, as he will indicate
below in his discussion of the raqiᶜa. He indicates this distinction between sublunar and supralunar matter by using the term
gerem to refer to the heavenly body rather than geshem (cf. Israel
Efros, The Problem of Space in Jewish Mediaeval Philosophy [New
York, 1917], p. 117; also see Guide 2:19.). "Body," he believes,
is said equivocally of the two (cf. above, 5:2:3, p. 193, l. 19f.).
As discussed above in notes #49 and #51, "body" refers both to
absolute dimensionality (when it lacks preservation of shape) and
to definite dimensionality (when it has preservation of shape).
The heavenly bodies, however, are the paradigmatic example of
definite dimensionality. Whereas the definite dimensions of sublunar bodies are subject to change because of the actions of the
contrary qualities, the definite dimensions of the heavenly bodies
remain perpetually unchanged because there are no contraries in
the supralunar world. It is in this sense that the term "body" is
said equivocally of sublunar and supralunar bodies.

255) I.e., the part of the body which does not preserve its
shape from which the sublunar world comes to be. This is a reference to Gen 1:7: "the water which is below the raqiᶜa (ha-mayim
ᵓasher mi-taḥat la-raqiᶜa)."

For his complete discussion of the meaning of raqiᶜa, see
above, 6:2:7.

The manuscripts consulted add the following at p. 429, l. 22,
after the words le-maṭah me-ha-raqiᶜa: ve-ha-ḥeleq ᵓasher (mi-
mav) le-maᶜlah me-ha-raqiᶜa (from the part of it which is above
the raqiᶜa). The additional phrase of the manuscripts can be
posited either to have been added for clarification of the meaning

of the original text or to have been omitted from the text
underlying the printed editions by scribal error.

256) Cf. Guide 2:39 (p. 352 of Pines translation) where
Maimonides writes:

> Among the things you ought to know is that the words,
> And He divided between the waters, and so on, do not
> refer merely to a division in place in which one part
> is located above and one below, while both have the
> same nature. The correct interpretation of these
> words is that He made a natural division between both
> of them—I mean with regard to their form—by means
> of the natural form with which he invested it, and
> bestowing upon the other part a different form, that
> latter part being water proper.

Gersonides agrees that the distinction described on the second
"day" is a formal one. He disagrees, however, with Maimonides'
assertion that it is also a spatial one (see below, in this chapter, p. 430, ll. 13ff.), and he does not think that the term
"water" on the second "day" has any relation to the element water,
except as the term is said analogously in both contexts with reference to the shared characteristic of indefinite dimensionality.
See 6:2:7 for his refutation of Maimonides' description of the
raqi^ca.

The distinguishing "nature" here is the nature of the elemental
forms which lower matter receives. The contrary qualities which
the elements possess lead to the process of coming to be and passing away to which all of the sublunar world is subject but to
which the heavenly body is not subject. (See above, note #49,
for a description of the way in which the composite existent
things come to be from the action of the contrary qualities of the
elemental forms.) The heavenly body has no potential to change or
to pass away because it has no contrary. (Cf. 6:1:16, where he
argues that the world as a whole cannot pass away because the
heavenly body, from which the sublunar world overflows, cannot pass
away.)

The process which he is describing here in which some of the
body which does not preserve its shape becomes the four elements
is discussed above, notes #49 and #51. As is argued there, the
most plausible reading of his intentions here is that body which
does not preserve its shape is absolute dimensional body, i.e.,
body which has tridimensionality but which has no actual definite
dimensions. He does not consider its indefinite dimensionality to
be a form. It is a disposition which persists prior to creation

and apart from the formal causation of the divine nomos. Though
the disposition of a thing is usually associated with its nature
and consequently with its form, Gersonides maintains in his argument in the first part of this treatise (6:1:17-18) that the disposition to dimensionality of this body is inherent in the material
receptacle on which the divine will works and is not to be associated with a specific form or nature. The body is therefore
properly described as "nothing," because it is formless and has no
actual existence of any kind. It is possible to understand the
"nature" which he says here is created to refer to a prior preparation of body which does not preserve its shape which gives it the
dimensionality it requires to serve as the substratum of the elemental forms (since definite dimensionality is the common characteristic of all of the elements). This interpretation is necessary,
however, only if body which does not preserve its shape is understood as nondimensional, and such an understanding leads to a number of problems. If, however, it is absolute dimensional body,
then it can properly be considered to be the substratum of the
elemental forms without further preparation. It is possible that
he intends this "nature," which he here says is the creation of
the elemental forms, to be the common characteristic of definite
dimensionality which all of the elements share so that absolute
dimensional body which does not preserve its shape acquires definite dimensions when it is informed by the elemental forms. This
is probably what he means to describe above, in chapter 2, in
his discussion of last form.

    257) Note that he is reading Gen 1:6 as follows: "God said:
Let there be the raqiᶜa (i.e., the heavenly body) in the midst of
water (i.e., body which does not preserve its shape) and let there
be a distinction (mavdil, i.e., the nature of the sublunar matter
to come to be and pass away because of the contrary qualities of
the elemental forms, which the heavenly body does not have) between
water (i.e., the part of body which does not preserve its shape
from which the heavenly body comes to be) and water (i.e., the part
of body which does not preserve its shape from which the sublunar
world comes to be)." According to his reading, the word mavdil
does not refer to the raqiᶜa. It is not the raqiᶜa (i.e., the
celestial sphere or spheres) which does the distinguishing. First
there is absolute dimensional body which does not preserve its
shape. From it, the heavenly body (raqiᶜa) is formed as a body

with perpetually unchanging definite dimensions. A separate part
of the process is the formation of the sublunar elements with the
definite dimensions of four concentric layers, but these definite
dimensions are subject to constant change. It is this potential
for change which distinguishes sublunar body from celestial body.
Similarly, he reads Gen 1:7 as referring to two distinct creative
processes: "God made the raqiᶜa, and He distinguished between the
supralunar and sublunar parts of body which does not preserve its
shape."

Though this seems to be the most likely understanding of his
reading of the second day based upon the present text, see below,
note #279, for another way to understand his reading.

258) Va-yehiy khen. Gen 1:7.

259) Gen 1:7.

260) Gen 1:7.

261) Gen 1:2. For a discussion of his understanding of tohu
and bohu, cf. above 6:2:2, and notes #49 and #51.

262) See above, note #235, for his reading of Gen 1:1, 2 after
the word be-reᵓshit. He reads the mention there of the heavenly
body and the sublunar elements as a parenthetical description of
what is created on the second "day." Because the positions of the
four concentric layers of the elements have already been described
(see his description of them above, 6:2:8, p. 428, ll. 32-35, and
his justification of his interpretation, 6:2:5-6), he is saying
here that there was no need to repeat it in the passage which
describes the second "day."

263) He makes this argument above, 6:2:7, p. 424, ll. 19-24.
As argued above, notes #49 and #51, it is most likely that his
term "preservation of shape" denotes the characteristic of definite
dimensionality. His examples, in 6:2:7, of things which are
"stretched out" (nirqaᶜ) are things whose definite dimensions are
not easily changed (beaten plates of gold and the visible part
of the earth which is higher than the water) or not changed at
all (the sky, i.e., the lowest celestial sphere).

By "an equivocal term" (shem meshutaf), he means, in this
context, a term which is said analogously (dimyon). Sublunar
things with fairly stable definite dimensions are analogous to the
raqiᶜa (the spheres) which has perpetual and unchanging dimensions.
On his use of analogy, cf. above, note #64.

264) He is referring to Gen 1:8, which he reads: "God called
the raqi^{c}a the heavens."   In his commentary, he writes (CT 10d,
ll. 27-32):

> The intention of (the term raqi^{c}a) is that it is a term
> of analogy between two places which do not move. They
> are the axes of the sphere, for the term is said with
> reference to a place. It is thus explained that the
> Lord, may He be exalted, set them in motion as soon as
> they were created, for it is with respect to motion
> that these two places are connected. An because they
> were given the nature to move perpetually without rest,
> it says that the Lord, may He be exalted, called the
> raqi^{c}a the heavens, because they have no potential at
> all for rest.

This passage reflects his view that all references in the text to
the calling of names refers to the creation of the unchanging
essence or definition of the thing named (cf. below, 6:2:8, p.
439, ll. 8-29). In his discussion, in the first treatise, of the
nature of human knowledge and the immortality of the acquired
intellect, he explains that the specific function of the hylic
intellect is to conceive the definitions of things, i.e., the
concept which exists in each thing which is its nature and which
it shares with all other members of its species (1:2, p. 16; 1:4,
p. 29; 1:10, pp. 63, 68; see below, notes #492, #495, #501, #502,
#504, #507, #508).

In the present case, the heavenly body is called by name
because its nature is to remain perpetually in the motions of its
definition.

265) Gen 1:8. On his understanding of the recurring phrase
va-yehiy ^{c}erev va-yehiy voqer, cf. above, note #245.

266) That is, the motions of the spheres in themselves combine
to cause the overflow to the sublunar world of a nomos which causes
the formation of the four concentric layers of the elements. The
activities of the stars, described on the fourth "day," which are
moved by the spheres, combine to cause the overflow to the sublunar world of a nomos which causes the interaction of the contrary
qualities of the elements and thereby the formation of composite
sublunar entities.

267) As is the case with the other six days of creation.

268) Gen 1:18.

269) That is, the four concentric layers of the elements which
are created on the second "day" are also not complete. The

elements do not exist simply and separately in this world but
rather exist in various stages of composition which are caused by
the nomos overflowing from the activities of the spheres and stars.
Since the stars have not yet been mentioned, this process of composition has not yet begun.

There is a possibility that, in addition to the fact that the
elemental forms represent a preliminary stage in the process of
the coming to be of sublunar existent things, they are incomplete
because they exist for the sake (ba'avur) of the other forms of
composite things. That is, they have no existence of their own in
the sublunar world after the process has been set in motion. (Cf.
above, notes #49 and #232 for a discussion of his references to
the elemental forms as extremely weak in existence and the closeness of their natures to the nature of privation.) In the first
part of this treatise, he uses ba'avur as a technical term denoting
one of the three characteristics of things which come to be, i.e.,
that there is something in its essence which exists for the sake
of something else (6:1:6, p. 310, 1. 4f.; cf. 6:1:9, where he shows
that the heavens have this characteristic).

He does not seem, however, to intend to identify here the
incompleteness of the elemental forms and the fact that they exist
for the sake of the other forms. Not all things which exist for
the sake of other things can be said to be incomplete without
these other things. Both the heavens and the visible part of the
earth, for example, exist for the sake of other things and yet
both are complete without them (cf. below, note #297). Though the
characteristic of being for the sake of something else reflects
that a thing has come to be, this characteristic does not entail
that that thing is imperfect (6:2:8, p. 434, 11. 30-32; 1. 35—
p. 435, 1. 18). Rather, it is the combination of the fact that
the elemental forms exist for the sake of the forms of composite
things and the fact that they do not have an existence of their
own apart from their existence in composite things that renders
them incomplete.

270) 4:6. The complete passage reads as follows (Soncino
translation):

> Why is 'that it was good' not written in connection with
> the second day? R. Johanan explained, and it was also
> thus taught in the name of R. Jose b. R. Ḥalafta:
> Because on it the Gehenna was created, (as it is writ-
> ten,) "For Tofteh is ordered from yesterday" (Isa. XXX,
> 33), which signifies a day to which there was a yester-
> day but not a day before yesterday. R. Ḥanina said:

Because in it a schism was created, (as it is written,)
"And let it divide the waters." R. Ṭabyomi said: If
because of a division made for the greater stability
and orderliness of the world, 'for it was good' is not
written in connection with that day, then how much the
more should this apply to a division which leads to
its confusion! R. Samuel b. Naḥman said: Because the
making of the waters was not finished: consequently 'for
it was good' is written twice in connection with the
third day, once in respect of the making of the waters
and a second time on account of the work done on that day.

271) That is, passing away and privation are characteristics
of the lower existent things because of the contrary primary
qualities of the elements which interact. These contraries are
created on the second "day." They are the distinction which is
created between the sublunar world and the supralunar world which
does not have them and thus is not subject to passing away and
privation (cf. above, note #257). In Gersonides' scheme, therefore, "heaven" is perpetual and unchanging existence (or rather
the perpetual existence which is a consequence of the perfect
conception of the separate intellects) and "hell" is subjection
to the process of coming to be and passing away to which all
material things are subject. As is clear from the rabbinic
passage, quoted above in note #270, the reference to Geihinnom
does not involve Gersonides' interpretation of it. Again, he
assumes that the rabbis read the Torah from the perspective of
Aristotelian physicists (see above, note #155).

272) The rabbinic statement, quoted above, note #270, refers
to the division of the waters on the second "day," with no mention
of contraries.

273) R. Samuel b. Naḥman's statement, quoted above, note #270,
speaks only of the "waters" and not of the "upper waters."
Indeed, it cannot refer to the "upper waters" because the "work"
to which he is referring is completed on the third day.

For Gersonides' identification of the "upper waters" as the
part of body which does not preserve its shape from which the
heavenly body is formed, and of the "lower waters" as the part
of that body from which the sublunar world is formed, see above
6:2:7, and 6:2:8, p. 429, ll. 19-22 (cf. above, note #254).

274) I.e., the word mavdil in Gen 1:6.

275) Gen 1:6.

276) Gen 1:7.

277) As explained above, note #257, he reads Gen 1:6 as a
description of two different creative processes on the second
"day." The first is the creation of the heavenly body described
as "Let there be a raqi^ca in the midst of the waters." The
second is the creation of the elemental forms which distinguish
the sublunar world from the supralunar world, which is described
as "Let there be a distinction between waters and waters." This
reading of verse 6 assumes that the word mavdil is the noun
"distinction" rather than the verb "distinguish" or "divide"
which has raqi^ca as its subject. This is a departure from the
more common assumption that both parts of the verse refer to the
raqi^ca which divides the upper world from the lower world. He
is defending his interpretation here with the assertion that the
second half of the verse (and the division described in verse 7)
would be superfluous if it referred to a division in place.
Rather, the raqi^ca does not divide. It is the heavenly body which
is distinguished from the sublunar world by the nature of the
latter which includes the existence of contraries.

Note that he is not denying that there is a division in
place between the heavenly body (raqi^ca) and the sublunar world
(lower waters). He is rather asserting that the creation of the
two makes that division in place clear and does not require further
elaboration. Thus, the distinction to which the text refers must
be another distinction, i.e., a distinction between the natures
of the sublunar and supralunar worlds.

278) Gen 1:7. For his own understanding of the meaning of
this phrase, see above, 6:2:8, p. 429, ll. 26-31.

279) That is, if all of verse 7 had been omitted except for
va-yehiy khen. In that case, it would be plausible to read the
text as referring to a division caused by the raqi^ca. As the text
actually reads, however, the distinction cannot refer to a division
in place.

Note that it is possible that he reads all of verse 6 as
referring to the raqi^ca and that he understands the word mavdil
as a verb denoting the division in place caused by the creation
of the heavenly spheres. He would then be saying that the distinction between the upper waters and the lower waters in verse 7 cannot be a superfluous repetition of that division in place but must
rather refer to a distinction between natures. This alternate
understanding is suggested by his statement here that the text's

meaning would be altered with the omission of verse 7. In either
case, his reading of the second "day" is that two distinct things
were created: the heavenly body and the elements of the sublunar
world.

280) Gen 1:7.

281) Gen 1:2. For an explanation of his understanding of
va-yehiy khen ("and it was so") in Gen 1:7 and of his reading of
Gen 1:2, see above, notes #235 and #262.

282) This unity is indicated by his reading of the second
"day" in two ways: a) both the heavenly body and the sublunar
matter come to be from the "waters", i.e., from the body which
does not preserve its shape; and b) the heavenly body and the sublunar world are referred to as "evening" and "morning" (Gen 1:8),
indicating that the heavens serve as the form and perfection of
the sublunar world (cf. above, 6:2:8, p. 429, ll. 32-34; note
#266).

283) Note his discussion of this issue in the first part of
this treatise (6:1:17, p. 368, ll. 7-16):

> It was possible for the Lord, may He be blessed, to give
> diverse forms or diverse dispositions to a matter which
> is one in itself. This is because this coming to be was
> willful. In this manner, it was possible for the stars to
> have diverse natures in what overflows from them by means
> of their illuminations, while their matter is one in
> itself, as explained above. It has thus been explained
> that the principle of all matters is one in number, for
> the body which is deprived of all nature cannot have
> parts which are diverse from one another. It is proper
> that this should be the case, for just as the principle
> of all the forms is a form which is one in number, simi-
> larly it is proper that the principle of all matters is
> one matter. For this reason, some of our predecessors
> considered that it was necessary that there be two
> divinities because they thought that there were two
> material principles—for lower matter and for the heaven-
> ly body.

Though he believes that both the sublunar and the supralunar
worlds come to be from body which does not preserve its shape
and that they are both material in some sense, he does not believe
that the matter of the heavenly body is identical with sublunar
matter, because sublunar matter is informed by hylic forms while
the matter of heavenly bodies is informed by separate forms which
do not use their matter as an instrument by means of which they
perform their functions. Thus the heavenly bodies are simple

matter, not the combination of substratum and form. For a discussion of celestial substance, see above, note #242.

Note that Maimonides (Guide 2:26) chooses to give an entirely
different emphasis to the same data. That is, though he and
Gersonides both hold similar views with regard to the differences
between sublunar and supralunar matter, Gersonides chooses to
emphasize the common origins of the two while Maimonides stresses
that the matter of the universe is not one. This difference is
a function of the fact that Maimonides believes in creation out
of nothing so that, in his view, sublunar and supralunar matter
do not have a common origin as they do according to Gersonides'
view. The difference between them is also reflected in their
respective views of the supralunar world. That is, Maimonides
concludes his examination of the diversity in the states of
affairs of the heavens by asserting that the supralunar world is
an effect of divine, purposeful causation and is thus not knowable (Guide 2:19). He therefore tends to stress the distinction
between supralunar body and the matter of the sublunar world.
Gersonides, on the other hand, although he also concludes that
the diversity in the heavens is an effect of divine, willful
causation, believes that the supralunar world is, to some extent,
knowable and that our observations of astronomical phenomena can
serve as evidence in support of a demonstration of creation
(6:1:6-9). He therefore tends to stress the similarities between
the fifth body of the heavens and the matter of the sublunar
world. Unlike Maimonides, his view of the universe does not allow
for acts of divine will—whether in the supralunar world or in
the marvels of the sublunar world—which are not a part of the
single and unchanging divine nomos which governs the entire world.

284) I.e., the third degree or "day."

285) Gen 1:9. Cf. above, note #134, for a discussion of his
view concerning the visible part of the earth. Given the natures
of the elements earth and water, the water should encompass the
earth as it did when the elemental forms first informed prime
matter. That part of the element earth which is elevated above
the water deviates from its nature.

286) 6:1:13; cf. 6:2:7, p. 424, ll. 20-22.

287) Ps 136:6. For his discussion of the meaning of the term
le-roqaᶜ see above, 6:2:7, p. 424, l. 20.

288) Gen 1:9. That is, va-yehiy khen ("and it was so") is
written to indicate the instantaneous actualization of the elevation of the earth.

289) Gen 1:10. In his commentary, he adds the following
comment to explain why the visible part of the earth is called by
name (CT 11a, 1. 29f.): "To comment that this part of the earth
is perpetually visible." This comment is based on his view that
when the Torah says God calls a thing by name, it is indicating
the unchanging nature of that thing. He is apparently saying,
therefore, that although the nature of the element earth is to move
downward through the element water, this visible part of the earth
was endowed with a different nature. As he will explain below,
this is one of the reasons why the elevation of the earth is
described prior to the description of the stars which are prior to
it in cause and in nature (6:2:8, p. 435, 1. 32 - p. 436, 1. 2).
That is, the nature of the visible part of the earth is not caused
by the nomos which overflows from the activities of the heavenly
bodies. That nomos, which includes the elemental forms, gives the
element earth the nature to move below the element water. The
visible part of the earth is rather related, in some sense, to the
divine will.

290) 6:2:3.

291) Gen 1:10. In his commentary, he adds the following
comment to explain why they are called by name (CT 11a, 1. 30f.):
"To comment that the element water would be in that place perpetually." This is again related to his understanding of what it
means to call something by name (cf. above, notes #264 and #289).

292) Meteorologica 2.3, especially 357b27-358a3.

293) 5:8. In his note to his translation of this text
(Soncino edition, p. 39), H. Freedman mentions Theodor's conjecture
that Aspamia refers to Apamea in the north of Palestine. M. A.
Mirkin, however, comments that the reference is to Spain (Midrash
Rabbah, with a commentary by M. A. Mirkin, 1:36 [Tel Aviv, 1968]).

294) Viz., "the gathering of waters He called Seas" (Gen 1:10).

295) In the Meteorologica 2.2.354b1-356b2, Aristotle argues
that, despite its saltiness, the sea is the natural place of the
element water. As Gersonides has already mentioned, (1. 5 above)
this argument is related to Aristotle's assertion that the sea

water is not salty by nature but rather acquires its taste from
the earth through which it passes. Gersonides is asserting that
the Torah is making a statement about the identity of the salt
water of the seas and the element water in order to answer questions such as the one Aristotle addresses. This is a clear example
of his conviction that the Torah contains the truth about the
nature of existent things which is accessible to those who are
sufficiently trained to understand its meaning, and that the truth
of the Torah is identical to the truth of speculation (see above,
note #1).

296) Gen 1:10.

297) He seems to be saying that the phrase, "And God saw that
it was good" (Gen 1:10) is said because the dry land is created
for the sake of the existence of the species of plant and animal
life that live on it. This would be inconsistent with his explanation above (6:2:8, p. 429, l. 35 - p. 430, l. 4) of why this phrase
is omitted in the description of the second "day." His explanation
there is twofold: that the description of the heavenly body is not
complete until the creation of the stars is mentioned on the fourth
"day;" and that the elemental forms, in themselves, are not in a
complete state because they are created for the sake of the rest of
the forms of composite existent things which are not described
until subsequent "days." Thus, he cannot mean here that "it was
good" refers to the fact that the dry land is for the sake of the
species that are on it, for though the creation of plants are mentioned on this "day," the animal species are not mentioned until
the sixth "day."

There are several ways to explain this apparent inconsistency.
One is to assume that it is an inconsistency. This is unlikely,
however, because there were other ways he could have explained the
omission of the phrase on the second "day." Note, for example,
his citation and interpretation above of the rabbinic explanations
of this omission which conclude the phrase is not said with reference to the second "day" because of the process of passing away
and privation which is initiated by the contrary qualities of the
elemental forms (p. 430, ll. 4-9). A second possibility is thus
that he prefers this latter explanation of the omission of this
phrase on the second "day," but neglects to mention that preference. (For another instance where he lists several alternative
explanations but neglects to explicitly state his preference, see

above, p. 429, ll. 6-15, where he discusses the meaning of "light"
and "darkness" on the first day. Though the more consistent
explanation and the one which he explicitly prefers in his commentary is the last one, he does not state that preference in our
text. See above note #242.) Thus, although the elemental forms
are for the sake of the other forms, they cannot be said to be for
their benefit as the dry land benefits the species which live on
it.

The ambiguity may derive, however, from the unique status
among sublunar things which he attributes to the elevated part of
the earth. As he mentions below, its existence cannot be attributed to the nomos which overflows from the heavenly bodies (6:2:8,
p. 435, l. 32 - p. 436, l. 2; cf. above, note #289). Inasmuch as
its nature—to remain above the water—is not the nature of the
element earth, he attributes it directly to God's will and desire
to allow lower existent species to survive. What such an attribution means is unclear, however. All creation can be attributed to
God's will and none of it departs from the nomos which is consequent upon that will (cf. above, note #234). In any case, his
inclusion of the elevated part of the earth in his list of things
with continuous existence in the first part of this treatise (cf.
above, note #134) is another indication of the special status he
gives it. (Cf. Meteorologica 2.3.356b3ff., where Aristotle discusses the perpetual existence of the sea, which is the other side
of this question.) We can thus conclude that the way in which the
elevated part of the earth is for the sake of species is different
than the way in which the elemental forms are for the sake of the
forms of composite existent things. Just as the heavenly bodies
exist for the sake of the sublunar world and yet derive no additional perfection from that which overflows from them to lower
existent things (6:2:8, p. 434, l. 35-p. 435, l. 18), it may be
inferred that the elevated part of the earth derives no additional
perfection from the benefits it confers upon the species which live
on it. Both the heavens and the elevated part of the earth have
continuous and perpetual existence and thus both are in a complete
state prior to the benefits which they cause. (Cf. below, 6:2:8,
p. 434, ll. 30-32; l. 35 - p. 435, l. 18, where he argues that the
more venerable thing exists for the sake of the less venerable
thing but does not acquire its perfection from the less venerable
thing.) The elemental forms, on the other hand, which cause the
formation of the elements, have no actual independent existence of

their own, but rather exist after the moment of creation only as
components of the forms of composite things. (On the weakness of
the existence of the elemental forms, see above, notes #49 and
#269.) Thus, the elements of which they are the forms have no
actual existence apart from the composite things for the sake of
which they exist, and their existence is properly said to be incomplete until those composite things come to be.

298) He is alluding to the words le-miyno and le-miynehu‎ᵓ in
Gen 1:11, 12, which he is reading as "according to its species."
The implicit contrast is to those plants which do not come to be
from their species but are rather spontaneously generated. The
creation of the latter, he has explained, is not directly attributed to God (cf. above, 6:2:8, p. 428, ll. 19-28; notes #229,
#231, and #234).

299) Gen 1:11.

300) I.e., the proper order with reference to hylic priority
or priority in order, in which the less perfect thing is prior to
the more perfect thing and should thus be mentioned first (cf.
above, note #215). The order in which things are described in the
Torah is important because it is the way in which the nature of
existent things is revealed to us, as he explains above, 6:2:8,
p. 427, l. 25-p. 428, l. 6 (see above, note #1).

301) He does not clearly state what it is about trees which
make them more perfect than other plants. He mentions that herbs
bear seed and that the tree produces fruit in which the seed comes
to be, but this is a paraphrase of Gen 1:11. His point, therefore,
seems to be that the order of the Torah's description is not random
but rather serves to indicate the priority in order of the less
perfect species to the more perfect species, and that the Torah's
mention of the manner in which these species produce seeds is a
reflection of its agreement with Aristotle that the true function
of a thing (which for plants is reproduction; cf. Historia
Animalium 8.1.588b24) corresponds to its form or soul (cf. below,
note #302). It thus mentions the true functions of plant species,
i.e., their manner of reproduction, to indicate the reasons for
their priority.

    For a further justification of his characterization of
seed-bearing herbs as less perfect than trees, note the additional
comment in the parallel passage of his commentary (CT 11a, ll.
47ff.):

It should be clear to you that the herb is deficient
when compared to the tree. This is because there are
many things in the (class of) herb(s) which come to
be from the mould. This is not the case with regard
to the (class of) tree(s).

302) Cf. De Anima 2.1.412a-413a10, where Aristotle states that
the form or the soul of a thing is "the first grade of actuality of
a natural body having life potentially in it" (412a27f., Oxford
translation). That is, the true function of a thing is the actualization of the soul of that thing, which is its actuality (412b9).
For example, if the eye had a soul, sight would have been its
soul (412b18). Thus, one can identify the form or soul or essence
of a thing by identifying its true function. Gersonides is saying
that the Torah's mention of the manner of reproduction of plant
species is its way of indicating their form or soul (cf. above,
note #301).

303) See his further discussion below (p. 431, l. 27-p. 432,
l. 4) for an investigation of what this sentence means.

304) Gen 1:12.

305) Gen 1:12.

306) Gen 1:12.

307) Gen 1:13.

308) Gen 1:13. For a discussion of his understanding of the
recurring phrase, va-yehiy ᶜerev va-yehiy voqer, see above, note
#245.

309) See above, note #297, for a discussion of the way in
which the elevated part of the earth is related to the species
which live upon it. If he is reading "evening" and "morning" here
as he reads it on the second "day" (6:2:8, p. 429, ll. 33-35),
then we can infer that, in some sense, the elevated part of the
earth is the form and perfection of the species which live upon it.
As discussed in note #297, the problem is that the elevated part
of the earth is not for the sake of these species in the same way
as the elemental forms are for the sake of the forms of composite
things (p. 430, l. 3f.) or the animals are for the sake of the
human species (p. 438, ll. 10-12). These latter examples of his
use of the term "baᶜavur" indicate the priority in order which the
less perfect thing has to the more perfect thing. It is conceivable that he thinks of the elevated part of the earth as prior in

order to the species which live upon it (including the human
species). Priority in order, however, entails posteriority in
nature (cf. above, note #27), and his characterization of the
elevated part of the earth seems to indicate that he thinks of its
nature as more venerable than deficient (cf. above, note #297).
Its unity with the species which live upon it, therefore, may
resemble the unity of the spheres with the sublunar world of which
they are the form and perfection.

310) In the first treatise he explains that the hierarchy of
forms which constitute the intelligible order of the sublunar
world is united in the conception of the Active Intellect.   (For a
discussion of the Active Intellect, see below, note #456.)   He
writes (1:12, p. 85, ll. 7-9):

> All of these intelligible forms are in the soul of the
> Active Intellect in the respect in which they are one
> in it.

That is, the Active Intellect knows the forms as they actually
are, abstracted from their material embodiments.   The human intellect which is hylic, on the other hand, does not conceive of them
in the actuality of their oneness in the intelligible order but
rather in their specific multiple embodiments in the material
world.   He writes (1:6, p. 37, ll. 27-34):

> We find that the Active Intellect also makes known to
> the hylic intellect the interrelated degrees of these
> intelligibles.   That is, it makes known that some of
> the forms are the perfection of others in a way that
> all of them end with a single form which is the per-
> fection of them, i.e., the human form, which prime
> matter receives by means of the rest of the forms which
> it has the potential to receive.   (The human form) is
> in the degree of perfection and form for them.   There-
> fore, it necessarily follows that the Active Intellect
> has knowledge of these orders with respect to their
> being a single order in their totality, and this is
> the respect in which they are one in it.

Thus, he is saying here that the forms of the various species
of plants are united in that they are all one in the intelligible
order in which they exist in themselves, abstracted from material
embodiment, and in that, within that intelligible order, the more
perfect forms are in the degree of the form to the less perfect.
(See above, note #215, for a discussion of his view of the relationships between the various degrees of perfection among hylic
forms.)   Their coming to be can thus be said to be one, even
though there are multiple instances of coming to be and passing

away as composite things come to be from the four elements and
from the actions of the contraries which are the qualities of the
elements. This is because the forms are interdependent and interrelated in their intelligible order, so that the sequence of composition is a single consequence of the causation of the intelligible
order upon prime matter.

311) I.e., on the third "day."

312) Gen 1:11.

313) ᶜal derekh peleᵓ. It is "marvelous" because a marvel is
something which conforms to the divine nomos and yet does not come
to be from something defined. According to natural custom, plants
come to be from seeds produced from their species. Their initial
coming to be without such seeds is therefore marvelous. For his
definition of marvels as unusual natural phenomena which conform
to the divine nomos of existent things but which do not come to be
from something defined, see below, 6:2:10, pp. 448-453, (cf.
above, notes #4 and #231).

314) Viz., the seeds which were created marvelously at the
moment of creation but which were not produced from their species.

315) His discussion here depends on his preliminary argument
above (6:2:8, p. 427, l. 22-p. 428, l. 18) that the sequence of
"days" of Gen 1:1-2:4 does not denote a temporal sequence. Rather,
the heavens and the sublunar world were created simultaneously
and instantaneously at the moment of God's creative will.

The issue here is both a question of textual interpretation
and of a concept which is basic to his understanding of the process
of creation. The textual question is twofold: a) In verse 11,
there is a description of God willing that the elevated part of
the earth should bear plant life. Verse 12 states that the earth
brought forth this plant life. The phrase "va-toṣeh ha-ᵓareṣ" is
problematic because it differs from other parts of creation, the
coming to be of which is attributed directly to God's "action"
after the statement of His will. This is a problem which he
directly addresses immediately below (p. 432, ll. 4-11). b) Though
Gen 1:12 states that the earth brought forth plant life, Gen 2:5
states that none of these plants sprouted until the earth was
watered and cultivated. This leads him to inquire about the sense
in which it can be said that plant life was created before it
sprouted. His answer is that the equivalents of the seeds of all

plant species were given to the earth at the moment of creation
but that the growth of these plants was temporally posterior to
that moment. Thus, verse 12 is a description of the potential or
disposition which the earth was given at the moment of creation.
This potential, however, was not actualized immediately, as is
indicated by the singular phrase, "va-toṣeh ha-ʾareṣ."

     The conceptual problem is also twofold. a) In all cases in
which the Torah describes the created species as fully developed,
the question arises as to whether this complete development was
instantaneously actualized. In the case of species of plant life,
he is saying that their sprouting was a temporally subsequent
development. He will state below (p. 432, 1. 10f.) that this is
only true of the plant species; all other things were created in a
complete state at the moment of creation. b) Given his understanding that the sequence of days does not indicate temporal priority
but rather priority in cause and in nature or priority in order
(cf. above, 6:2:2, 6:2:8, p. 427, 1. 25-p. 428, 1. 6; note #27),
the description of the elevation of the earth and the plant species
on third "day," prior to the description of the stars on the fourth
"day," is problematic, since neither is prior in either sense to
the stars. He deals with this problem below (p. 435, 1. 18-p. 436,
1. 18) and explains there that the description of the elevation of
the earth precedes the description of the stars in order to indicate that the former is not caused by the latter. He adds there
(p. 436, 11. 12-18) that a description of the species of plant
life is included with the description of the earth's elevation in
order to indicate, in part, how the elevated earth is the cause,
in some way, of the existence of the species which live upon it.
His statement here that the coming to be of plants at the moment
of creation does not involve their subsequent sprouting sheds
light on his explanation below. That is, the description in verse
12 of their actualization refers to later events. Thus, the
description of their coming to be does not really precede the
description of the coming to be of the stars, the actualization of
which was instantaneous.

     316) Gen 2:5.

     317) Gen 1:11.

     318) Gen 1:12.

     319) 12:4. The complete passage reads as follows (Soncino
translation):

R. Judah and R. Nehemiah discussed this passage. R.
Judah said: 'And the heaven and the earth were
finished' in their own time, 'and all their host' in
their own time. Said R. Nehemiah to him: But it is
written, 'These are the generations of the heaven and
of the earth be-hibbaram (when they were created),'
which means: they are (now) as when they were (first)
created, i.e. on the very day they were created they
brought forth their generations. R. Judah countered:
Yet surely it is written, 'And there was evening and
there was morning, one day...a second day...a third
day...a fourth day...a fifth day...a sixth day'? Said
R. Nehemiah: They were like those who gather figs,
when each appears in its own time. R. Berekiah
observed in confirmation of the view of R. Nehemiah:
'And the earth brought forth, etc.' (Gen. I, 12),
implies something which was already stored within it.

In his Commentary to the Torah, Gersonides expands on this
midrash in the context of his argument that the Genesis narrative
does not denote temporal priority. He writes (CT 9b, 11. 12-16):

The sages compared the appearance of some things prior
to others in the account of the work of creation to
one who plants diverse seeds in the earth. Some of
them sprout before others. Similarly, they said that
the state of affairs of the coming to be of the world
was such that everything came to be simultaneously
from the Lord, may He be exalted, but that some things
appeared before others.

Though he follows this with the statement of his preferred
understanding of the sequence of "days"—i.e., that they denote
nontemporal priority—he is citing the rabbis here in support of
his claim that, with regard to the species of plants, only the
potential for their actualization was created at the moment of
creation.

320) Gen 1:12.

321) I.e., the seeds were not literally planted. Rather, the
creation of the disposition in the earth to sprout the species of
plants is similar to the depositing of seeds in the earth (cf.
above, note #313). Again he is assuming that the rabbis agree
with his interpretation. They knew, he assumes, that God did not
actually deposit seeds in the earth. Thus, they must have meant
the word "deposited" to be taken figuratively.

322) Gen. Rab. 12:4. The word "toledot" ("generations") in
this passage belongs to the previous statement, in our current
editions of Genesis Rabbah. (It is also included by the manuscripts
consulted.) It is possible that his use of the word is a subject
heading and that he intends the beginning of the passage to be read

as follows: "'The generations' (Gen 2:4).   The earth (was
created) on the first day."   This is unlikely, however, because in
no sense does he believe that the earth was created on the first
"day."   Thus, whether or not this confusion was conscious and
purposeful, it does serve to alter the meaning of Beit Hillel's
statement in a way that makes it agree with Gersonides' position.
That is, according to his reading, it is not the earth that Beit
Hillel asserts was created on the first day.   It is rather the
generations of the earth, i.e., the potential for them to come to
be at a later time.   He may understand this statement in one of
two ways: a) Beit Hillel does not intend the use of days to refer
to the specific, numbered sequence of Genesis, since it agrees
that that sequence does not refer to temporal priority.   Rather,
it means to assert that the species of plant life were brought
forth later at a variety of times which correspond to the pace
which each species respectively requires to sprout.   b) The reference of Beit Hillel to "the generations of the earth" refers to
the forms of the plant species which are not actualized immediately
but the potentials for which were created immediately at the moment
of creation.   "The first day" of this passage would thus denote
the moment of creation which includes all six "days."   The first
interpretation is preferable because he states immediately below
(p. 432, l. 3f.) that they intended that the sprouting occurred
"some time" after the creation of this potential in the earth, and
because it does not have to deal with the way he understands Beit
Hillel's rather explicit reference to the third day as the time of
sprouting.

    Note that he ignores the rest of Beit Hillel's statement which
deals with the potentials deposited in the heavens and in the sea,
presumably because it cannot be interpreted in a way that conforms
to his interpretation.

    324) God knows the plant species before their material and
individual actualization, because He knows their natures or definitions rather than their individual embodiments.   He knows those
natures insofar as they are one in the divine nomos.   (See above,
note #310, for a discussion of the nature of this unity.)   It is
these natures to which he is referring when he speaks about the
potential or the disposition which was placed in the earth.   The
seed of a plant species, or the equivalent thereof, possesses the
form or the nature of that species prior to the material actualization which occurs in its sprouting.

325) I.e., because the creation of the plant species did not involve their immediate sprouting (and not because God knew that they were good).

326) Gen 1:7.

327) Gen 1:16.

328) Gen 1:21.

329) Gen 1:25.

330) Gen 1:27.

331) Gen 1:12.

332) I.e., at the moment of creation, since the "days" are not temporal designations and since all things (except the plants) were created simultaneously and instantaneously. Because the species of plants were not immediately actualized, he is saying, the Torah does not directly say that God created or made them. Such statements imply instantaneous actualization of the divine will, because God does not act. Rather, He wills and His will is immediately realized. As explained above, notes #226 and #234, he believes that there is only one instance of divine will. It is at the moment of creation and it is a single volition to overflow to other existent things. That is, God does not will the creation of each of the many species of existent things. Rather, as a consequence of His will to share some of His goodness and grace with other existent things, the divine nomos overflows from Him. That divine nomos includes the forms of all the species. Thus, it does not say that God created or made the plants, because the completion of their creation is not immediate. (Cf. CT 15b, l. 45 - 15c, l. 6, where he explains that the plant species require the cultivation of the soil and rain. In the initial absence of both of these factors, the plant species sprouted slowly and the natural world, as we know it, was only completed after a long period of time following the moment of creation.) It does say, however, that "God said" that there should be plants (Gen 1:11), because God's speech denotes His will (6:2:8, p. 429, ll. 16-18) and the creation of the natures of the plant species is part of the divine nomos which overflows from His will.

333) This paragraph is a further elaboration of the argument which he has just completed. That is, he has just explained why it is not said of the plants that God made them while it does say

that God created or made the other things. He now must discuss
why it does not say that God made the light. (That it does not
say that He made the elemental forms on the second "day" is presumably due to the weakness of their existence, as discussed above,
note #260. Its failure to say that God created the elevation of
the earth on the third "day" remains unexplained but is probably
related to the anomalous nature of the visible part of the earth,
as discussed above, note #297. These are the only other excep-
tions.)

334) He identifies the "light" of the first "day" with the
separate intellects above, 6:2:5, p. 423, ll. 11-35, and 6:2:8,
p. 429, l. lf. He defines them as the forms of the heavenly
bodies above, 6:2:8, p. 429, ll. 3-6 (cf. above, note #242).

335) I.e., in this case, the heavenly bodies. The process of
coming to be and passing away is caused by the actions of the contrary qualities which the elements possess. It is thus something
to which material substances are subject since they are all composed
of the four elements. Forms, on the other hand, are not subject
to this process. What passes away in any given change is the substance, which is composed of a material substratum and the form
which gives it its nature. The change occurs when one form is
replaced by another, contrary form as the form of the material
substratum. Though the form which is replaced no longer has the
particular material embodiment which it had before the change, it
cannot be said to pass away. Similarly, the new form cannot be
said to come to be in itself. Rather, it has "come to be" insofar
as it has a new particular material embodiment. Both forms, as
all forms, exist apart from their material instantiations. Their
multiplicity is a function of the different material substrata of
which they are the forms. Abstracted from their substrata, each
form is single and all forms are one in the divine nomos.
The separate forms of the heavenly bodies, unlike the hylic
forms of the sublunar world which require material instruments
to perform their functions, are not, in some sense, embodied in
that of which they are the forms. Their creation is thus mentioned on a different "day" than the creation of the heavenly
bodies. Note the comment in this regard in his commentary (CT 10c,
ll. 52ff.):

> It places the creation of the spheres in the second
> degree of coming to be and does not include their crea-
> tion with the creation of the angels which are their

form. This is to indicate that their forms, i.e., the
separate intellects, do not cleave to them as hylic
forms cleave to matter. Rather, their forms are separate. Therefore, it relates the command of (the separate forms') creation to the first day and the creation
of spheres to the second day.

The Torah does not state that God made or created them, however,
because those phrases, Gersonides is asserting, refer to the process of coming to be, and forms do not come to be insofar as they
are forms.

336) Note that he is not using the term "connected" (niqshar)
here in a material or spatial sense. No form, whether hylic or
separate, can be said to be connected in this way to that of which
it is the form, because forms are not material. They are thus not
"in" the things they inform. His point here, therefore, is that
one should not mistakenly think that separate forms are distinct
from hylic forms because they are not connected to bodies while
hylic forms are so connected. Rather, they are both connected in
a nonmaterial way, i.e., they are the perfection of which their
material embodiments are the approximations.

337) See above, 5:3:6.

338) For example, the form of a human being requires a material
human embodiment to perform the functions specific to human nature.
For human conception to occur, an eye is needed to perceive sensible objects from which concepts can be abstracted (see below,
6:2:8, p. 433, ll. 18-25, and notes #455, #456 and #491). None of
the separate intellects, on the other hand, perform their specific
function of self-conception by means of the heavenly bodies. The
motion of each of the heavenly bodies, which is a consequence of
the conception of each of the separate intellects, is thus not the
function which is specific to that separate intellect. It is a
secondary consequence of the true function of self-conception; a
consequence which is necessary for the existence of the sublunar
world but which is not essential to the separate intellect itself.

As mentioned above, note #215, the separate intellect
conceives of itself and of the single, simple motion which overflows from it. As he states below (6:2:8, p. 440, ll. 2-7), the
intellects are aware of the imperfection of their conceptions in
relation to the perfect divine conception and thus subject themselves to the divine nomos.

339) Gen 1:12. He here returns to the question with which he
dealt above (p. 432, ll. 4-11) and offers another explanation of
why the Torah does not say that God made or created the species of
plants.

340) Though both plants and animals have a nutritive power or
soul, only animals also have appetitive, sensory and locomotive
powers (cf. De Anima 2.2-3). Thus, he is arguing, the Torah does
not say that God made the plant species because their complete
development requires nothing beyond the form of the nutritive soul,
something which is presumably very low in the hierarchy of forms
in the divine nomos. Animals are said to be made by God, on the
other hand, because their development involves other, more perfect
forms.

341) I.e., the nutritive power of an animal embryo must be
augmented subsequently by locomotion, sensation, etc.

342) I.e., of animals.

343) I.e., the fourth degree or "day."

344) Gufim. On the nature of the material substance of the
heavenly bodies, see above, note #254. At least here and in l. 30
below Gersonides' use of the term guf does not support our hypothesis there that he usually avoids the term geshem in referring
to the heavenly bodies and instead uses the term gerem in order to
be precise about the differences between sublunar and supralunar
body. It may be that he uses the terms geshem and gerem only when
he is clearly distinguishing between sublunar and supralunar bodies.
Elsewhere, he employs guf to refer to the element earth (6:2:5,
p. 423, l. 8), to lifeless, motionless bodies (6:2:8, p. 435, l.
10), and to the human body when it is contrasted with the human
soul (6:2:9, p. 443, ll. 15, 16, 19).

345) Gen 1:14.

346) As explained above, notes #136 and #223, the term "stars"
(kokhavim) includes the sun and the moon, the planets and those
bodies which we call "stars." His reference here to "the rest of
the stars" implicitly assumes that all of these are kokhavim.

347) Raṣah bimṣi'utam. God creates in a single act of will,
as discussed above, notes #226 and #234.

348) He is referring to Gen 1:14: le-havdil bein ha-yom
u-vein ha-laylah. He reads the biblical description of the fourth

"day" as specifically referring to three different purposes of
the stars: a) to distinguish between "day" and "night," i.e., to
generate, by the variation in influence of each star, the contrary
qualities of the elements, the action of which leads to the coming
to be of lower existent things from prime matter and the elemental
forms; b) to be "signs" of the singular influences that each star
has upon the sublunar world; and c) to illumine the earth. Here
he begins his discussion of the first of these purposes.

     Note that his emphasis here on the benefits which the sublunar
world derives from the heavenly bodies reflects his argument above
in the first part of this treatise that the varied activities of
the heavens cannot be explained as a necessary consequence of their
nature but are rather clearly for the sake of the nomos which overflows from these activities to lower existent things. Therefore,
he argues, though the existence of the heavens is continuous, the
heavens were nevertheless created, since existence for the sake of
something else is a characteristic of things which come to be as
the effect of an agent (6:1:5-9).

     349) The opposites to which he refers here are the contrary
qualities which the four elements possess, as explained above in
notes #49 and #167. The influence of the supralunar bodies upon
the sublunar world occurs in that they each cause the coming to
be of certain contrary qualities in the sublunar world. Note his
more explicit discussion in the parallel passage of his commentary
(CT 11c, 11. 26ff.):

> There is generated from them in this lower world
> opposite natural things in the four seasons which are
> generated from the star. That is, when the sun is
> above the horizon, the air and the fire predominate;
> when it is below (the horizon), the earth and the
> water predominate. This is very clear with regard to
> the sun. Similarly, it is proper that we understand
> that this state of affairs (applies) to each star.
> That is, opposite things occur from it in respect to
> the day and the night which are generated from it.

     350) His point is that "day" and "night" are terms which denote
variations in the influence of a star which do not necessarily
correspond to twenty four hour cycles of time. As the "day" of
the sun refers both to its daily periods above the horizon and to
its seasonal periods among the northern constellations (since the
inhabited part of the earth is in the northern hemisphere), similarly the "day" of other stars refers to their respective periods
above the horizon and in the north. As the influence of a star

grows weaker and stronger, contrary qualities are generated in the
sublunar world. For example, during the "day" of the sun the
qualities of heat and dryness predominate, while the qualities of
cold and moisture predominate when solar influence weakens and
lunar influence predominates. Cf. his explanation in his Commentary to the Torah (11c, ll. 2ff.).

For a discussion of all the factors which affect the strength
of the influence of a star upon the earth, see above, 5:2:8, p.
207f. He lists there six self-evident principles: 1) The stars
perform diverse functions in the ways in which they influence the
earth. 2) The diversity of their functions is affected by their
diverse locations in the spheres. 3) The longer a star remains in
one place, the stronger is its influence. 4) The variation of a
star's influence is affected by its inclinations north and south.
5) The greater the illumination of a star, the stronger its
influence. 6) The closer a star is to the earth, the stronger is
its influence.

In his article, "The Medieval Hebrew Tradition in Astronomy"
(Journal of the American Oriental Society 85(1965):146), Bernard
R. Goldstein mentions that in 1148 Abraham Ibn Ezra translated
The Treatise on Eclipses by Masha²allah, in which the influence of
the stars upon the earth is compared to the way in which a magnet
attracts iron. Gersonides' discussion of the factors affecting
celestial influences can be read as supporting that analogy,
though his emphasis in 5:2:8 (p. 207, ll. 29ff.) and in the first
part of this treatise is on the transmission of these influences
through the illuminations of each star (cf. Guide 2:12).

351) He is referring to the second part of Gen 1:14 in which
the luminaries are called "signs" (²otot). Each star serves as a
sign for its particular influence on the sublunar world.

352) Gen 1:14. In both the Leipzig and the Riva di Trento
editions, the order of the words shanim and yamim is inverted,
apparently without significance. The manuscripts consulted disagree with the printed editions and agree with the text of Genesis.

353) See above, note #350, for a discussion of factors
involved in the length and the strength of a given star's influence.

354) Cf. his explanation in his Commentary to the Torah
(11b, ll. 38ff.) of the term ²otot:

"For signs." These are the actions which are ordered by
the heavenly bodies in this lower world which the stars
indicate, so that each of them is individuated in the
way that is explained in Astrology. To indicate that
this is the case, (the Torah) says, "Do not be dismayed
at the signs of the heavens" (Jer 10:2), and "Do you
know the ordinance of the heavens? Can you establish
their rule on the earth?" (Job 38:33). In our explanation of natural science and in the second and sixth
treatises of The Wars of the Lord, we have explained
beyond a doubt that everything that is generated in this
lower world is ordered from the heavenly bodies. In
relation to this order, it is possible that knowledge of
these occurrences can reach a person in a dream or in
divination or in prophecy, because human choice is capable in some way of altering that order, as we explained
there. That the deficiency which occurs in the science
of astrology is in respect to our shortcomings, not in
respect to the state of affairs in itself, (is indicated
by) its statement, "Do you know the ordinances of the
heavens? Can you establish their rule on earth?"
(Job 38:33).

His references are to 2:2, p. 95, ll. 15ff. and to 6:1:5-9.

355) I.e., that the stars effect the actions of contrary
qualities in the sublunar world according to the alternating
degrees of the strength ("day") and the weakness ("night") of
their respective influences; and that each star is associated with
("is a sign of") its own singular action upon the sublunar world.

356) He is referring to Gen 1:15: "They shall serve as
luminaries in the raqiᶜa of the heavens to illuminate the earth."

357) I.e., by allowing the species whose nature it is to see
to perform its function.

358) The manuscripts consulted add the word viy-kavein after
the word me-ha-maziq at p. 433, l. 23. According to the manuscripts, the translation should add "and its orienting itself"
before "to that which is beneficial."

Cf. CT 14a, ll. 26ff., quoted below, note #491; De Anima
3.7, 3.13.435b21ff.; and Guide 2:4, where Maimonides defines the
seeking of the agreeable and the flight from the disagreeable as
the "nature" of a thing.

359) See above, 6:2:5, for his discussion of the connection
between the perception of light and the conception of the intelligible world. Cf. Topica 2.7.113a32f. (Oxford translation): "It
is through the sensation of sight that we recognize the Form
present in each individual." Cf. also Metaphysica 1.1.980a27,
where Aristotle states that the sense of sight gives us the most
knowledge.

As discussed in notes #3, #338, #455 and #456, human beings acquire true knowledge of concepts by inducing them from their perceptions of individual instances of those concepts.

360) I.e., the alternation of their influences upon the sublunar world ("day" and "night"); the influence of each of them on the sublunar world for different periods of time; and the illumination of the earth.

361) Note that ha-geramin ha-shemiymiyim here (heavenly bodies) is inclusive of kokhavim (stars) above in l. 26, and may refer to stars and spheres. See above, note #136.

362) In 6:1:7 above, he makes this argument as part of his greater argument that the heavens came to be. Because everything within the heavens acts for the sake of the perfection of lower existent things in the most perfect possible way, and because everything that acts for the sake of some other thing is necessarily the effect of an agent, therefore the heavens and everything in them are the effect of an agent and must have come to be (p. 310, l.7-p. 312, l. 14). His list there of the various characteristics of the heavenly bodies, each of which acts in the most perfect possible way, is more complete than his list here. It includes the following: The distance of the heavenly body from the earth. The magnitude of the stars. The shape of the spheres of a star, so that the distance of a given star from the earth sometimes varies and so that its speed varies. The order of the spheres of the stars. The diversity in the illuminations of the stars. The place of a star in its sphere relative to the north and south. The number of spheres of a star. The number of stars in the outermost sphere. The fact that some stars radiate their own light and other reflect light. The changes in the phases of the moon. The place of the Milky Way in the sphere of the fixed stars. The magnitude of body which does not preserve its shape which is between the spheres of one star and the spheres of the next star in order to prevent the confusion of the motions of the heavenly bodies. The total number of spheres and stars.

His point there is that all of these factors combine to form the most perfect possible overflow of the divine nomos to lower existent things so that the slightest deviation in the order of the celestial world would cause the sublunar world to pass away (cf. CT 11d, 11. 23ff.; 5:2:9). His allusion here seems to be a

suggestion that the Torah, in referring to these three types of
actions by means of which the heavenly bodies influence the sublunar world, means to suggest a teleological form of the argument
for the creation of the world and for the existence of God (cf.
Guide 3:13, p. 449 of Pines translation). That is, the existence
of all of these characteristics of the supralunar world cannot be
explained as a necessary consequence of the nature of the heavens
and therefore must have come to be from a volitional cause (cf.
above, 6:1:8). The Torah emphasizes this point in enumerating the
ways in which the sublunar world depends upon every characteristic
of the heavenly bodies, he is suggesting, to show that the supralunar world exists in the most perfect possible way and that its
cause must be the most perfect cause. This would be one instance
in support of his claim that, with regard to the creation of the
world, the text of Genesis itself leads one to the truth of the
investigation (see above, notes #1 and #6).

In emphasizing the fact that the heavenly bodies move for
the sake of the perfection of the sublunar world, he departs from
the perspective of Maimonides. Maimonides argues against Aristotle's assertion that the final purpose of all things in the universe is the perfection and the perpetuation of the sublunar, and
particularly the human, species. He rejects the notion that God
needed the heavens as instruments for the creation of human beings.
He therefore concludes that the heavens were created for their own
sake and not for the sake of something else (Guide 3:13).

In contrast to Maimonides' position, Gersonides accepts the
Aristotelian view of the teleological nature of the universe and
shows in the first part of this treatise that, based upon Aristotle's view, the heavens, and hence the world as a whole, can be
demonstrated to have been generated (6:1:6-9). In response to
Maimonides' reluctance to posit that the heavens, which are more
venerable than and prior in cause and in nature to the human
species, act for the sake of the human species, Gersonides argues
below that that which is more venerable always acts for the sake
of that which is less venerable but that it does not acquire any
perfection from that action (6:2:8, p. 434, ll. 35ff.). Thus,
though he disagrees with Maimonides' view that the heavens do not
act for the sake of the sublunar world, he would agree with
Maimonides' view that the heavens exist primarily for their own
sake.

363) He is referring to Gen 1:15, "and it was so" (va-yehiy
khen), which he takes in all cases to refer to the instantaneous
actualization of the divine will.

364) Gen 1:16.

365) His premise here is that one of the factors which
determines the strength of the influence of a heavenly body upon
the sublunar world is its magnitude. The greater its magnitude,
the stronger its influence. In his discussion of this issue
above (5:2:8, p. 207f.; summarized in note #350), he does not
mention the magnitude of a star as one of the factors which determine the degree of influence. He does mention, however, the
strength of its illumination, and presumably the sizes of the sun
and the moon contribute to their strong illuminations.

366) He expands upon the nature of this rule or dominance in
his Commentary to the Torah (11c, 11. 9ff.), where he writes:

> "To rule the day." (Gen 1:16) This is the governance
> over the actions of the rest of the stars. It is
> generally recognized that the actions of the sun and
> the moon are more apparent and visible in this lower
> world than are the actions of the rest of the stars.
> In the science of Astrology the way that the sun rules
> the day and the moon rules the night is mentioned in
> the laws of the births of human beings. Nevertheless,
> it is clear that the rest of the stars have some rule
> and governance in the day and at night, as is generally
> recognized by one who speculates a bit in Astrology.

Thus, we can infer that he does not mean here to suggest that the
sun and the moon govern the actions of the other stars (which are
in higher spheres). Rather, the influence of the sun and the moon
on the sublunar world can be said to predominate over the influences
of the other stars.

367) In his commentary (CT 11c, 1. 20), he refers to the first
part of the fifth treatise for his discussion of the ways in which
the sun rules over the moon. It is likely that his discussion of
the rule of the sun and the moon over the rest of the stars is
also in 5:1.

368) Gen 1:16.

369) His reference is most likely to the first part of Treatise
Five. The referents of the phrase ha-kokhavim ᵓasher la-hem
("their stars") is unclear. Based upon his explanation in the
parallel passage of his commentary (CT 11c, 11. 9ff., quoted above,

note #366), he probably intends to say that the day's stars and
the night's stars also govern the day and night of the sublunar
world, though their rule is weaker than that of the sun and the
moon. The reference may also be to the sun and the moon. That
is, the stars of the sun, i.e., those stars which are above the
horizon when the sun is above the horizon, and the stars of the
moon. His meaning is the same in both cases.

370) ᶜAsᵓam. He does not seem to distinguish between the
terms ᶜasah ("to make"), baraᵓ ("to create") and himṣiᵓ ("to bring
into existence"). Note, for example, his consecutive use of all
three terms above, 6:2:8, p. 433, ll. 27, 32, 33.

371) Gen 1:17: "to illumine the earth."

372) Gen 1:18.

373) 6:2:8, p. 432, l. 31; p. 433, l. 5. It is the diverse
and fluctuating influences of each of the stars (to which he takes
the Torah's mention of "day" and "night" to refer) which accounts
for the diversity among members of sublunar species, i.e., their
accidental qualities.

374) Gen 1:18.

375) Gen 1:18. A star rules when it is above the horizon, as
does the sun. See above, p. 433, l. 2 and note #350.

In assuming that verses 17 and 18 are a recapitulation of the
three actions of the heavenly bodies which were first mentioned in
verses 14 and 15, he is compelled to alter their order. That is,
the illuminating function of verse 17 corresponds to the parallel
statement in verse 15. His interpretation of the statement in
verse 18 that they "rule the day and the night" corresponds to his
understanding of the term "signs" in verse 14. That is, different
stars exert singular influences for different periods of time.
The division of light and darkness in verse 18 corresponds to the
parallel division between day and night in verse 14—as a reference
to the fluctuations in a given star's influence.

Note that the division between light and darkness to which he
is referring is not a distinction made by the sun and the moon.
As he interprets "day" and "night" above (p. 432, ll. 35ff.) as
referring respectively to the maximal and minimal degrees of
influence of each star, similarly here "light" and "darkness"
refer respectively to the times when each star is above and below

the horizon. As explained above, note #366, he believes that the
Torah is saying that all stars illuminate, all stars rule over
the sublunar world, and all stars fluctuate in their influence.
Thus, he is reading Gen 1:17-18 as follows: God set all the stars
in the raqiᶜa of the heavens (i.e., the spheres; cf. above 6:2:7)
to illuminate the earth, to rule at different times ("by day and
by night"), and to fluctuate in their degrees of influence, depending on whether they were above or below the horizon ("to divide
the light from the darkness").

376) 6:2:8, p. 433, ll. 6-17.

377) Gen 1:18.

378) Gen 1:14.

379) I.e., that stars ruled for daily periods of time and not
for shorter and longer periods of time.

380) I.e., "the day" and "the night" of Gen 1:14.

381) Gen 1:18.

382) Gen 1:18.

383) Gen 1:14.

384) Gen 1:14. His earlier explanation is on p. 433, ll.
6-17. The connection which he makes between the two verses is
that the stars serve as "signs" (1:14) in that each of them repre-
sents its singular influence and that it serves as a "sign" when
it is visible, above the horizon (1:18—its "light").

385) Gen 1:18.

386) I.e., that their actions would influence the sublunar
world.

387) I.e., the nomos which orders the sublunar world and which
overflows from the activities of the heavenly bodies.

388) As he states elsewhere (2:1, p. 92, l. 8f.; 6:1:6, p. 309,
l. 32f.; 6:1:9, p. 321, ll. 30ff.; 6:1:13, p. 350, l. 15f.;
6:2:12, p. 454, ll. 16ff.) accidents occur only infrequently, for
short periods of time and in few instances (cf. Physica 2.5.
196b10ff.; De Caelo 2.5.287b24; Guide 2:20). Insofar as the divine
nomos which overflows from the stars to lower existent things has
none of these characteristics, it cannot be said to be purposeless
in an accidental way. Insofar as the activities of the heavenly
bodies do not follow necessarily from their nature or essence, as

he argues above, 6:1:8, the nomos which overflows from their activities cannot be said to be purposeless in a necessary way. Thus,
the correct conclusion is that they were created by the Lord for
the purpose of the perfection of the sublunar world.

389) Gen 1:19. On his understanding of va-yehiy ᶜerev va-yehiy
voqer, see above, note #245.

390) nimos, seder and yosher function here and elsewhere as
synonyms which refer together to that which overflows to the sublunar world from the heavenly bodies and ultimately from God's
will (cf. 6:2:8, p. 440, l. 17; 6:2:10, p. 444, ll. 12, 13; 6:1:3,
p. 296, l. 11, where he uses ṭov, seder and yosher; also cf. the
explanation of Norbert M. Samuelson, Gersonides. The Wars of the
Lord. Treatise Three. On God's Knowledge [Toronto, 1977] p. 100,
n. 13). Nimos is a term which designates political, social or
natural law. In this context, it refers to the laws of nature
which result from the hierarchy of forms as they overflow to the
sublunar world by means of the action of the heavenly bodies, which
cause the actions of the contrary qualities of the elemental forms,
which in turn cause prime matter to be informed by the forms of
sublunar species. Seder refers to the order which results from
this process. Yosher is the most difficult of the three terms to
translate. We translate it as "rightness" because of its basic
meaning, "to go straight." Samuelson translates it as "arrangement." In several places, Gersonides uses related terms to mean
"to direct" (6:2:1, p. 419, ll. 21, 26, 27; 6:2:2, p. 420, l. 16;
6:2:8, p. 436, l. 11; p. 441, l. 20; 6:2:12, p. 458, l. 2), so
that yosher might properly be translated as "correct direction."

For his most extensive description of the way in which all of
the motions of the heavenly bodies cooperate to form the most perfect possible nomos which then overflows to lower existence, see
above, 6:1:7, pp. 310ff. It is this cooperation to form a single
nomos to which he takes the implicit unity of "evening" and "morning" in Gen 1:19 to refer (cf. above, p. 429, l. 15).

391) I.e., there are two respects in which there is a unity of
diverse characteristics in the heavenly bodies.

392) He is interpreting "morning" and "evening" here in a way
that corresponds to the way he interpreted "day" and "night"
(Gen 1:14) and "light" and "darkness" (Gen 1:18) above. That is,
morning, day and light refer to the period of a given star's
strongest influence and evening, night and darkness refer to its

period of weakest influence (cf. above, p. 432, l. 35-p. 433, l. 5;
p. 434, ll. 6-13).

His reference here to the actions of the stars upon the
visible part of the earth is based upon his assumption that the
elevated, visible part of the earth is primarily in the northern
hemisphere and that it is in the north that human civilization
exists. Thus, the period in which the influence of a star is
strongest is the time in which it is in the north and when it is
above the horizon. There seems to be some confusion here which is
based upon the equivocal nature of the term nigleh ("visible").
In the first part of this treatise (6:1:13) he vacillates between
talking about the visible part of the earth as that part of the
earth which is elevated above the seas and as that elevated part
of the earth which is elevated above the seas during the day,
i.e., when light renders it visible. Thus, in arguing against
Averroes' claim that the existence of dry land is a necessary
consequence of the actions of the heavenly bodies since there are
more stars in the north and it is their heat which dries the
water in the north, Gersonides refutes Averroes' claim by stating
that, if dry land were caused by the heat of the stars, the earth
should be visible for twenty four hours (6:1:13, p. 351, l. 24-p.
352, l. 11). Used in this sense, "visible" can only mean visible
to the human eye because of daylight.

Because he uses the term "visible" in two different ways, the
intent of his statement here needs to be examined. It would seem
that the diverse actions of the stars affect the state of affairs
of the entire sublunar world rather than the visible part of the
earth alone. For example, the divine nomos which overflows from
the heavenly bodies governs the species of fish in the sea as well
as the species which live on dry land. If we assume that he uses
the term "visible" here to refer to the elevated part of the earth,
and not to the elevated part of the earth when it is visible by
daylight, then it is clear that the terms "evening" and "morning"
have no relation to the periods of a day. He is not saying that
the influence of the stars is strongest before noon. Rather, the
Torah refers to the period when a star's influence is strongest as
its "morning." That he specifies that the "morning" of a star is
the period when a star's influence is strongest in the visible part
of the earth is a further elaboration of his statements that the
actions of the heavens were created by divine will for the purpose
of governing the sublunar world (p. 433, l. 29f.; cf. note #362) and
that all of the lower sublunar species are for the sake of the human
species (6:1:27, p. 405, l. 4f.; 6:2:8, p. 438, ll. 10-12; see above,

note #215). Since the human species lives on the visible part of
the earth which is in the north, the respective and fluctuating
influences of the stars are measured in terms of their effects
upon that part of the sublunar world in which humans live.

393) Kavod. Jacob Klatzkin defines this term as the measure
of the star's body and the magnitude of its light (Oṣar Ha-Munaḥim
Ha-Filosofim Ve-Antologiyah Filosofit [New York, 1968] 2:62). As
explained above, note #251, the relative degree of the venerability
of a separate intellect, as Gersonides describes it in 5:3:8,
p. 273, is determined by the speed of its sphere's motion, the
number of stars in its sphere, and the size of the star in its
sphere. We can reasonably infer that the venerability of a star
itself is determined by its speed as well as its size and the
strength of its illumination. The greatest variation occurs in
the disparity between the sun and the moon, and the rest of the
stars. The sun and the moon are both larger than the rest and
have much stronger illuminations (p. 433, ll. 33ff.; cf. CT 11c,
ll. 9ff.) In addition, the light of the sun is approximately
50,000 times as great as the light of the moon (CT 11c, ll. 16ff.).

394) In his exposition of the fourth "day" of creation. That
is, that the heavenly bodies were created to perform three actions
for the sublunar world (p. 432, l. 28-p. 434, l. 29; cf. above,
5:2:3 and 6:1:7).

395) The venerable cannot be for the sake of the inferior,
according to this argument, because that would entail that the
venerable would be dependent for its perfection on the inferior.
In this case, the end of the heavenly bodies would be the perfection of the sublunar world and, as a consequence, the heavenly
bodies could not perform their true function without the existence
of the sublunar world. If this were the case, the sublunar world
could be said to be the end or the final cause, and hence the
perfection, of the heavenly bodies, which would make it more venerable than them (cf. Metaphysica 5.2.1013b27; Tahafut Al-Tahafut
15:484f., p. 295 of van den Bergh translation).

Cf. Guide 3:13 for Maimonides' argument that the heavens do
not exist for the sake of the existence of men. Maimonides'
conclusion is that each species exists for its own sake and that
all things were created in accordance with the divine intention,
the final end of which is beyond our ability to conceive (see
above, note #362).

396) For his discussion of priority in cause and in nature,
see above, 6:2:2. His phrase here, "prior in cause and in existence," functions in an equivalent way. This is the fourth sense of
priority which he enumerates in 6:2:2 (p. 420, ll. 21ff.), which
corresponds, as explained above, notes #27 and #214, to Aristotle's
fifth sense of the term "prior" in the Categoriae 12, i.e., when
the existence of the cause implies the existence of the effect.
The heavens are prior in this sense to the sublunar world because
it is the combination of all of their activities which produces
the nomos which rules lower existent things. The existence of
the heavens, therefore, is a cause of the existence of the sublunar
world.

Note that in referring to this priority as "priority in
cause and in existence," Gersonides may be reflecting the issue
with which he will deal immediately below when he addresses the
first doubt. That is, Aristotle's second sense of priority in the
Categoriae is priority in existence, i.e., when the existence of
that which is prior implies the existence of that which is posterior but the converse is not true. Aristotle's fifth sense, priority in nature, occurs when the existence of that which is prior and
the existence of that which is posterior reciprocally imply each
other, but when the existence of that which is prior causes the
existence of that which is posterior. In asserting that the actions
of the heavenly bodies are for the sake of the perfection of the
existence of the sublunar world, Gersonides will address the question of whether there is a reciprocal implication of existence.
That is, the existence of the sublunar world can be said to imply
the existence of the heavens, since the actions of the heavens to
perfect the sublunar world would be in vain without the existence
of the sublunar world. In his omission of "priority in existence"
in his enumeration of the senses of the term "priority" in 6:2:2,
Gersonides may have been rejecting the notion that there is such a
thing as nonreciprocal implication of existence. Thus, though the
heavens are prior in cause and in nature to the sublunar world, the
existence of each implies the existence of the other, since a cause
cannot fulfill its function without the existence of that which is
caused. His response to the first doubt below will be based on this
assumption. What will remain for him to explain is that reciprocal
implication of existence does not entail reciprocal causation.

397) 6:1:9, where he explains that the heavens move for the
sake of lower existent things and that they thus possess a
characteristic of things which come to be. Thus, the spheres move

for the sake of the composite motion of the stars in order to form
the nomos of lower existence, and the shapes, distances, sizes,
degrees of illuminations and inclinations of the stars all make
sublunar existence possible. He argues there that the motions of
the spheres must necessarily be for the sake of something else,
because they cannot move to fulfill their own needs (since they
need nothing to perfect their existence) and they cannot be moving
to flee from their contraries (since there are no contraries in
the supralunar world). They cannot be moving because it is natural
and necessary for living things to move, as Aristotle claims,
because living things in the sublunar world move in the sublunar
world to perfect their existence. Useless motion is contrary to
natural law. Nor can they be moving for the sake of the pleasure
they might derive from conceiving, as humans derive pleasure in
conceiving motion, because, unlike human conception, the conception
of the spheres is actual and involves no motion. In addition, even
if they did need motion for the sake of being alive or of conception, they would not need to move in a way that perfects sublunar
existence. Furthermore, motion inhibits conception. Thus, he
argues, there is no way to posit that the motions of the spheres are
for the sake of their own conception unless we say that they conceive of the divine nomos and they consequently desire to move in a
way that sublunar existence will overflow from them in the most
perfect possible way. In that case, however, they would be moving
for the sake of lower existent things.

Note that when he speaks of the conception of the spheres in
6:1:9, he is really referring to the conception of the separate
intellects which move the spheres (see above, notes #215 and #251).
Though Maimonides does distinguish in the Guide between the separate intellect of a sphere and the sphere's intellect (Guide 2:4,
p. 258 of Pines translation; 2:10, p. 271 of Pines translation),
Gersonides makes no such distinction. When he addresses the issue
directly, in 5:3:6 above, he does speak about the conception of
the spheres, but he makes it clear there that he thinks that that
conception is intelligible and not hylic. That is, it is a
continuous conception of its motion in its totality, not a hylic
conception which conceives successively of individual concepts
which are particularized in matter. Thus, the conception of a
sphere cannot be said to have another intellect which can be distinguished from its separate intellect.

It is on the basis of this discussion in the first part of
this treatise that he will now respond to the first doubt.

398) <u>Yashpiy^ca</u>. The parallel passage in the commentary (CT
12a, 1. 10) and the manuscripts consulted have <u>yashlim</u> (perfects).

Cf. <u>Guide</u> 2:11 (p. 275f. of Pines translation) for Maimonides'
parallel explanation of how a more noble thing can act for the sake
of a less noble thing through an overflow of a residue of its perfection.   Maimonides does not, however, conclude that the celestial
motions caused by the conceptions of the separate intellects are
for the sake of the sublunar world, as discussed above in note #362.

399) See below, 6:2:10, p. 451, ll. 14ff., where he explains
that divine providence extends to individual human beings in proportion to their proximity to the degree of the Active Intellect.
He refers there to his discussions in the second treatise on the
nature of prophecy (2:6, pp. 104ff.) and in the fourth treatise on
divine providence (4:4-5, pp. 164ff.).

400) That is, he agrees with the premise of the first doubt as
he relates it above, p. 434, 1. 32f., insofar as it refers to a
case in which X acts for the sake of Y, and X acquires its perfection from Y.   In that case, it would be false to say that X is
more venerable than Y.   His response is based on his claim that the
heavens do not acquire their perfection from the sublunar world even
though they do act for its sake.   Since they acquire no perfection
from the sublunar world, the latter cannot be said to be their final
cause.

Cf. above (5:3:6, p. 262, 1. 31-p. 263, 1. 10), where he
explains that each of the separate intellects does not conceive
of its sphere's position at every moment.   Rather, it conceives
of the general and single concept of perpetual, circular motion as
a singer conceives of the song he is singing and not of every note.
He notes there that if we were to posit that the separate intellects did conceive of the exact position of their spheres in their
contingent motion, then we would have to infer that the intellects
needed their effects insofar as their effects were the objects of
their conception.   As they do not conceive of their spheres' position, they similarly do not conceive of the existence of the sublunar world which overflows from the nomos which is formed from the
totality of their conceptions and motions.   Since each intellect
does not conceive of the entire nomos which overflows to the sublunar world, but rather conceives only of the single circular
motion of its own sphere, the separate intellects and the heavenly
bodies cannot be said to need or to derive perfection from the sublunar world which they benefit.

401) The intended implication is presumably that the supralunar world's _activities_ are not for its own sake. It is not clear, however, how he justifies this distinction. If it is the case, as he claims immediately below, that it is the nature of the heavenly bodies to move and to act, insofar as they are alive, and that the heavenly bodies fulfill their nature by acting for the sake of the sublunar world, then it is unclear how the spheres and their movers can be said to exist for their own sake. Their natures would seem to require something other than themselves for the sake of which they can act, since their own perfection requires no action.

It would seem therefore that the argument which follows does not depend on his assertion here that "the spheres and their movers exist for the sake of themselves." Rather, he is arguing that the fact that they do fulfill their function by acting for the sake of lower existent things does not entail that they acquire their perfection from lower existent things. Their final cause is not the sublunar world which benefits from their actions but is rather the divine nomos which the separate intellects long to conceive and the conception of which causes the respective motions of each of their spheres (see above, note #214). None of the movers of the spheres conceives of the entire nomos which overflows from the composite motions of the spheres to the sublunar world. Their end, from which they acquire their perfection, is thus the divine nomos. What overflows from them to the sublunar world can be said to be accidental to their natures.

402) Cf. _De Caelo_ 2.12. In the first part of this treatise, he rejects the argument, which he attributes to Aristotle, that the motions of the heavenly bodies are for their own sake in that it is the nature of living things to move. He does so by asserting that this principle holds only in cases in which the living thing is moving to perfect itself. In the case of the heavenly bodies and their movers, however, this cannot be the case, since they are actual and perfect in themselves (6:1:9, p. 321, l. 23-p. 322, l. 2). His statement here bypasses this issue. That is, he is assuming the motion of the heavenly bodies and is asserting only that it would not be proper for them to move without purpose or benefit.

His failure here to consider the possibility that it would have been most proper for there to have been no motion at all in the supralunar world, given the natures of the heavenly bodies and their movers (though he does mention this in the parallel passage of his commentary, CT 12a, ll. 18-20), is a further indication that he considers the end of supralunar motion to be the divine nomos and not the perfection of the sublunar world. That is, he seems to be engaged in an explanation of how the divine nomos overflows through the supralunar world to the sublunar world, and his underlying assumption is that the supralunar bodies and movers act in a way that is proper not to their own natures in themselves but to the divine will. For example, in their pursuit of their ultimate end, i.e., the most perfect possible conception of the intelligible world, human beings sustain their physical needs by consuming a certain number of individual members of the animal species. If we did not do so, those species might die out by overpopulating their natural environments. Thus, the human species may be said to act for the sake of the survival of species which are hierarchically lower than it while it is pursuing its true end of conception. Nevertheless, the occurrence of human actions for the sake of lower species does not entail that the final cause of human action is the perpetuation of lower species. Rather, the divine nomos rules in a way that different species are interdependent. In the same way, in their conception of the divine nomos which is their ultimate end, the separate intellects cause the motions of the heavenly bodies which serve to perfect lower existent things. Though their end is not action for the sake of lower species, their pursuit of their end results in such a benefit. Thus, the propriety which Gersonides mentions here—which entails that natural actions not be purposeless—is a reference to what is proper for the divine nomos rather than what is proper for the separate intellects in themselves.

Note that Gersonides makes the distinction very explicit between the end of the heavens and their movers and the fact their motions yield a benefit for the sake of the sublunar world in his argument for creation in the first part of this treatise. That is, his list of the three characteristics of generated things (6:1:6-9) distinguishes between the (first) characteristic of having a final cause and the (third) characteristic of acting for the sake of some other thing. Though he explains there (6:1:9) that anything which acts for the sake of some other thing necessarily has a final cause, the two characteristics are not identical. But when he seeks to show that the heavens have a final cause (6:1:7), what he shows is that their motions benefit the sublunar world. There, as here, we must understand him as saying that the heavens move for

the sake of the sublunar world because of their final cause, i.e.,
the divine nomos whose purpose it is to preserve the order of the
world.

403) He addresses this problem above, 6:1:9, p. 321, ll. 28ff.
Useless activities of humans such as dancing, he says there, occur
only for short periods of time. Since the motions of the heavens
are perpetual and unchanging, however, a purposeless motion would
persist perpetually and would reflect negatively upon the wisdom
of the divine nomos. There are no accidents in the supralunar
world.

404) The objection was that it is false to assert that the
activities of the heavenly bodies are for the sake of lower existent things, because this would mean that the heavens acquired their
perfection from lower existent things and that they would therefore
not be more venerable than the inferior sublunar world. The solution of this doubt was his argument that the heavens exist for
their own sake and that the overflow from their activities to the
sublunar world serves the purpose of the divine nomos and does not
have the purpose of perfecting the heavenly bodies and their movers
themselves. This solution depends on the fact that the world was
generated. If the world were not generated, things in the world
could have no purpose outside of their natures. The heavens would
exist by necessity. If this were the case, it would be impossible
to explain their nonessential properties. They could not occur
accidentally, because they are perpetual and good (see above,
6:1:7, p. 315, ll. 8ff.). Thus, all nonessential properties of
the heavens are demonstrations that the heavens must have been
generated by will and choice (6:1:8).

405) 6:1:9, where he shows the failure of Aristotle's
attempts to explain the motions of the spheres as the necessary
consequence of natural causes. Since their motions are not a
consequence of their natures, he argues there, they must have been
generated by will and choice for the sake of perfecting lower
existent things.

406) I.e., "That it would have been proper, according to this
natural order, for this coming to be (of the stars) to have been
related to the third day, since the heavens and the stars are
prior in cause and in existence to the elements and to that which
comes to be from them" (p. 434, ll. 33-35).

407) See his Commentary to the Torah 2a, ll. 12ff. and 2c,
ll. 16ff., for his opinion that the human intellect is incapable
of perfectly conceiving the wisdom of the Torah (cf. above, notes
#1 and #3). The Torah is the instrument through which God
instructs us according to our abilities so that we may improve our
conception of the wisdom of existent things. Insofar as human
conception is imperfect even at its best, we can never fully understand the Torah's meaning.

408) CT 2a, ll. 6-12, where he writes:

> Together with His overseeing of (human) existence in
> the marvelous way in which He oversaw it in (His crea-
> tion of) the dispositions and powers of his organs and
> in the instruments which He gave him to preserve his
> existence, He also oversaw him in His directing him to
> true perfection which is the fruit of every human being
> and for the sake of which the forms which are found in
> this lower matter exist. This occurred from Him in the
> giving of this divine Torah which is the nomos which
> perfectly moves those who occupy themselves with it to
> true success.

Cf. above, 6:2:1, p. 419, ll. 2-15.

409) For the way in which the Torah functions to guide us to
the truth of the question of the generation of the world, see
above, 6:2:1, p. 419, ll. 16-29.

410) That is, the Torah serves its pedagogical purposes by
getting us to pause and ask the right questions. Without the
guidance of the Torah, he is saying, we would remain hopelessly
lost in our pursuit of speculative truth. Averroes, with whom
Gersonides shares much in common regarding the relationship of
reason and revelation and the function which revealed Scripture
serves in guiding philosophers, makes a similar comment in his
Kitāb faṣl al-maqāl, where he writes (8:11-12):

> The reason why we have received in Scripture texts
> whose apparent meanings contradict each other is in
> order to draw the attention of those who are well
> grounded in science to the interpretation which
> reconciles them.

The translation is that of George F. Hourani, Averroes: On the
Harmony of Religion and Philosophy (London, 1961), p. 51. In his
note to this passage, Hourani cites a similar remark by Avicenna
(p. 95, n. 73).

411) Cf. Metereologica 2.3.360a7, where Aristotle refers to the
drying function of the sun on earth. In 6:1:13, p. 351, ll. 24ff.,

Gersonides refers to Aristotle's assertion that dry land exists
because the heat of the sun predominates in the north. Because
this assertion is flawed by its neglect of the fact that the sun's
heat predominates in the south as well (where the earth is not
visible), he says that Averroes added the numerous number of stars
in the north as additional causes of the drying of the visible
part of the earth (p. 352, ll. 2ff.). Both Aristotle and Averroes
would agree, however, that the existence of dry land is caused by
the nature of the heavenly bodies. For a summary of Gersonides'
refutation of this claim, see above, note #392.

The significance of this issue lies in his assertion that the
nature of the visible part of the earth constitutes an argument in
support of the generation of the world. As one of the things whose
existence is continuous, the visible part of the earth is the subject of his investigation in the first part of this treatise. He
argues there that if it can be shown that those things with continuous existence have the characteristics of things which come to
be, then the world as a whole must have come to be (6:1:5). He
shows that the visible part of the earth possesses those characteristics, one of which is that it has aspects which are not a necessary consequence of its nature, in that it is elevated above the
water (6:1:6 and 13). If, however, we were to assume that the dry
land came to be because of the natures of the heavenly bodies and
of the elements earth and water, as Aristotle and Averroes assume,
then this argument for the generation of the world would fail.
Thus, the Torah mentions the creation of dry land before it mentions the creation of the stars in order to indicate that the former did not proceed necessarily from the latter.

In the parallel passage of his commentary, he adds the
following (CT 12a, l. 49-12b, l. 1):

> It is impossible for this coming to be (of the visible
> part of the earth) to be related to the stars, because
> if this were the case, the place of the visible part of
> the earth would be the complete rotation, for these
> stars rotate completely around the part of the earth
> which is below them in a single relation. We do not
> find this to be the case. Rather we find that the visi-
> ble part of the earth is not greater than half of the
> circumference of that visible place.

412) I.e., on the third "day."

413) I.e., on the fourth "day."

414) I.e., on the visible part of the earth. Cf. above 6:1:13,
p. 350, ll. 5-7; 6:2:8, p. 431, l. 10f.; and note #296.

415) The problem which he is addressing here is that the Torah
describes the creation of the plant species on the third day as
well as the creation of the visible part of the earth. His explanation of the mention of the creation of the visible part of the
earth prior to the mention of the creation of the stars, however,
does not explain the prior mention of the creation of the plant
species the existence of which, unlike the visible part of the
earth, is related to the nomos which overflows from the heavenly
bodies. His additional explanation here is that, in mentioning
the plant species with the visible part of the earth, the Torah is
teaching us something about why the earth was elevated above the
water contrary to the natures of these two elements. That is, the
earth was elevated for the sake of the existence of the plant
species, which therefore are mentioned even though they are caused
by the divine nomos (cf. CT 11a, ll. 17-20).

416) Cf. above, p. 431, l. 22f., where he locates the unity of
"evening" and the "morning" of the third "day" (Gen 1:13) in the
fact that the appearance of the earth is for the sake of those
things which come to be on it.

417) Which is discussed on the second "day." In this context,
the term ha-gerem ha-shemiymiy refers to the creation of the
spheres alone out of the body which does not preserve its shape.
Cf. above, 6:2:8, p. 429, ll. 19-34, and note #136.

418) I.e., that the stars exist for the sake of the spheres,
as he explains below, p. 436, l. 9f. Note that the phrase baᶜavur
ᶜaṣmutam here and the phrase ᵓel ᶜaṣmutam below in line 10 are
ambiguous syntactically. Thus, it is possible to infer, on the
basis of this passage, that the erroneous assumption to which he is
referring is that the spheres are for the sake of the stars. This
reading is not impossible. He may be suggesting that though the
spheres do move the stars with their rotations, the spheres do not
rotate for the sake of moving the stars, i.e., their spherical
rotations are perfect in themselves and their final cause or purpose is their separate movers and not the stars. Though our text
can be read this way, other statements of Gersonides indicate that
he does think that the spheres' motions are for the sake of moving
the stars (see, e.g., 5:2:2, p. 192, l. 1). On either reading of

the phrase, however, his point is that the Torah wants to indicate that the relationships between the spheres and the stars are not a necessary consequence of their natures.

419) That is, the primary intention of the creation of the stars would have been thought to be the perfection of the spheres. Only secondarily would their function have been to perfect the nomos of lower existent things. If this were the case, one could argue that the activities of the stars follow necessarily from the nature of the supralunar world. In that case, the part of his argument for creation based upon the nature of the supralunar world would be invalidated (cf. 6:1:7 and 8).

His phrase here is ʿal ha-kavanah ha-shenit which may be understood as "by a second intention." That is, he may be suggesting that if the Torah had not warned us against assuming that the stars existed to perfect the spheres, we might have been led to a dualistic belief that God did not create the supralunar and sublunar worlds in a united way. See above, 6:2:8, p. 430, ll. 24-29, for an indication of his concern with this issue. Alternately, he may be suggesting that we might have been led to a belief that God created with more than one act of will.

420) In his response to the first doubt above (p. 434, l. 35-p. 435, l. 18; cf. notes #401 and #402), he argues that the spheres and their movers exist for their own sake but that they nevertheless benefit lower existent things through their own functions. They do not, however, derive any perfection from the benefits which overflow from them to lower existent things.

He seems to be refining that point here. That is, the stars, the activities of which are the aspect of the supralunar world from which the divine nomos overflows to lower existent things, do not perfect the spheres. The spheres are perfect without the stars. Thus, as he argues in the first part of this treatise (6:1:8), the stars are nonessential characteristics of the heavenly body. Their diverse sizes, colors, radiations, etc. do not follow necessarily from the nature of the heavens. For this reason, the heavens do not derive perfection from their activities and from the consequences of their activities, i.e., the perfection of the sublunar world.

Note, however, that he is not arguing that spheres, unlike stars, exist in a way that is essential to the nature of their movers. Though it is the nature of each of the separate intellects

to move its sphere in a perfect spherical motion as a consequence
of its attempt to conceive the divine nomos (cf. above, note #215),
he notes in the first part of this treatise that the variation in
quantities among the spheres does not follow necessarily from their
nature or from the nature of their movers (6:1:7, p. 317, 11.
12ff.). Thus, the characteristics of the spheres as well as the
stars constitute evidence for the generation of the heavens. His
comments here are not intended to distinguish between spheres and
stars in this respect. Rather, he is saying that the hiatus
between the Torah's discussion of the creation of the spheres on
the second "day" and its discussion of the creation of the stars
on the fourth "day" is intended to cause us to reflect upon the
characteristics of the heavenly body which do not follow necessarily
from its nature.

421) That is, the sequence of the Torah's discussion helps us
to see that the heavens possess many nonessential properties and
that the spheres and the stars must function for the sake of lower
existent things, since their activities do not perfect themselves.
These are characteristics of things which come to be, as he explains
in the first part of this treatise (6:1:6-9). Thus, because the
heavens possess the characteristics of things which come to be, the
universe as a whole must have been generated, because it is impossible for the world to have existed prior to the coming to be of
the heavens (6:1:5). Cf. Guide 2:19, for Maimonides' argument that
the state of affairs of the heavens can only be explained as the
consequence of purposeful action and not of necessity.

422) On the second "day."

423) For his interpretation of the second "day" in this way,
see above, p. 429, 11. 19ff. and note #256. For a discussion of
his understanding of the elemental forms, also cf. notes #49 and
#51.

424) That is, on the second "day," part of the body which does
not preserve its shape from which the sublunar world comes to be
is given the elemental forms, which exist in this prior stage in
concentric, noncomposite layers. This prior stage does not designate temporal priority since the sequence of the six "days" of
creation is not a temporal sequence. Rather, the reception by
lower matter of the forms of the elements enables it to receive the
divine nomos which overflows from the supralunar world through the
actions of the contrary qualities of the elements. Through the

actions of these contraries upon each other, the process of coming
to be and passing away is initiated in which the lower matter is
informed by all of the forms of lower existent things. Insofar as
the elements do not actually exist in the sublunar world in noncomposite form, the elemental forms can be described as "close to
privation." They exist for the sake of the forms of existent
things which are the "perfection" to which he refers here.

425) Which are one of the things which come to be as a result
of the actions of the contrary qualities of the elements.

426) Cf. above, p. 431, l. 23, and notes #297 and #309.

427) I.e., the discussion on the third "day" of the creation of
the elevated part of the earth and of the plant species.

428) On the fourth "day."

429) I.e., the fifth "day."

430) Gen 1:20.

431) He is expanding upon the terms le-miynehem and le-miynehu
("According to their [its] species") in Gen 1:21. He infers two
points from these terms: a) that the Torah is referring to the
coming to be of the various fish and bird species; and b) that the
Torah does not mention the creation of those species which do not
come to be from their own species, i.e., those organisms which are
spontaneously generated from the mould. For his explanation of
the omission of spontaneous generation, see above, 6:2:8, p. 428,
ll. 19-28 (cf. notes #229-#232).

432) Gen 1:21.

433) See below, 6:2:8, p. 438, ll. 5-12, where he is explicit
that the good occurs when a thing performs the purpose for the
sake of which it exists. In the present case, the species of fish
and birds can be said to be good because they exist for the sake
of those species to which they are hylically prior and ultimately
for the sake of the human species. On hylic priority, see above,
6:2:8, p. 427, l. 31-p. 428, l. 3 and note #215.

434) ḥaniynah. The world is created through divine grace
inasmuch as it was not a necessary consequence of God's nature.
Rather, He created the world by choice, because of His volition
that part of His perfection overflow to other existent things
(cf. above, 6:1:18, p. 377, ll. 3-7; 6:2:8, p. 435, ll. 1-7).

Divine grace should not, however, be taken to be distinct from
divine will. Rather it is an aspect of the single action of the
divine will in its instantaneous creation of the universe—the
aspect that we conceive when we contemplate the goodness of the
universe and when we understand that God does not need His creation.
His creation is thus an unmerited, unnecessary, gracious gift.
(See J. Klatzkin ᵓOṣar Ha-Munaḥim Ha-Filosofim 1:316, where he
defines ḥanan as "natan matanat ḥinam.") Thus, when Gersonides
uses this term here and in l. 29 below, he refers to the goodness
and grace of creation. Elsewhere (6:2:9, p. 433, l. 14; 6:2:12,
p. 456, l. 11) he speaks of the goodness, grace and providence
which are characteristic of marvels. With regard to both the laws
of the created world and marvels, he is not suggesting that divine
grace acts apart from divine will but rather that the causes and
consequences of the divine will are gracious.

435) Cf. De Partibus Animalium.

436) On the limitations of human knowledge, see above, notes
#3, #232, #310. Cf. CT 2a, ll. 15-21, where he writes:

> It is impossible for us to conceive with perfection
> the existence of existent things in the way that they
> (exist) in wisdom and grace. Rather we conceive lit-
> tle of the wisdom of their nature as is clear to one
> who speculates extensively in the science of existent
> things and knows the relation of the order through
> which we conceive of existent things to the intelli-
> gible order from which their existence develops. We
> have expanded upon this assertion in the first and
> fifth treatises of The Wars of the Lord in our inves-
> tigation of whether it is possible for the intellect
> in us to reach the level of the Active Intellect.

437) The Riva di Trento edition has ha-ᵓareṣ for ha-mayim, as
does the Pococke manuscript. The manuscript of the Bibliothèque
Nationale agrees with the Leipzig edition.

438) Gen 1:22.

439) Gen 1:23. On his understanding of the phrase va-yehiy
ᶜerev va-yehiy voqer, see above, notes #245 and #309. He considers
the species of fish and birds to be "united" in the sense that
they are on a higher level than plant species but on a lower level
than species of walking animals. The latter are closest to the
human species and their respective creations are mentioned on the
same day (cf. CT 12b, ll. 15-17).

440) Cf. above, 6:2:8, p. 428, ll. 1ff., where he explains
that fish produce imperfect eggs and birds produce perfect eggs.
As explained there, note #217, the level of a species corresponds
to the efficiency with which it reproduces by nature.

Also, cf. CT 12b, ll. 3ff. for a discussion of the hierarchy
of the species. He cites a rabbinic comment (b. Ḥullin 27b)
there (l. 14) that birds are intermediate between fish and walking
animals. This is another instance of his assumption of identity
of the truths of the Torah and speculation.

441) I.e., the classes of fish and birds. A class (sug)
consists of the variety of different species in each case, viz.,
a genus.

442) I.e., the species of walking animals which do not receive
this blessing on the sixth "day."

443) Cf. above, 6:2:8, p. 428, ll. 1ff. and CT 12b, ll. 3ff.

444) In the first treatise (1:7, p. 49, ll. 30ff.), Gersonides
discusses the various "instruments" (kelim) with which the different sublunar species are endowed by nature from the Active Intellect and which insure their preservation. His list of these
instruments includes: the different faculties of the soul; different kinds of limbs which allow predators to obtain food; and
instinctive behavior patterns such as those which bees possess.
In his discussion there, he also mentions different aspects of the
sublunar world which insure the preservation of the human species,
such as the existence of wool to be used for clothing. While the
precise phenomenon to which he is referring here is open to speculation, it is clearly some organic or behavioral characteristic
which birds and fish possess by nature, such as their hard shells
or their instinctive affinity for protected breeding grounds.
Divine providence, as he explains in the fourth treatise, does not
refer to the personal overseeing of individual members of species
but rather to the nature which species possess and which enable
them to perpetuate their own existence. Insofar as they receive
their natures from the divine nomos which overflows from the supralunar world and ultimately from God, God can figuratively be said
to have "given" them their natures and to exercise providence over
them (see above, note #217).

445) That is, the human species reproduces with the development
of the fetus within the body of the mother as the species of

walking animals do (cf. above, 6:2:8, p. 428, l. 3; p. 437, ll.
1, 3). He has just explained that the walking animals therefore
did not require the additional providence over their survival
which birds and fish require to protect their eggs. He therefore
must now explain that the statement, "Be fruitful and multiply"
does not denote the blessing of additional divine providence when
it is said of the human species (Gen 1:28) as it does when it is
said of birds and fish (Gen 1:22).

   446) Gen 1:28.

   447) CT 12b, ll. 26-40, where he writes:

> Another reason which requires that this statement is a
> commandment and not the giving of the nature to pro-
> create is that this activity, i.e., the joining of
> male and female, is the choice of man, for a man has
> the potential to do this activity or not to do it. It
> is also possible for him to do it without being fruit-
> ful when he "cohabits naturally but scatters it with-
> out" (Gen. Rab. 85:5), as our rabbis, may their mem-
> ories be for a blessing, said concerning Onan with
> regard to what the Torah relates about him: "Whenever
> he joined with his brother's wife, he let it spoil on
> the ground" (Gen 38:9). This is not the case with the
> rest of the animals. The Lord, may He be blessed, pre-
> ferred one of the two alternative choices so that the
> choice would necessarily be a commandment for him and
> not his nature. This being the case, the statement is
> undoubtedly a commandment. This is mentioned here
> because it accords with the degree of perfection of
> human perfection, for in this way the human species
> endures. Because it mentions here the creation of the
> other things which are born from their species and the
> causes which help them to preserve their species so
> that existence will be extended, it also mentions this
> commandment with the mention of the creation of man by
> the Lord.

Thus, the human species does not require additional divine
providence to perpetuate the species with respect to its biological
functions, insofar as a fetus develops within the mother's womb
and is not subject to the dangers which imperil the egg of a fish
or of a bird. The human species does need the commandment to
procreate, however, because the human species alone has the choice
to procreate and does not do so instinctively as do the lower
species.

   Also see CT 13a, ll. 29ff., where he discusses the halakhic
specifications of the commandment to reproduce. On the distinction
between the giving of a commandment and the giving of a nature, see
also CT 12d, l. 24.

   448) I.e., the sixth degree or "day." Gen 1:24ff.

449) I.e., He created, through His single act of will, all these species simultaneously at the moment of creation. Note that the manuscripts consulted omit the world ha-gedolim (large) at p. 432, l. 11. The manuscript reading concurs with this following statement that the creation of all walking animals, large and small, is being discussed.

450) Gen 1:25.

451) The animal species can be said to have a divine nature insofar as their forms are a part of the divine nomos which overflows to them through the Active Intellect. They can be said to be "good" insofar as they are part of the divine plan the intention of which culminates with the human species, for the sake of which the animal species exist. See above, note #215, and his statement in the first treatise (1:6, p. 37, ll. 29ff.):

> Some of the forms are the perfection of others in a way that all end with a single form which is their perfection, i.e., the human form, for it is (the human form) which prime matter receives by means of the other forms which it has the potential to receive, and it is (the human form) which is in the degree of perfection and form for them.

Cf. 1:6, p. 40, ll. 20ff.

452) Gen 1:26. He shows his acquaintance with the rabbinic view that the human species partly resembles both upper and lower beings in his citation of Gen. Rab. 12:8 above, 6:2:7, p. 427. In his commentary on this verse (CT 12d, l. 3), he refers to the view of Maimonides that the human intellect is related in some way to the world of the angels. Cf. Guide 1:1 (Pines translation, p. 22).

453) Gen 1:28.

454) Ve-khein hayah. The Riva di Trento edition has ve-khein raṣah, which may be a dittographic error, since the next word is roṣeh. The parallel passage in the commentary (CT 13a, l. 9) and the manuscripts consulted have ve-khein ᶜasah (And He did so.).

455) Sekhel ha-hiyulaᵓniy. Treatise I is devoted to a discussion of the nature of the hylic intellect and to the question of whether the human soul can become immortal and everlasting through the development of the hylic intellect. For a discussion of this treatise, see Seymour Feldman, "Gersonides on the Possibility of Conjunction with the Agent Intellect," AJS Review 3(1978):99-120.

Briefly, Gersonides explains in the first treatise that the hylic intellect is the disposition of the human soul to acquire concepts. It is not an actually existent substance but rather a disposition. In the hylic intellect all concepts have a potential existence. Thus, it can be said that the hylic intellect has the potential to conceive the nomos of existent things and that such conception is its end. These potential conceptions are actualized by the Active Intellect when the hylic intellect apprehends hylic forms, i.e., the forms of material existent things, by abstracting their true, general conceptions from their material instantiations. When conceptions are actualized in this way in the human intellect, they are referred to as the "acquired intellect."

Thus, he is saying here that God created the human species with the potential to conceive through the disposition of the hylic intellect, and that conception is the function which defines the human form. This is his understanding of the statement in Gen 1:27 that humans were created in the image of God.

Note his expanded discussion in his commentary to the second chapter of Genesis. He asserts there that the gan (garden) is an allusion to the hylic intellect, for as the plants in the garden were potentially man's, so are the conceptions which exist poten-tially in the hylic intellect (CT 14b, ll. 41ff.). The nature which leads him to the acquisition of actual conceptions is the manifest goodness, order and rightness of lower existent things, which leads man to investigate the intelligible order of sublunar existence (CT 14d, ll. 22ff.).

456) As he explains in the first treatise, the conceptions which the human intellect acquires are identical to the conception which the Active Intellect has of the order of lower existent things. In fact, these conceptions exist primarily in the soul of the Active Intellect and it is this actual existence which serves as both the formal and efficient cause of the actualization of the conceptions in the hylic intellect. Thus, the human intellect is related to the Active Intellect. And, insofar as the Active Intel-lect conceives of the nomos which overflows from the actions of the heavenly bodies and which is a combination of the conceptions of each of the separate movers, the human intellect can also be said to be related to the other separate intellects.

He qualifies this assertion here by saying that "the human intellect is related in some way" for a number of reasons. First, as he states in the first treatise, the Active Intellect knows the

heavenly bodies and their movers as an effect knows its cause (1:7,
p. 51). Though an effect can know its cause by knowing its own
nature and its relation to its cause, this knowledge is of a weak
sort. Thus, our knowledge of both the heavens and their movers
and of the Active Intellect is necessarily weak. Second, the
human intellect acquires conceptions of lower existent things in
their multiplicity, while the Active Intellect knows them in
respect to their being one in the order of existent things (1:6,
p. 37f.; 1:12, p. 86f.). Thus, though a human intellect, as it
accumulates true conceptions, may gain a progressively better
conception of the way in which all lower existent things are
interrelated in the providential governance which overflows from
the Active Intellect, it can never know that nomos as its cause
knows it. As a result of our dependence upon material embodiments
of the forms, our knowledge is such that we proceed by abstracting
each form individually and by then inferring the total plan which
we can never fully conceive. This leads to the third consideration:
The human intellect can never acquire a complete knowledge of all
aspects of all species of existent things (1:12, p. 85f.). It is
for these reasons that Gersonides argues in the first treatise
against the possibility of the conjunction or union of the human
intellect with the Active Intellect.

457) Gen 1:27.

458) He substitutes va-yeḥezqu bah for ve-khivshuha in Gen 1:28.
His motivation for doing so may be revealed in part by the following comment in the parallel passage of his commentary (CT 13a, 1.
16f.), where he adds:

> That is, He decreed at their creation that man would
> be commanded with this when a recipient was found
> through whom it would be proper to give the Torah.

Part of the intention of this comment is to clarify the relationship between the giving of the commandments at Sinai and those
commandments, such as piryah ve-rivyah, which are mentioned prior
to Sinai, as will be explained below, note #460. Nevertheless,
it appears from this comment that he may be using the term ḥozeq
to mean "a high degree of existence" as well as or rather than
"strength" or "dominance" (cf. Klatzkin, ᵓOṣar Ha-Munaḥim
Ha-Filosofiyim 1:280). That is, the human species dominates the
earth by its acquisition of conceptions and its consequent worthi-
ness to receive divine revelation.

459) Gen 1:28.

460) Note his discussion above (6:2:8, p. 436, ll. 33ff.; cf. notes #444-447) concerning the difference between the statement to be fruitful and multiply relating to the species of fish and birds (Gen 1:22) and the apparently identical statement here (Gen 1:28). He interprets the first statement to refer to the extra divine providence which the species of fish and birds needed for the perpetuation of their existence because they reproduce by laying eggs outside their bodies (see above, notes #217, #444, #445 and #447). The second statement, regarding human beings, on the other hand, is a commandment, because the human species does not need providence in this way. The danger to the perpetuation of the human species lies in human choice. Since humans can choose not to procreate, they required a commandment. Thus, his use of the term providence here (1. 23) does not refer to the statement "be fruitful and multiply" but rather to the statement "fill the earth", as he explains immediately below.

In his commentary, he deals extensively with the issue of commandents, such as "be fruitful and multiply," which are reported in the Torah to have been given prior to Sinai (CT 12b, ll. 41ff.; 12d, ll. 25ff.; 13a, ll. 22ff.). His position there is that all of the Torah in its entirety was given to Moses on Sinai. The Torah is a single nomos through which one is guided to a single purpose, i.e., human felicity, and is thus given once by a single cause at a single time. Only Moses received the entire Torah because only his intellect was sufficiently developed. The prophecy of other prophets is incomplete and partial according to the respective deficiencies of their intellects. Thus, any part of the Torah which was given through another prophet requires verification through Moses at Sinai.

461) I.e., in one section of the elevated part of the earth rather than in all of its parts.

462) 6:1:19, p. 380, ll. 20-33.

463) CT 22a, ll. 17ff. Also see his theory of the development of languages, 6:1:15, p. 356f.

464) Gen 1:28.

465) For other of his comments about the human species as the end, purpose, perfection and form of lower species, see 1:6, p. 37, ll. 29ff. (quoted above, note #451); 1:12, p. 86, ll. 8ff.(quoted

above, note #215); and CT 12d, ll. 16ff., where he refers these
comments to this verse.

466) In the parallel passage of his commentary, he adds (CT
12d, ll. 19ff.):

> The Lord, may He be blessed, blessed them by giving
> them this rulership, because one finds that many of the
> animals which are very necessary for human work are much
> stronger than human beings. If it were not for this
> rulership which human beings have over them, the end for
> the sake of which (these animals) exist would not be
> realized for humans from them.

467) He is paraphrasing Gen 1:29. He inserts the terms ṭeva^c
(nature) and koaḥ (power or potential) into the verse. The nature
of a thing is what that thing is by definition. The power or
potential of a thing is the abilities of the thing. Since what
a thing can do is determined by its nature, the two are usually
identical. Usually, the nature of a thing is defined by its
potential functions (cf. De Caelo 2.3.286a9). For example, the
human form or nature is defined by its hylic intellect, which is
what distinguishes the human soul from the souls of lower species
(cf. CT 14a, ll. 30ff.). Thus, human nature is defined by its
specific conceptual function (see above, note #358).

In the present case, it is interesting to note that he adds
in his commentary that this nature, given to humans to eat plants
as food, is a nature and not a commandment (CT 12d, l. 24). That
is, the human disposition to eat various forms of plant life is
to be contrasted with the human disposition to procreate. As he
explains above (6:2:8, p. 436, ll. 33ff.), humans have a choice
in procreating so that the divine decree to be fruitful and
multiply is a commandment and not the bestowing of a nature. By
contrast, it can be inferred that humans have no choice in eating
plants but that it is part of their nature.

468) See his discussion in 1:7, ll. 11ff., where he states
that the Active Intellect oversees the preservation of the human
species by giving humans the power to cultivate the soil and to
improve foods by cooking them. Humans need these abilities because
plants in their natural, uncooked states and in their wild, uncul-
tivated growth would not satisfy human nutritional needs and would
not ensure the preservation of the species (cf. 5:3:6, p. 260, ll.
12-19).

In the parallel passage of the commentary (CT 12d, ll. 25ff.),
he addresses the problem that occurs when one infers that the
divine will changes from Adam to Noah in that Adam is given a
vegeterian diet here while Noah is given meat as well (Gen 9:3).
He rejects rabbinic statements which suggest the possibility of a
change in divine will (Gen. Rab. 34:13), citing Maimonides'
instructions to follow the true rather than the apparent meaning
of Scripture (cf. above, notes #1, #6, #20). The present instance
is, for him, a clearcut case in which the apparent meaning of the
Scriptural text must be disregarded if it suggests that God's will
can change.

469) Natan. The Riva di Trento edition and the Pococke
manuscript have ꜣeten, the first person imperfect form of the
verb. This transforms the statement which follows into another
quote placed in God's mouth, as is the case in Gen 1:30 which is
being paraphrased.

470) Gen 1:30.

471) On the unchanging and instantaneous actualization of the
divine will, see above, notes #240, #288, #315, #332 and #468.

472) I.e., the creation of food.

473) This statement should not be interpreted as a suggestion
that he believes that a species can perish. Such a belief would
directly conflict with many explicit statements which he makes
elsewhere throughout The Wars (see, for example, 6:1:13, p. 353,
ll. 5ff.). That is, each of the species is everlasting though its
individual members come to be and pass away. The preservation of
each species is overseen by the providence of the Active Intellect
which has provided each with the powers it needs to survive. Thus,
his statement here ha-zeman ha-ꜣefshariy ("for the time that is
possible") must refer to the preservation of the existence of
individual members of species through the power given them to find
the proper nutrition.

474) Gen 1:31.

475) Gen 1:31.

476) The end of all lower existent things is the human species,
as discussed above, notes #215, #451 and #465.

477) Gen 1:31. On his interpretation of the meaning of the
recurring phrase, va-yehiy ꜥerev va-yehiy voqer, see above, notes
#245, #249, #265, #308, #309.

478) I.e., the human species is served by lower land animal species (cf. above, notes #215, #451 and #465). These are thus two different degrees of existence which are united in their inter-relationship.

479) Gen 1:31.

480) Gen 1:26.

481) Gen 1:11.

482) Gen 1:20.

483) Gen 1:24.

484) Cf. above, note #215, for a discussion of hylic forms. They are to be distinguished from separate forms in that they require material instruments to perform their specific function while separate forms have no such requirement. See his discussion above, 1:9, p. 58f., relating to the epistemological distinction between intelligible forms and hylic forms as each of them exists in the human intellect, a distinction which he attributes to Avicenna. Insofar as the form of a material object is hylic, the existence of that form is connected to the coming to be and passing away of its material embodiment. Thus, insofar as an intellect apprehends a form as hylic, the knowledge of that form will pass away with the passing away of its matter. Once, however, the intellect is able to abstract the hylic form from its matter and to conceptualize it as an intelligible form which has a conceptual existence apart from its many material instantiations, that concept exists independently of its hylic existence.

In light of this discussion, his meaning in the present statement is twofold. First, all sublunar species other than the human species have only hylic forms insofar as their forms cannot perform their function without their material instantiation. But this is also true, in part, of the human species. That is, the human form is hylic insofar as it requires material human beings to perform its function. Second, all lower forms of life cannot conceptually abstract forms from their sense perceptions. To the extent that the human intellect can do so, it can be said that part of its existence is not hylic but is rather related to the upper beings whose knowledge consists of separate forms and who are therefore immortal in that they are not connected to the coming to be and passing away of the hylic embodiments of their concepts.

485) For his understanding of the way in which the hierarchy of species comes to be from the elemental forms, see above, notes #49, #51, and #215.

486) See above, notes #455, #456 and #484, for a discussion of the way that the potential concepts in the hylic intellect are actualized by the Active Intellect when a person abstracts hylic forms and conceptualizes them into non-hylic, separate forms.

487) Qoh 12:7. He discusses this verse in his commentary to Qohelet (Peirush ʿal Ḥamesh Megillot [Riva di Trento, 1660; Reprinted Jerusalem], p. 35c), where he takes this statement as a warning to us to strive for perfection while we are alive in our material embodiment. He does not, however, explicitly interpret this verse there, as he does here, to refer to the relationship between the human intellect and the separate intellects. Note in this regard that the manuscript #723 of the Bibliothèque Nationale has be-ʾamro (in [the Torah's] saying) for kemo she-biʾarnu (as we explained). Thus, the reading of this manuscript does not assume that he has explained the verse in this way in his commentary to Qohelet.

In his discussion of the term ruaḥ above, 6:2:6, he lists the human soul as one of the senses of the term. Thus, we may infer that he is reading this verse as an allusion to that part of the human intellect which, having acquired true conceptions, "returns to God" in the sense that it becomes partially united with the conception of the Active Intellect.

488) b. Ḥag. 16a; Gen. Rab. 8:11; 12:8; 14:3; Lev. Rab. 9:9; Tanḥuma Ber. 1:15; ʾAbot R. Nat. 37; Pesiq. R. 43.

489) Le-haʿir. That is, the Torah's use of the plural form, "Let us make man" in verse 26. On the way the Torah functions to arouse us to the truth, see above, notes #1 and #410.

490) I.e., in chapter three of Genesis.

491) His discussion of the Garden of Eden story in his commentary interprets that story as a description of the way the human intellect can achieve its end of true conception and the obstacles which deter it from achieving that end. What follows is a translation of his introduction to that interpretation, which precedes his word-by-word exegesis of the story (CT 14a, ll. 1-32):

The intended purpose in (The Torah's similitudes),
according to what appears to us, is to make known the
instruments which the Lord, may He be blessed, gave to
man to bring him to spiritual success, through which we
have everlasting life. Our explanation here encompasses
everything which supports the following story (i.e.,
Gen 3:1-24) until the passage (which begins), "And Adam
knew his wife, Eve" (Gen 4:1).

That is, it is explained in De Anima that the
human intellect, at the beginning of its creation, is
naked (ᶜarum) of all conceptions which it conceives,
and that it is the Active Intellect from which its conceptions overflow by means of the sense, the imaginative
power, and the power of memory. This overflow, which
overflows to it in making known to it the deep secrets
of existence, resembles lightning or the fiery ever-
turning sword (Gen 3:24), which shines at one time and
is hidden at another time because of the difficulty of
reaching the isolation which the human intellect requires
from the other powers of the soul in this manner of
conception, as we explained in our explanation of The
Song of Songs.

The Master the Guide also discussed this in his
venerable book, The Guide of the Perplexed, and we
explained it in the first (treatise) of The Wars of the
Lord, i.e., that the success which reaches man is in
his conception of the nomos, order and rightness of
existent things, as far as that is possible for him.
In this way, his intellect lives an everlasting life.
Most of what can be known to him of the secrets of
existence is that which is in this lower world, i.e.,
its intelligible order. But his conception of the
heavens and that which is above them in degree is weak
because of the distance between his existence and their
existence in essence and in place.

It is explained in De Anima that the imaginative
power and the power of desire moves the animal to or
away from that towards which or away from which it is
moved. This imagination apprehends one of the perceptible things and the power of desire is aroused
from that apprehension so that the animal moves to
approach or to flee from that object of perception
which the imaginative power apprehends. In this way,
it occurs that a man follows after bodily pleasures
which distance him from his perfection. This power of
desire is the evil inclination and the imaginative power
is that which directs him.

Thus, it is clear to you that the imaginative
power is an instrument for the realization of perfection
for man and is also an instrument which distances (him)
from perfection. This occurs in different respects
which are intended in his nature, which is to reach perfection. It is also clear that there are human appre-
hensions which man does not have insofar as he is man
but which he shares in common, in some way, with animals—
i.e., the apprehension of good and evil.

With this as an introduction, he interprets each of the terms in
the story as aspects of the Torah's instruction to us with regard
to the realization of true success.

492) <u>Sekhel ha-niqneh</u>. In the first treatise, he explains that though the hylic intellect is only a disposition with potential conceptions (1:5), when these conceptions are actualized, the actual conceptions form the acquired intellect. This acquired intellect is everlasting because its actual conceptions do not come to be or pass away but rather exist continuously in actuality in the soul of the Active Intellect. They are only generated in respect to themselves (1:10). Thus, the acquired intellect can be said to be separate (1:11).

493) Gen 2:7.

494) See above, notes #455, #456, #484 and #492.

495) The rest of the animals only have hylic souls which apprehend hylic forms and which thus pass away with the passing away of the material instantiations of those hylic forms (cf. CT 14b, l. 17). The human soul, on the other hand, insofar as it can acquire abstracted separate conceptions which are not connected to matter, is everlasting (cf. CT 14c, l. 10f.).

496) Gen 1:24.

497) The "self-evident" nature of his distinction between two instances of the phrase <u>nefesh ḥayah</u> in Gen 1:24 and 2:7 is yet another instance of his presupposition that the Torah cannot be read as contradicting the demonstrated conclusions of reason. In this case, it is obvious that the soul of the human species is different than the soul of land animals. Therefore, the Torah must be read in this light.

498) Gen 2:7.

499) Gen 1:26, 27. At no point does he read these verses as suggesting in a literal way that man was created in the image of God. He interprets the divine aspect of the human soul suggested in these verses to refer to the everlasting nature of the acquired intellect which is related to the separate intellects, i.e., the upper beings (<u>ha-ᶜelyonim</u>), insofar as it acquires separate conceptions.

500) Gen 2:19f.

501) As discussed above, notes #264, #289 and #291, the Torah's use of the term "name" is a way of indicating the perpetual, unchanging nature of the thing named (cf. CT 10a, ll. 45ff.). He makes this explicit in the parallel passage of his commentary to this verse, where he states (CT 14b, ll. 21ff.):

When (the Torah) says that "whatever Adam called
each living creature, that would be its name" (Gen
2:19),...it does not intend that the names Adam employed
were called according to conventional language alone,
apart from their indicating the essence of this thing
called by this name. Rather, the intention of calling
by name is that which indicates the essence of each
thing. The names which have this state of affairs are
definitions.

(The rabbis) said in Genesis Rabbah (17:4): When
the Lord came to create the first human being, He took
counsel with the ministering angels. He said to them:
Let us make man (Gen 1:26). They said to Him: What
will be the nature of this man? He said to them: His
wisdom will exceed yours. He brought birds, animals
and beasts before them and said to them: What should
the name of this be? But they did not know. He brought
them before Adam and said to Him: What should the name
of this be? He said: This is an ox and this is an ass
and this is a horse and this is a camel, etc.

(The rabbis) indicate to you that the calling of
these names is a marvelous wisdom. Now if the calling
of them were according to conventional language alone,
there would be no wisdom in it, because he could call by
any name he chose.... But when we posit that these names
(refer to) the essence of the things named by these
names, there is wisdom in this which should not be hidden from any of the men of speculation. Therefore, (the
rabbis), may their memories be for a blessing, related
the calling of these names to a marvelous wisdom and
said that for everything which man calls by name in this
way, that name is a soul in which life exists in itself.
That name is the conception of the thing named by it,
and these conceptions are everlasting when they reach
man, as we explained in the first (treatise) of The Wars
of the Lord.

Note that he may be citing Genesis Rabbah here in support of
another of his theses. That is, the separate intellects which move
the spheres, to which he generally takes the term "angels" to refer,
do not conceive of all of the forms in the nomos of lower existent
things. Each of them conceives only of God, itself and the motions
of its specific sphere (cf. above, note #224). Only the Active
Intellect conceives of the nomos which overflows from the combination of all of the motions of the spheres, and even the Active
Intellect conceives of the forms of existence things only insofar
as they are each a part of the one nomos (1:6). He may thus be
interpreting the distinction which this midrash makes to refer to
the difference between human conception and the conception of the
separate intellects.

502) The specific function of the hylic intellect is to
conceive definitions (1:4, p. 29, ll. 7ff.) which make known the

essence of the individual in which the definition inheres (1:10,
p. 63, 11. 31ff.; p. 68, 1. 32f.). It is a general nature which
exists in each individual which is defined by it, and through it
each individual can be conceived as one (1:2, p. 16, 11. 11ff.;
11. 32ff.).

503) This is his interpretive reading of the latter part of
Gen 2:19, based on his assumption that the phrase nefesh ḥayah in
this verse has the meaning of the phrase in Gen 2:7 and not in
Gen 1:24 (see above, note #497).

504) The respective terms are: ṣiyur (apprehension) and
haʾamatah (verification). He distinguishes between the two terms
in the first treatise, where he associates apprehension with a
knowledge of definitions and states that it is prior to verification, which is a judgment about objects of apprehension (1:10,
p. 63, 1. 22-p. 64, 1. 20). Elsewhere, in the context of investigating the question of the immortality of the acquired intellect,
he states that the acquired intellect is composed of two species of
perfection: apprehension and verification. Apprehension has no
connection with material things which exist outside the soul but
is rather the knowledge of the order which exists perpetually in
the soul of the Active Intellect, i.e., the knowledge of forms
abstracted from their hylic embodiments. Verification, by contrast,
is connected with material substances which exist outside the soul
because it is composed of intellect and sense. Thus, he concludes
that the perfection which the Active Intellect actualizes in the
acquired intellect is that of apprehension alone, since it is only
in the process of apprehension that human conceptions are abstracted
from hylic forms (1:11, p. 82, 11. 3-18).

Based upon his use of these terms in the first treatise, we
may infer that he is saying here that the acquired intellect is
everlasting insofar as it is composed of conceptions which have
been apprehended, i.e., have been conceived as definitions which
have a separate existence apart from their material instantiations.
Though the acquired intellect has another function—that of veri-
fying the nature of material substances by judging them in light
of their definitions—it is not everlasting by virtue of this
function. This is because verification is connected to material
substances and anything so connected comes to be and passes away
with the coming to be and passing away of material things.

505) Gen 2:20.

506) Cf. above, note #232, for a discussion of this term.

507) 1:13, p. 89f. He asserts there that, insofar as the
Active Intellect conceives of all things in respect to their being
part of one nomos, and insofar as the degree of human felicity is
related to the extent that one's acquired intellect approximates
the conception of the Active Intellect, one ought to strive to
acquire the greatest possible number of true conceptions. The more
one conceives of the nomos of existent things, the more one conceives of their oneness as the Active Intellect does, and greater
joy and success is correlated to the unity of one's conception.
Thus, one ought to begin by conceiving the lower existent species
and should then proceed from conception to conception and from one
degree of existence to the next.

508) In 1:8 above, he lists three different views of his
philosophic predecessors concerning the immortality of the human
intellect. The first, which he attributes to Alexander of Aphrodisias, Themistius and Averroes (according to the latter's discussions in his Epitome to De Anima and his three letters), is that
it is possible for the hylic intellect to be immortal when it
reaches the degree of perfection at which it conceives of conceptions which are intellect in themselves (i.e., separate), particularly the Active Intellect. It cannot gain immortality, however,
by conceiving conceptions of lower existent things, because,
according to this view, such conceptions come to be and pass away.
The second view, which he attributes to Avicenna and his followers
(as Averroes reports their views in his Epitome to De Anima), is
that the acquired intellect is everlasting, because neither conceptions of lower existent things nor the hylic intellect come to
be and pass away. The third view, which he attributes to Alfarabi,
is that it is impossible for the hylic intellect to become immortal
and everlasting, because the hylic intellect itself comes to be
and that which comes to be must pass away.

While it is unclear to whom Gersonides is referring here, it
is interesting to note that, unlike his practice with regard to
other subjects of discussion, he does not refer in the first treatise to the position of Maimonides on the immortality of the soul.
While Maimonides seems to have held views resembling his own with
regard to the immortality of the acquired intellect and the
perishability of the hylic intellect (Guide 1:68, 70; Yad, Hilkhot
Yesodei Ha-Torah 4:9, Hilkhot Teshuvah 8:2; cf. the discussion of

Harry Blumberg, "The Problem of Immortality in Avicenna, Maimonides
and St. Thomas Aquinas," Harry Austryn Wolfson Jubilee Volume,
edited by Saul Lieberman [Jerusalem, 1965], pp. 174-180), he can be
interpreted in the Guide to have accepted Ibn Bajja's view that
the immortality of the acquired intellect is not individual.
(Guide 1:74, seventh way. See the discussion of Shlomo Pines in
his introductory essay, "The Philosophic Sources of The Guide of
the Perplexed" to his translation of the Guide, p. ciiif. For a
more complete exposition of the views of Ibn Bajja, see Alexander
Altmann, "Ibn Bajja on Man's Ultimate Felicity," Studes in Religious Philosophy and Mysticism [Ithaca, 1969], pp. 73-107.) Thus,
the present passage may be an oblique reference to the position of
Maimonides who, if Pines is correct, would have disagreed with
Gersonides on the question of individual immortality. Maimonides
attributes the source of this view to Ibn Bajja (Guide 1:74), so
that the latter may be the philosopher who Gersonides believes has
blinded Maimonides.

509) For his discussion of the purpose of the Torah, see CT
2aff. and note #1 above.

510) I.e., the seventh "day," Gen 2:1-3.

511) I.e., in the way that it was instantaneously actualized
by a single act of divine will, as described on the first six
"days."

512) In the parallel passage of his commentary, he adds the
following comment at this point (CT 13c, ll. 29ff.): "For
example, a house, when it is built, endures if the builder is
absent."

513) Zoᵓt ha-hasagah ha-nikhbedet she-be-hasagot. In the
parallel passage of his commentary, he writes (CT 13c, ll. 31ff.):
"On the seventh day, the Lord, may He be blessed, desired the
intelligible order of created things so that that desire is the
cause of the continuing duration of existence."

Note that the manuscripts consulted insert the following after
ṣerikhah ᵓel ha-poᶜel tamid (needs its cause perpetually) and
before ve-zeh ᵓamnam (This occurs), at p. 439, l. 34: yaᶜamideha
ve-yishmereha ve-ᵓofen haᶜamadat ha-Shem yitbarakh ha-ᶜolam huᵓ
she-huᵓ yasig ᶜaṣmuto tamid (to sustain it and to preserve it.
The way that the Lord, may He be blessed, sustains the world is
that He perpetually conceives of Himself.). If we follow the

manuscript reading, as Touati advises, then our translation at
439, 1. 35 should read "when He perpetually" for "when it perpetually." As noted below in note #515, the manuscript readings suggest that he is polemically engaged here in asserting that the
separate intellects move the spheres because of their conceptions
of the perfect divine nomos of God's self-conception and not
because of their conceptions of the relatively imperfect nomos in
their own souls.

514) Ḥesheq. He is using this as a technical term which
denotes that which motivates a thing to realize its own end. As
discussed above, note #215, he conceives of the universe as a
hierarachical order in which each species has been given a natural,
specific function which is its end. In the supralunar world, as
he will explain immediately below, each of the separate intellects
has the desire to conceive of the perfect divine nomos as perfectly as it possibly can. The consequence of this desire is that
each separate intellect moves its sphere according to its conception of the divine nomos and that the combination of these supralunar motions overflows through the Active Intellect to the sublunar world which is governed by that nomos. In the sublunar
world, the hierarchical order takes the form of hylic priority, in
which it is the function of each species to serve those species
which are hylically posterior to it and in which all sublunar
species as a whole serve the human species and contribute to its
realization of its end—the acquisition of true conceptions. In
each case, a species can be said to fulfill its function in the
hierarchical order because of its respective desire for the divine
nomos, which is its final cause. This desire is most apparent,
however, among separate intellects and in the part of the human
soul which is related to the separate intellects—i.e., the
acquisition of true conceptions by the actualization of potential
conceptions in the hylic intellect (cf. 5:3:7; CT 13c, 11. 4ff.).

515) Cf. his explanation of this phenomenon in his commentary,
where he writes (CT 13c, 11. 15-23):

> This desire which the Lord, may He be exalted, has for
> this intelligible order is the cause of its perpetual
> apprehension of the Lord, may He be exalted. In this
> apprehension, this existence is preserved in its defi-
> nition, as is clear to one who emphasizes speculation
> about divine things. The reason for this is that the
> separate intellects desire to resemble their creator
> so that there can also proceed from them the cause,

form and end (of existence). They apprehend this
order according to their degrees and they desire to
do what that order decrees, according to the actions
which the Lord, may He be exalted, gave to them for
the perfection and preservation of the world. On
account of this apprehension, the spheres are moved
in the way that they are moved and in this way all
(sublunar) existent things are perfected.

On the deficiency of the conception of the separate intellects in
relation to the perfect conception of the First Cause, see his
discussion in 5:3:12, pp. 278ff.

Note that the manuscripts consulted read min ha-sheqer for
min ha-ḥesheq at p. 440, l. 2. This accords with the additional
phrase of the manuscripts immediately above, noted in note #513.
That is, according to the manuscript reading, this sentence would
read as follows: "For it is false that (the movers) have this
wonderful desire in respect to the imperfect nomos which is in
their souls." This reading would suggest that Gersonides is
arguing polemically against the view of Averroes that the separate
intellects move their spheres because, in themselves, they know
that their perfection is in circular motion. (See Averroes' Long
Commentary on the Metaphysics, edited by Bouyges, p. 1595; cf.
H. A. Wolfson, "Averroes' Lost Treatise on the Prime Mover,"
Hebrew Union College Annual 23.1(1950-1951):683-710. Whereas
Averroes identifies God as the First Mover of the outermost sphere,
Gersonides rejects this view above, 5:3:11. In our text here,
revised according to the manuscripts, he is asserting that the
separate intellects move out of their desire for the perfect divine
nomos and not as a result of their own self-conception (cf. Guide
1:69).

516) His reference to the soul of the Lord should not be taken
to suggest that God is composite in any sense. It is to be taken
figuratively, as when he speaks of the souls of the separate intellects. Among the faculties of the soul in lower existent things is
the rational faculty, i.e., the power to conceive. Insofar as God
is pure, perfect conception conceiving itself (cf. 5:3:12, p. 279),
He may be described figuratively as having a soul (cf. De Anima
2.3). His soul, however, is nothing other than His essence (cf.
5:3:12, pp. 280ff.; 6:2:8, p. 430, ll. 29ff.).

517) See above, 6:1:7, p. 310, l. 22-p. 312, l. 14, where he
makes this argument in great detail. Also see below, 6:2:12, p.
456, ll. 8ff.

518) That is, through their desire to resemble the divine
nomos, they move their spheres and stars, and through these
motions the divine nomos overflows to lower existent things (cf.
above, notes #215, #251 and #514).

519) Gen 2:1.

520) Gen 2:2. As he will argue below, he wants to translate
va-yekhal in this verse as "desired." See above, note #514, on
the term ḥesheq. His motivation in arguing for this translation is
clearly to avoid the problems consequent upon the alternative
translation which suggests that God must have been performing some
work which He ceased on the seventh day. Gersonides, in reading
the account of the first six "days" as referring to an instantaneous
actualization of a single act of divine will, would rather understand va-yekhal as referring to God's relation to the world after
the moment of its creation. As the First Cause of the nomos of
existent things, God perpetually knows all existent things as they
are united in the divine nomos. He knows them in this way in the
process of knowing Himself, since the divine nomos is that which
overflows from His conception (5:3:12, pp. 278ff.). Thus, there
is no action involved in the creation of the first six "days"—
apart from a single act of the divine will—and there is no cessation of action to be described on the seventh "day." Rather, after
having willed the existence of the universe, God knows it perpetually and perfectly, and it is this knowledge which sustains the
world.

His use of the term ḥesheq ("desire") to translate va-yekhal,
however, has its own problems. As mentioned above, note #514,
ḥesheq is a term which denotes the motivation of a thing to perform its own end. To say that God desires the world in this sense
would seem to entail that this desire is part of His activity—
that it fulfills Him. He deals with this problem below (6:2:8,
p. 440, ll. 26ff.), where he attempts to explicate the difference
between divine and human desire. We may also assume that his
argument above (6:2:8, p. 434, ll. 35ff.)—where he argues that
God and the supralunar world perfect the sublunar world without
acquiring their perfection from it—also applies here. That is,
since God acquires no perfection from the world, it cannot be said
to be His end. (See above, notes #400, #401). Thus, he must be
using the term ḥesheq equivocally with reference to God as he
suggests in his discussions below, p. 440, ll. 26ff. We may

assume that it is for this reason that he remarks below that he
prefers another interpretation of va-yekhal to this one (6:2:8,
p. 441, l. 4f.).

521) As he explains in the third treatise, God does not know
the multiple, material embodiments of the forms of the divine
nomos. He knows all species of things insofar as they are one in
their form, and He knows all forms insofar as they are one in the
divine nomos. He knows them through His single act of self-
conception. His clarification here is designed to explain that
God can be said to desire only the conception of creation and not
all existent things that come to be as a result of that conception.

522) I.e., in the way that he has described above (6:2:8,
p. 439, ll. 34ff.)—that God's conception of the divine nomos
causes the separate intellects to move the spheres and stars as
they do and that all of creation overflows from these motions
(cf. above, notes #215, #514, #515).

523) The manuscripts consulted insert the following after ᵓelu
and before ha-meṣiyᵓut at p. 440, l. 19: ha-peᶜulot ᵓasher ᶜasah
(be-ᶜet) ḥidusho ha-ᶜolam kiy kevar natan (ha-)ṭevaᶜ (be-)nimṣaᵓot
le-hamshikh. A translation based upon the manuscript reading
would read as follows:

> In the way that He is, it is not necessary (for Him)
> to do anything (with His desire), as is the case with
> these (other) causes which He made at (the moment)
> that He generated the world. This is because He gave
> existent things (the) nature to continue existence,
> viz., the perpetual desire which the movers of the
> heavenly bodies possess to be subjected...

In this case, the manuscript reading is easier than the text
which underlies the printed editions, though the latter is not
impossible.

524) Gen 2:3. In his commentary (CT 12b, ll. 41ff.; 12d, ll.
25ff.; 13a, ll. 22ff.), he gives an explicit explanation of his
understanding that all of the commandments, including those which
the Torah mentions prior to Sinai, were given all at once at
Sinai through the prophecy of Moses. In the case of the commandment to be fruitful and multiply, the commandment is mentioned
earlier because it was needed immediately for the preservation of
the human species. The commandment of circumcision, given to
Abraham, was to be used as a sign of the covenant prior to Sinai.
We may assume that he regards the statement here about the Sabbath
as an explanation of the commandment which was not given until Sinai.

525) The "kind of actions" which were caused at the moment of the instantaneous actualization of creation came to be through a single act of divine will. Subsequent to the moment of creation, things come to be by natural custom, i.e., according to their natures (CT 13c, 1. 33f.). Though these natures were willed at creation, subsequent functioning does not require further acts of divine will. Rather, in conceiving the nomos which perpetually overflows from Him and which contains the natures of all things, God sustains the world by allowing it to follow natural custom (cf. below, 6:2:10, p. 452, 11. 5-19).

The distinction between the willful coming to be which occurred at the moment of creation and the natural coming to be which occurs thereafter serves as a basis in the first part of this treatise for his refutation of arguments for the eternity of the world which rely on an analogy between the characteristics of instances of coming to be in this world and the coming to be of the world as a whole (cf. above, note #240).

526) Gen 2:2.

527) Va-tekhal. 2 Sam 13:39.

528) Kaltah. Ps 84:3.

529) Va-tekhal. 2 Sam 13:39.

530) In that the verb, va-tekhal, is feminine and suggests therefore a feminine subject such as "soul." In our passage, however, va-yekhal has a masculine gender and thus does not imply the soul of God as its subject.

531) Through the sensory power of the soul, animals and human beings alike are able to perceive good and evil and are able to pursue that which is pleasant and flee from that which is unpleasant (CT 14a, 11. 26ff.; cf. above, 6:2:8, p. 433, 1. 32f.). In the case of the lower species, this power of the soul can itself be identified with their desire (ḥesheq), i.e., with their motivation to fulfill their end which is the perpetuation of their species in a way that the human species can be properly served. The human soul also has a rational power by which it can acquire true conceptions of the things it perceives (see above, notes #455, #456, #491). The desire of the human soul, i.e., its motivation to fulfill its function of true conception, occurs as a consequence fo its perception of the apparent order of lower existent things and its longing to conceive them truly in their oneness (CT 14a, 11. 1ff.).

532) On the unitary, noncomposite nature of God, see above,
5:3:12, pp. 280ff.

533) Gen 2:2.

534) Gen 2:2.

535) That is, the term va-yekhal in Gen 2:2 can be taken to
mean "completion" in the sense that the world is complete after
the moment of creation through its perpetual preservation through
natural custom. Thus, the verse may signify that God rendered
creation complete by perpetually subjecting it to the natural custom inherent in the divine nomos. It may not be taken, however,
to mean either that God finished performing an overt, physical,
creative act or that the physical processes which were caused by
the divine will at the moment of creation ceased on the seventh
day. He rejects the interpretation which suggests that the verse
refers back to the sixth day (CT 13b, ll. 41ff.; cf. b. Meg. 9a)
because the statement would thus be superfluous and there are no
gratuitous parts of the Torah. In any case, since he does not
understand the "days" of the creation narrative as temporal designations, there is no way for the seventh degree to have a temporal
significance. Rather, it is a description of the degree of
existence which exists perpetually after the moment of creation.

Note his description above (6:1:9, p. 322, l. 13) of the
separate intellects' conception of the spheres as "rest" (menuḥah).
He describes their conception in this way because it is actual and
perpetual and it does not involve the motion from potentiality to
actuality that is involved in the human acquisition of conceptions.
(Though he refers there to the conception of the spheres, it must
be assumed that he means to refer to the conception of the separate
intellects, as explained above, note #397.) He may thus be associa-
ting this restful, perpetual conception of the separate intellects,
from which the natural order of existence overflows, with the rest
of Gen 2:2-3. Alternately, God's perpetual self-conception may be
described as His rest.

536) She-yeḥalqu ʾelav. The manuscripts consulted read she-
yeḥeshqu ʾeleha (to desire [His degree of existence]). The manuscript reading, which Touati recommends, corresponds to Gersonides'
statements above, p. 439, ll. 34ff.; p. 440, ll. 13, 20. That is,
the separate intellects conceive of the divine nomos and desire to
be subjected to it and thus to move their spheres in accordance
with it.

We have not translated the text here, however, according to the easier, manuscript reading for the following reasons. First, he is here offering an alternate interpretation of the term va-yekhal in Gen 2:2 which does not involve the notion of desire—a notion which is problematic, as discussed above, note #520. He may thus be avoiding the term intentionally. Second, the text as it stands makes sense. That is, in the subjection of the separate intellects to the divine nomos, they are differentiated in degree so that some can be said to be more venerable than others (see above, 6:2:8, p. 429, ll. 11ff.; notes #242 and #251). Though the separate intellects cannot be differentiated in themselves insofar as they are separate, they are differentiated in terms of the variations of the spheres which are the objects of their conception. Since they have no need for the spheres which they conceive in order to perfect their own existence (see above, 6:2:8, p. 435, ll. 8ff.; p. 436, ll. 5ff.; notes #401, #418, #419 and #420), the cause of their differentiation, he may be saying here, is their desire to serve as the instruments of the overflow of the divine nomos to the sublunar world.

537) That is, the sense is one whether we understand va-yekhal to mean that God desired the created world in the sense that He conceives its nomos perpetually in His self-conception and thus causes the separate intellects to desire to be subjected to Him, or that God completed creation by causing, through the perfection of His existence, the separate intellects to move their respective spheres. In neither case is there an implication of a cessation of overt divine work, nor an implication that God can be described as subject to a temporal sequence. Both interpretations rather refer to the distinction between the coming to be of the world by divine volition at the moment of creation and the subsequent perpetual preservation of the world's existence through the natural custom which inheres in the divine nomos.

538) See above, note #520, for a discussion of the problems involved with the (first) translation of va-yekhal as "desired."

539) Loʾ tikhleh ve-loʾ tifsoq. Though both of these terms can be translated synonymously to mean "to cease" or "to stop," we have translated klh in its passive voice and with its sense of destruction (cf. below, 6:2:13, p. 462, ll. 5, 17). This is because he distinguishes, in his argument in the first part of this treatise (6:1:16) against the possibility that the created world may pass

away, between natural passing away and passing away as a consequence
of the volition of an agent. His use of two terms here may thus
be intended to include both types of passing away, though he uses
neither of these terms in his discussion of the issue above, in
6:1:16.

540) 6:1:16.

541) Ma^caseh be-re^ɔshit. See above, note #2, for a discussion
of his use of this term.

542) That is, the meaning of the creation narrative in Genesis,
when it is properly understood as explained in 6:2:1-8 above, is
identical to the conclusions which he demonstrated philosophically
in 6:1.

543) See above, note #1, for a full discussion of his view of
the relationship of the truth as it is divinely revealed in Scripture and the truth as it is realized through rational demonstration.

544) At the conclusion of his discussion of the creation
narrative in his commentary, he takes a more reverent attitude to
his predecessors. He writes (CT 13d, ll. 41ff.):

> It is proper that we should not fail to give thanks to
> our predecessors for their discussions of the account
> of creation. Even though their (interpretations) will
> be found to be very distant from the intention (of the
> Torah) which we have found here—as you will see in that
> which the Master the Guide explained of this in his
> venerable book, The Guide of the Perplexed and (which
> the sage, Rabbi Abraham ibn Ezra (explained) in his com-
> mentary to the Torah—they nevertheless were the cause,
> in some way, which established us in the truth of this
> (question).

Note, however, that he does not credit Maimonides or Ibn Ezra in
his commentary with having reached correct views on the question
of creation. He merely acknowledges his debt to them for having
laid the groundwork for his own investigation of the question,
though they themselves did not arrive at true conclusions.

His confidence here that the text of the Torah clearly
supports his interpretation of it accords with his statement above,
(6:2:1, p. 419, ll. 16ff.; cf. note #1) and immediately below
(p. 441, ll. 19ff.) that it was the Torah's narrative of creation
which guided him in his quest for the speculative demonstration
of the truth of creation. This may thus be taken as a paradigmatic
instance of how the Torah performs its primary function of leading
the human intellect to its ultimate felicity, the acquisition of
true conceptions.

This confidence, however, should not be taken as an indication that he believes that his interpretation of the text is so clear that anyone reading the first chapter of Genesis would be led to his interpretation. He is well aware of the fact that his interpretation does not reflect the obvious meaning of the text. He begins the paragraph by addressing one who is involved in speculation. That is, anyone who properly prepares himself in his studies and understands the basic principles of logic, the natural sciences and metaphysics, and who is also sensitive to the way in which the Torah guides the speculator with its hints, allusions and apparent inconsistencies and contradictions, will conclude that the Torah bears witness to his interpretation. As he concludes in his commentary (CT 13d, 11. 49ff.), these matters are difficult and deep. They are secrets of the Torah which require a great deal of disciplined preparation and investigation before they can be properly conceived.

545) This is a difficult clause. It is his practice throughout the book to begin his discussion of each issue with an investigation and an evaluation of the views of his predecessors, with whom he inevitably disagrees and whom he subsequently corrects. Yet, he seems to be saying here that the views of his predecessors need not be cited. We may infer that he does not regard the preceding interpretation of the text as a demonstration on par with the preceding philosophical demonstrations which do require a careful and comprehensive examination of all of the arguments. Insofar as the exegetical enterprise differs in nature from the speculative demonstration, it does not require the citation of preceding, incorrect interpretations. Those incorrect interpretations may be said to be false primarily because they are subject to speculative refutation. Once the view of Maimonides on the question of creation, for example, has been refuted by philosophical demonstration in the first part of this treatise, it is clear that his exegesis of Scripture will be incorrect, because the Torah does not teach falsehoods. There is thus no need to review his interpretation of the text.

546) See above, notes #1 and #410, for a discussion of how the Torah functions in this way.

The manuscripts consulted have he²iyr for he^c iyr at p. 441, 1. 20, which would alter the translation here to: "It enlightens our eyes." Though Touati recommends the manuscript reading, we

have retained the reading of the text underlying the printed
editions, because Gersonides often uses the term ha^carah to
describe the way in which the Torah stimulates the speculator
to see the truth as a function of its purpose of guiding the
human species to its ultimate felicity, viz., true conception
(cf. above, 6:2:8, p. 435, ll. 21, 23; p. 436, l. 9; p. 438,
l. 27).

547) The manuscripts consulted have be-zo^ɔt ha-haysharah for
ha-meyashrah. The manuscript reading is easier, but the meaning
of the text remains essentially unchanged in either case.

APPENDIX A

The Pagination of the Notes to the Commentary

Note	Page	Note	Page	Note	Page
#1	148-154	#56	212	#111	223
#2	154-156	#57	213	#112	227
#3	156	#58	213	#113	227
#4	157-161	#59	213	#114	227
#5	161-162	#60	219	#115	227
#6	166	#61	219	#116	227
#7	166-167	#62	219	#117	227
#8	167	#63	219	#118	227
#9	167	#64	219	#119	227
#10	167	#65	219	#120	227
#11	167	#66	219	#121	227
#12	167-168	#67	219-220	#122	227
#13	168	#68	220	#123	227
#14	168	#69	220	#124	227
#15	168	#70	220	#125	227
#16	168	#71	220	#126	228
#17	168	#72	220-221	#127	228
#18	169	#73	221	#128	228
#19	169	#74	221	#129	228-229
#20	169-170	#75	221	#130	229-230
#21	170	#76	221	#131	237
#22	170	#77	221	#132	237
#23	170	#78	221	#133	237
#24	170	#79	221	#134	237-238
#25	173	#80	221	#135	238
#26	173	#81	221	#136	238-239
#27	173-178	#82	221	#137	239
#28	178	#83	221	#138	239
#29	178	#84	222	#139	239
#30	178	#85	222	#140	239
#31	178	#86	222	#141	239
#32	178	#87	222	#142	239
#33	178	#88	222	#143	239-240
#34	178	#89	222	#144	240
#35	178	#90	222	#145	240
#36	178	#91	222	#146	240
#37	178-180	#92	222	#147	240-241
#38	180	#93	222	#148	241
#39	180	#94	222	#149	241
#40	180	#95	222	#150	241
#41	180	#96	222	#151	241
#42	180	#97	222	#152	241-242
#43	182	#98	223	#153	242-243
#44	182	#99	223	#154	243
#45	182	#100	223	#155	243-244
#46	182	#101	223	#156	244
#47	182	#102	223	#157	244
#48	185	#103	223	#158	244
#49	185-206	#104	223	#159	244
#50	206-207	#105	223	#160	245
#51	207-211	#106	223	#161	245
#52	211	#107	223	#162	245
#53	211-212	#108	223	#163	245
#54	212	#109	223	#164	245
#55	212	#110	223	#165	245

SELECTED BIBLIOGRAPHY

1. Primary Sources

A. Printed Works of Gersonides

Peirush ᶜal Ha-Torah (Commentary on the Torah). Mantua, 1480.

Peirush ᶜal Ha-Torah (Commentary on the Torah). Venice, 1547.

Peirush ᶜal Ḥamesh Megillot (Commentary on the Five Scrolls).
    Riva di Trento, 1559/60. Reprinted: Koenigsburg, 1860.

Sefer Maᶜaseh Ḥoshev. Edited and translated by Gerson Lange.
    Frankfurt am Main: Louis Golde, 1909.

Sefer Milḥamot Ha-Shem (The Wars of the Lord). Riva di Trento,
    1560.

Sefer Milḥamot Ha-Shem (The Wars of the Lord). Leipzig, 1866.
    Reprinted: Berlin, 1923.

Shaᶜarei Ṣedeq (The Gates of Righteousness). Jerusalem, 1884.
    (Attributed to Gersonides.)

B. Gersonides' Works in Manuscript

Sefer Milḥamot Ha-Shem (The Wars of the Lord).

    Bibliothèque Nationale, Paris. Hebrew manuscript #723.

    Bodleian Library, Oxford. Pococke #376.

    Vatican Library, The Vatican. Urbinate #28.

Supercommentaries on Averroes' Works

Epitome of "De Anima." Bibliothèque Nationale, Paris. Hebrew
    manuscript #919.

Epitome of "Parva Naturalia." Bodleian Library, Oxford. Opp.
    mss. add. 38.

Epitomes of "Physica," "De Caelo," "De Generatione et Corrup-
    tione," "Meteorologica," "De Sensu." Hebrew University,
    Jerusalem. 4°1095.

Middle Commentary on "De Caelo." Biblioteca Palatina, Parma.
    #805.

Middle Commentary on "Organon." Bibliothèque Nationale, Paris.
    Hebrew manuscript #958.

Middle Commentary on "Physica." Bibliothèque Nationale, Paris.
    Hebrew manuscript #963.

Middle Commentary on "Topica." Bayerische Staatsbibliothek,
    Munich. #26.

C. Translations of and Commentaries to Gersonides' Works

Bleich, J. David. _Providence and the Philosophy of Gersonides_.
New York: Yeshiva University Press, 1973.

Kellerman, Benzion. _Die Kampfe Gottes von Lewi ben Gerson_.
2 volumes. Berlin: Mayer & Muller, 1914-1916.

Lassen, Abraham. _The Commentary of Levi ben Gersom on the Book
of Job_. New York: Bloch, 1946.

Samuelson, Norbert M. _Gersonides. The Wars of the Lord.
Treatise Three: On God's Knowledge_. Toronto: Pontifical
Institute of Mediaeval Studies, 1977.

Touati, Charles. _Les Guerres du Seigneur: Livres III et IV_.
Paris: Mouton, 1968.

D. Other Authors

Aquinas, Saint Thomas. _Basic Writings of Saint Thomas Aquinas_.
Edited and annotated, with an introduction, by Anton C.
Pegis. 2 volumes. New York: Random House, 1945.

_____. _Summa Contra Gentiles. Book Two: Creation_.
Translated, with an introduction and notes, by James F.
Anderson. New York: Doubleday, 1956. Reprinted: Notre
Dame: Notre Dame University Press, 1975.

Aristotle. _The Works of Aristotle_. Translated into English
under the editorship of W. D. Ross. 10 volumes. Oxford:
The Clarendon Press, 1908-1931.

_____. _Aristotle's "Categories" and "De Interpretatione."_
Translated with notes by J. L. Ackrill. Oxford: The
Clarendon Press, 1963.

_____. _Aristotle's "De Anima": Books II, III_. Translated
with introduction and notes by D. W. Hamlyn. Oxford: The
Clarendon Press, 1968.

_____. _Aristotle's "Physics."_ Translated with commen-
taries and glossary by Hippocrates G. Apostle. Blooming-
ton: Indiana University Press, 1969.

_____. _Aristotle's "Physics": Books I and II_. Translated
with introduction and notes by W. Charlton. Oxford: The
Clarendon Press, 1970.

_____. _Aristotle's "Metaphysics."_ Translated with commen-
taries and glossary by Hippocrates G. Apostle. Blooming-
ton: Indiana University Press, 1966.

Averroes. _Die Epitome der Metaphysik des Averroes_. Translated
with introduction and commentary by Simon van den Bergh.
Leiden: E. J. Brill, 1924.

_____. _Long Commentary on the Metaphysics_. Edited by M.
Bouyges. Beyrouth, 1938-1948.

_____. Averroes' Tahafut Al-Tahafut (The Incoherence of the Incoherence). 2 volumes. Translated with introduction and notes by Simon van den Bergh. Oxford: University Press, 1954.

_____. Kitab Fasl Al-Maqal. Edited by George Hourani. Leiden: E. J. Brill, 1959.

_____. On the Harmony of Religion and Philosophy. A translation with introduction and notes of Kitab Fasl Al-Maqal by George F. Hourani. London: Luzac, 1961.

_____. Averroes on Plato's Republic. Translated with introduction and notes by Ralph Lerner. Ithaca, N.Y.: Cornell University Press, 1974.

_____. Averroes' Middle Commentary on Porphyry's "Isagoge" and on Aristotle's "Categories". Hebrew text edited and translated by Herbert A. Davidson. 2 volumes. Corpus Commentarium Averrois in Aristotelem, volume 1, edited by H. A. Wolfson, David Baneth and F. H. Fobes. Cambridge, Mass.: Mediaeval Academy of America, 1969.

_____. Averrois Cordubensis Commentarium Medium in Aristotelis De Generatione et Corruptione Libros. Latin text edited by F. H. Fobes. Corpus Commentarium Averrois in Aristotelem, volume 4, 1, edited by H. A. Wolfson, David Baneth and F. H. Fobes. Cambridge, Mass.: Mediaeval Academy of America, 1956.

_____. Averroes on Aristotle's "De Generatione et Corruptione": Middle Commentary and Epitome. Hebrew text edited and translated from the original Arabic and the Hebrew and Latin versions with notes and introduction by Samuel Kurland. 2 volumes. Corpus Commentarium Averrois in Aristotelem, volume 4, 1-2, edited by H. A. Wolfson, David Baneth and F. H. Fobes. Cambridge, Mass.: Mediaeval Academy of America, 1958.

_____. Averrois Cordubensis Commentarium Magnum in Aristotelis De Anima Libros. Edited with introduction and notes by F. Stuart Crawford. Corpus Commentarium Averrois in Aristotelem, volume 6, 1, edited by H. A. Wolfson, David Baneth and F. H. Fobes. Cambridge, Mass.: Mediaeval Academy of America, 1953.

_____. Averrois Cordubensis Compendia Librorum Aristotelis Qui Parva Naturalia Vocantur. Edited with introduction and notes by A. L. Shields. Corpus Commentarium Averrois in Aristotelem, volume 7, edited by H. A. Wolfson, David Baneth and F. H. Fobes. Cambridge, Mass.: Mediaeval Academy of America, 1949.

_____. Averroes' Epitome of "Parva Naturalia." Arabic text and Hebrew version edited and original Arabic text translated by Harry Blumberg. 3 volumes. Corpus Commentarium Averrois in Aristotelem, volume 7, edited by H. A. Wolfson, David Baneth and F. H. Fobes. Cambridge, Mass.: Mediaeval Academy of America, 1954, 1961, 1972.

Bar Ḥiyya, Abraham. Sefer Hegyon Ha-Nefesh (The Meditation of the Sad Soul). Edited by E. Freimann with introductions by E. Freimann and S. J. L. Rapoport. Leipzig, 1860. Reprinted: Jerusalem, 1967.

_____. The Meditation of the Sad Soul. Translated with an introduction by Geoffrey Wigoder. New York: Schocken, 1969.

_____. Sefer Ṣurat Ha-ᵓareṣ Ve-tavnit Ha-shamayim (The Form of the Earth and the Structure of the Heavenly Orbs). Edited by M. Jaffe and Jonathan ben Joseph. Offenbach, 1720.

_____. La obra Forma de la Tierra. Translation into Spanish with introduction and notes by José M. Millás Vallicrosa. Madrid/Barcelona, 1956.

Crescas, Ḥasdai. ᵓOr Ha-Shem (The Light of the Lord). Ferrara, 1555.

Ibn Daᵓud, Abraham. Sefer Ha-ᵓEmunah Ha-Ramah (The Exalted Faith). Edited with notes by S. Weil. Frankfurt am Main: Wellerstein, 1852. Reprinted: Jerusalem, 1967.

Ibn Ezra, Abraham. Peirushei Ha-Torah (Commentary on the Torah). 3 volumes. Edited with introduction and notes by Asher Weiser. Jerusalem: Mossad Harav Kook, 1976.

Kimḥi, David. Peirush Rabbi David Kimḥi ᶜal Ha-Torah. Edited with notes by Moshe Kamelhar. Jerusalem: Mossad Harav Kook, 1970.

_____. The Commentary of David Kimḥi on Isaiah. Edited with introduction and notes by Louis Finkelstein. New York: Columbia University Press, 1926.

Maimonides, Moses. Dalalat Al-Hairin. (The Guide of the Perplexed). Edited by I. Joel. Jerusalem: Junovich, 1929.

_____. Moreh Ha-Nevukhim (The Guide of the Perplexed). Translated into Hebrew by Samuel Ibn Tibbon, with five commentaries: Efodi, Shem Tov, Crescas, Abravanel and Hanarboni. New York: Om Publishing Company, 1946.

_____. Le Guide des égarés (The Guide of the Perplexed). 3 volumes. Translated into French with notes and commentary by Solomon Munk. Paris: A. Franck, 1856-66.

_____. The Guide of the Perplexed. Translated and annotated by Michael Friedlander. London, 1881. Reprinted: New York: Hebrew Publishing Co., 1910.

_____. The Guide of the Perplexed. Translated with introduction and notes by Shlomo Pines. Chicago: University of Chicago Press, 1963.

_____. Moreh Ha-Nevukhim (The Guide of the Perplexed). 2 volumes. Original Arabic and Hebrew translation by Joseph Kafiḥ. Jerusalem: Mossad Harav Kook, 1972.

_____. Mishnah ʿim Peirush Rabbeinu Mosheh ben Maimon
(Commentary to the Mishnah). 3 volumes. Translated
into Hebrew by Joseph Kafiḥ. Jerusalem: Mossad Harav
Kook, 1968.

Midrash Ha-Gadol: Bereʾshit. Edited by M. Margulies.
    Jerusalem, 1947.

Midrash Lekaḥ Tov. Edited by S. Buber. Vilna, 1880.
    Reprinted: Jerusalem, 1960.

Midrash Mishlei. Edited by S. Buber. Vilna, 1893.

Midrash Rabbah. Vilna, 1878. Reprinted: New York, 1952.

Midrash Tanḥuma. Jerusalem: Levin-Epstein, 1974.

Midrash Tehillim. Edited by S. Buber. Vilna, 1891. Reprinted:
    Jerusalem, 1966.

Pesikta Rabbati. Edited by M. Friedman. Vienna, 1880.
    Reprinted: Tel Aviv: Esther, 1963.

Pirkei de-Rabbi Eliezer. Warsaw, 1852. Reprinted: Jerusalem,
    1970.

Plato. Collected Dialogues. Edited by Edith Hamilton and
    Huntington Cairns. Princeton: Princeton University
    Press, 1961.

_____. Plato's Cosmology: The "Timaeus" of Plato. Translated
    with commentary by Frances M. Cornford. New York: Har-
    court, Brace & Co., 1937.

Ramban (Moses ben Naḥman). Commentary to the Torah in
    Miqraʾot Gedolot. New York: Pardes, 1951.

Rashi (Solomon ben Isaac). Rashi ʿal Ha-Torah. Edited by
    Abraham Berliner, 1905. Reprinted: Jerusalem: Feldheim,
    1970.

Rashbam (Samuel ben Meʾir). Peirush La-Torah. Edited by D.
    Rosin. Breslau, 1881.

Saadia ben Joseph. Peirush Rabbeinu Saʿadiyah Gaʾon ʿal
    Ha-Torah. Edited with introduction and notes by Joseph
    Kafiḥ. Jerusalem: Mossad Harav Kook, 1964.

_____. The Book of Beliefs and Opinions.
    Translation of Kitab al-ʾAmanat wal-Iʿtiḳadat with intro-
    duction and notes by Samuel Rosenblatt. New Haven: Yale
    University Press, 1948.

Sefer Aggadat Bereʾshit. Bet Ha-Midrasch, volume 4. Edited
    by Adolph Jellinek. Jerusalem: Wahrman, 1967.

Sforno, Obadiah ben Jacob. Commentary to the Torah in
    Miqraʾot Gedolot. New York: Pardes, 1951.

Seder ʿOlam Rabbah. Vilna, 1894.

Themistius. _Themistii In Libros Aristotelis De Caelo._
Paraphrasis, Hebraice (translated by Zeraḥiah b. Isaac
Gracian) _et Latine._ Edited by Samuel Landauer. Berolini,
1902.

_____. _Themistii In Aristotelis Metaphysicorum Librum Λ_
Paraphrasis. Hebraice (translated by Moses b. Samuel Ibn
Tibbon) _et Latine._ Edited by Samuel Landauer. Berolini,
1903.

Yalqut Shimᶜoniy. Jerusalem, 1960.

2. Secondary Sources

A. On Creation in Gersonides

Epstein, Isadore. "Das Problem des göttlichen Willens in der
Schöpfung nach Maimonides, Gersonides, und Crescas."
Monatsschrift für Geschichte und Wissenschaft des
Judenthums 75(1931):335-347.

Feldman, Seymour. "Gersonides' Proofs for the Creation of the
Universe." _Proceedings of the American Academy for_
Jewish Research 35(1967):113-137.

_____. "Platonic Themes in Gersonides' Cosmology." In
Salo Wittmayer Baron Jubilee Volume, pp. 383-405. Jerusalem: American Academy for Jewish Research, 1975.

Kellner, Menahem M. "Gersonides and the Problem of Willful
Creation." Paper read at the Annual Conference of the
Association for Jewish Studies, December, 1976.

Touati, Charles. _La pensée philosophique et théologique de_
Gersonide. Paris: Les Editions de Minuit, 1973.

Weil, Isidore. _Philosophie religieuse de Levi-ben-Gerson._
Paris: Ladrange, 1868.

B. On Gersonides

Adlerblum, Nima H. _A Study of Gersonides in His Proper_
Perspective. New York: Columbia University Press, 1926.

_____. "Gersonides in Jewish Thinking of Tomorrow." In
Israel of Tomorrow, edited by Leo Jung, pp. 289-306. New
York: Herald Square Press, 1946.

Alègre, Leon. _Levi-ben-Gerson._ Bagnols: A. Baile, 1880.

Bertola, Ermenegildo. "Levi Gersonide e la logica Arabo-
Giudaica." In _Pier Lombardo_ 5, 3-4(1961):55-68. _Revista_
di teologia, filosofia, e cultura mediovale of the
Seminario S. Gaudenzio. Novara, Italy.

Blumenkranz, Bernhard. _Auteurs juifs en France médiévale:_
leur oeuvre imprimée. Toulouse, 1975.

Broyde, Isaac. "Levi ben Gershon." Jewish Encyclopedia
    8:26-32. New York, 1904.

Carlebach, Joseph. Levi ben Gerson als Mathematiker. Berlin,
    1910.

Curtze, Maximilien. "Die Abhandlung des Levi ben Gerson über
    Trigonometrie und der Jacobstab." Bibliotheca Mathematica,
    n.s., 12, 4(1898):97-112.

_____. "Urkunden zur Geschichte der Trigonometrie im
    Christlichen Mittelalter." Bibliotheca Mathematica,
    3rd series, 1(1900):321-416.

Espenshade, Pamela H. "A Text on Trigonometry by Levi ben
    Gerson." The Mathematics Teacher 60(1967):628-637.

Feldman, Seymour. "Gersonides on the Possibility of Conjunction
    with the Agent Intellect." AJS Review 3(1978):99-120.

Fletcher, Harris. "Milton and Ben Gerson." Journal of
    English and Germanic Philology 29 (1930):41-52.

Goldstein, Bernard R. "The Medieval Hebrew Tradition in
    Astronomy." Journal of the American Oriental Society
    85(1965):145-148.

_____. "Preliminary Remarks on Levi ben Gerson's
    Contributions to Astronomy." Proceedings of the Israeli
    Academy of Science and Humanities 3(1969):239-254.

_____. "Some Medieval Reports of Venus and Mercury
    Transits." Centaurus 14, 1(1969):49-59.

_____. "Levi ben Gerson's Lunar Model." Centaurus 16
    (1972):257-284.

_____. "Theory and Observation in Medieval Astronomy."
    Isis 63(1972):39-47.

_____. "Levi ben Gerson's Preliminary Lunar Model."
    Centaurus 18(1974):275-288.

_____. The Astronomical Tables of Rabbi Levi ben Gerson.
    Transactions of the Connecticut Academy of Arts and
    Sciences, volume 45. Hamden, Connecticut: Shoestring
    Press, 1975.

_____. "Levi ben Gerson's Analysis of Precession."
    Journal for the History of Astronomy 6(1975):31-41.

_____. "Astronomical and Astrological Themes in the
    Philosophical Works of Levi ben Gerson." Archives Inter-
    nationales d'Histoire des Sciences 29(1976):221-224.

_____. "Levi ben Gerson: On Instrumental Errors and the
    Transversal Scale. Journal for the History of Astronomy
    8(1977):102-112.

_____. "The Role of Science in the Jewish Community in
   Fourteenth-Century France." In Machaut's World: Science
   and Art in the Fourteenth-Century, edited by M. P. Cosman
   and Bruce Chandler, pp. 34-49. Annals of the New York
   Academy of Sciences, volume 314. New York: New York
   Academy of Sciences, 1978.

Grüll, Benjamin. Die Lehre von Kosmos bei Maimuni und
   Gersonides. Lemberg: A. Goldman, 1901.

Guillemain, B. "Citoyens, Juifs et Courtisans dans l'Avignon
   en XIVe siècle." In Comptes Rendu du 86e Congrès National
   du Sociétés Savantes, Montpellier, 1961, pp. 147-160.
   Paris: Gautier-Villars, 1962.

Guttman, Julius. "Levi ben Gersons Theorie des Begriffs."
   In Festschrift zum 75 Jahringen Bestehung des Jud. Theol.
   Seminars 2:131-149. Breslau, 1929. Translated as "Torat
   Ha-musag shel Ralbag." In Dat U-Madda^c, edited by S. H.
   Bergman and Nathan Rotenstreich, pp. 136-148. Jerusalem:
   Magnes Press, 1955.

Heinemann, Isaac. Ṭaᶜamei Ha-Miṣvot Be-Sifrut Yisraʾel
   1:97-101. Jerusalem, 1954.

Hoffman, E. "Levi ben Gerson als Religionsphilosoph."
   Monatsschrift für Geschichte und Wissenschaft des Judenthums 10(1860).

Husik, Isaac. A History of Mediaeval Jewish Philosophy.
   Philadelphia: Jewish Publication Society of America,
   1916.

_____. "Studies in Gersonides." Jewish Quarterly Review,
   n.s., 7(1916/17):553-594; 8(1917/18):113-156, 231-268.

_____. "Gersonides." In Philosophical Essays, edited by
   Milton C. Nahm and Leo Strauss, pp. 172-185. Oxford:
   Basil Blackwell, 1952.

Joel, Manuel. Lewi ben Gerson (Gersonides) als Religionsphilosoph; ein Beitrag zur Geschichte de Philosophie und
   der philosophischen Exegese des Mittelalters. Breslau:
   Schletter, 1862. First published in Monatsschrift für
   Geschichte und Wissenschaft des Judenthums 10(1860) &
   11(1861).

_____. "Notizen zu Levi ben Gerson." Monatsschrift für
   Geschichte und Wissenschaft des Judenthums 9(1859):
   223-226.

Karo, Jakob. Kritische Untersuchungen zu Levi ben Gersons
   (Ralbag) Widerlegung des Aristotelischen Zeitbegriffs.
   Leipzig: Albert Teicher, 1935.

Kellner, Menahem M. "Gersonides, Providence and the Rabbinic
   Tradition." Journal of the American Academy of Religion
   42(1974):673-685.

_____. "Gersonides and His Cultured Despisers: Arama and Abravanel." Journal of Medieval and Renaissance Studies 6(1976):269-296.

_____. "Maimonides and Gersonides on Mosaic Prophecy." Speculum 52(1977):62-79.

_____. "R. Levi Ben Gerson: A Bibliographical Essay." Studies in Bibliography and Booklore 12(1979):13-23.

_____. "Gersonides on Miracles, the Messiah and Resurrection." Daat 4(Winter, 1980):5-34.

Leibowitz, Joshua O. "Cardiological Comments on Geriatrics in Ecclesiastes by Levi ben Gerson, 1328." Dapim Refuiim 25, 1-6(January-June, 1966):3-16.

Levi, Israel. "Un recueil de consultations inedits de rabbins de la France meridionale." Revue des Études Juives 43 (1901):237-250; 44(1902):73-86.

Marx, Alexander. "The Scientific Work of Some Outstanding Medieval Jewish Scholars." In Essays and Studies in Memory of Linda R. Miller, edited by Israel Davidson, pp. 117-170. New York: The Jewish Theological Seminary of America, 1938.

Neubauer, Adolf. Medieval Jewish Chronicles, 1:97-99, 106, 110 & 2:240. Oxford, 1895. Reprinted in 1967.

Pines, Shlomo. "Scholasticism after Thomas Aquinas and the Teachings of Hasdai Crescas and his Predecessors." Proceedings of the Israel Academy of Sciences and Humanities 1(1967):1-101.

Rabinovitch, Nachum L. "Rabbi Levi ben Gershon and the Origins of Mathematical Induction." Archive for the History of Exact Sciences 6(1970):237-248.

_____. "Early Antecedents of Error Theory." Archive for the History of Exact Sciences 13(1974):348-358.

Renan, Ernest & Neubauer, Adolph. Les écrivains juifs français du XIVe siècle. Histoire litteraire de la France, volume 26. Paris, 1877.

Samuelson, Norbert M. "On Knowing God: Maimonides, Gersonides and the Philosophy of Religion." Judaism 18(1969):64-77.

_____. "Philosophic and Religious Authority in the Thought of Maimonides and Gersonides." CCAR Journal 17(1969):31-43.

_____. "The Problem of Free Will in Maimonides, Gersonides and Aquinas." CCAR Journal 17(1970):2-20.

_____. "Gersonides' Account of God's Knowledge of Particulars." Journal of the History of Philosophy 10 (1972):399-416.

_____. "The Problem of Future Contingents in Medieval
    Jewish Philosophy." Studies in Medieval Culture 6-7
    (1976):71-82.

Sarfatti, Gad B. Mathematical Terminology in the Hebrew
    Scientific Literature of the Middle Ages (Hebrew).
    Jerusalem: Magnes Press, 1968.

Sarton, George. Introduction to the History of Science.
    Washington: Carnegie Institute, 1947.

Schatzmiller, Yosef. "Suggestion and Addenda to Gallia
    Judaica" (Hebrew). Kiryat Sefer 45, 4(September, 1970):
    607-610.

_____. "Gersonides and the Jewish Community of Orange
    in His Day" (Hebrew). In Studies in the History of the
    Jewish People and the Land of Israel, edited by B. Oded,
    et. al., volume 2, pp. 111-126. Haifa, 1972.

_____. "Some Further Information About Gersonides and
    the Jewish Community of Orange in His Day" (Hebrew). In
    Studies in the History of the Jewish People and the Land
    of Israel, edited by B. Oded, et. al., volume 3, pp. 139-
    143. Haifa, 1974.

Silverman, David W. "Dreams, Divination and Prophecy:
    Gersonides and the Problem of Precognition." In The
    Samuel Friedland Lectures: 1967-74, pp. 99-120. New
    York: The Jewish Theological Seminary of America, 1974.

_____. The Problem of Prophecy in Gersonides. Ph.D.
    dissertation, Columbia University, 1975.

Steinschneider, Moritz. Die Hebräischen Uebersetzungen des
    Mittelalters und die Juden als Dolmetcher. 2 volumes.
    Berlin, 1893. Reprinted: Graz, 1956.

_____. "Zu Levi ben Gerson." Magazin für die
    Wissenschaft des Judenthums 14(1899):139-155.

_____. "Levi ben Gerson." In Gesammelte Schriften
    1:233-270. Berlin: M. Poppelauer, 1925.

Stitskin, Leon. "Ralbag's Introduction to the Book of Job."
    Tradition 6, 1. Reprinted in A Treasury of Tradition,
    edited by M. Lamm & W. Wurzberger, pp. 370-374. New
    York: Hebrew Publishing Company, 1967.

Teicher, Jacob. "Studi Preliminari Sulla Dottrina Della
    Conoscenza di Gersonide." Rendiconte della Reale Accademia
    Nazionale dei Lincei 8(1932):500-510. Reprinted in
    Medieval Jewish Philosophy, edited by Steven T. Katz.
    New York: Arno Press, 1980.

Touati, Charles. "Les idées philosophiques et théologiques de
    Gersonide (1288-1344) dans ses commentaires bibliques."
    Revue des sciences religieuses 27(1954):335-367.

_____. "Quatre compositions liturgiques de Gersondie."
    Revue des études juives 117(1958):97-105.

_____. "La controverse de 1303-1306 autour des études
philosophiques et scientifiques." Revue des études juives
127(1968):21-37.

_____. "Le problème de l'inerrance prophétique dans le
théologie juive du Moyen Age." Revue de l'histoire des
religions 174(1968):169-187.

_____. "La lumiere de l'Intellect, creation du Premier Jour:
L'éxegèse de Genèse 1:1-3 chez Gersonide." In In Princi-
pio: Interpretations des premiers versets de la Genèse,
pp. 37-45. Paris: Presses Universitaires de France,
1973.

Vajda, Georges. Introduction à la pensée juive du moyen age.
Paris: J. Vrin, 1947.

Ventura, Moise. "Belief in Providence According to Gersonides"
(Hebrew). In Minḥah le-Avraham (a festschrift for
Abraham Elmaleh), pp. 12-21. Jerusalem, 1959.

Werner, Eric, and Sonne, Isaiah. "The Philosophy and Theory
of Music in Judeo-Arabic Literature." Hebrew Union
College Annual 17(1942-43):511-572.

Wolfson, Harry Austryn. "Maimonides and Gersonides on Divine
Attributes as Ambiguous Terms." In Mordecai M. Kaplan
Jubilee Volume, pp. 515-530. New York: The Jewish
Theological Seminary of America, 1953. Reprinted in
Studies in the History of Philosophy and Religion, edited
by Isadore Twersky and George H. Williams, volume 2,
pp. 231-246. Cambridge, Mass.: Harvard University Press,
1977.

C. On Creation

Al-Alousi, Husâm Muhi Eldin. The Problem of Creation in
Islamic Thought: Qurᶜan, Hadith, Commentaries and Kalam.
Baghdad: National Printing & Publishing Co., 1965.

Allard, Michel. "Le rationalisme d'Averroes d'apres un étude
sur la création." Bulletin d'études orientales 14(1954):
7-59.

Altmann, Alexander. "A Note on the Rabbinic Doctrine of
Creation." Journal of Jewish Studies 7(1956):195-206.

Craig, William Lane. The Kalām Cosmological Argument. New
York: Harper & Row, 1979.

Davidson, Herbert A. "John Philoponus as a Source of Medieval
Islamic and Jewish Proofs for Creation." Journal of the
American Oriental Society 89(1969):357-391.

Diesendruck, Z. "Saadya's Formulation of the Time Argument
for Creation." In Jewish Studies in Memory of G. A.
Kohut. New York, 1935.

Duhem, Pierre. Le système du monde: Histoire des doctrines
cosmologiques de Platon à Copernic. Paris: Librarie
Scientifique Humaine, 1954.

Efros, Israel I. "Saadya's Second Theory of Creation in its
     Relation to Pythagoreanism and Platonism." In Louis
     Ginzberg Memorial Volume, English section, pp. 133-142.
     New York: American Academy for Jewish Research, 1945.

Fakhry, Majid. "The 'Antinomy' of the Eternity of the World
     in Averroes, Maimonides and Aquinas." In Studies in
     Maimonides and Saint Thomas Aquinas, edited by Jacob I.
     Dienstag, pp. 107-123. New York: Ktav, 1975.

Hyman, Arthur. "Aristotle's 'First Matter' and Avicenna's
     and Averroes' 'Corporeal Form.'." In Harry Austryn
     Wolfson Jubilee Volume, edited by Saul Lieberman, pp. 385-
     406. Jerusalem: American Academy for Jewish Research,
     1965.

Kravitz, Leonard. "The Revealed and the Concealed: Providence,
     Prophecy, Miracles and Creation in the Guide." CCAR
     Journal 17(10/1969):1-30.

Kovach, F. J. "The Question of the Eternity of the World in
     St. Bonaventure and St. Thomas—A Critical Analysis."
     Southwestern Journal of Philosophy 5(1974):141-172.

Macdonald, D. B. "Continuous Re-creation and Atomic Time in
     Muslim Scholastic Theology." Isis 9(1927):326-344.

Marmura, Michael E. The Conflict Over the World's Pre-eternity
     in the "Tahafuts" of Al-Ghazali and Ibn Rushd. Ph.D.
     dissertation, University of Michigan, 1959.

_____. "The Logical Role of the Argument from Time in the
     Tahafut's Second Proof for the World's Pre-eternity."
     Muslim World 49(1959):306-314.

Nasr, Seyyed Hossein. An Introduction to Islamic Cosmological
     Doctrines. Boulder, Colorado: Shambhala, 1978.

Nuriel, Abraham. "On the Creation of the World and its
     Eternity According to Maimonides" (Hebrew). Tarbiz 33
     (1964):372-387.

Prijs, Leo, ed. Abraham Ibn Esra's Kommentar zu Genesis
     Kapitel I. Weisbaden: F. Steiner, 1973.

Rahman, Fazlur. "The Eternity of the World and the Heavenly
     Bodies in Post-Avicennan Philosophy." In Essays on
     Islamic Philosophy and Science, edited by George F.
     Hourani, pp. 222-237. Albany: State University of New
     York Press, 1975.

Wolfson, Harry Austryn. "The Problem of the Origin of Matter
     in Medieval Jewish Philosophy and Its Analogy to the
     Modern Problem of the Origin of Life." Proceedings of the
     International Congress of Philosophy (Philadelphia), 1926,
     pp. 602-608. Reprinted in Studies in the History of
     Philosophy and Religion, edited by Isadore Twersky and
     George H. Williams, volume 2, pp. 491-496. Cambridge,
     Mass.: Harvard University Press, 1977.

_____. "The Platonic, Aristotelian and Stoic Theories of
Creation in Hallevi and Maimonides." In Essays in Honour
of the Very Rev. Dr. J. H. Hertz, pp. 427-442. London,
1942. Reprinted in Studies in the History of Philosophy
and Religion, edited by Isadore Twersky and George H.
Williams, volume 1, pp. 234-249. Cambridge, Mass.:
Harvard University Press, 1973.

_____. "The Kalam Arguments for Creation in Saadia, Averroes,
Maimonides and St. Thomas." In Saadia Anniversary Volume:
Texts and Studies 2:197-245. New York: American Academy
for Jewish Research, 1943.

_____. "The Meaning of Ex Nihilo in the Church Fathers,
Arabic and Hebrew Philosophy, and St. Thomas." In
Medieval Studies in Honor of J. D. M. Ford, pp. 355-370.
Cambridge, Mass. : Harvard University Press, 1943.
Reprinted in Studies in the History of Philosophy and
Religion, edited by Isadore Twersky and George, H.
Williams, volume 1, pp. 207-221. Cambridge, Mass.:
Harvard University Press, 1973.

_____. "The Kalam Problem of Nonexistence and Saadia's
Second Theory of Creation." Jewish Quarterly Review,
n.s., 36.4(1946):371-391. Reprinted in Studies in the
History of Philosophy and Religion, edited by Isadore
Twersky and George H. Williams, volume 2, pp. 338-358.
Cambridge, Mass.: Harvard University Press, 1977.

_____. "Atomism in Saadia." Jewish Quarterly Review,
n.s., 37.2(1946):107-124. Reprinted in Studies in the
History of Philosophy and Religion, edited by Isadore
Twersky and George H. Williams, volume 2, pp. 359-376.
Cambridge, Mass.: Harvard University Press, 1977.

_____. "Arabic and Hebrew Terms for Matter and Elements with
Especial Reference to Saadia." Jewish Quarterly Review
38.1(1947):47-61. Reprinted in Studies in the History
of Philosophy and Religion, edited by Isadore Twersky and
George H. Williams, volume 2, pp. 377-392. Cambridge,
Mass.: Harvard University Press, 1977.

_____. "Emanation and Creation Ex Nihilo in Crescas"
(Hebrew). In Sefer Assaf, pp. 230-236. Jerusalem:
Magnes Press, 1953. Reprinted in Studies in the History
of Philosophy and Religion, edited by Isadore Twersky and
George H. Williams, volume 2, pp. 623-629. Cambridge,
Mass.: Harvard University Press, 1977.

_____. "The Meaning of Ex Nihilo in Isaac Israeli." Jewish
Quarterly Review, n.s., 50(1959):1-12. Reprinted in
Studies in the History of Philosophy and Religion, edited
by Isadore Twersky and George H. Williams, volume 1,
pp. 222-233. Cambridge, Mass.: Harvard University Press,
1973.

_____. "Plato's Pre-existent Matter in Patristic Philosophy."
In The Classical Tradition, edited by L. Wallach, pp.
409-420. Ithaca, N.Y.: Cornell University Press, 1966.
Reprinted in Studies in the History of Philosophy and
Religion, edited by Isadore Twersky and George H. Williams,
volume 1, pp. 170-181. Cambridge, Mass.: Harvard University Press, 1973.

394   GERSONIDES ON CREATION

_____. "Patristic Argument Against the Eternity of the
World." Harvard Theological Review 59(1966):351-361.
Reprinted in Studies in the History of Philosophy and
Religion, edited by Isadore Twersky and George H.
Williams, volume 1, pp. 170-181. Cambridge, Mass.:
Harvard University Press, 1973.

_____. "The Idenification of Ex Nihilo with Emanation in
Gregory of Nyssa." Harvard Theological Review 63(1970):
53-60. Reprinted in Studies in the History of Philosophy
and Religion, edited by Isadore Twersky and George H.
Williams, volume 1, pp. 199-206. Cambridge, Mass.:
Harvard University Press, 1973.

_____. The Philosophy of the Kalam. Cambridge, Mass.:
Harvard University Press, 1976.

D. On Related Issues

Anscombe, G. E. M. Intention. Ithaca, N.Y.: Cornell
University Press, 1957.

Anscombe, G. E. M., and Geach, P. T. Three Philosophers.
Ithaca, N.Y.: Cornell University Press, 1961.

Altmann, Alexander. "Ibn Bajja on Man's Ultimate Felicity."
In Studies in Religious Philosophy and Mysticism,
pp. 73-107. Ithaca, N.Y.: Cornell University Press,
1969.

_____. "Maimonides and Thomas Aquinas: Natural or Divine
Prophecy?" AJS Review 3(1978):1-19.

Arberry, A. J. Revelation and Reason in Islam. London, 1957.

Berman, Lawrence V. Ibn Bajjah and Maimonides: A Chapter in
the History of Political Philosophy (Hebrew). Ph.D.
dissertation, Hebrew University, 1959. Reprinted: Tel
Aviv: Jacob Twersky, n.d.

_____. "The Political Interpretation of the Maxim: The
Purpose of Philosophy is the Imitation of God." Studia
Islamica 15(1962):53-63.

_____. "A Reexamination of Maimonides' 'Statement on
Political Science.'." Journal of the American Oriental
Society 89(1969):106-112.

_____. "Maimonides, Disciple of Alfarabi." Israel Oriental
Studies 4(1974):154-177.

Blanchet, Louis-Émile. "L'infini dans les pensées Juive et
Arabe." Laval théologique et philosophique 32(1976):
11-21.

Blumberg, Harry, "The Problem of Immortality in Avicenna,
Maimonides and St. Thomas Aquinas." In Harry Austryn
Wolfson Jubilee Volume, edited by Saul Lieberman, pp. 174-
180. Jerusalem: American Academy for Jewish Research,
1965.

Blumenthal, David R. "On the Intellect and the Rational Soul."
    Journal of the History of Philosophy 15(1977):207-211.

Bolzano, B. The Paradoxes of the Infinite. Translated by
    D. A. Steele. New Haven: Yale University Press, 1950.

Bostock, David. "Aristotle, Zeno, and the Potential Infinite."
    Proceedings of the Aristotelian Society 73(1972-73):
    37-51.

Conway, D. A. "Possibility and Infinite Time: A Logical
    Paradox in St. Thomas' Third Way." International Philo-
    sophical Quarterly 14(1974):201-208.

Davidson, Herbert. "Maimonides' Shemonah Peraqim and
    Alfarabi's Fuṣūl Al-Madanī." Proceedings of the American
    Academy for Jewish Research 31(1963):33-50.

_____. "Arguments from the Concept of Particularization in
    Arabic Philosophy." Philosophy East and West 18(1968):
    299-314.

Efros, Israel I. The Problem of Space in Jewish Mediaeval
    Philosophy. New York: Columbia University Press, 1917.

_____. Philosophical Terms in the "More Nebukim." New York:
    Columbia University Press, 1924.

Fackenheim, Emil. "The Possibility of the Universe in
    Al-Farabi, Ibn Sina, and Maimonides." Proceedings of the
    American Academy for Jewish Research 5(1946-47):39-70.

Fakhry, Majid. Islamic Occasionalism and Its Critique by
    Averroes and Aquinas. London: George Allen & Unwin, 1958.

_____. A History of Islamic Philosophy. New York: Columbia
    University Press, 1970.

Friedlander, Michael. Essays on the Writings of Abraham Ibn
    Ezra. London: Society of Hebrew Literature, 1977.
    Reprinted: Jerusalem, 1964.

Gauthier, Léon. Ibn Rochd. Paris: Presses Universitaires de
    France, 1948.

Gilson, Etiènne. Reason and Revelation in the Middle Ages.
    New York, 1938.

Golb, N., ed. "The Hebrew Translation of Averroes' 'Fasl al-
    maqāl'." Proceedings of the American Academy for Jewish
    Research 25(1956):91-113; 26(1957):41-64.

Goldstein, Bernard R. "The Arabic Version of Ptolemy's
    Planetary Hypothesis." Proceedings of the American
    Philosophical Society, n.s., 57, part 4. Philadelphia,
    1967.

_____. "Ibn Mu'adh's Treatise on Twilight and the Height
    of the Atmosphere." Archive for the History of Exact
    Sciences 17(1977):97-118.

Golomb, Morris. A Critical Study of Abraham Ibn Ezra's
    Pentateuchal Introductions. D.H.S. dissertation, Hebrew
    Union College—Jewish Institute of Religion, 1970.

Goldstein, Helen Tunik. "Averroes on the Structure and Function
    of Physics VII, 1." In Harry Austryn Wolfson Jubilee
    Volume, edited by Saul Lieberman, pp. 335-355. Jerusalem:
    American Academy for Jewish Research, 1965.

Grant, Edward. "Scientific Thought in Fourteenth-Century
    Paris: Jean Buridan and Nicole Oresme." In Machaut's
    World: Science and Art in the Fourteenth Century, edited
    by M. P. Cosman and Bruce Chandler, pp. 105-124. Annals
    of the New York Academy of Sciences, volume 314. New
    York, 1978.

Greive, Hermann. Studien zum judischen Neuplatonismus: die
    Religions-philosophie des Abraham Ibn Ezra. Berlin &
    New York: W. de Gruyter, 1973.

Guttmann, Julius. Philosophies of Judaism. Translated by
    David W. Silverman. New York: Doubleday, 1964.

Hart, W. D. "The Potential Infinite." Proceedings of the
    Aristotelian Society 76(1976):247-264.

Hartman, David. Maimonides: Torah and the Philosophic Quest.
    Philadelphia: The Jewish Publication Society of America,
    1976.

Harvey, Steven. Averroes on the Principles of Nature: The
    "Middle Commentary" on "Physics" I-II. Ph.D. disserta-
    tion, Harvard University, 1977.

Heller, Joseph. "Maimonides' Theory of Miracle." In Between
    East and West, edited by Alexander Altmann, pp. 112-127.
    London: East & West Library, 1958.

Husik, Isaac. "Averroes on the Metaphysics of Aristotle."
    The Philosophical Review 18(1909):416-428. Reprinted in
    Philosophical Essays, edited by Milton C. Nahm and Leo
    Strauss, pp. 160-171. Oxford: Basil Blackwell, 1952.

_____. "Maimonides and Spinoza on the Interpretation of the
    Bible." Journal of the American Oriental Society,
    supplement no. 1, 55(1935):22-40. Reprinted in Philosoph-
    ical Essays, edited by Milton C. Nahm and Leo Strauss,
    pp. 141-159. Oxford: Basil Blackwell, 1952.

_____. "Averroes on the Metaphysics of Aristotle." In Jewish
    Studies in Memory of G. A. Kohut, edited by Salo W. Baron
    and Alexander Marx, pp. 370-378. New York, 1935.

Ivry, Alfred. "Averroes on Intellection and Conjunction."
    Journal of the American Oriental Society 86(1966):76-85.

Klatzkin, Jacob. ʾOṣar Ha-Munaḥim Ha-Filosofim Ve-ʾAntologiyah
    Filosofit. 2 volumes. New York: Feldheim, 1968.

Klein-Braslavy, Sarah. "The Reality of Time and the Primordial
    Period in Medieval Jewish Philosophy" (Hebrew). Tarbiz
    45. 1-2(1975/1976):106-127.

Koyré, A. "Le vide et l'espace infini au XIVe siècle."
    Archives d'histoire doctrinale et literaire du moyen age
    25(1949):45-91.

Lerner, Ralph. "Maimonides' Letter on Astrology." History of
    Religions 8(1968):143-158.

Lerner, Ralph, and Mahdi, Muhsin, eds. Medieval Political
    Philosophy: A Sourcebook. Ithaca, N.Y.: Cornell
    University Press, 1963.

Levy, Raphael. The Astrological Works of Abraham Ibn Ezra.
    Baltimore: The John Hopkins Press, 1927.

Lindberg, David C., ed. Science in the Middle Ages. Chicago
    & London: University of Chicago Press, 1978.

McMullin, Ernan, ed. The Concept of Matter in Greek and
    Medieval Philosophy. Notre Dame: University of Notre
    Dame Press, 1963.

Mahdi, Muhsin. "Alfarabi Against Philoponus." Journal of
    Near Eastern Studies 26(1967):233-260.

Melammed, Ezra Zion. Mefarshei Ha-Miqra³. 2 volumes.
    Jerusalem: Magnes Press, 1975.

Marx, Alexander. "The Correspondence Between the Rabbis of
    Southern France and Maimonides About Astrology." Hebrew
    Union College Annual 3(1926):311-358.

Oles, M. Arthur. A Translation of the Commentary of Abraham
    Ibn Ezra on Genesis with a Critical Introduction. Ph.D.
    dissertation, Hebrew Union College—Jewish Institute of
    Religion, 1958.

Owens, Joseph. The Doctrine of Being in the Aristotelian
    "Metaphysics". Toronto: Pontifical Institute of
    Mediaeval Studies, 1951.

Pines, Shlomo. "An Arabic Summary of a Lost Work of John
    Philoponus." Israel Oriental Studies 2(1972):320-352.

Popper, Karl. "On the Possibility of an Infinite Past: A
    Reply to Whitrow." British Journal for the Philosophy
    of Sciences 29(1978):47-48.

Rabinovitch, Nachum L. Probability and Statistical Inference
    in Ancient and Medieval Jewish Literature. Toronto:
    University of Toronto Press, 1973.

Romano, D. "La transmission des sciences arabes par les Juifs
    en Languedoc." In Juifs et Judaisme de Languedoc, edited
    by M. H. Vicaire and B. Blumenkranz, pp. 363-386. Cahiers
    de Fanjeaux, volume 12. Toulouse: E. Privat, 1967.

Rosenberg, Shalom. Logic and Ontology in Jewish Philosophy in
    the Fourteenth Century. Ph.D. dissertation, Hebrew
    University, 1973.

Sambursky, Shmuel. The Physical World of the Greeks. Translated by Merton Dagut. London: Routledge & Kegan Paul,
   1956.

_____. The Physical World of Late Antiquity. London:
   Routledge & Kegan Paul, 1962.

_____. "Note on John Philoponus' Rejection of the
   Infinite." In Islamic Philosophy and the Classical
   Tradition, edited by S. M. Stern, Albert Hourani, and
   Vivian Brown, pp. 351-353. Columbia, S.C.: University
   of South Carolina Press, 1972.

Sambursky, Shmuel, and Pines, Shlomo. The Concept of Time in
   Late Neoplatonism. Jerusalem: The Israel Academy of
   Sciences and Humanities, 1971.

Samuelson, Norbert M. "Causation and Choice in the Philosophy
   of Ibn Daud." In The Divine Helmsman: Studies on God's
   Control of Human Events, edited by J. L. Crenshaw and
   Samuel Sandmel, pp. 223-233. New York: Ktav.

Sirat, Colette. Les théories des visions surnaturelles dans
   la pensée juive du moyen-âge. Leiden: E. J. Brill,
   1969.

Solmsen, Friedrich. "Aristotle and Prime Matter." Journal of
   the History of Ideas 19(1958):243-252.

_____. Aristotle's System of the Physical World. Cornell
   Studies in Classical Philology, volume 33. Ithaca, N.Y.:
   Cornell University Press, 1960.

Spinoza, Benedicto de. A Theologico-Political Treatise and A
   Political Treatise. Translated with an introduction by
   R. H. M. Elwes. New York: Dover, 1955.

Stitskin, Leon D. Judaism as a Philosophy: The Philosophy of
   Abraham bar Hiyya (1065-1143). New York: Bloch, 1960.

Strauss, Leo. "Quelques remarques sur la Science Politique de
   Maimonides et de Farabi." Revue des études juives 100
   (1936):1-37.

_____. "Farabi's Plato." In Louis Ginzberg Jubilee Volume,
   edited by Saul Lieberman, et. al., pp. 357-393. New York:
   American Academy for Jewish Research, 1945.

_____. "How Farabi Read Plato's Laws." In Melanges Louis
   Massignon 3:319-344. Damascus: Institut Francais de
   Damas, 1957.

_____. Persecution and the Art of Writing. Glencoe, Ill.:
   The Free Press, 1952.

_____. "How to Begin to Study The Guide of the Perplexed."
   In The Guide of the Perplexed, translated with an intro-
   duction by Shlomo Pines, pp. xi-lvi. Chicago: The
   University of Chicago Press, 1963.

_____. "Notes on Maimonides' Book of Knowledge." In Studies in Religion and Mysticism Presented to Gershom G. Scholem, edited by E. E. Urbach, R. J. Zwi Werblowsky and Ch. Wirszubski, pp. 269-283. Jerusalem: Magnes Press, 1967.

Swinburne, R. G. Space and Time. London: Macmillan, 1968.

_____. The Concept of Miracle, London: Macmillan, 1970.

Twersky, Isadore. Introduction to the Code of Maimonides. New Haven: Yale University Press, 1980.

Urbach, Ephraim E. Ḥazal: Pirqei ᵓEmunot Ve-Deᶜot. Jerusalem: Magnes Press, 1971. Translated as The Sages: Their Concepts and Beliefs by Israel Abrahams, 2 volumes. Jerusalem: Magnes Press, 1975.

Whitrow, G. J. "On the Impossibility of an Infinite Past." British Journal for the Philosophy of Science 29(1978): 39-45.

Wolfson, Harry Austryn. Crescas' Critique of Aristotle. Cambridge, Mass.: Harvard University Press, 1929.

_____. "Hallevi and Maimonides on Design, Chance and Necessity." Proceedings of the American Academy for Jewish Research 11(1941):105-163. Reprinted in Studies in the History of Philosophy and Religion, edited by Isadore Twersky and George H. Williams, volume 2, pp. 1-59. Cambridge, Mass.: Harvard University Press, 1977.

_____. "The Double Faith Theory in Saadia, Averroes and St. Thomas." Jewish Quarterly Review, n.s., 33(1942):231-264. Reprinted in Studies in the History of Philosophy and Religion, edited by Isadore Twersky and George H. Williams, volume 1, pp. 583-618. Cambridge, Mass.: Harvard University Press, 1973.

_____. Philo: Foundations of Religious Philosophy in Judaism, Christianity and Islam. 2 volumes. Cambridge, Mass.: Harvard University Press, 1947.

_____. "Averroes' Lost Treatise on the Prime Mover." Hebrew Union College Annual 23(1951):683-710. Reprinted in Studies in the History of Philosophy and Religion, edited by Isadore Twersky and George H. Williams, volume 1, pp. 402-429. Cambridge, Mass.: Harvard University Press, 1973.

_____. The Philosophy of the Church Fathers. Cambridge, Mass.: Harvard University Press, 1956.

_____. Repercussions of the Kalam in Jewish Philosophy. Cambridge, Mass.: Harvard University Press, 1979.

INDEX OF NAMES

INDEX OF TECHNICAL TERMS

413